Penguin True Crime
Who Killed Hanratty?

A writer and journalist, Paul Foot wrote ⟨...⟩
and was editor of the paper during 1974 ⟨...⟩
the *Daily Mirror* in 1979. He was named journalist of the Year
(Granada's 'What the Papers Say' Awards) for 1972 and
Campaigning Journalist of the Year (British Press Awards) in
1980. He has written two other books about suspected injustice:
The Helen Smith Story, inquiring into the mysterious death of a
British nurse in Jeddah, and *Murder at the Farm* (Penguin, 1988),
investigating the murder of Carl Bridgewater and the subsequent
convictions. His other books include *Immigration and Race in Brit-
ish Politcs* (1965), *The Politics of Harold Wilson* (1968), *The Rise of
Enoch Powell* (1969), *Why You Should Be a Socialist* (1977) and
Red Shelley (1981).

PAUL FOOT

Who
Killed
Hanratty?

PENGUIN BOOKS

PENGUIN BOOKS

Published by the Penguin Group
27 Wrights Lane, London w8 5TZ, England
Viking Penguin Inc., 40 West 23rd Street, New York, New York 10010, USA
Penguin Books Australia Ltd, Ringwood, Victoria, Australia
Penguin Books Canada Ltd, 2801 John Street, Markham, Ontario, Canada L3R 1B4
Penguin Books (NZ) Ltd, 182–190 Wairau Road, Auckland 10, New Zealand

Penguin Books Ltd, Registered Offices: Harmondsworth, Middlesex, England

First published by Jonathan Cape 1971
Published in paperback, with a postscript, by Granada 1973
Published with a further postscript by Penguin Books 1988
10 9 8 7 6 5 4 3 2 1

Made and printed in Great Britain by
Richard Clay Ltd, Bungay, Suffolk
Set in Ehrhardt

CONTENTS

LIST OF ILLUSTRATIONS

Diary of Events

1961

August

    5th. Hanratty's hair dyed dark by Carol France.

    22nd. 9.30 p.m. approx. Murderer climbs into car at Dorney Reach.

    23rd. 3 a.m. approx. Murder at Deadman's Hill.

    6.30 p.m. approx. Car found at Ilford.

    24th. Edward Blackhall, John Skillett and James Trower all make statements about car.

    Mrs Audrey Willis held up by gunman at Old Knebworth.

    (9 p.m.) Murder gun found under back seat of bus.

    27th. Peter Alphon interviewed at Highbury police station.

    29th. Two Identikit pictures issued.

    31st. Mrs Gregsten identifies Hanratty as her husband's murderer — from Mr Ewer's shop.

    Valerie Storie moved from Bedford to Guy's. Changes description of murderer's eyes.

September

    1st. Mr Ewer sees Hanratty again, and informs Scotland Yard.

    Hanratty traced to florist, and name of mother established.

    4th. James Hanratty leaves for Ireland.

    5th. Garage attendant who served murder car found.

    7th. Mrs Dalal attacked at Richmond.

    11th. Two cartridge cases from murder weapon found in Vienna Hotel, Maida Vale.

    Police headquarters set up in Broadway House.

    13th. Mr Acott interviews Mrs Alphon, Peter Alphon's mother.

    15th. First statement of Vienna Hotel manager Nudds — mentioning Alphon and Hanratty but incriminating neither.

20th. Mrs Gregsten visits Valerie Storie at Guy's.

21st. Nudds's second statement implicating Alphon.

22nd. (afternoon) Acott interviews Mrs Alphon again.

(afternoon) Press conference announcing murder hunt for Alphon.

Nation-wide murder hunt.

(midnight) Alphon gives himself up at Cannon Row.

23rd. Identity parades at Scotland Yard.

Attended by Blackhall, Mrs Dalal, Nudds and others.

24th. Identity parade at Guy's before Valerie Storie. Alphon not picked out.

Alphon held on Mrs Dalal assault charge.

25th. Discussion between police and D.P.P.

Nudds's third statement exonerating Alphon.

26th. Acott, Oxford visit Hanratty home in Kingsbury.

29th. Alphon released on bail.

Acott, Oxford go to Dublin. Airports 'sealed'.

October

3rd. Alphon released without charge. Costs paid.

James Hanratty senior goes to Scotland Yard with birthday card from his son, postmarked London.

6th. Hanratty rings Acott at Scotland Yard.

Drives to Manchester, takes train to Liverpool.

7th. Rings Acott again from Liverpool.

11th. Leaves Liverpool.

(11 p.m.) Arrested in Blackpool.

12th. Two interviews with Acott, Oxford.

Travels to Bedford with police.

13th. Identification parade. Skillett, Trower identify Hanratty.

14th. Identification parade at Stoke Mandeville. Valerie Storie identifies Hanratty. Hanratty charged with A6 murder.

November

22nd. Hearing starts at Ampthill.

Langdale makes statement to prison officer about confession.

December

1st. Langdale interviewed by Acott.

5th. Hearing ends without Langdale giving evidence.

Hanratty committed for trial at Old Bailey.

1962

January

2nd. Case switched to Bedford.

22nd. Trial opens at Bedford.

29th. Hanratty instructs lawyers to 'run' the Rhyl alibi.

February

9th. Defence opens. Trevor Dutton makes statement in Rhyl.

11th. Jean Justice first meet Peter Alphon.

17th. Hanratty's conviction and sentence to death.

19th. Mrs Walker, Mrs Vincent make statements in Rhyl.

21st. Mr Larman makes statement about Rhyl.

March

13th. Hanratty appeal turned down.

16th. Charles France, prosecution witness, commits suicide.

18th. Peter Alphon arrested for being drunk and disorderly at the Regent Palace Hotel.

April

2nd. Reprieve refused by Home Secretary.

Mrs Willis held up again in Old Knebworth.

4th. Hanratty executed at Bedford.

May

21st. Carol France, prosecution witness, takes overdose of drugs.

August

22nd. Alphon goes to the Hanrattys' house and offers to 'compensate' for the death of their son.

23rd. Incident at Green Park station. Fracas between Alphon, Mrs Hanratty and Justice.

Justice undertakes never to see Alphon again.

October

27th. 'Green Park' assault case at Bow St. Alphon acquitted.

October to May, 1963

First batch of phone calls between Alphon and Justice.

August 2nd, 1963

Commons debate on Fenner Brockway's motion for an inquiry.

March 18th, 1964

First mention of X by Alphon in phone call with Justice.

October 16th, 1964
    Justice's book published.

October 21st, 1965
    Russell's book published.

August 4th, 1966
    House of Lords debate on Russell motion.

August 25th, 1966
    Alphon convicted at Marylebone magistrates' court for making
    annoying telephone calls to Russell and Frank Justice. Bound
    over in his own recognizance not to repeat the calls.

September 14th, 1966
    Publication in *Queen* of Alphon's confessions on tape.

November 7th, 1966
    Panorama programme on case. Alphon denies guilt.

November 14th, 1966
    Mrs Walker, Mrs Vincent statements first mentioned in press.

January 30th, 1967
    Nimmo Inquiry into Rhyl alibi set up.

May 12th, 1967
    Alphon confession in Paris.

May 17th, 1967
    Confession repeated on I.T.N.'s Dateline.

May 21st, 1967
    Confession withdrawn in *People*.

June 7th, 1967
    Hanratty parents travel to Rhyl. Take statements.

June 11th, 1967
    Statements published in *Sunday Times*.

July 13th, 1967
    Supt Nimmo sent again to Rhyl.

September 2nd, 1967
    Alphon convicted at Marylebone of breaking recognizance not
    to make annoying calls.
    Withdraws confession on oath.

September 28th, 1967
    First Alphon letter to Home Secretary restating confession to
    the murder.
November 1st, 1967
    Roy Jenkins refuses public inquiry.

November 16th, 1967
    Frost Programme on case.

May 24th, 1968
    Hanrattys travel to Rhyl again. Collect more statements.

September 15th, 1968 (approx.)
    Hanrattys receive all defence papers.

September 29th, 1968
    Sunday Times article revealing Larman's statement on Rhyl
    alibi.

March 7th, 1969
    Alphon letter to the Home Secretary naming Mr X as the
    prime mover in the murder.

Introduction

This is the fourth book in English about the A6 murder and its aftermath. In 1963, a year after the verdict, Penguin Books published a short Penguin Special entitled *The A6 Murder: Regina v. James Hanratty; The Semblance of Truth* by the barrister and legal journalist Mr Louis Blom-Cooper. Mr Blom-Cooper's book appeared to settle many of the doubts about James Hanratty's guilt. My estimate of the book will become clear later.

In late 1964, the Paris publishers Olympia Press published a book entitled *Murder versus Murder* by Jean Justice. The book named Peter Alphon as the A6 killer and, no doubt because of that, was not published in England. The following year Lord Russell of Liverpool's persuasive book *Deadman's Hill: Was Hanratty Guilty?* was published by Secker and Warburg after being turned down on grounds of libel by Gollancz. The state of public knowledge about the case at the time and, more important, the libel laws, restricted Lord Russell to a refutation of the case against Hanratty as presented at his trial. Lord Russell introduced little or no new evidence to support his thesis that Hanratty was innocent, and avoided incriminating references to Peter Alphon.

The most comprehensive account of the case in book form to date is *Le Crime de la Route A6* (Laffont, Paris, 1968), also by Jean Justice, which is written and published in French.

Since Lord Russell's book was published, the case which he argued has been reinforced by new developments connected with Hanratty's alibi at Rhyl and with the behaviour of Peter Louis Alphon. This book is an attempt to codify this new information as well as to restate the case made by Lord Russell in greater detail — a task which has been made much easier by the availability of the defence papers.

The material for this book has come from four main sources. First, there are the defence papers, handed over to the Hanrattys in 1968. These include a copy of the transcript of the trial, held in January and February 1962, which is some 600,000 words long (about the size of eight full-scale novels); the depositions taken after the hearing before the magistrates at Ampthill in November and December 1961; statements by witnesses (including Hanratty); and photographs, maps and other documents.

Secondly, I have delved deep into newspapers, local and national. In this connection I am grateful to Mr E. R. C. Lintott, chief librarian at the *Daily Mirror* and his deputy, Mr Harry Cox, who gave me access to their library's comprehensive cuttings on the case, and to Mr Fred Sayer, chief librarian of the *Sunday Times*, who did likewise. I have interviewed several journalists connected with the case, all of whom surprised me by insisting on Hanratty's guilt. The press in general has been universally hostile to the attempts to reopen the A6 case, and not one leading crime correspondent has questioned the verdict. The only exception has been the *Sunday Times*, whose editor, Mr Harold Evans, has opened up his news-paper to each new development in the case. Mr Evans came to the *Sunday Times* from the *Northern Echo* in Darlington, which paper, under his editorship, gave every encouragement to the campaign to clear the name of Timothy Evans, convicted in 1950 for the murder of his child. The sophisticated scepticism which greeted that cam-paign came to an end in 1966 when Evans received a posthumous free pardon.

Thirdly, I have relied to a considerable extent on tape-recorded conversations involving Mr Peter Alphon, and on my own relation-ship with him over the last three years. Mr Alphon has known for more than two years that I have been working on this book, and has spoken to me freely in that knowledge.

Finally, I have attempted to interview all the important witnesses at the trial and all those who have subsequently come forward with evidence about the A6 murder.

From the prosecution witnesses I have not received the maximum co-operation.

In November 1969, for instance, I wrote to Miss Valerie Storie requesting an interview. My letter explained that I had no wish to distress her further, and that I was fully aware of her attitude at the trial and afterwards. I would not, I explained, have disturbed her at all, were it not for an interview she gave to the *Sunday Express* on August 29th, 1965, when Lord Russell's book was completed. 'Lord Russell', she said, 'has not talked to me once. And I was the only witness.' Miss Storie's mother was also quoted as saying, 'Lord Russell should have contacted us.' I received no reply to my letter, and wrote again when the book was almost completed in July 1970. Once again, there was no reply.

In November 1969, I also wrote to Mr Robert Acott, the officer in charge of the case. The previous summer, Mr Acott had suddenly and mysteriously left the police force after a long and distinguished career in which he had risen to the post of Deputy Commander. Some explanation for his premature retirement came in Mr Acott's reply to me some weeks later, which ran as follows:

December 14th, 1969

Dear Mr Foot,

        I see by the date of your letter that you have been kept waiting three weeks for a reply. I am extremely sorry, but I have only just returned from a tour.

Since August 1961, rarely has a week passed when I have not been called upon to speak or write on the A6 murder. To escape this and the persistent publicity, which for more than eight years had affected not only my private life but those of my family, I decided to retire from the Force and fall into oblivion indulging my interests and pastimes with my family and close friends. I have decided to have nothing to do with that case and on that I am adamant. Three months after retiring I am more than ever convinced that my decision is the right one. It is for this and other reasons, which I feel sure you will understand and appreciate, that I must decline your offer as I have several others recently. Let me add that I do value your courtesy in approaching me before going to print. So many are unlike you.

                Yours sincerely,

                      B. ACOTT

The two chief prosecution witnesses did not want to see me, and the third, Mr Charles France, was dead. I spent an uncomfortable evening in December 1969 with Mrs France and two of her brothers, all of whom were anxious not to discuss the case in public.

Similarly, I have not been able to discuss the case with Mrs Gregsten, the wife of the murder victim, or her family. My letters to her and to her brother-in-law, Mr William Ewer, requesting interviews were not answered. I spent many hours and pounds in bribes on ex-prisoners in an attempt to find George Nudds, another main prosecution witness. Nudds uses aliases so freely that he is almost impossible to trace.

Prosecution witnesses who have agreed to speak to me (and to whom I am grateful) are Mr John Skillett, Mr Edward Blackhall, Mrs Louise Anderson, Mr Cecil Harding, Mr Robert Crocker, Mr George Pratt, Mr Ernest Brine and Mr Arthur Embleton.

Witnesses for the defence have been more helpful. I have to thank a large number of people in Rhyl who have helped me in the course of four visits to the town in four years. All these people, and many others in London, Liverpool and Bedford gave up time without benefit to themselves.

In November 1969, I wrote to the Home Secretary, Mr James Callaghan, with three requests. First, I asked to see the documents about the case which were not made public at the trial, of which, as Home Office spokesmen have made clear in both Houses of Parliament, there are a great many. Secondly, I requested an interview with any Home Office official who had dealt with the case. And lastly I asked if I could see and publish the last letters of Charles France, which have always been kept secret. Several weeks later I received the following reply signed by Mr Callaghan's private secretary:

Dear Mr Foot,

       The Home Secretary has asked me to thank you for your letter of 21st November about the case of the A6 murder and to say that he is sorry that you have not had an earlier reply.

All Home Office criminal case papers are closed to public inspection for a period of 100 years under the provisions of the Public Records Acts and the Orders made by the Lord Chancellor under section 5(1) of the Act of 1958. At the inquest into the death of Mr Charles France the coroner decided that the letters he left before he died should not be made public, although two Members of Parliament have been permitted to see copies of them at the Home Office as an exceptional measure and against assurances that they would not disclose their contents. They do not however cast any doubt on the veracity of the evidence he gave at Hanratty's trial. The Home Secretary would be prepared to extend that concession to you on receipt of a similar assurance; but after careful consideration he regrets that he does not feel able to go further than this. You will appreciate that Home Office papers on capital cases have been disclosed only in the most exceptional circumstances and never in a case as recent or controversial as this. Similarly it would be contrary to long established practice for officials to discuss an individual capital case in the way you envisage.

I remain convinced that many of the gaps in the case which are not filled in this book could be filled after access to the unsaid evidence and unpublished statements in the Home Office. It is now clear that only a public inquiry will release them. In July 1970, however, despite a change of government, I was permitted to see the last letters of Charles France on the ludicrous condition that I could not comment on them.

This book has been written without the co-operation of the defence lawyers at the time of Hanratty's trial—Mr Kleinman, Hanratty's solicitor, and Mr Michael Sherrard, his counsel. In July 1970, when the book was nearly completed, I wrote long letters to both lawyers requesting an interview on any terms they suggested. I approached the lawyers with some caution. An article I had written in the *Sunday Times* in September 1968 had annoyed both of them. Angry letters were sent to the *Sunday Times* talking of legal action if aspects of the article were repeated.

In my letters in July 1970 I made it plain that I considered the conduct of Hanratty's case to have been more than adequate, and, excepting one or two details, above criticism. I do not take the view that Hanratty was badly defended, nor that his conviction was in any way the fault of his lawyers. Indeed, I regard criticism of his lawyers as a decoy to divert attention from the real reasons for his conviction.

After consulting Mr Sherrard, Mr Kleinman wrote to me to the effect that he and Mr Sherrard would consider what they could do to help me if I showed them the complete manuscript of my book in advance of publication. After much thought, I decided not to show the lawyers copies of the book before publication, and therefore to forfeit interviews with them.

This book has been written at the request and with the help of the A6 Murder Committee. This committee has no constitution. Membership of it is not formal. Its meetings are sporadic and unrecorded, and it has never at any time had more than a dozen active supporters. Yet it has sustained a vigorous campaign over many years whose only dynamic has been the determination of a few individuals.

Of these the most persistent and fanatical is Mr Jean Justice. His role in the campaign will emerge from the narrative. For nine years, the A6 murder and what he regards as its unjust sequel has been the main motivation of Mr Justice's existence. He has badgered and infuriated almost everyone connected with the case. As a result, he has had to put up with abuse and harassment on a wide scale. Yet more than anyone else outside the Hanratty family Justice has kept the case alive. This book, certainly, could not have been written without his help. He has made freely available his tape-recordings, his documents and his panoramic knowledge of the case. After knowing him for five years I am more convinced than ever that he is nearer the truth than all the 'normal' journalists, commentators and policemen who have abused and ridiculed him.

Justice's friend, Jeremy Fox, has also contributed enormously to the work of the A6 Committee. Mr Fox has spent not merely time and energy but also considerable sums of money on the A6 Committee's campaign. When the Hanratty family travelled to Rhyl in 1968 to seek witnesses for their son's alibi, Fox paid all the bills. He has contributed with incessant generosity to the costs of public meetings and advertisements in newspapers. He too has put everything he knows about the case at my disposal and corrected many points in the manuscript.

I am grateful too to other members of the Committee – Mr Michael Fogarty-Waul who accompanied me on important visits to witnesses in Slough, Ealing and Paddington; to Dr David Lewes, a Bedford surgeon who attended every day of Hanratty's trial and has ever since played a prominent part in the campaign to clear his name; to Mr Barney Berkson, a Birkenhead solicitor, whose friendship with Lord Russell of Liverpool brought him into the case and who has always been ready to help with free legal advice; to Mr Charles Irish and Mr Julian Howell; to Mr Tony Mason, a freelance journalist in Slough, who is almost the only journalist in the country consistently to have questioned the A6 verdict from the outset; and to Lord and Lady Russell for nourishing my interest when it was first aroused.

Lastly, I have to thank Mr and Mrs Hanratty and their sons, Michael, Richard and Peter. James Hanratty senior has lived in Kingsbury for more than twenty-five years working as a dustman and engineering worker. Until 1961, he and his wife Mary had lived an ordinary working-class existence, bringing up a large family in a council house on meagre, if secure wages. Neither of them before that year had ever been in a court room.

Suddenly in October 1961 they were wrenched out of this environment in circumstances too appalling to be imagined. Their eldest son was arrested for murder, tried, convicted and hanged. Mr Hanratty was not at that time an opponent of capital punishment. He believed that men who killed deserved to be killed. Alone with his son in a cell soon after the arrest, he asked him if he had committed the murder. 'He looked me straight in the eye,' he says today, 'and said, "No, Dad, I didn't".' That was enough for Mr Hanratty. Since that day, he, his wife and sons have committed themselves to carry out their son's last wish and clear his name.

It has been hard, unprofitable work. On innumerable occasions both parents have visited the Home Office with new grounds for a public inquiry, only to be rebuffed. They have demonstrated outside the House of Commons, and spoken, Sunday after Sunday, in Hyde Park. They have addressed at least half a dozen public meetings which they have helped to organize. Twice they have travelled to Rhyl to search for alibi witnesses. In the spring of 1969 they gave up two weeks' pay to stand in Whitehall with placards proclaiming their son's innocence, and to hand out leaflets to passers-by. Michael Hanratty, a printer, and his brothers Richard, a bus conductor, and Peter, a factory storeman have supported their parents loyally throughout their campaign.

The Hanratty parents have made available to me all the defence papers in their son's case. Everything I have asked for has been freely volunteered. The book has been written primarily because of Jim and Mary Hanratty, and it is a mark of the respect and affection in which I hold them.

September 4th, 1970   PAUL FOOT

PART ONE

The Murder and The Murder Hunt

1

A Tale of Two Suspects

The marriage between Michael and Janet Gregsten had been deteriorating for several months before the summer of 1961. They had been married when Mr Gregsten was working as a research scientist at the Fire Research Station at Borehamwood, and had set up home in a block of flats at Abbots Langley, near Watford. In 1956, Gregsten started work at the Road Research Laboratory at Langley, near Slough, and it was after their second son was born in 1959 that the couple began to drift apart. In the spring of 1960 Gregsten took lodgings near his work with Mr and Mrs Edward Cox at 50 Farnham Road, Slough, and travelled to Abbots Langley to see his family at weekends. After leaving the Coxes in Slough, he took a flat in Windsor. From time to time during the year before he was murdered in August 1961, Gregsten returned to Abbots Langley to try to patch up his marriage, usually without success. He sought advice from a marriage guidance counsellor as well as from a Harley Street psychiatrist. For several months before his death, Gregsten had been having a love affair with a young research assistant at the Laboratory where he worked – Valerie Storie.

Miss Storie shared his passion for motor cars and motor rallies and the pair took part in several of the latter. While Gregsten was in lodgings in Slough and Windsor, he would see Valerie Storie often, sometimes daily. He was always welcome at the Stories' home at Anthony Way, Cippenham, near Slough, even after, as Valerie Storie later revealed, 'someone tittle-tattled to my mother' that Gregsten was married.

Janet Gregsten was irritated and depressed by her husband's affair with Miss Storie. She and her family did everything in their power to discourage the relationship. At one stage, the director of the Road Research Laboratory received a letter complaining of the relationship, and called the couple to his office to advise against the liaison. Miss Storie told him sharply to mind his own business. Other attempts at sabotaging the relationship had been made. Gregsten's landlord at Windsor had been visited and advised not to let the flat as Gregsten was a married man.

All this, however, was to no avail. The affair between Gregsten and Miss Storie was not to be deflected. 'By now', wrote Miss Storie, referring to the latter half of August 1961, 'Mike discussed marriage pretty freely. He told me he wanted to marry me if ever he became free to do so.' (*Today*, June 2nd, 1962.) Gregsten had in fact taken legal advice about a possible divorce, but Mrs Gregsten was having none of it. 'It is true', she told the *People* several months after her husband's murder, 'that our marriage was at its lowest ebb. But so far as I was concerned, there was no question of divorce.' (The *People*, February 18th, 1962.)

Early in August 1961, Michael Gregsten, his wife and sons went on holiday to Swanage. At the same time, Valerie Storie took a holiday in Majorca with her friend, Ann Binks. The period immediately after the holiday was regarded by everyone concerned as crucial to the future of the marriage. Everything hinged on whether or not Gregsten, who had temporarily returned to live at home, renewed his affair with Valerie Storie.

On Tuesday, August 22nd, 1961, Michael Gregsten spent most of the day at his flat at Abbots Langley. He left the house at about 4.30 p.m., telling his wife that he would be back late. He was driving a grey 1956 Morris Minor which belonged, jointly, to his mother and to his aunt, both of whom lived in Golders Green. He drove first to the Road Research Laboratory where he picked up Valerie Storie. They then drove into Cippenham where Gregsten had his hair cut and Miss Storie did some shopping. They called in at Valerie's house for tea, and left about 8 p.m. for their favourite pub, the Old Station Inn at Taplow, on the Bath Road (the A4) between Slough and Maidenhead. The proprietress, Mrs Mary Lanz, told the press on the day after the murder that Michael and Valerie had often been to the pub.

'They had', she said, 'been coming in here for about four months. Some weeks they would come in every night, but never at weekends.' (*Windsor, Slough and Eton Express*, August 25th, 1961.)

The couple had one drink each and spent about an hour studying maps for a rally they were planning for the Road Research Laboratory's Social Club. The pub quickly filled up, and at about 9 p.m., the couple left and drove back down the A4 towards Slough. They turned right down Huntercombe Lane and drove through the little village of Dorney and round in a half circle till they came to a cornfield off Marsh Lane, which also runs down from the A4. The long, large cornfield stretches from Marsh Lane to the River Thames. Although less than a mile from one of the busiest main roads in Britain, it is relatively desolate, and, particularly on summer evenings, was a favourite spot for courting couples. Mrs Nellie Climo, who lived and still lives with her husband in a small house in Marsh Lane adjoining the field, tells me that she was so fed up with the 'Lovers' Lane' traffic that she persuaded her husband to put a gate at the entrance to the field.

Michael Gregsten and Valerie Storie had been to the field many times before. In evidence later Miss Storie was asked:

Q. Had you been to that same place before?
A. Yes.
Q. About how often?
A. Only a couple of times during the last three months. (Trial transcript, vol. II, p. 43.)

Moreover, in her articles for *Today* magazine, written several months later, she wrote:

We had been in the car to that particular spot quite a few times. In the summer we had parked the car and wandered down to the river to watch the boats go through the locks. We always enjoyed our evenings by the river. (*Today*, June 9th, 1962.)

Just as often, however, they did not wander down to the river, but stayed in the car. 'The car', Miss Storie wrote later, 'seemed so snug and reassuring. A private world.' (*Today*, June 9th, 1962.)

Certainly the couple had visited the field shortly before leaving for their holidays. In her deposition taken three months later, Miss Storie declared: 'About three weeks before the 22nd August, I went to the cornfield at Dorney Reach.'

Lighting up time on the evening of August 22nd, 1961, was at 8.35 p.m. As the couple drove into the cornfield it was rapidly getting dark. They stayed there for about half an hour, by which time it was almost completely dark.

There was then a sharp tap on the window of the driver's side. Looking sideways, Valerie Storie said later, she 'could see a man standing there ... could not see his head ... from shoulders more or less down to his waist'. He was wearing 'a dark suit, a white shirt and a tie'. (Vol II, p. 44.) 'This was', she wrote, 'no farmer or farmer's lad – it was someone immaculately dressed, standing perfectly still.' As Gregsten began to wind down the window, the man thrust a gun inside the car. Valerie Storie's immediate reaction, as she wrote later, was that the whole thing was a joke.

'I kept thinking ... this doesn't happen to ordinary people ... It happened to all sorts of queer people who lead queer strange lives. Not to Michael and me. Not to two ordinary law-abiding people ... It seemed so farcical, so utterly ridiculous that I almost wanted to giggle.' (*Today*, June 2nd, 1962.)

Gregsten's attitude, however, again according to Miss Storie, was rather different.

'I have told you how close we were,' she wrote. 'How I could sense every one of Michael's moods. This time I could sense that he was worried, almost frightened. When that knock came at the window of our car as we sat chatting together in that cornfield near Taplow, I felt as if someone had exploded a bomb.' (*Today*, June 9th, 1962.)

Then the man spoke. 'This is a hold-up,' he said. 'I am a desperate man. I have been on the run for four months. If you do as I tell you, you will be all right.'

The man got into the back of the car through the rear door, having forced Gregsten to hand over the ignition keys.

For all this, and for what happened over the next few hours we have only the evidence of Miss Storie. What follows is an account of the facts which are not in doubt and have never been challenged.

From the back of the car, the man said that he was hungry, that he had not eaten for two days, that the gun was 'a ·38', that he had bullets in his pocket. When asked what he wanted, he said: 'It is all right; there is no hurry.'

After about five minutes, the man ordered Gregsten to drive farther into the field and park close to a reaper, which was covered by a tarpaulin. The car remained there for about two hours.

The man then asked for watches and money. He took watches

from Miss Storie and from Gregsten, and gave them back later. He pocketed three pounds from Gregsten's wallet, but Miss Storie managed to take seven pounds out of her shopping basket and put them in her bra. He kept referring to his hunger, and was pressed to take the car and get something to eat. He was also pressed, if he wished to avoid notice, to make good his escape while it was still dark. To most of these questions he replied that there was 'no hurry' and that he would wait until daybreak.

The man said little about himself, save that he had been in institutions since the age of eight, that he had been to remand homes and Borstal, that he had done 'C.T.' (corrective training), and that the next thing he would get would be 'P.D.' (preventive detention). He also said that he had lived with the rich, and that he knew the Bear Hotel, Maidenhead. As for Miss Storie and Mr Gregsten, he asked them whether they were married and whether they knew the area. He seemed to want to know little else about them.

At about 10.30, the back door of one of the houses adjoining the field opened, and a man came out into his back yard and started to put away a bicycle. The man in the back of the car grew nervous and warned the couple that if anyone came over to them, they should say nothing. At about 11.30, he became restless and said he wanted food. He told Gregsten to get out of the car and into the boot. He took a rug from the car, and put it into the boot so that Gregsten would be more comfortable. While the two men were outside inspecting the boot, Valerie Storie ripped the strap which bound the back seat to the boot, thus ensuring that if Gregsten was put into the boot, he would be able to clamber into the inside of the car.

Gregsten and Valerie Storie pleaded with the man not to put Gregsten into the boot because a small hole in the exhaust pipe was letting out fumes which could be lethal for someone in the boot. The man agreed at once, and decided instead that Gregsten should drive the car. The car came out of the field, turned left up Marsh Lane and turned right on to the A4 towards Slough. It arrived in Slough at about 11.45 p.m., and stopped briefly beside a milk machine at Nevill and Griffin's Dairy. No one, however, had any sixpences, so the drive continued through Slough, Hayes and Greenford, where Gregsten was told to turn right towards London through Harrow and Stanmore. Near London Airport, the car turned into a Regent garage, where, on his passenger's instructions, Gregsten asked for two gallons which were put into the car by an elderly attendant. In Stanmore, Gregsten was allowed to get out of the car, cross the road and buy some cigarettes from a machine. Gregsten meanwhile, without his passenger's knowledge, had been flashing his reversing light. At one stage, in the Harrow area, a car passed and its passengers pointed at the back of the car, upon which Gregsten and the man got out of the car and walked round the back. The man could find nothing wrong, and so they climbed in and resumed their journey.

They travelled north from Stanmore through Aldenham and Park Street, which was a terminal of the recently built M1. They joined the A5 to St Albans, and from St Albans they took the A6 to Luton and Bedford. It was now about 1.30 a.m. and the volume of traffic had considerably diminished. The man in the back of the car had stopped talking about food and was talking instead about sleep. He wanted, he said, 'to have a kip'. As the car drove through the dark villages on the A6 beyond Luton, the man in the back kept looking out of the left-hand window, searching for somewhere to park off the main road. Twice he made Gregsten turn off to the left, but each time he found the place unsatisfactory, and the car continued down the A6. Finally, it passed through the village of Clophill and climbed Deadman's Hill on the other side. The sign 'Deadman's Hill' flashed in luminous lights in front of them. At the top of the hill there was a picnickers' lay-by, into which Gregsten was ordered to turn the car. Silent now, and frightened, Gregsten refused, and drove past. The man then became angry and forced him to turn in the road and drive back. Again, Gregsten drove past and again the man ordered him to do a U-turn and drive into the lay-by. The car was driven up a concrete strip parallel to the A6. When he reached the end of the strip, Gregsten was instructed to turn the car round so that it faced in the direction of Luton and London, and to turn off all the lights.

The man said that he was going to 'kip' and would therefore have to tie them up. There was then some discussion as to what to use for rope. Again, the two begged him not to shoot, but to take the car and run away with it. He replied: 'If I was going to shoot you, I would have done it before now.' He then searched around for something with which to tie up the couple, and even went again with Gregsten to the back of the car to search the tool-kit for rope.

When he returned, he tied Miss Storie's wrists with Gregsten's tie. He then asked Gregsten to pass him over the duffle bag of laundry which was in the front of the car. Gregsten picked up the bag, and, turning to his left, started to lift it over the front seat. He may well have tried to hurl the bag at the man in the back. Instantly, the man fired two shots into the side and back of Gregsten's head which killed him instantly.

The noise was shattering. Valerie Storie screamed: 'You shot him, you bastard. Why did you do that?' to which he replied: 'He frightened me. He moved too quick. I got frightened.' Miss Storie then shouted about getting a doctor for Gregsten, and the man replied with a sentence he had used throughout the journey. 'Be quiet will you,' he said, 'I am finking.' As before, Miss Storie noticed that he could not pronounce 'th'.

For several minutes, perhaps a quarter of an hour, Miss Storie and the man engaged in a near-hysterical conversation as to whether Gregsten was dead. Eventually, the man ordered her to turn round and kiss him, which, after some protest, she did. As she turned for the first time towards him, his face was lit in the headlights of a passing car. He then forced her to join him in the back of the car, where he assaulted her. She noticed that he was wearing black nylon gloves, one of which he removed during the assault.

After the assault, she again pleaded with him to take the car and leave her. Instead he forced her to pull Gregsten from the car. Gregsten's body was too heavy for her, and the man helped by taking hold of his legs. They dragged the body on to the concrete, and, after taking her basket from the car, Miss Storie sat down beside Gregsten, once more begging the man to leave them. Once more, he said: 'There is no hurry,' and asked her to start the car for him and show him how the gears worked. This she did, and again returned to Gregsten's body. The car's engine stopped. Again she started it and showed him how to work the gears. The man walked indecisively back and forth from the car. Miss Storie pulled out a pound from her mackintosh pocket and told him to take it and go. He took it, walked a few paces, turned and, at a range of about six or eight feet, fired a volley of shots in her direction. She felt the use of her legs go, and fell over. There was a pause, and she heard a clicking sound as though he was reloading. Then another volley of shots came in her direction, all of which, she thought, passed over her head. The man then walked towards her and touched her, while she lay, not breathing, pretending to be dead.

After a few moments he kicked her slightly, walked back to the car, put on the headlights and drove off towards Luton.

Valerie Storie found that she could not move her legs or her body. She waved her petticoat to try to attract the attention of a passing car. Several times, cars passed her without noticing her, and eventually she lost consciousness.

Three hours later, at about 6.45 a.m., a farm labourer called Sidney Burton was walking along the A6 to his work at Clophill. He heard a groan from the lay-by, ran down and found the couple. He ran down the road and found an Oxford undergraduate called John Kerr, who lived in Bedford, and had taken a summer vacation job for the Ministry of Transport counting the number of cars travelling along the A6. Kerr ran to the lay-by, and Miss Storie urged him to flag down a car. He ran into the road, stopped two cars, and told them urgently to get an ambulance and the police. Returning to the girl, he pulled down her skirt and covered her with a jacket. Before the ambulance arrived, she gasped out a few facts about her ordeal. Kerr jotted down the gist of what the girl told him on the back of one of his enumerator forms. (This he handed to a senior police officer at about 8 a.m.) By this time the lay-by was buzzing with activity. At 6.55 a.m. one of the drivers flagged down by Kerr had telephoned the police from the R.A.C. call-box on Deadman's Hill. A few minutes after 7 a.m., Police Inspector Milborrow arrived with a sergeant and a constable from Bedford Police Station. Milborrow spoke to Valerie Storie, and, some three minutes later, went down to the R.A.C. call-box and released to the nation's police the registration number of the grey Morris Minor. By 7.30, Miss Storie had been put in an ambulance and taken to Bedford General Hospital.

As can be seen from her conversations with John Kerr and with Police Inspector Milborrow, Valerie Storie was able to speak coherently about the appalling events of the previous night. Her ambulance was accompanied to Bedford Hospital by senior police officers, including Detective Chief Inspector Harold Whiffen of the Bedfordshire police, who was stationed at Luton, and Woman Inspector Arnett of the same force. Miss Storie was admitted to the hospital at about 7.45 a.m. Mr Andrew Pollen, a consultant ortho-paedic surgeon at Bedford Hospital, examined her and ordered an immediate blood transfusion. 'Her lower limbs', says Mr Pollen's statement, 'were completely paralysed. There were other serious wounds, and, according to the X-rays which were taken, two bullets still inside the body.'

Mr Pollen's examination started at about 9.45 a.m., and lasted about twenty minutes. His statement, under cross-examination at the hearing, goes on:

> I spoke to her and asked her questions. She understood and gave remarkably clear answers ... I did not discuss the man with her. The information I referred to as coming from her was to the effect that she had been raped. She said that it was under threat of the gun. She did not give me any details at all of the person who had done it. At the time I spoke to her she was compos mentis ...

If Mr Pollen did not talk to Miss Storie about her assailant, someone else did. Mr Pollen's statement continued:

> There were a number of police officers present in the hospital when I first examined her. They included Chief Inspector Whiffen and Woman Inspector Arnett. *I allowed them to take a statement from her.* Her general condition was serious. She was able to talk at intervals. *She was capable of giving a statement.* (My italics.)

The bullets which hit Valerie Storie had passed near enough to the spinal column to shut out much of the pain and shock which, had the spinal column not been affected, would have killed her or at least knocked her out. The long-term effect of the bullets was ruinous, but in the short term, as the ambulance took her to Bedford Hospital and as she was being examined there, Miss Storie was 'compos mentis'. 'That morning', wrote Valerie Storie later, 'through the pain, I heard policemen's voices and saw the doctors leaning over me. I began to tell my fantastic story. Miraculously, I could remember every detail. Because I was paralysed, this took most of the shock, and I was able to tell my story quite coherently.' (*Today*, June 9th, 1962.) Police officers therefore were able to take from her a statement about the murder and about the man who had done it.

That statement, made while her recollection of the murder was freshest, *has never been made available*. None of the police officers who took it were asked about it either at the magistrates' hearing or at the trial. No one outside the Home Office except the officers themselves know what sort of description Miss Storie gave of the man who, *that same morning*, had murdered her lover, and assaulted and shot her. Chief Inspector Whiffen, who appeared briefly at the trial to give evidence on another matter, was not asked by prosecution or defence about the statement which he took from Valerie Storie on the morning of the murder and which he must have written down, at least in note form. Woman Inspector Arnett appeared neither at the trial nor at the magistrates' hearing.

At the time, however, Miss Storie's description whispered to Chief Inspector Whiffen and his associates was treated with the greatest urgency. Almost at once, a description of the killer, which must have been based on Valerie Storie's statement, was circulated to the press and to police stations throughout the country. The description was printed prominently in that day's (August 23rd) evening papers, most of which carried the story of the murder as its page-one lead. The papers, needless to say, had sent their representatives to Deadman's Hill. The only man willing to talk to them there was John Kerr, the undergraduate, who, until later in the day, continued with his job as traffic enumerator. The description which emerged from the Bedford Hospital could then be compared with the statements of John Kerr about what Miss Storie had said to him about her assailant in the lay-by while waiting for the ambulance.

In the London *Evening News* on the afternoon of August 23rd, John Kerr was quoted as saying:

> She told me that as they passed through Slough at 9.30 last night, a man thumbed a lift. They picked him up, and on the journey they noticed he had staring eyes.

The *Evening News* gave the following description of the killer:

> He is aged about 30, 5 ft. 6 ins., of medium build, wearing a dark brown suit. He has dark hair, a pale face and deep-set brown eyes. He talks with an East End accent.

The morning papers the following day (Thursday, August 24th) repeated this description. The *Daily Mirror* had:

> The shot girl, Valerie Storie, was able to give a description of the killer, who, she said, thumbed a lift. And last night Scotland Yard's murder squad stepped up an all-out hunt in the London

area for a man described as: 'Aged about 30; 5 ft. 6 ins.; pale, clean-shaven face, dark brown hair and deep-set brown eyes.'

The *Daily Mail*'s description ran:

About 30; 5 ft. 6 ins. tall; medium build; deep-set brown eyes; dark hair and pale-faced. He is wearing a dark lounge suit and speaks with a Cockney accent.

Daily Telegraph readers were told:

Police say they wish to interview a man about 5 ft. 6 ins. tall, of medium build with dark hair and pale face. He has deep-set brown eyes.

The *Daily Herald*, which shared with the *Telegraph* the most extensive and original coverage of the case, stated:

The injured girl spoke to John [Kerr]. What she said gave detectives valuable clues to the killer. In her story, gasped out to John, Valerie talked of the gunman's staring eyes. The gunman is described as about 30, 5 ft. 6 ins. tall, of medium build. He has dark hair and deep-set brown eyes.

This description, common to all the newspapers, came from Miss Storie, and *from no one else*. As the *Windsor, Slough and Eton Express* (August 25th) put it:

The *only description* of the man wanted for questioning by the police is the one given by Miss Storie in her gravely ill condition.

Nor was the description the only aspect of Miss Storie's statement whispered from her bed at Bedford General Hospital which reached the newspapers the following morning. So full was her account of the murder that almost all the newspapers, in choosing their lead story for the morning of August 24th, chose the A6 murder, as it was already called, in preference to stories of increased tension in Berlin and of the expulsion of the Electrical Trades Union by the Trades Union Congress.

She said [wrote Robert Traini of the *Daily Herald*] that when they reached a common at Dorney Cross—15 miles from Slough —a man hitched a lift. Inside the car he pulled a gun and ordered them to take a roundabout route. They drove about 30 miles. Finally, the gunman told Mr Gregsten to drive into the lay-by off the A6. There he fired five shots at Mr Gregsten. Two went through his head and killed him. Then the gunman ordered Valerie into the back of the car where she struggled with him.

She was kept in the car for a long time. At about 3 a.m. the man fired a number of shots at her, and threw her body out of the car with Mr Gregsten's body. Valerie had been shot at least twice in the chest.

Almost all the papers carried all or part of this story. The detail did not vary. Most of them reported faithfully that the gunman had been 'given a lift'. The *Express* talked of 'lonely Dorney Common, where, it is believed, they picked up a hitch-hiker'; the *Daily Sketch* of a 'crazed hitch-hiker'. Rhona Churchill of the *Daily Mail* reckoned that: 'The murder of Michael Gregsten by a hitch-hiker is going to make many hospitable drivers refuse in future to give lifts to wayside strangers.'

The Royal Automobile Club was so impressed by these reports that it put out a statement warning motorists 'not to give lifts'.

The information that the gunman had hitched a lift was, as it later turned out, false. Its effect, however, was to divert the attention of the press from two important possibilities. The 'chance hitch-hiker' story ruled out the possibility that the murder had been planned: that Michael Gregsten and Valerie Storie were the targets of a prearranged plot. Secondly, if the murderer was a chance hitch-hiker, the relationship between Gregsten and Miss Storie had nothing to do with the murder. If they had been driving along and picking up hitch-hikers, nothing could be said or inferred about their relationship, save only that they were planning a motor rally.

Thus the breakdown in the Gregstens' marriage received scant publicity in a press not normally renowned for its squeamishness about reporting the details of people's private lives. The press were led even further astray by statements from loyal friends and relatives of the Gregstens and Miss Storie which conflicted sharply with the facts. Miss Ann Binks, for instance, Miss Storie's closest friend, was quickly besieged by journalists. She told them that the relationship between Valerie and Michael had been purely platonic.

The *Daily Telegraph* (August 24th) reported: 'The Gregstens were described by neighbours as a devoted couple'—a description which seemed to conflict with the information in the same article that: 'Mr Gregsten lived at a separate address from his wife.'

Mr Roy Catton, who lived next door to Mrs Gregsten and who like Mrs Gregsten was a prominent performer for the Abbots Langley Players, told the *Daily Sketch*: 'Mr and Mrs Gregsten were a happy couple. This week-end Mike decorated the kitchen.'

Mrs Marjorie Storie, who knew perfectly well that her daughter was in love with Gregsten, was quoted in the *Daily Herald* as saying: 'There was nothing between them.' Mrs Storie reinforced the 'hitch-hiker' theory with the information, printed in the *Daily Sketch*, that: 'Michael was so kind-hearted he would give anyone a lift.'

The local press, which could have been expected to give some clue to the background of the main participants, was even less informative. Only the *Windsor, Slough and Eton Express*, in its Slough edition, printed the facts about Gregsten living in lodgings in Slough for more than a year before the murder. The *Slough Observer* printed nothing of interest about either Gregsten or Miss Storie. The *Watford and West Herts Post* reported:

> It was with his mother that he lived at Slough during the week because of the distance of his place of work from his Abbotts Langley home. (August 31st, 1961.)

This was very odd, since Mr Gregsten's mother lived at Golders Green, which is farther from Slough than Abbots Langley. The *Langley Times* reported that Mrs Janet Gregsten had left her home after the murder and was 'staying with friends' in London. Both the press and the police from the outset of the inquiry started from the assumption that this was a chance encounter, that the two people in the car might have been anyone, and that the murderer therefore was some sort of 'moon maniac'. 'Detectives', surmised the *Daily Mail* crime correspondent, 'are not ignoring the possibility that the crazed gunman is a killer for thrills.' (August 25th.) 'Detectives believe', wrote Robert Traini of the *Daily Herald*, 'that the killer has a lust for blood. There seems no reasonable motive for the crime.' (August 24th.)

One further aspect of the reports following the murder conflicted sharply with later evidence. Nowhere in those early reports was the word 'rape' mentioned. 'The gunman', reported the *Daily Herald*, 'ordered Valerie into the back of the car where she struggled with him.' The *Daily Mail*'s version was: 'Then he forced Miss Storie into the back seat and attempted to assault her.' According to the *Daily Mirror*, the gunman 'attacked' Miss Storie. Most papers did not mention the incident at all.

At 3 p.m. on the afternoon after the murder the officer in charge of the murder inquiry arrived at Deadman's Hill. He was Detective Superintendent Robert Acott of Scotland Yard's Murder Squad. Acott had been a policeman for twenty-eight years, and had started on the beat in Harlesden, north-west London. He had been a bomber pilot during the war, and was awarded the D.F.C. for consistent bravery. His career in the Flying Squad and in the Murder Squad had been marked by displays of personal courage. While with the Flying Squad he had led an ambush against an armed gang of bullion raiders. He had led the group of Murder Squad officers who had charged into the hotel bedroom of the police-killer, Günter Podola. He had personally arrested Victor Terry, the Worthing bank killer.

At about 6.30 on the same evening, Mr Alan Madwar took his dog for a walk down Avondale Crescent, Ilford, Essex. Radio bulletins throughout the day had been circulating descriptions of the murder car, including its registration number, ever since Police Inspector Milborrow had sent it out from Deadman's Hill at eight minutes past seven that morning. Mr Madwar noticed that the number appeared on the number plate of a grey Morris Minor parked in Avondale Crescent. Immediately, he phoned the police and before long the Crescent was swarming with policemen, police photographers and ballistics experts. The car was spattered with blood, and the front number plate had been damaged. Mr Sidney Lawrence who lived in the corner house on the Crescent, in the house outside which the car was parked, told the press that he had seen the car outside his house at 7.45 that morning but had thought nothing of it. 'I think', he said, 'that the man must have got the car into the Crescent very quietly during the night.' (*Daily Herald*, August 24th, 1961.)

The policeman who first arrived at the car ensured that no one touched it until Mr Lewis Nickolls, the director of the Metropolitan Police Laboratory at New Scotland Yard arrived to take possession.

Mr Nickolls found two cartridge cases in the car. He found two clots of blood on the floor, and a rug draped over the driver's seat.

The car itself, though obviously the murder car, surrendered no clues to the murderer's identity. There were no fingerprints save those of Gregsten and Miss Storie and very few fibres of clothing or human hair on the rug or in the back seat. Yet the finding of the car in Avondale Crescent led to four important witnesses. Early the following morning – August 24th – plainclothes policemen started extensive inquiries in the Redbridge area. As people came out of their houses to go to work, they were approached and asked if they had seen anything out of the ordinary on the previous morning.

Shortly after 7 a.m. that morning, as on other mornings previously, Mr James Trower, then working in an engineering factory, called at the house of Paddy Hogan, who lived above Green's Stores in Redbridge Lane, to give him a lift to their common place of work. Trower knocked up Hogan and the two were about to get into Trower's car when they were approached by plainclothes policemen who asked if they had seen anything unusual the previous morning. Both men answered in the negative, and drove off. As they drove, Trower mentioned a small, grey car the previous morning which had made a grinding noise when the driver changed gears. Hogan advised him, if he remembered anything about the incident, to go back and tell the police. Trower turned back and told one of the policemen that early the previous morning he had seen a Morris grinding its gears. That night, Trower made a full statement to the police.

Later that morning, after reading a description of the car in the newspapers, Edward Blackhall, a dry-cleaner of Church Road, Lower Dunton Road, near Brentwood, telephoned Walthamstow police station to say that the previous morning he had, as usual, been given a lift to work in the car of an engineering foreman called John Skillett who worked at Stratford. In the course of their journey down Eastern Avenue, he said, they had encountered a grey Morris Minor which was being driven extremely badly. Both Blackhall and Skillett were whisked to Scotland Yard where Blackhall immediately identified the murder car as the one they had encountered the previous morning. He identified it by three red Scotch Tape strips on the back bumper and a torn green label on the back window.

Both men then told the police how they had been travelling down Eastern Avenue from east to west on the morning of August 23rd.

They were approaching red traffic lights at the corner of Ley Street and Eastern Avenue when suddenly the car which they identified whisked past them on the inside, and skidded in front of them, stopping just behind an Austin A40, and barely missing Skillett's car. When the lights turned green, the Morris shot off into the inside lane again, crossed the lights and careered down the dual carriageway which follows. As Skillett continued driving in the fast lane, both men noticed that the Morris had got stuck behind a green bus and was trying to pull out in front of them. Eventually, they allowed the Morris to pull out, and caught up with it a few hundred yards farther on at the roundabout at Gants Hill. As the Morris slowed down at the roundabout, Skillett steered his car level, asked Blackhall to pull down the window, and shouted across at the driver of the Morris: 'Are you fucking mad or something? You ought to get off the fucking road.' The driver turned towards them and laughed.

The cars moved off from the roundabout, with the Morris several cars in front. When the Morris got to Redbridge Station, it suddenly, without signalling, turned right across the intersection of the dual carriageway into Redbridge Lane, just beyond Redbridge Station.

This was plainly the murder car, and the man driving the car was plainly the murderer. Deadman's Hill is some seventy miles from Ilford, but the route is not on main roads and a bad driver at night could not be expected to do the journey in much less than three hours. The murderer left Deadman's Hill at about 3.30 a.m. Skillett noticed as they were driving past Newbury Hospital that its clock showed exactly 7 a.m. Skillett and Blackhall were important witnesses. Nothing was released to the press about their statements but they were warned by the police that they might be required at short notice to attend identity parades. On the evening of August 24th, they were allowed to go home.

That same evening, the police were presented with another major clue. Mr Edwin Cooke, a bus cleaner for London Transport, was working on the buses at Rye Lane garage, Peckham. Mr Cooke was a 'pick-up' man, whose job was to pick up by hand any objects which would not go through the vacuum pipe with which the buses were cleaned. Several years previously, Mr Cooke had found two dead rats under the upstairs back seat of a bus. Since that day, it had always been his practice to lift the back seat of a bus, where he had often found smaller objects. Lifting the seat of a 36A bus on August 24th, 1961, he saw some loose bullets and a handkerchief. Under the handkerchief was a revolver, fully loaded, and five boxes of ammunition.

Almost immediately, the gun and ammunition were handed over to Detective Sergeant Frederick Parrish of 'L' Division of the Metropolitan Police, who in turn handed them over to the Forensic Science Laboratory at Scotland Yard.

It did not take Mr Nickolls and his experts long to discover that this was the gun with which Michael Gregsten had been killed. The morning papers on Saturday, August 26th, carried detailed descriptions of the gun and appeals for anyone who knew anything about it to come forward. The police offered an amnesty to anyone assisting with information about the gun. In the meantime, they focused their attention on the 36A bus and its route. Mr Cooke, the pick-up man, told them that he was certain that the gun was not there on the evening of August 23rd, the day after the murder. Police then discovered that the 36A bus had made two journeys on the 24th. The first, in the early morning, had been from Rye Lane, Peckham, to Kilburn Lane, near the Kilburn High Road, returning via Marble Arch and Paddington Station (departure 5.40 a.m., arrival Kilburn 6.32 a.m.; departure Kilburn 6.39 a.m., arrival Rye Lane, after a break at Victoria, approximately 8.55 a.m.). The second journey was in south London only, from Rye Lane (departure 3.43 p.m.) to Brockley Rise and Victoria arriving back at Rye Lane at 7.23 p.m. The gun, therefore, had been left under the back seat either early in the morning anywhere between Peckham and Kilburn, or in the afternoon in south London, or (much less likely) while the bus was waiting in the forecourt of Rye Lane garage for most of the day.

By the Saturday morning (August 26th) Valerie Storie was beginning to fill in the details of the crime. She explained that the man in the car was not, as originally described in her story, a 'hitch-hiker'. According to the *Daily Herald* (August 26th), 'He (Superintendent Acott) identified the spot at Dorney Reach, near Taplow, Bucks, where the gunman forced his way into the car — a cornfield gateway.'

Yet there was still no indication as to why the murder had been committed. The conflict in the minds of the men conducting the murder inquiry was well summarized by two newspaper reports.

The *Daily Mirror* took one view: 'Now Scotland Yard believe they are looking for a gun maniac with no settled home.' The *Daily Mail*'s Owen Summers had somewhat different information: 'Police are considering a theory that though Mr Gregsten and Valerie did not know the killer, he may have known them. The killer may have become attracted to Valerie after seeing her with Gregsten at some time.' (August 26th.) This is the only suggestion in print at any stage during the inquiry that there was some previous connection between the murderer and his victims.

'The net', reported the *News of the World* on Sunday, August 27th, 'is closing on the terrified killer of the A6.' The reason for this confidence was the continuing improvement in the health of Valerie Storie, who had told the police that she was quite confident of her ability to identify her lover's killer. Her confidence led Superintendent Acott to make use of a new technique for assisting inquiries in criminal investigations – the Identikit picture. An Identikit is obtained by interviewing relevant witnesses about the facial characteristics of the man required. The interviewer has at his disposal some five hundred transparent slides of every facial feature each of which he shows to the witness until the witness agrees on a likeness. The whole is then put together into one photograph, and issued to the public.

The Identikit had already been used extensively in America. Its advantages, provided that the witnesses can remember outstanding physical characteristics of the wanted person, are obvious. It has however several drawbacks. Slight shifts in memory can produce marked differences between the picture produced and the hunted man. The issue of an Identikit picture, moreover, invariably results in innumerable telephone calls from all over the country, and a consequent waste of energy and resources in tracking down futile 'leads'. Nevertheless, Detective Sergeant Jock Mackle, Scotland Yard's expert in the Identikit technique, was summoned to Valerie Storie's bedside at Bedford General Hospital on Saturday, August 26th, where he started an exhaustive inquiry with his Identikit slides.

Even before the Identikit pictures were issued, the police had been attempting to cope with the usual flood of calls which follow sensational crimes. No one will ever know how many people were interviewed as a result of random, well-intentioned or crackpot telephone calls imparting 'information' about the A6 murderer. Such calls had been encouraged by the detectives in charge of the murder investigation. London's *Evening Standard*, for instance, on the day after the murder, reported: 'Landladies have been asked if any lodgers did not return on Tuesday night or have behaved in an agitated manner since.

At midday on Sunday, August 27th, Superintendent Acott appealed further to landladies. 'Do you have a lodger', ran the Scotland Yard statement, 'who has not stirred out for the past few days?' (*Daily Sketch*, August 28th, 1961.)

Several times in the weeks following the murder detectives repeated this plea, which had at least one interesting response. On Sunday, August 27th, Mr Peter Sims, the manager of the Alexandra Court Hotel in Seven Sisters Road, Finsbury Park, was approached by one of his permanent guests, a middle-aged schoolteacher called Miss Perkins. She was, she told him, extremely disturbed by the behaviour of the man in the room next to hers – No. 80 on the second floor. She had been unable to sleep at nights because the man had paced up and down the room, rummaging in his wardrobe, talking to himself and rattling metallic objects. She had noticed that he had been in his room almost continuously for about five days and on one occasion she had tried the door to ask him to be quieter at night. The door was locked and her knock produced no response.

Mr Sims, who is now the proprietor of the Kenhouse Hotel at Amersham in Buckinghamshire, then kept watch on the man, who had booked into the hotel in the early evening of August 23rd in the name of Frederick Durrant, and had given an address in Horsham. He had not come down for a meal since he had booked in four days previously. After a further discussion with Miss Perkins, Mr Sims telephoned the local police station at Blackstock Road, Highbury. Almost immediately, Detective Sergeant Arthur Kilner and a constable arrived, went up to Mr Durrant's room and asked him if he would come down to the police station for 'routine inquiries'. Mr Durrant politely agreed. At the police station, he revealed that his real name was Peter Louis Alphon.

Asked where he had spent the previous Tuesday night, Mr Alphon explained that he had been to see his mother in Streatham and had spent the night at the Vienna Hotel, Sutherland Avenue, Maida Vale, where he had registered in the name of Frederick Durrant. Sergeant Kilner phoned the Vienna Hotel and established that a man had signed in in the name of Durrant for the night of August 22nd. The hotel manager said that as far as he could remember Durrant had been in the hotel all night. The Highbury police discovered that Alphon led a nomadic existence, keeping very much to himself, moving from hotel to hotel, and making a living out of selling almanacs from door to door. His father, they found, worked as a records clerk in Scotland Yard's Aliens Department.

Sergeant Kilner interviewed Alphon for about two hours, and took from him a long statement about his movements on every day of the previous week. The sergeant must have noticed one very curious feature about the statement. At no time during the week, apparently, had Alphon met anyone except, fleetingly, his mother. He said he had gone for walks, notably in Richmond and Barnes, and had spent many hours in cinemas. On Monday, August 21st, he had spent the night under the pier at Southend. On Tuesday the 22nd, in the evening, he had booked in at the Vienna Hotel through the Broadway House Hotel in Dorset Square near Baker Street (the two hotels were in the same group). He had then travelled to Streatham, and met his mother on the corner of Gleneagle Road, where she lived. He had not gone to the house because he 'did not get on' with his father. He had then returned by Underground to the Vienna Hotel, where he had arrived about 11 p.m. The following day—the 23rd—he had met his mother for lunch, gone for a walk, and gone to a cinema. He had spent Thursday, Friday and Saturday entirely on his own—going for walks and going to cinemas. The statement seemed to satisfy the Highbury police. Alphon was released at about 10 p.m.

When Alphon returned, on his own initiative, to the police station the next day to see if they wanted anything more from him, the police, he wrote later, 'didn't seem particularly interested' (*Daily Express*, October 4th, 1961). His statement was sent in to the A6 'murder room' at Scotland Yard.

After August 27th, the attention of detectives in charge of the inquiry was concentrated almost exclusively on the forthcoming publication of the Identikit portraits of the killer. According to the *Daily Herald* on the Monday morning, August 28th, 'Scotland Yard are putting the finishing touches to the killer's face. The hunt for the man—said by police psychiatrists to have a split mind—will be stepped up to become the biggest manhunt ever seen in Britain.'

Detective Sergeant Mackle and his assistants had been having a little trouble with the Identikit. Miss Storie had been helpful and coherent, but her description did not seem to fit the descriptions which Mr Mackle had obtained from the other witnesses. At any rate, the Identikit pictures had very little in common. The more Superintendent Acott puzzled over the pictures, the more it became obvious that a composite was impossible. A compromise was therefore reached. The picture selected by Valerie Storie was published unchanged. The other three (or four) pictures were amalgamated, and published as one. The two final pictures, which differed sharply, appeared on television on the night of Tuesday, August 29th, and were published in the morning newspapers of Wednesday, August 30th.

There is no way of telling how many witnesses helped with the Identikit pictures, or who they were. The *Daily Express* on the morning of the Identikit's publication was specific. The pictures, announced a staff reporter, were 'built up by five people who had seen him'. The *Daily Mail* reported that the second photograph had been made up 'with the help of secret witnesses whose identity the Murder Squad are not revealing'. The *Daily Mirror*, on the other hand, reported that both pictures had been put together by four witnesses *'including Valerie'*.

Three of these 'secret witnesses' can be identified at once. Mr Skillett helped police with the Identikit, and was very unhappy with the published result. So did Mr Blackhall, and Mr Trower. If the *Mirror* was right, and four people helped with the Identikit including Miss Storie, that was all. If the *Daily Express* was right, however, there was another person who helped with the Identikit picture whose name has never been revealed.

No official explanation was given by Scotland Yard for the issuing of two different pictures, except that one had been put together by Miss Storie, the other by 'other witnesses'. The nearest to an official explanation was that given by the *Liverpool Echo* (August 30th): 'It is believed that one of the pictures represents an after-dark impression – probably given by Valerie Storie – and the other a daylight impression.'

The Identikit pictures were greeted by the press with a mixture of faith and scepticism. The *Daily Express* loyally reported that: 'the main features of the hunted man can be seen in each picture.' In the sense that each picture showed a face with two eyes, a nose, a mouth, two ears and hair, the *Daily Express* was right. Otherwise, the two faces differed in almost every respect. The *Daily Telegraph* (August 30th) was nearer the truth:

> They [the pictures] differ considerably in general feature. The first, on the left, has long straight hair brushed back, with his right eyebrow a little higher than the other. The eyes appear hooded and the nose straight. The mouth has thin lips and the ears are fairly large.
>
> In the second, which has more pronounced colouring and detail, the gunman is shown to have black, wavy hair and his eyes are more deeply set with bushier eyebrows.

There were other differences. The nose in the first picture is straight and slim. In the second picture it is large and flat. In the second picture, the lips are thicker and the ears less pronounced. There were however two features which were the same in both faces. The right eyebrow in both was higher and slightly bushier than the left eyebrow. Where did the bushy eyebrow originate? Mr Acott explained later: 'The feature of the bushy eyebrow in the Identikit photo must have come from Miss Storie.' (Deposition in Ampthill Magistrates' Court, December 5th, 1961.)

Miss Storie vehemently denied that she had ever emphasized a bushy or thicker eyebrow, and so Mr Acott was forced to retract. *No one*, he explained at the trial, had emphasized a bushy eyebrow. It had appeared in the Identikit pictures without one of the named witnesses – Skillett, Trower, Blackhall or Valerie Storie mentioning it at all. Could it have been that another witness, a fifth composer of the Identikit, had emphasized the bushy eyebrow?

The other similar feature was even more important. 'Both pictures', said the *Daily Telegraph*, 'are similar in as much as they are dominated by strong, staring eyes.' What were the colour of these eyes? In those far-off days before colour television and even before colour supplements, Identikit photographs were not produced in colour. Darkness and lightness, on the other hand, could be shown by shading. The hair, for instance, in the first Identikit picture of the A6 murderer was ostensibly lighter than in the second. What about the eyes?

'Yesterday', concluded the *Liverpool Echo* of August 30th, 'two Identikit pictures were issued giving two impressions by witnesses of the killer's facial appearance. *Each was dominated by dark staring eyes.*' (My italics.)

This fitted the original description given to police by Miss Storie to the effect that her assailant had 'deep-set brown eyes'. Both Identikit pictures show dark, staring eyes. The *Daily Sketch* article on the Identikit photographs reminded its readers: 'The wanted man is about 30 years old and five and a half feet tall. He has dark hair, pale face, deeply-set brown eyes.' (August 30th.)

The British public, no doubt anxious to assist police in their hunt for the A6 murderer, were confronted with two photographs of entirely different faces, which had only two common features. One, the bushy eyebrows, had not been mentioned by any of the witnesses who saw the killer, and the other, the dark eyes, was shortly to be retracted and changed.

Small wonder, then, that the publication of the Identikit pictures was followed by hundreds, if not thousands of phone calls to police stations all over the country giving useless information. One such call, however, was rather more significant than it seemed at the time. It concerned a young man called James Hanratty.

James Hanratty, who was twenty-five, had spent most of the previous seven years in prison. In September 1954, when he was eighteen, he was put on probation for a year for taking and driving away a motor car without consent and without being insured. Hardly had he finished his probation than he was up again at the Middlesex Sessions for housebreaking and stealing property. After a few months' freedom following that imprisonment, he was sent to prison again in July 1957—once again, for stealing a car. Almost immediately after his release, he was sentenced, in March 1958, to three years' corrective training—again for car stealing.

He left Manchester prison, after serving every day of his three years, on March 24th, 1961. He travelled to London, and immediately contacted his former associates. In Ealing he was 'fixed up' with a couple of suits and an *ex gratia* payment of £25, and during the Easter weekend that year (March 31st to April 3rd), he robbed a house in Wood Lane, Ruislip, leaving his fingerprints on the frame of the ground-floor window, which he had broken. After the robbery, he fled to Durham where he worked for a week in an engineering factory.

His family, meanwhile, were worried about him. His father, James Hanratty senior, had worked for twenty-six years for the local authority cleansing department where he was a foreman. He had persuaded the council to employ his son when the latter left school in 1951, but the boy had run away. As their son got deeper in trouble with the police, his parents did their best to encourage him to 'go straight'. They saw him only briefly after his release from Manchester, and had not had time to discuss plans for his future. His mother was therefore delighted when, on April 13th, he arrived on the doorstep of their home at Sycamore Grove in Kingsbury, north London, announcing his decision to 'give it one more try'.

His father, determined 'to give the boy a chance', left his job with the council, sacrificing his pension rights. He and his son then set up their own window-cleaning business. With his pension contribution money, Mr Hanratty senior bought window-cleaning equipment, and the two James Hanrattys started to tout for business on the Kingsbury estates. In the following three months, they built up a strenuous, profitable 'round'. Mr Hanratty still remembers his son's pleasure at their business success. During the rest of April, the whole of May and June and the first two weeks in July, James Hanratty did not spend a night away from home.

In the second week in July, Mr and Mrs Hanratty went away for a week's holiday in Southsea, leaving their son to look after the business. On the Thursday of the week they were away, Hanratty abandoned his window-cleaning equipment in a customer's garden, and vanished. His parents did not see him again until he was charged for the A6 murder three months later.

On an impulse, freed for a moment from the influence of his parents, Hanratty had gone on a spree in the West End. His brother Michael recalls today how easily his elder brother could be conned into committing petty crimes from which others prospered and he suffered. Before long, he had fallen prey to the bribes and patter of the Soho underworld.

Almost at once he stole a car, and headed for the Midlands with a fellow thief. They had a puncture at Shrewsbury and, as a police officer approached and asked for their licence, Hanratty ran away, leaving the police officer holding his accomplice. Hanratty hitched a lift, first to Cardiff, and then by lorry northwards until after many hours' walking, and almost without money, he arrived on July 25th in Rhyl.

He wandered disconsolately on to the front and down to the fairground, and got a 'start' as a temporary worker on the dodgem cars. A fairground worker got him a job, befriended him and put him up for the night. The following morning he left Rhyl and made his way back to London.

Shortly after returning from Rhyl, at the Rehearsal Club in Archer Street, Soho, he bumped into an old associate called Charles 'Dixie' France. France offered Hanratty accommodation in his house, and for much of July, August and September of that year, Hanratty slept on the sofa in the Frances' sitting-room. France helped him value the jewellery he was stealing, and introduced him to receivers. During July and August Hanratty had a number of successes with burglaries, mainly in the Northwood and Stanmore areas. He said later that in that time he stole goods to the value of some two thousand pounds.

At the time of the issue of the Identikit pictures in connection with the A6 murder, Hanratty was staying with his friend Charles 'Dixie' France. He and Mr and Mrs France were watching the television when the Identikit pictures were flashed on the screen. According to one of Hanratty's statements to his lawyers after his arrest, Mrs France remarked how much the pictures looked like him.

If Mrs France did say something to that effect, it was very surprising. Hanratty had a box-like square face. Both the Identikit faces were oval. His hair was not slicked back as in the first identity picture, nor brushed back as in the second. It fell forward at the front and could not be brushed back because of a 'widow's peak' on his forehead. His eyes were not dark. They were light blue. How Mrs France arrived at the conclusion that the Identikit picture resembled her guest remains a mystery.

Hanratty was still staying with the Frances two days later, on the morning of Thursday, August 31st, when he was first identified as the A6 killer – in most unusual circumstances.

On that morning, Hanratty left the Frances' house at Boundary Road, Swiss Cottage, and walked up to the Finchley Road. He turned left and walked the hundred yards or so to Swiss Cottage tube station which then included an arcade of shops. In the arcade was an umbrella shop owned by a north London antique dealer called William Ewer. Mr Ewer's wife was the sister of Janet Gregsten, and Mr and Mrs Ewer had gone out of their way to take care of Mrs Gregsten and shelter her from prying journalists in the days after her husband was murdered. The story can now be taken up by Peter Duffy, a crime reporter on the *Daily*

Sketch who reported the whole A6 case but who could not, by the rules governing contempt of court, publish this story until after a verdict had been arrived at. The story therefore appeared in the *Daily Sketch* of February 19th, two days after Hanratty's conviction. It was the main story on the back page and it was headed:

AMAZING STORY OF MRS GREGSTEN'S INTUITION.
SHE SAW HIM AT THE CLEANERS.

The amazing intuition of Janet Gregsten, widow of A6 murder victim Michael Gregsten, helped to put James Hanratty on trial for his life.

Only eight days after the murder – when Scotland Yard were without a positive clue to the killer – Mrs Gregsten pointed to Hanratty and said:

'That's the man the police are looking for.'

Mrs Gregsten's 50-year-old brother-in-law, Mr William Ewer, had taken her to his antique shop in the station arcade at Swiss Cottage, North London, to try to help her to get over the tragedy which struck her life.

On the morning of August 31st, Mrs Gregsten was standing in the shop window helping Mr Ewer to hang a picture – a Wilson Steer interior. Suddenly she clutched Mr Ewer's arm and pointed through the window to a man with jet black hair walking into a Burtol cleaner's shop only two yards across the arcade.

'That's the man. He fits the description,' she said.

'But it's more than that. I've got an overpowering feeling that it's him.'

Said Mr Ewer last night: 'I calmed her down and told her she was overwrought. But she was so convinced about what she had seen that I went into the cleaners later and talked to the manageress.'

She told me the man had brought a green suit in on August 21st to have a tear in the coat mended and the trousers tapered. He had called in that day to ask if it was ready. He gave the name J. Ryan, and an address in St John's Wood.'

Neither Mr Ewer nor the police knew then that J. Ryan was an alias of James Hanratty and that, immediately after the murder, he stayed in the road named with his friend, Charles 'Dixie' France – only a mile away from the cleaners.

Said Mr Ewer: 'So convinced was I about what Janet had seen that I vowed then to search for the man myself. I had to find him again!'

Mr Ewer's hunt, according to the story, did not last long. The next day he went to a café in the Finchley Road. As he sat drinking a cup of tea and pondering the almost hopelessness of the A6 murder he spotted a pair of hand-made Italian shoes.

'My eyes travelled upwards to a well-cut blue suit. Then I found myself staring into those blue eyes again. It was the same man.'

Stunned by this miracle, according to the story, Mr Ewer decided to follow the man. He watched him go into a florist's shop in the Finchley Road. Then, acting on an impulse, he rang Scotland Yard. 'A Squad car arrived. I introduced myself and told the police the story.' The police (the article does not say *which* police) then made inquiries at the florist's shop, and the manageress there, a Mrs Dorothy Morrell, told them that the man had come in on September 1st and said he wanted to send some roses to his mother – a Mrs Hanratty of 12 Sycamore Grove, Kingsbury.

The article continues:

A report was made to Scotland Yard. But the Murder Squad had never heard of Jimmy Ryan. They had never heard of the address in Sycamore Grove, Kingsbury, which was the home of his mother. But Bill Ewer could not rest. Almost daily, he went out looking for the man with the staring eyes.

He walked into the shop of a business associate – 58-year-old Mrs Louise Anderson, who has an antique business in Greek Street, Soho.

He did not know that Hanratty, whom Mrs Anderson had befriended, had been in the shop only that morning.

On the same day as the *Sketch* article, a very similar article appeared in the *Daily Mail* by Bernard Jordan.

The publication of these articles was the first indication that Scotland Yard had Hanratty's name and his alias long before they started to hunt him as the murderer. The articles presented a series of coincidences which would strain the credulity of the most gullible mystic. The only description of the murderer had been released on the day of the murder, and did not fit Hanratty. Neither of the

Identikit pictures resembled Hanratty. Yet here was Mrs Gregsten 'identifying' James Hanratty as he walked into the cleaners opposite her brother-in-law's shop. The coincidence was compounded when Hanratty appeared the next day in the same café as Mr Ewer and went into a florist's shop, giving the address of his parents. Finally, Hanratty had been 'befriended' by Mrs Louise Anderson, a 'friend and business associate' of William Ewer.

What was it exactly which enabled Mrs Gregsten to recognize Hanratty as her husband's killer and put her brother-in-law on his trail? The *Daily Mail* is explicit:

> The face in the crowd that caught the eye of Janet Gregsten left her gasping.
>
> Was it – could it be – the face of the man who only eight days before had cold-bloodedly murdered her husband? She saw the blue staring eyes when she looked suddenly out of the window of a tiny antique shop in Swiss Cottage. It was a flash of intuitive recognition.
>
> The face of the man who went into the cleaner's shop next door was, she felt sure, the face that Valerie Storie had described to police as that of the A6 killer.

It was those *blue, staring eyes*, apparently, which convinced Mrs Gregsten that this was the face that Valerie Storie had described to the police as that of the killer.

Yet up to that morning, August 31st, neither in her detailed conversations with policemen nor with the Identikit experts had Valerie Storie spoken of the killer's blue eyes. On the contrary, she had told police after the murder that the killer had 'deep-set brown eyes'. The Identikit pictures and the descriptions which preceded them had included 'deep-set brown eyes'. In no newspaper, radio broadcast or television bulletin had blue eyes been mentioned as a characteristic of the A6 killer. Yet here was Mrs Gregsten identifying a man as the A6 killer because of his blue eyes; and here was her brother-in-law, William Ewer, on the hunt for the blue-eyed man who, he was convinced by his sister-in-law, had something to do with the murder.

Mr Ewer has on a number of occasions protested to journalists that the *Sketch* story was not accurate. He protested to the deputy editor of *Queen*, which magazine reproduced the gist of the article in September 1966, and he protested in the same terms to two

Sunday Times reporters in December of the same year. It is not clear which aspects of the *Daily Sketch* article Mr Ewer regards as inaccurate. Peter Duffy, on the other hand, is confident that his story was accurate. He confirmed it not only to me but also in public on a B.B.C. Panorama programme in November 1966. At any rate, the crucial aspect of the story – that the police were put on the trail of James Hanratty – is confirmed in both the *Daily Sketch* and the *Daily Mail* by the woman in the Finchley Road flower shop, Mrs Dorothy Morrell. Mrs Morrell, who was still the manageress at Caters when I interviewed her in August 1970, remembers the visit of Hanratty very well, and confirms that, soon afterwards, inquiries were made about him by two plainclothes policemen.

While William Ewer was rushing about the Finchley Road on the morning of August 31st following the blue-eyed man who had left the cleaner's shop, Valerie Storie was lying in bed in Bedford General Hospital. Her condition had improved by this time, and doctors advised that she should be moved to Guy's Hospital, London, which had better facilities for treating her. At midday on the 31st she was transferred under strict security precautions by ambulance, accompanied by a policewoman. As she travelled in the ambulance, the police at Bedford issued a new description of the murderer, which was published in the later editions of that day's evening papers. In the description, the colour of the murderer's eyes had changed completely. The *Liverpool Echo*'s front-page report declared:

MAN WITH 'ICY-BLUE SAUCER-LIKE EYES' SOUGHT.
New Description issued to Police.

The man being sought for the killing of Michael Gregsten and the wounding of Valerie Storie in their car at Deadman's Hill on the A6 eight days ago has 'large, icy-blue, saucer-like eyes'. This feature was included in a new description issued today by Bedfordshire County Police at Bedford.
The man they are looking for is aged 25 to 30, about 5 ft. 6 ins. tall and proportionate build. He has dark brown hair, is clean shaven and has a pale smooth face.
Detective Superintendent Barron said the wanted man had 'large, icy-blue, saucer-like eyes'.

The morning papers of September 1st faithfully carried the 'icy-blue eyes' description, but most of them did not mention that this represented a sharp change from the previous descriptions. The *Daily Mail* reported that the description was 'amended', and the *Daily Mirror* referred to a 'corrected description'. Only the *Daily Express* gave some clue as to where the change originated: 'Miss Storie was transferred yesterday to Guy's Hospital from Bedford. Before she left Bedford she *remembered something more* about the killer's appearance. He had "icy-blue, saucer-like eyes", she told detectives at her bedside.' (My italics.)

Miss Storie was not, however, 'remembering something more'. She was remembering something entirely different to what she had originally remembered – that the murderer had 'deep-set brown eyes'. She was changing her description of the murderer to include his 'saucer-like blue eyes' only a few hours after Janet Gregsten and Bill Ewer had 'identified' Hanratty, who had wide blue eyes, as the murderer. The police, who would in normal circumstances be more than a little cautious about so sharp a change of mind, immediately put out the new description and stuck to it until the case was closed.

Almost immediately, it seemed, the Murder Squad were on the trail of their newly described suspect. On September 1st, Superintendent Acott returned to Bedford from London and directed the search to 'a man he believes may be able to help inquiries with the hi-jack murder ... police now have a description of the man' (*Daily Mail*, September 2nd). 'The name of a man', wrote Robert Traini of the *Daily Herald* (September 2nd), 'with large, icy-blue eyes who may be the A6 killer was given to a special squad of detectives last night.' 'The man who supplied the information', said the *Daily Express* of the same day, 'was given a special police guard. Forty detectives in East London were given the wanted man's name and were told to check immediately with his relatives and friends to trace his latest whereabouts.' All this hullabaloo came to nothing, as a small report in the *Daily Express* pointed out two days later (September 4th). 'The East End man', it said, 'has been ruled out.'

It was now a fortnight since the murder. Despite total co-operation from the press, Superintendent Acott and his detectives were no further forward in the murder hunt. By now they had abandoned any suggestion that the murder was planned. 'Detectives', said the

Sunday Pictorial on September 3rd, 'are convinced he is a moon-mad murderer with a complete contempt for death and a warped attitude towards sex.' On September 5th, the London *Evening Standard* voiced the current view of the Murder Squad: 'The A6 killer is in London. He is a sadist. At any moment he may strike again.'

These fears appeared to be confirmed on September 7th when a Richmond housewife, Mrs Meike Dalal, opened her door to a man who said he was answering her advertisement in the paper for a room to let. She took him upstairs to show him the room, where he immediately tried to assault her, shouting: 'I am the A6 killer.' He hit her on the head, attempted to tie her hands and lift her skirt, but she struggled free and screamed, and he charged out of the house. A window cleaner on a neighbouring house saw the man running down the street. Mrs Dalal described the man to the police as in his twenties, slightly shorter than she was, with dark brown hair plastered back, wearing a white shirt, no tie and a new white 'shortie' mackintosh. She thought his eyes were brown.

On the same day, the newspapers announced that the police had run to ground the garage man who, according to Miss Storie, had filled the murder car with petrol about two and a half hours before the murder. He was Mr Harry Hirons, aged eighty, who remembered filling the car, and recalled that Gregsten, in a vain attempt to attract attention, had twice changed his order for the number of gallons required. Yet Hirons told police that he did not get a good look at the man in the back of the car, and his discovery was scant reward for the thousands of hours spent in checking the route which the murder car had taken on the night of August 22nd–23rd.

On Monday, September 11th, nearly three weeks after the murder, the Murder Squad at last got a clue which led them to suspects. Throughout the day at Guy's Hospital, Valerie Storie talked to police officers through a tape-recorder. Five hours of her account of the murder night were carefully recorded. Scraps of what she said were thrown to the hungry newspaper reporters. 'From 9.30 to 11.30 on the murder night', reported the *Telegraph* next morning, 'all three sat in the cornfield near Dorney Reach, talking.' 'The killer', wrote the *Daily Mail*, 'talked for two hours before shooting. And in those two hours he spoke about himself.'

'They promised to give him the Morris 1000 car in which they had offered him a lift. They offered him money. He refused that too.' (*Daily Herald*.) The *Daily Telegraph* recorded: 'Miss Storie has told police that she would easily recognize the murderer.'

It was while Valerie Storie was talking into the tape-recorder that the vital clue was discovered. Mr Robert Crocker was the manager of four London hotels, the chief of which was the Broadway House Hotel near Baker Street. One of the hotels in Mr Crocker's charge was the Vienna Hotel in Sutherland Avenue, Maida Vale. That hotel was managed by a Spanish couple, Mr and Mrs Galves, who were assisted by a man called William Nudds, aged fifty-three, and a woman named Florence Snell with whom Nudds was living. The Galves and the Nudds had not been getting on very well, and in the early morning of that Monday, Mr Crocker went down to the Vienna Hotel, discovered some money missing from the till and sacked the Nudds instantly, with a week's money, insisting that they leave the hotel at once.

Mr Crocker then decided to go on a 'tour of inspection' of the hotel with Mrs Galves. He visited all the bedrooms, checking damage to furniture. When he came to room 24, a big room in the basement, Crocker leant down to rip off a piece of material hanging from one of the armchairs. As he did so, something fell off the chair. It was, he noticed at once, a ·38 cartridge case. (He had had extensive experience of such weapons during his war service.) Mrs Galves pointed out another cartridge case on the chair. Crocker remembered the call from Highbury Police Station a fortnight previously about a man staying in the Vienna Hotel. So he rang the Highbury police and told them about the cartridge cases. 'I wondered', he told me when I interviewed him in July 1970, 'whether to fling the cases in the bin and have done with it – but I thought they might be important.' Ten minutes later, Police Constable Copp from Harrow Road police station arrived, took the cases and handed them over to Mr Nickolls at Scotland Yard's forensic laboratory. It took Mr Nickolls only a few hours to discover that these were cartridge cases whose bullets had been fired by the A6 murder gun.

As soon as Superintendent Acott was told about the cartridge cases, he descended with all his staff on the Vienna Hotel and even set up a headquarters of his murder inquiry in the front room of the Broadway House. No mention of the cartridge cases was made in the press or on radio or television. The only sign that the inquiry had been given a boost was a report in the *Telegraph* on Thursday,

September 14th, that the previous day Superintendent Acott had returned 'on a surprise visit to London to take personal charge of the inquiry'. From that day onwards the Vienna Hotel and its ill-kept records became central to the murder hunt.

Meanwhile, on another front, it appeared from one provincial newspaper report that the police had narrowed the field of suspects:

> Every police force in Britain last night received the names and descriptions of two men who are wanted for questioning about the A6 murder. Photographs of the two men were picked out from a number of criminal record pictures by the young woman who was shot on the road at the time her companion, Michael Gregsten, was killed. It is essential that these two suspects should be found. (*Yorkshire Post*, September 15th, 1961.)

The *Yorkshire Post* had got it wrong, but only slightly. The 'two suspects' had been picked not by Valerie Storie but by James Trower, the Redbridge engineering worker, who had agreed to look through Scotland Yard's photograph album to see if he could identify the man he had seen in the murder car.

Trower duly picked out three pictures. One of them had to be discounted when it was discovered he had spent the night of the murder in prison. The other two were quickly found, and quickly eliminated. Police faith in Mr Trower's ability to identify the murderer never wavered.

Mr Acott, however, was busy with other matters. He was urgently studying the records of the Vienna Hotel and was also talking to the Galves and the Nudds.

No one, the Superintendent discovered, had stayed in room No. 24 on the night of the murder. On the night before the murder, August 21st–22nd, one man had slept in the room, giving his name as J. Ryan and his address as 72 Wood Lane, Kingsbury. According to the records, only one other person had slept in the room before the cartridge cases were found — an Indian called Rapur who had stayed in the room on the night of August 30th.

A brief glance through the case records, however, showed that the Vienna Hotel had cropped up once before in the murder hunt. On August 27th, only four days after the murder, Peter Alphon, questioned at Highbury because of his curious behaviour after the murder, had said that he had signed in, in the name of Durrant, at the Vienna Hotel on the night of the murder, and stayed there all night. He also said that he had been with his mother at Streatham from about 9.15 p.m. until about 10 p.m.

There were therefore two names on the Vienna Hotel register which immediately required investigation: James Ryan and Frederick Durrant. Ryan had booked for the 21st–22nd and Durrant had booked for the 22nd–23rd – the murder night.

On September 13th, Acott himself interviewed Alphon's mother who agreed that she had seen him and given him a suitcase on the murder night.

At the Vienna Hotel itself, Mr and Mrs Galves, Acott discovered, were of little assistance since they spoke only Spanish. Mr Acott came to rely increasingly on William George Richard Nudds, whom Acott then knew under the name he was using at the time, Jack Glickberg.

It was unfortunate for everyone concerned that Nudds was so crucial a witness. To start with, he had a number of aliases – Edward Baker, Edward Bartlett, David 'Jazzer' Beaumont, George Knight, William Itter, and George Nudds (and William Nudds, which, he later testified on oath, was his real name). He had spent most of his life in prison, usually for fraud. In prison he had acquired a considerable reputation. A report in the *Empire News* some nine years previously began:

> Behind the bars of Parkhurst prison, Britain's toughest jail, David Beaumont is serving a sentence of nine years preventive detention, and on every day of that sentence he goes in terror of his life. Gaol mobsters have threatened to get him for informing on one of them ... (*Empire News*, July 20th, 1952.)

The story of 'Jazzer' Beaumont's 'courage' began in 1947 when he gave evidence against a fellow prisoner before visiting magistrates about a slashing incident in the prison. Some years later, at Parkhurst, he gave similar evidence against a fellow prisoner and was transferred under threat of attack. Mr Marcus Lipton, M.P. for Brixton, took up his case, and he was moved to the hospital wing at Parkhurst.

During my inquiries into this case, I received a long and helpful letter from a Mr Edward Kelly of Whetstone Lane, Birkenhead. Mr Kelly was writing 'about the credibility of the prosecution witness Nudds, alias Beaumont, an ex-P.D. prisoner with me at Parkhurst in 1952'.

'The man Nudds', writes Mr Kelly, 'was a notorious informer, what the prisons call a "mixer", and during his "time" he was constantly being threatened, attacked and placed under protection by the prison authorities.' Mr Kelly goes on to explain how, acting on instructions, Nudds deliberately planted two letters asking for money to be illegally sent in to him on two hospital officers, who were later arrested, convicted at the Isle of Wight magistrates' court and sacked.

Mr Kelly wrote to Hanratty's defence counsel at the time of the trial giving this information about Nudds, but refused to give evidence at the trial because he was then wanted for another crime. He is, he writes, happy to give evidence at a public inquiry. 'The case', he writes, 'has always intrigued me because I know what Nudds was capable of, and although I thought Hanratty guilty at the time, there is always for me a big question mark.'

Throughout his evidence at this trial, Nudds protested that he was attempting to 'go straight'. Yet in October 1962, eight months after the trial ended, he was again convicted for fraud and sentenced to six years in prison. Once again, his safety was in question, and once again he had to be transferred—this time to Strangeways Prison, Manchester, where he spent most of his time in the special protection wing. The most accurate description of Nudds comes from the man himself. 'I am', he once told a newspaper, 'the most hated man in Britain. They call me The Squealer.' (*Empire News*, August 3rd, 1958.)

When Mr Acott first interviewed Nudds shortly after the cartridge cases had been found in the Vienna Hotel, he did not know that he was talking to 'The Squealer'. The first statement which Nudds made to Acott on September 15th was signed J. Glickberg and gave the wrong date of birth (February 4th, 1915, instead of January 16th, 1908).

The statement concentrated first on the booking of J. Ryan, and described how the man calling himself Ryan was sent over to the Vienna Hotel by the Broadway House Hotel between 9 p.m. and 11 p.m. on the evening of Monday, August 21st. The statement continued:

Mr Ryan was instructed to add to his particulars in the

hotel register, which he did, and I showed him into his room. There are a number of beds in this room and he occupied the bed on the left hand side as you go in the door. The bed is set back in an alcove. I informed Mr Ryan that breakfast was from 8 a.m. to 10 a.m. in the morning. I closed the door of the room and left Mr Ryan there.

At about 7.45 a.m. Mr Ryan came up the following morning to the dining room and was served with breakfast which he ate. He left soon after breakfast. It would be about 8.30 when he left. He returned a few minutes later and said he had forgotten something in his room. He asked me if he could return there and I allowed him to do so and didn't go with him. He was gone a few minutes and reappeared from the basement and asked me how he could get to Queensway. I told him to walk to Harrow Road, which is about half a mile away, and get a number 36 bus.

I have been shown our hotel receipt book, and in particular an entry dated 21st August, 1961, which relates to Mr Ryan and numbered 6776. This receipt is in my handwriting. I cannot remember if Mr Ryan paid me on the night he arrived or whether I made the receipt out on the night he came in readiness to give it to him when he paid the following morning. He did in fact settle the bill.

There followed a long description of Ryan with the assurance: 'I would definitely identify the man again.'

This statement was, of course, extremely damaging to Ryan. The reference to the 36 bus was dramatically relevant, for the gun had been found under the back seat of a 36A bus.

Mr Nudds was also required to make a statement about Mr Durrant (Alphon). It ran as follows:

I have been shown another entry in the hotel register signed F. Durrant, 7 Hurst Avenue, Horsham, Sussex, and dated 22nd August, 1961. I remember this particular man and booking as my wife had told me he had phoned earlier in the day. He arrived very late in the evening. I think about 11.30 p.m. to midnight. He was dealt with by my wife, but I saw him and stood by while my wife dealt with him. My wife took him to his room. I didn't see him again until the following morning when I went to his room to see if he wanted breakfast. He was in room 6, which is on the second floor of the hotel and is a single room. He told me he didn't want breakfast and he stayed in his room as far as I know until about noon when he left.

There then follows an accurate description of Alphon and the fact that he had with him a medium-size brown suitcase. The statement ends with the passage:

Although the entry in the register shows this man as being there on the 22nd August, 1961, I would not be absolutely certain that he came in on that night as the date appears to have been filled in by Mrs Galves.

With the exception of this last 'let-out' passage, the statement substantiates Alphon's original alibi. Nudds's 'wife', Florence Snell, made a statement similar to her 'husband's, though she said nothing about Queensway or a 36 bus in relation to Hanratty's departure from the hotel.

The position on September 15th regarding the two suspects was as follows. Nudds's statement partially implicated Ryan, and partially exonerated Alphon. Acott's interview with Mrs Alphon on the 13th also, at least partially, exonerated Alphon. If the *Sketch* and *Mail* articles on February 19th, 1962, were right, the Murder Squad should have had some record of the telephone call from Mr Ewer on September 1st which had led to a man called Ryan, who had sent flowers to his mother, a Mrs Hanratty, in Sycamore Grove, Kingsbury.

Of all this, the public knew nothing. Either because they were kept in the dark, or because they were under instructions to say nothing, the press remained silent about the cartridge cases, the Vienna Hotel, Nudds, the Galves, Alphon and Ryan. According to the *Sunday Pictorial* of September 17th, the police were still looking for a 'moon maniac'. The paper printed a 'warning' from Scotland Yard to women not to walk out alone at night, since 'a new full-moon cycle begins on Tuesday – just a month after the murder'.

September 16th, 17th, 18th and 19th, 1961, were perhaps the most important days in the whole murder inquiry. During those days, the A6 murder hunt went almost unreported in the press or on television. There is no reference to these days at the hearing or at the trial. Yet something happened at some time during those days which influenced Mr Acott and his advisers to turn their full attention to Peter Alphon.

On Monday, September 18th, Murder Squad detectives descended in large numbers on the Alexandra Court Hotel in Finsbury Park, and detailed statements were taken from the manager, the ladies in the room next to the one Alphon had occupied, chambermaids, waiters and receptionists. On the same day Detective Sergeant Kilner of the Highbury police handed over to Mr Nickolls of the forensic laboratory at Scotland Yard a pillowcase from the hotel – presumably one on which Alphon had slept.

The decision to hunt for Alphon was, on the face of it, surprising. Nudds's first statement three days earlier had exonerated Alphon, and presented him with an alibi for the night of the murder. Alphon himself, answering questions by police on August 27th, had corroborated this alibi and said that at the time the murderer was climbing into Gregsten's car at Dorney Reach, he had been visiting his mother in Streatham. In spite of all this, the police decided to hunt for Alphon.

When was the decision made? On September 23rd, the *Daily Mirror* reported:

> Detectives under Murder Squad Superintendent Bob Acott have been closely on his [Alphon's] track for three days. They have traced him to several small hotels in the London area. He stayed at one of them for four days at the end of August.

Mrs Buckman of 7 Hurst Road, Horsham, with whom Alphon had stayed while a child and whose address he had given at the Vienna Hotel, was visited by the police on September 20th, but was unable to help them as to Alphon's whereabouts.

While these initial, unsuccessful and unpublicized attempts to find Alphon were going on, Valerie Storie was visited at Guy's Hospital by her dead lover's widow, Janet Gregsten. The meeting between the two women received several inches of predictably gushing publicity in the press, including the *Daily Mirror*'s 'first picture of Valerie since the murder'. Mrs Gregsten, who had done everything in her power to break up the relationship between her husband and Valerie Storie, explained to the *Daily Express* her reasons for visiting Valerie in hospital. Valerie, she said, had sent a message asking Mrs Gregsten to visit her. 'I wanted to see her.

She is my friend. She and my husband had a lot in common. They were very keen on cars and rallies.' (*Daily Express*, September 21st, 1961.) The *Daily Mail* the following day (September 22nd) printed a more detailed story than the other newspapers about the conversation between the two women:

> Mrs Gregsten revealed for the first time the inside story.
> 'Valerie [Mrs Gregsten was quoted as saying] told me what happened. They were parked on the roadside when this man tapped at the window, Mike, my husband, wound the window half down and the man stuck a gun in and told them: "Open the door". The man was in his thirties and reasonably dressed. He spoke with a Cockney accent, but the most important feature was his eyes. They were blue and staring.' (*Daily Mail*, September 22nd, 1961.)

One man who was clearly unimpressed by this reminder about the killer's blue eyes was Superintendent Robert Acott who was leading a desperate hunt for his Number One Suspect—Mr Peter Alphon, whose eyes were deep-set and hazel.

On the morning of September 21st, Mr Nudds was hauled out of his house and escorted to Scotland Yard, where he was interviewed for most of the day. At 5.10 in the afternoon, he signed a statement about the register and booking at the hotel at the time of the murder which was entirely different to his statement of September 15th, six days earlier.

Nudds's second statement ran as follows:

> Since I made my last statement to you on 15th September 1961 I realise that what I told you in that first statement was wrong. I was confused and made an honest mistake about the booking and arrival of the man named Durrant that I then told you about. I am now perfectly clear about everything that happened at the Vienna Hotel in regard to Durrant.
> At about 11 a.m. on Tuesday, 22nd August 1961, my wife told me she had just received a booking from a man who gave the name of Durrant and asked for a room for one night. I made an entry in the hotel diary which is used for recording bookings on page 234 under Tuesday, 22nd August, 1961, which read 'Mr Durrant, One Night'.
> I saw Durrant arrive at the Vienna Hotel at 1 p.m. on 22nd

August, 1961. My wife and I were together at the reception desk. He was given the key to his room and was shown to his room by my wife. At 1 p.m. when I booked Durrant into the hotel I could see by the hotel booking sheet that we had no single or small rooms to offer him. We never turn a guest away if it is at all possible to accommodate him, and so, in accordance with general practice at the hotel, I allotted him room No. 24, which is a large room in the basement containing two double and one single beds.

I explained to Durrant the position of the hotel accommodation and pointed out to him 1) that although the normal charge for bed and breakfast for a single person for one night was £1.7.6. the charge for occupying a large room like room No. 24 was £2.15.0. and 2) if other guests arrived later that day or night he would have to agree to others sharing room No. 24 with him. Durrant agreed to these terms and I and my wife took him to room No. 24 and gave him the key to that room.

When we entered room No. 24, Durrant chose the single bed, which is in the alcove immediately to the left of the door as one enters the room, and he put his suitcase on the armchair which is at the foot of the bed behind a narrow partition which prevents the chair being seen from the doorway. The basement room is level with a park which looks like an ordinary garden when one looks out of the window. Durrant asked me what was outside the window, and I said a park. He walked round the room and said to me: 'I don't like a basement. I prefer a room upstairs'. I said to Durrant: 'All our single rooms are booked, but if one should become vacant, I'll let you have it, and move you into it.'

Durrant left his case in room 24, the key of which he had already been given, and we all went back to the reception desk. He paid me £1.7.6. and agreed that if he had to spend the night in the large room he would pay the extra money to make up the £2.15.0. before he left the hotel the next day. I was therefore unable to give him a receipt then as the transaction was not completed, and I would have done so next day when I knew for certain whether it was to be £1.7.6. or £2.15.0.

To cover myself with the hotel accounts, I added 'Deposit £1.7.6.' to the previous entry, 'Mr Durrant, one night', which I had made in the hotel diary on page 234 when Durrant made his initial booking by telephone that morning. The word 'deposit' in front of £1.7.6. shows that this is the amount of money I received from Mr Durrant, but was only a deposit towards the amount of £2.15.0. which Durrant would have had to pay had he occupied room 24 all night.

Durrant was in a hurry to get out of the hotel, and I cannot remember whether or not he signed the hotel register that day, but I rather feel on reflection that it was left for him to sign early next day. This is not an uncommon practice with guests who are in a hurry and that would explain why Durrant's interest in the hotel register is the last entry under 22.8.1961, and I know that a good number of the dates in the first column used to be put in by the Spanish woman Mrs Galves when she was checking the register for her accounts in the mornings. At that time, I noticed that Durrant had a smart appearance, something like a commercial traveller, wore neat clothes and a clean white shirt, was well shaven and had hair neatly smoothed down with grease. He was, however, in a bit of a flurry and certainly in a hurry to get out of the hotel. Durrant told me that he was going out and would not be back until late. When I asked him how late, he replied 'I may be very late. Do not wait up for me.'

I then explained to him that the key he had to his room fitted the street door to the hotel, and I asked him, if the hotel was locked when he returned, not to ring the front door bell and disturb us or the guests, but to unlock the street door with his room key, be sure to close the door behind him, and find his way to his room. I also told Durrant to tip-toe into his room in case we had to put another guest into that room, and I also pointed out to him that if, through a cancellation we managed to find him a single room I would notify him if he returned after we had gone to bed, by pinning a note for him on the door of room 24 or on the reception desk, telling him his new room number and where it would be.

When we had finished this business at the desk, Durrant left us to go to his room No. 24, but I remember now that he came up shortly afterwards and went straight out of the hotel, and he was not wearing a hat or overcoat and I do not think he was carrying anything at the time. Some time during that evening, pretty late, and probably between 9 p.m. and 11 p.m.,

Mr Pichler, my employer and owner of the hotel, telephoned me from the Broadway House Hotel and told me that the booking he had previously given us for Mr Bell and to whom we had already allotted room No. 6, a room on the second floor containing one single bed, could now be cancelled.

My wife and I sat up late that night, as was our usual custom, watching television and talking together while we waited in case there were any late guests arriving at the hotel. We sat in the lounge, which is next to the reception hall and desk, and from that position we could see and hear anyone entering or leaving the hotel. At 2 a.m., on the morning of the 23rd August, my wife and I decided to go to bed.

At that time Durrant was the only guest who had not returned to the hotel. The rest of the guests had long retired to their rooms and none were in the public rooms of the hotel. Before retiring to bed, I and my wife decided to leave a note for Durrant, notifying him of the change of his room. At the reception desk I took a sheet of pale blue paper from a scribbling pad which we keep for such purposes on the reception desk, and on it I wrote with my Biro pen the heading 'Mr Durrant' in large letters which I underlined, and underneath this I wrote, 'I have been able to change your room to a single – No. 6. Herewith the key to the door. Manager'. I placed this note on the top of the pen tray in the centre of the reception desk where it could not be missed by anyone coming to the reception desk. I and my wife went to our room in the basement and retired to bed. As always, we left a small light on over the reception desk.

My wife and I got up at 7 a.m. that morning, 23rd August, 1961, and we both went to the kitchen which is next door to our room in the basement, and we spent the next hour in the kitchen preparing breakfasts for the guests. At 8.0 a.m. my wife went upstairs to the dining room on the ground floor and she was then engaged on her own serving breakfasts to the guests. This necessitated her coming down to me in the kitchen from time to time, collecting a breakfast and taking it upstairs to a guest, and for the next hour and a half she would have been fully occupied in these duties and would have spent much of that time in the basement kitchen with me preparing tea trays and collecting breakfasts. This was a particularly busy morning as the hotel was particularly full. I remained in the kitchen until about 9.50 a.m. when I asked my wife whether there were any more breakfasts wanted.

When she told me there was only one who had not had breakfast, and that was Mr Durrant in room No. 6, I went up to room No. 6 to ask Mr Durrant whether he was going to have breakfast. I knocked on the door of No. 6 but got no reply, so I opened the door with my pass key and looked inside the room. I saw Mr Durrant standing by his bed and pulling on his trousers. I cannot remember now whether the bed was made or unmade, but I do remember that a suitcase lay open on the bed, and I can remember that it contained what appeared to be dirty linen.

I asked Mr Durrant if he wanted any breakfast, and he appeared to be agitated when he said 'No, No, I do not want any'. He appeared dishevelled. His hair was ruffled and he was in need of a shave, and very different from the Durrant when booking him into the hotel the previous day. I said to him: 'Did you sleep well?' and he said 'yes'. I said to him: 'What time did you get in last night?' Durrant said: '11 o'clock'. I left the room and went back to my wife in the dining room. I said to her: 'No. 6 does not want any breakfast. It looks as if he has been drinking last night. He told me he came in at 11 o'clock.' She said: 'He could not, or we would have seen him. He could not have got our note then and would not be in No. 6 now'.

At about 11.45 a.m. I saw my wife and Mrs Galves, who were making beds upstairs, and I asked them if they had finished with the rooms. My wife replied: 'No, we have got one more, No. 6: he is still in his room'. I told them to go to No. 6 and tell him that unless he vacated his room by noon he would be charged for another night's lodging.

I did not see Mr Durrant again, and I was told a little later by my wife that he had left the hotel. This statement I have now made is a true account of what happened in the Vienna Hotel on 22nd and 23rd August, 1961. The statements I have made to you before have been inaccurate as to detail because I was confused in my mind as to the comings and goings of the many guests that were using the hotel at that period, but what I have now told you is correct.

In order to clear up any confusion there may have been earlier between Ryan who went into room No. 24 and spent the night of the 21/22 August there, I want to point out the differences between him and Durrant, who entered room No. 24 at about 1 p.m. on 22nd August, 1961, after Ryan had vacated that room at about 8.30 a.m. that morning. Durrant is five or six years older than Ryan; he is about two inches taller than Ryan; he is bigger in build than Ryan; although they both had dark-coloured hair, Ryan had a quiff which gave him the appearance of having more hair standing up in the air. Whereas Ryan had an accent, possibly Irish, Durrant had no accent, and was better spoken than Ryan; though they were more or less dressed in equivalent clothes, Ryan was dressed in the style of a younger man; while Durrant carried a suitcase, Ryan carried a brown holdall and a portable radio with a shoulder strap. The most important difference between the two men was that Ryan was at all times cool, calm and composed, and left our hotel like a normal man who had had a breakfast after a full night's sleep and was leaving for work; whereas Durrant was flurried, hurried and agitated. This statement has been read to me and it is true.

Signed: J. Glickberg. 21st September, 1961.

This is the statement which emerged from the wretched Nudds in that first eight-hour interview at Scotland Yard. Nudds later explained what the session was like:

> I stayed there about eight hours and I went through a course of questioning which you only see on films. It takes place in America. I had never believed this was done to a prisoner in this country. This happened to me. I was confused and I said one thing and then said another. I carried on, but it did not suffice. (Transcript, vol. V, p. 54.)

The alibi which Nudds had supplied for Alphon on August 27th, after the telephone call from Highbury, and in his first statement to the police on September 15th, was comprehensively contradicted by his second statement on September 21st. To some extent the statement fitted the hotel documents which had been seized and studied by the police. These included the relevant pages of the hotel register, signed by the guests; a hotel diary in which the manager recorded bookings as they came in on the phone; and a booking sheet in which the overall position as to bookings was recorded on a large chart.

The hotel register is signed on August 21st by J. Ryan, 72 Wood Lane, Kingsbury, and Ryan is recorded on the chart as the only occupant for room 24 on August 21st. The last signature in the register for August 22nd is Durrant, 7 Hurst Lane, Horsham, marked down for room 6 (1 person). The name Ryan does not appear in the hotel diary, but in the diary for August 22nd the last entry reads as follows:

> 6   Mr Durrant.   1 Night.   Deposit: £1.7.6.

There is also a receipt book with carbon copies of receipts issued to guests. Receipt No. 6776 was made out to Ryan for £1.7.6. on August 22nd. There is no receipt recorded for Durrant. The lack of a receipt fits the second statement. The second statement also seems to fit the theory that Durrant booked into a large room, where the bill might come to more than £1.7.6., but paid that amount in the hope that a single room would become available.

There were, however, two aspects of the documents which did not fit the second statement and which showed that even if its essence was true, some details were false. For instance, Nudds's second statement says that he received a telephone call from the Broadway House Hotel late in the evening to the effect that a Mr Bell had cancelled his booking, and, in the hotel diary, the entry: *1 s*[single] *Mr Bell 1 Night Deposit £1*, had been scored out as if the booking had been cancelled. In the hotel register, however, there was a signature for Mr Bell, who, apparently, spent a happy night on August 22nd in room 9. The story about the cancellation of room 6 by Bell was false. If Nudds's second story was essentially true, it was embellished to connect Alphon with the murder.

The crucial question remains: why did Nudds make this statement, so clearly implicating Alphon in the crime and so clearly destroying his alibi? It is scarcely credible that the statement was offered voluntarily to the police. Nudds was not the sort of man to go of his own accord to Scotland Yard to make a second statement because he felt he had made a mistake in his first statement. Nudds's own explanation, given in court, was characteristically unsatisfactory. He told the hearing at Ampthill and the jury at Bedford that he had made his statement implicating Alphon because he wanted to help the police, and had assumed that the police suspected Alphon.

'The reason why I jumped to the conclusion that they wanted Durrant for the murder', he said at Ampthill, 'was because we had a telephone call from Highbury police station asking us just to confirm whether Durrant had stayed at the hotel that night, the 22nd August ... We all jumped to the conclusion that the police must want this man in connection with the murder.'

The telephone call from Highbury police station, was, as we have seen, on August 27th. If Nudds was so anxious to help the police, and if he had jumped to the conclusion that Alphon (Durrant) was the man the police wanted, why did he not implicate Alphon in his *first* statement on September 15th?

The truth, almost certainly, was that some time between the 15th and 21st something happened which convinced the police that Alphon, not Ryan, was their man. The police may have received casual information on the underworld network. They may have been impressed by psychologists' advice after close study of Valerie Storie's description of the killer. At some time between September 15th and September 21st there must have been some clue or some information which propelled the inquiry towards Alphon and which led detectives to believe that Nudds's first statement providing an alibi for Alphon was false.

The detectives in charge of the A6 murder inquiry were not fools. They were men who understood as well as anyone in the country how much their case could be damaged by the chopping and changing of statements by one of their chief witnesses. They would never for a moment have accepted Nudds's new story unless they had other information of substance which led them to believe that his second statement was, in essence, true; that Alphon had not in fact spent the night at the Vienna Hotel; that Alphon had committed the A6 murder.

After Nudds left Scotland Yard on the evening of September 21st Mr Acott acted quickly. The following morning (September 22nd), he called on Mr Felix Alphon, who worked in the records department of Scotland Yard, and explained to him that they were looking for his son as a suspect for the A6 murder. 'Some of the officers', reported the *Daily Telegraph* of September 23rd, 'went with Mr Alphon to get his wife, who was taken to the Yard for the matter to be explained to her.' What Mrs Alphon had to say was crucial to the inquiry. In his original statement to police at Highbury,

Alphon had said that he had visited his mother at about 9.15 on the evening of August 22nd.

Acott had spoken to Mrs Alphon on September 13th, and had, apparently, been satisfied by what she told him. Now, however, he was no longer satisfied. And in the course of the interview with her that morning, he must have been convinced that Alphon's 'mother alibi' was false. How Mr Acott assured himself on that point is not clear. Mrs Alphon, obviously, was very upset. After the interview, according to the *Daily Express*, 'Mrs Alphon collapsed ... ' A 'Scotland Yard spokesman' was quoted as saying: 'Mrs Alphon has taken it very badly. We are having to call a doctor.' (*Daily Express*, September 23rd, 1961.)

The alibi, however, was smashed. 'Alphon's mother', reported Peter Duffy of the *Daily Sketch*, 'told detectives that he last visited their home in Gleneagle Road, Streatham, two months ago.' (*Daily Sketch*, September 23rd, 1961.)

The police were now certain of their man. Peter Alphon, they knew, from their detailed inquiries at the Alexandra Court Hotel, had behaved oddly in the days immediately following the murder. Alphon, they realized, knew the Slough area and was a regular attender at the Slough dog-track. Alphon had told them that he had spent the night with his mother and at the Vienna Hotel. Both these assurances the police now knew to be lies. According to Nudds's second statement, he had not arrived at the Vienna Hotel until the early hours of the morning. In the morning he had behaved oddly. Police information about Alphon's character and appearance, which by that time was considerable, seemed to fit Valerie Storie's description of the killer. They knew that Alphon studied weird philosophies; that he was a Fascist; that he was a nomad wandering from hotel to hotel. Finally, perhaps most important, Alphon looked uncannily like the Identikit picture drawn up by Valerie Storie. His hair was slicked back with grease. His eyes were deep-set and staring (though neither icy-blue nor saucer-like nor brown). Apart from the colour of his eyes, he fitted Valerie's *original* description given at Bedford Hospital.

Mr Acott, at any rate, must have been as near certain as he ever hoped to be. He decided without further ado to resort to a rare practice: the public appeal. In all police hunts for suspects, especially in murder hunts, the officers in charge are chary of releasing the suspect's name. Despite the carefully worded formula about 'helping police with their inquiries', the release of the name of a man later found to be innocent is dangerous. Not only does it damage that person's reputation and peace of mind. It betrays that the inquiry was open to error.

In this case, however, Mr Acott did not hesitate. Soon after dismissing Mrs Alphon, he summoned a press conference and outlined what the *Daily Telegraph* described as 'one of the most detailed appeals ever issued'. The statement was sent to all news-papers with urgent appeals from Acott that it be given the utmost prominence. It ran as follows:

In relation to the murder of Michael John Gregsten, who was shot on the A6 road at Deadman's Hill, Clophill, Bedfordshire, during the night of August 22–23, 1961, it is desired to trace the following described man, who may be able to assist police in this inquiry:

Peter Louis Alphon, 31, born Croydon, Surrey, 30.8.30. 5 ft. 9 ins. to 10 ins.; slim build; complexion pale; hair dark brown, brushed back and flat; eyes hazel; straight small nose; thin lips; rounded chin; well spoken, speaks like a Londoner, and in a quiet voice.

Dressed in a double-breasted dark blue blazer, dark clerical grey trousers, white shirt, no hat or coat. May be in possession of an off-white three-quarter length raincoat, known as a shortie, and which has a bright red lining cape shoulders back and front, slit pockets and side vents.

This man has done no regular work for several years, but is believed to have had casual employment as a waiter or barman in public houses and hotels in London and the home counties.

He is known to frequent Streatham, Victoria, Putney, Hammer-smith, Finsbury Park, Highbury, Holloway, Richmond, Maida Vale, Kilburn, Northolt and Kingsbury.

It is known that he is a keen student of theology, theosophy,* and astrology, and has been a frequent visitor to public reference libraries in London, borrowing books on these subjects. He is also a regular attender at greyhound tracks in

---

* Theosophy was accurately described in the *Daily Telegraph* the next day as 'a system of philosophy or mysticism which proposes to attain intercourse with God and super-spirits and consequent super-human knowledge'.

London and the Home Counties, particularly at Slough, Bucks, and Southend, Essex.

Anyone with information about Alphon was asked at the end of the statement to telephone Bedford Police or Scotland Yard, and the telephone numbers were supplied.

The statement was printed faithfully on the front page of the late editions of the evening newspapers on September 22nd. It was splashed on the London *Evening News* front page with a massive headline: A6 MURDER: THE POLICE SEEK A MAN'S HELP. That evening B.B.C. Television News broadcast an interview between their reporter, Peter Woods, and Superintendent Acott.

'Mr Acott', said Peter Woods, 'I gather that now you have a man in mind who might be able to help you in your inquiries.' 'Yes,' said Mr Acott, earnestly. 'He is Peter Louis Alphon.' Prompted by Peter Woods, Mr Acott ran through the description of Alphon. Few who saw the broadcast can have doubted that, at that stage, Acott regarded Alphon as the killer.

The appeal did not stop at newspaper and television coverage. At Slough dog-track that Saturday afternoon the police appealed through the loudspeakers for information about Alphon (*Slough Observer*, September 25th). Small wonder that the *Sketch*'s Peter Duffy could reflect on that afternoon's frantic search as 'the biggest police search in recent years in London and the Home Counties. Every policeman, across a 60-mile belt from Southend to Maidenhead, Berks, was on the look out for Alphon.' (*Daily Sketch*, September 23rd, 1961.)

This was a remarkable manhunt, which employed every available method of publicity, regardless of the consequences. It smacked of the confidence in the Bedford Murder Room that their man was within their grasp. Soon after launching the appeal, a smiling Superintendent Acott went to visit Valerie Storie at Guy's Hospital. He stayed there for about three-quarters of an hour 'discussing the inquiries' (*Daily Telegraph*, September 23rd, 1961). There is no record as to what was said, but there can be little doubt that Miss Storie was told that the net was closing on her assailant. If Miss Storie read the description of the wanted man in the police press release, she might have been prompted to ask why the police were searching with such confidence for a man with hazel eyes, when she herself had recently described the killer's eyes as 'large, icy-blue

and saucer-like'. If she did make any such inquiry, she would
have been quickly reassured. As Superintendent Acott said in
Ampthill magistrates' court two months later: 'Valerie Storie's
description of the man with icy-blue eyes was only part of the
description. It is not one we would depend on. We would not
depend on any individual details unless it were something such as a
deformity.'

The size and extent of the murder hunt for Peter Louis Alphon
contrasts strikingly with Mr Acott's explanation for it at the trial
of James Hanratty four months later. He was asked: 'If you really
relied on the description given by Miss Storie, how could you have
begun to think that this was the man whom you should interview
in connection with this murder?'

Mr Acott said:

Because we were then left with two very strong suspects –
Alphon and Ryan ... One had to be eliminated. *The only one we
could eliminate was Alphon.* At the same time, one has to take
into consideration the second statement of the Glickbergs or
Nudds or Snells which not only broke Alphon's alibi, but
showed it to be a fabricated one. (Vol. X, p. 25.)

A little later on, Acott said:

Despite my knowledge at this time of the difference in
description between Alphon and the wanted man, with the
Glickbergs' statements I had no alternative but to get Alphon
in and eliminate him, and that is exactly what happened; and,
of course, as I was confident, he was not picked out by any of the
witnesses.

Q. If those were your views, why did you not go for suspect
   No. 1 first – the man Ryan?
A. He was an unknown quantity at that moment; he was
   merely a name. Alphon, I had identified. (Vol. X, p. 26.)

And much later on, in re-examination, Acott re-emphasized the
point:

Q. At that time had the man who booked in as Ryan at the
   Vienna Hotel, Room 24, on the 21st with a false address
   of 72 Wood Lane, Kingsbury, been identified?
A. No, he had not. (Vol. XI, p. 47.)

Acott's approach can be summed up in his words at the trial: 'I did not think Alphon had done it.' (Vol. X, p. 27.) Neither this, nor his reasons for unleashing a murder hunt against Alphon, is plausible when related to the facts at the time.

Up to that time, police had interviewed perhaps a score of suspects. As early as September 1st, the *Bedford Times* had reported: 'So far ... about 12 people have been taken into police stations for questioning about their movements on the night of the murder, but they were all released when police were satisfied that they were not connected with it.'

During the first three weeks in September, largely as a result of the Identikit fiasco, there were several other such interviews. It is worth recalling, for instance, the information given to the police by 'an East End' man about 'a man with large icy-blue eyes who may be the A6 killer'. The man who gave the information was given a special police guard and a squad of forty detectives was put on his trail. Two days later, the man was found, interviewed for several hours and released. Until September 22nd, all the suspects had been found and eliminated without publicity, as is the usual practice in criminal investigations.

Peter Louis Alphon was not a difficult man to find. The police were keeping watch on a number of boarding houses where he was likely to stay. They knew the firm for which he was selling almanacs. They knew his parents. All these people were co-operating with them. They could have been certain of finding him within a few days. If Mr Acott was 'confident' that such an interrogation would lead to Alphon's 'elimination' from his inquiries, why did he go to the almost unprecedented step of calling a press conference, issuing a press release, commandeering loudspeakers at dog-tracks and appearing on television to *name* the suspect? Everything about the brief hunt for Alphon during the afternoon of September 22nd indicated that Superintendent Acott and his advising officers were confident that they had identified the killer.

Nor was it sufficient for Mr Acott to explain away this murder hunt on the grounds of Mr Nudds's second statement. For Nudds's second statement did not arise from an overpowering urge to retract. Nudds did not appear at Scotland Yard on September 21st clamouring to change his original statement. On the contrary, Nudds was sought out and taken to Scotland Yard where he was told to tell the police the truth. Acott's explanation as to why he did not seek out Ryan before launching a nation-wide hunt for Alphon – that at that time Ryan was just a name to him – was a shocking commentary on the efficiency of the Murder Squad's classification. Mr William Ewer, following up his sister-in-law's miraculous identification at Swiss Cottage, had put the police on the trail of a man who gave his name at a cleaner's shop as J. Ryan, and, the following day, sent flowers to his mother, who was called Hanratty and lived at 12 Sycamore Grove. The name Hanratty could have been quickly checked in the police files, for James Hanratty was already wanted for robberies in Ruislip and North-wood. If such a check had been made, of course, it would have revealed that Hanratty had no record of violence or sex crimes. He was not a 'moon maniac'.

The search for Alphon ended earlier than expected. At midnight on the night of September 22nd–23rd, Peter Alphon phoned the *Daily Mirror* and the *Daily Express* from a call-box outside Scotland Yard. He was, he told the newspapers, about to give himself up in order to clear his name. The police, he said, had mistakenly got it into their heads that he had something to do with the A6 murder.

After meeting a reporter, Alphon walked into Scotland Yard through the Derby gate. Superintendent Acott and Detective Sergeant Oxford were contacted at their homes, and rushed to the Yard to confront Peter Alphon in an interview room.

Alphon's surrender in so shrewdly public a manner caused consternation at newspaper offices, notably at the *Daily Mail*, where crime reporters, after getting a tip-off from the police, had been spending several days preparing a mammoth 'background' article on Peter Alphon whom they assumed to be the A6 murderer. As soon as Mr Acott named Alphon in his murder-hunt press release on the afternoon of the 22nd, the *Daily Mail* felt free to publish their background piece under a huge headline on the front page, with the article carrying over at length on to page 2. The article avoided the obvious libel of saying that Alphon was a murder suspect, but its style and content clearly indicated the author's assumption that Alphon had done the murder. FROM MISFIT TO MYSTIC, it was headed, and it quoted, among others, a former school friend called Ron Knight, of East Barnet, Herts, as saying: 'I remember him as a misfit. He wasn't in the same pattern as the rest of us.' Miss Ethel Taylor, the landlady of the house where Alphon's parents lived was also quoted as saying: 'Peter never lived here. I haven't seen him for several months.' The *Daily Mirror* carried a similar, shorter, article.

As soon as Alphon gave himself up, declaring that he had nothing to do with the murder, the respective editors of both papers panicked. The pieces were instantly removed. The removal of the *Daily Mail* piece in particular required heavy newspaper surgery, but the fear of legal action in the event of Alphon not being the murderer overruled all other considerations. As a result, the article appeared only in the small-circulation first editions of the newspaper and is not available today.

The printing of the *Daily Mail* article suggested perhaps more than anything else that the hunt for Alphon was not, as Mr Acott later told the court, merely a hunt for one of two suspects. The article indicated that the newspapers had been tipped off that Alphon was the man police were hunting as the number one suspect, indeed *the only* suspect. Only with such advance information would the *Daily Mail* have dared publish their article. Moreover, the article indicated that Alphon was the suspect *before* Nudds's second statement. The substantial information about Alphon in the *Mail* article could not have been gleaned and prepared in the single day available to reporters after Nudds signed his statement on September 21st. *Daily Mail* reporters almost certainly knew for at least three days that Alphon was the suspect.

One news item in the *Daily Mail*, however, which was not removed from the later editions read as follows: 'Mrs Janet Gregsten, widow of the A6 victim, last night visited Miss Storie for the second time in Guy's Hospital, London.'

This short item, which appeared in other newspapers, was not accompanied by any of the long accounts about what was said between the two women which had appeared in the press the previous day (September 21st). (As we have seen, Mrs Gregsten had, amid much publicity, visited Valerie Storie on the 20th September.) On September 22nd, the evening papers carried the announcement of the hunt for Alphon. That evening, Mrs Gregsten went again to visit Valerie Storie at Guy's.

While the newspaper editors were desperately changing their front pages, Peter Alphon was being interrogated by Superintendent Acott and Sergeant Oxford. There are two conflicting accounts of this interview—one from Alphon himself on the front page of the

Daily Express of October 4th; the other from Messrs Acott and Oxford at the trial.

Peter Alphon wrote:

> I was escorted up to Mr Acott's office — just two desks, three chairs and a filing cabinet — where the real interrogation started. Mr Acott sat behind his desk. I sat in front of him, and Detective Sergeant Oxford sat at the other table making notes.
>
> The questions came fast. Every facet of my personal life. Had I a wife? I told them I wasn't earning enough to marry. Again and again, they came back to the night of the A6 murder which I had spent at the Hotel Vienna at Maida Vale. I knew they already had a full statement of all my activities in the previous 12 days. At intervals of about half an hour, Mr Acott and the detective sergeant would get up and leave the office ... Then a plainclothes man would come in and urge me to help all I could. Each time it was a different man. I can tell you it was an ordeal ...
>
> On and on the questioning went until nine o'clock in the morning. I had had no sleep. They had offered me a meal at about six o'clock, but I was unable to sleep. I felt utterly exhausted and defeated.

Detective Sergeant Oxford's impression of that interview is given in the following section from the trial transcript:

Q. Were you present when Alphon was interrogated?

A. Yes.

Q. Were there intervals during the interrogation when you and Mr Acott would get up and leave the office?

A. No.

Q. Three or four times during the night?

A. I think on two occasions I took Alphon to the toilet.

Q. Apart from that?

A. No.

Q. And on those occasions or any occasion during the interrogation would a plainclothes man come in and urge him to help all he could?

A. No. Superintendent Acott and I were the only persons there.

Q. How long did the interrogation of Mr Alphon last? ...

A. Three and a quarter hours: from 2 a.m. to 5.15 a.m. on the 23rd September ...

Q. Would you have said that as the interrogation of Alphon proceeded, you and Acott would not accept a word he said?

A. No.

Q. Or that the more he tried to clear up the dreadful mess, the blacker things looked for him?

A. No. As the interview progressed things began to look a little brighter for him. (Vol. XI, p. 60.)

Alphon's story is one of a ruthless interrogation lasting seven hours in which 'the more I tried to clear up the dreadful mess, the blacker things looked for me'; Oxford's of a mild interview lasting three and a quarter hours in which things got better for Alphon as they went along. Mr Acott said that by the time the preliminary inquiries were over he was satisfied that Alphon was not the killer.

Neither police officer was able to say *how* things got better for Alphon as things went on. Certainly, he could not have produced a credible alibi. That had already been destroyed by Nudds and his mother.

Despite Acott's and Oxford's assurances that things looked good for Alphon as the Saturday morning (September 23rd) broke, they decided to go to the trouble and expense of putting him on a series of identification parades, the first of which were held at Cannon Row police station on the afternoon of Saturday, September 23rd.

The *Evening Standard* of September 23rd reported that 'cars with two men and two women' had arrived for the identity parades. The *News of the World* the next day reported that 'people from Bedfordshire and from Richmond, Surrey, attended'. The *Observer*, which carried the fullest report, said that there were 'four inspections, two by men, two by women'. These included, according to the *Observer*, Mr Hirons, the garage attendant who had filled the murder car with petrol when the killer was in the back seat; and 'two women from Slough who had seen the car with a passenger in it leaving a hotel near Dorney, Slough'. The *Sunday Express* referred to 'four mystery witnesses'.

In a letter to me the Home Office has flatly refused to release the names of any witnesses on this parade. Mr Acott, in his description at the trial of the parades on the 23rd, said that there were four witnesses and Mr and Mrs Nudds—who were 'alibi witnesses'. From reports of the trial and of the magistrates' hearing it is certain that Mr and Mrs Nudds, Mr Blackhall and Mrs Dalal, from

Richmond, attended the parade. So, possibly, did a Mr Philip Dyerson, a window cleaner who had seen Mrs Dalal's assailant rush away from her house after the assault. If the *Observer* was right, another witness was Hirons. Mr Skillett, who was driving in the same car as Mr Blackhall, was not available to attend the parade. Nor was Mr Trower, who had seen the murder car in Ilford.

The only witness to pick out Alphon was Nudds, who tapped two of the men on the identity parade, one of whom was Alphon, murmuring 'one of these could be him'. 'Mrs Nudds', Florence Snell, who, according to Nudds's first statement had met Alphon at the door of the Vienna Hotel late at night, had signed him in and taken him up to his room, did not pick him out from the parade. Mr Blackhall picked out someone entirely different. Mrs Dalal did not pick anyone out, but collapsed behind the screen and named Alphon to the police as the man who had attempted to rape her on September 7th.

After the parades, the *Evening News* correspondent, who had been waiting at the Yard, dashed back to Fleet Street to file a report which just caught the last edition. 'Peter Alphon', it ran, 'was still with the Yard today. It is thought that he will probably continue to help the police for many hours, *and is expected to travel to Ampthill this evening.*' (*Evening News*, September 23rd, 1961, my italics.)

There was only one reason why Alphon should 'travel to Ampthill': to be charged with the murder. The A6 murder charge, according to the rules of demarcation which then obtained in the British police, would have to be made in the tiny courthouse at Ampthill, Bedfordshire – the nearest court to the scene of the crime. The report in the *Evening News* was an indication that Alphon was likely to be charged that evening. The report must be contrasted with Mr Acott's breezy assurance at the trial: 'It was fairly early on in that interview [with Alphon] in the early morning of September 23rd that I was satisfied in my own mind that this was not the suspect out of these two.'

The *Evening News* report was a trifle premature. There was one more identity parade which had to be undergone before any charge could be brought against any suspect. The *Evening Standard* on that evening of Saturday 23rd, reported: 'At one time police considered holding an identity parade at Guy's Hospital, where Miss Storie is seriously ill.' The day before, Miss Storie had been operated on, and two bullets removed from her body. The bullets were lodged just beneath the skin near the right shoulder blade, and the operation was performed under a local anaesthetic.

The operation was completely successful, and Miss Storie showed no ill effects. But doctors at Guy's suggested to Mr Acott and his colleagues that they postpone the identity parade until the following day, Sunday, September 24th.

Early that Sunday morning, a police van drew up at the Union Jack Club in Waterloo. Police entered the club and asked for nine volunteers in civilian clothes to serve on an identity parade. These were taken to Guy's Hospital. A separate van brought Peter Alphon. The men were taken into the hospital and given cardboard placards with a number on each. They were then shepherded into the Ruth Ward where Valerie Storie lay, behind screens.

She had recovered from her operation. Dr Ian Rennie, who had been looking after her since she arrived at Guy's more than three weeks previously, described her condition on the morning of the identity parade as 'very keyed up, very tense, but not flustered and quite clear in her mind'. He said on oath at Ampthill:

> I am quite satisfied that Miss Storie was in a fit condition to go through with the identification parade on the 24th September ... I am quite satisfied that she was in possession of her mental faculties on that occasion.

Mr Acott, in the words of the *Daily Mail*, 'stood by her bedside'. Dr Rennie was also present. There was however no solicitor or other representative for Peter Alphon.

The *Daily Telegraph*, which, as usual, printed the most detailed report of the identification parade, included one very remarkable detail:

> As hospital staff started to move the curtains, it was pointed out that one of the men had no tie. The remainder of the line were asked to remove their ties, and did so.

The man without the tie must have been Peter Alphon. The *Daily Herald* on the 26th recorded that Alphon had gone to the Yard 'wearing an open-necked shirt and blazer'. The *Daily Sketch* on September 23rd, the day before the identity parade, printed on its front page a large picture described as an 'artist's impression of the man whose description was issued by Scotland Yard'. The picture was no more than a photograph of Peter Alphon with the face blacked out. The shirt was open at the neck.

If Valerie Storie had seen the impression, her attention would no doubt have been drawn to the only man on the parade without a tie. Fortunately for Alphon, however, just before the curtains were drawn, someone noticed the discrepancy and the nine men took off their ties. When the curtains were finally drawn, Miss Storie was confronted by the ten men. For between five and seven minutes, her eyes wandered up and down the line.

> Her eyes [wrote Alphon later] began travelling along the line, each person in turn. Two or three times, she slowly scanned the line. It dawned on me she wasn't quite sure of herself. I began to get hot under the collar. Eventually her gaze fell on me and stayed. I thought another great mistake was about to be made. She looked round us one by one. Suddenly she spoke. It was not my number. (*Daily Express*, October 4th, 1961.)

Able Seaman Alan Bainbridge, who was one of the servicemen on the parade, gave a statement about the parade to several of the papers, in all of which he was quoted as saying: 'As the screen was pulled back I heard her break down crying.' (*Daily Express*, September 25th, 1961.) As soon as she discovered from Acott that the man she had picked out was not the man he was seeking, Miss Storie broke down almost uncontrollably, shouting: 'I've made a mistake! I've made a mistake!' (*Daily Telegraph*, September 25th, 1961.) Exactly what sort of a mistake she thought she had made was clarified later – by Miss Storie herself at the trial:

Q. You now know, do you not, that there was a man on that parade called Peter Alphon?
A. I know now.
Q. And when it appeared that you had identified some other person on that parade did you not afterwards say that there was a fair resemblance between Alphon and the man who attacked you?
A. When am I supposed to have said that?
Q. Some time after that parade?
A. Some time afterwards, yes.
Q. Can you tell us to whom you made this observation?

A. In the first instance, I believe it was a doctor at Stoke Mandeville
  hospital.
Q. And later?
A. I am not sure whether it was Superintendent Acott or not.
Q. May it have been Superintendent Acott?
A. It may have been, but I do not remember. (Vol. III, p. 22.)

At any rate, soon after the parade, Valerie Storie said that the man
she picked out looked like the newspaper photographs of Peter
Alphon, which appeared in the press after his release.

When Miss Storie failed to pick Peter Alphon from the identity
parade the case against him, apparently so powerful a few hours
earlier, suddenly crumbled. Positive identification was important to
a possible prosecution but lack of identification was even more
important to a possible defence. However strong the evidence
against Alphon, however flimsy and fabricated his alibi, the only
witness to the murder had failed to pick him out from a row of ten
men.

Mr Acott told the trial court at Bedford some months later that
'he never expected' Miss Storie to pick out Alphon, and that Alphon
was dropped from the murder inquiry as soon as Miss Storie failed
to pick him out.

Q. What time was he released from custody and when?
A. 2 p.m. You are talking about my custody of course.
Q. Yes.
A. Yes. 24th September.
Q. At what time?
A. 2 p.m. (Vol. X, p. 29.)

This was, however, a quibble. Alphon was driven back to
Scotland Yard, while detectives anxiously discussed their next move.
In the meantime, Alphon was bundled off to Brixton prison where
he was held on charges of assaulting and causing grievous bodily
harm to Mrs Dalal of Richmond.

He was not charged with the A6 murder, but he was still in
custody. On the following day, September 25th, an urgent conference was called to decide his fate. 'Last night', reported the *Daily
Sketch* of September 26th, 'top Scotland Yard detectives and solicitors of the Director of Public Prosecutions office held a 5-hour
conference on the A6 murder.' The *Daily Mail* also reported this
conference, which, it said, took ninety minutes.

Detectives do not normally call in officials of the Director of Public Prosecutions unless to discuss a potential prosecution, and the likelihood of its success. At that time, September 25th, a case had been built up against only one man — Peter Alphon. There can be little doubt that this high-level and top-secret conference between 'top detectives' and 'representatives of the Director of Public Prosecutions' discussed the case against Alphon, and the likelihood of charges against Alphon resulting in conviction. If Alphon had already been ruled out of the inquiry, it is difficult to appreciate why there should have been such protracted discussions with the Director of Public Prosecutions.

What *was* the case against Alphon at that stage? His alibi was destroyed — by his mother, by Nudds, and by Florence Snell's failure to identify him. He had deliberately lied about it. He looked like the Identikit picture drawn up by Valerie Storie. He had behaved oddly after the murder. He had been identified by Mrs Dalal as her assailant. On the other hand, he had not been identified by either Blackhall or Miss Storie.

It is a fair assumption that the Director of Public Prosecutions' solicitors advised that the case against Alphon was too slim and that a prosecution without Miss Storie's identification was bound to fail. Alphon, in the meantime, remained in custody on the Richmond charge. On the morning after the identity parade (Monday 25th) he was charged at Mortlake magistrates' court with inflicting grievous bodily harm on Mrs Dalal. He pleaded not guilty and asked for bail to substantiate his alibi. Bail was opposed by the police, and refused. Alphon was locked up in Brixton prison. If more evidence came to light to implicate Alphon in the A6 murder, he was still available to the authorities. In effect, however, Miss Storie's failure to identify Peter Alphon had eliminated him from Mr Acott's inquiries.

Before Mr Acott could hunt for another suspect, however, he had to resort to another, even longer interview with his most co-operative witness, 'The Squealer' Nudds.

Accordingly, on September 25th — the same day as the conference with the D.P.P. — Nudds found himself once more at Scotland Yard for another of those interrogations which, he believed, only took place on the films. The *Daily Express* (September 26th) reported:

A man who has assisted police in the A6 murder case spent seven hours at Scotland Yard yesterday ... Line by line the man's original statement to the police was read over by Superintendent Acott. Then the man was asked further questions. The Superintendent hoped he would be able to remember other incidents on the night of the murder ...

It was following Valerie Storie's comments to detectives at the identification parade that Superintendent Acott summoned the man for the further interview.

As with the first 'interview' at Scotland Yard, there was nothing voluntary about Nudds's appearance there. He did not arrive, his conscience troubling him, to change everything he had said before. He was hauled in. Mr Acott started by saying that in his view Nudds's second statement was nonsense, and damaging nonsense at that. Nudds's reply was most revealing. 'You must', he said in horror, 'be kidding.' Mr Acott, however, was not kidding. He interviewed Nudds for another seven hours, at the end of which Nudds signed another statement, his third in ten days. Mercifully, it was shorter than the second statement.

Because of my past bad record, I have been trying to go straight with the help of Mrs Snell, ever since I came out of Oxford prison in 1958. In order to keep straight, I had always wanted to help police and had helped police on some occasions with information. When police came to the Vienna Hotel making enquiries about the murder and checking on the movements of the guest named Durrant, I jumped to the conclusion that they wanted Durrant for the murder. After I and my wife had made our first statements, police continued to question us and check the hotel books and it was obvious to me that when we had said that Durrant had booked into the Vienna Hotel at 11 p.m. on 22nd August 1961, and had stayed that night in Room No. 6, this information did not fit in with their investigations which also covered the movements of the occupant of Room No. 24.

It was then that I decided that I could do myself a good turn by helping the police in an important job by giving them the information they appeared to want. I made up the story which is contained in my second statement of the 21st September, 1961, and gave it to the police ...

After I left Scotland Yard that night I went home and told Mrs. Snell what I had done and told her that she would have to make another statement next day and that statement would have to agree with mine or we would be in serious trouble ...

I have given this matter a lot of thought during the last few days and especially since we had to go on an identity parade on Saturday 23rd September and I can see now that I have put myself and Mrs Snell in a very dangerous position. I can no longer continue to offer this false evidence in a case as serious as murder where a man's life is at stake, and I want now to withdraw unreservedly every word of that second statement.

In addition, I want to make it clear that the whole of the first statement is true and correct to the best of my recollection. Lastly, I want you to believe that Mrs. Snell only made her second statement because I made her believe that it was the only way to save us both getting into trouble, but she agreed, unwisely, to do everything to help me. This statement has been read to me and it is true.

Signed: WILLIAM GEORGE RICHARD NUDDS

The double somersault was complete. After 'a lot of thought', Mr Nudds and Mrs Snell decided to withdraw completely the statements implicating Peter Alphon and return to their original statements which provided him with an alibi. Perhaps the best comment on Nudds's behaviour between September 15th and September 25th came during the trial four months later:

MR SHERRARD. Can you remember, when you were using the name Beaumont and were known as 'Jazzer' Beaumont, how it came about that you got that nickname 'Jazzer'?
MR NUDDS. Yes, years ago I used to do quite a lot of dancing ...
S. Someone would play a tune and you would dance?
N. No. (Vol. V, p. 25.)

Nudds's third statement, as far as Mr Acott was concerned, removed the stain of guilt from Alphon and cleared the decks for the hunt for the second suspect, Ryan.

Who was Ryan? Both Mr Acott and Mr Oxford later testified that on September 24th they did not know who Ryan was. He was 'only a name'. Sergeant Oxford also testified: 'Actually, on the 25th September we had in fact identified the man Ryan as being possibly Hanratty.' (Vol. XII, p. 2.)

Miraculously, on the day after Alphon was eliminated at Valerie

Storie's identification parade, the identity of Ryan became known to the police. How were they able to discover so quickly that Ryan was Hanratty?

One way could have been through Mr George Pratt, who lived at the address given by Ryan when he signed the register at the Vienna Hotel — 72, Wood Lane, Kingsbury. Mr Pratt, at some stage, was visited by police. He told them that he had just received a bill from a car hire company in Dublin addressed to a J. Ryan. No one of that name, he said, had ever lived at his address.

When I interviewed Mr Pratt on August 23rd, 1970, he was emphatic that he had no idea who had sent the bill from Ireland. He knew the Hanratty family vaguely, but none of them had ever been inside his house. No one, as far as he knew, had ever used his address falsely before, and he could give the police no clue as to Ryan's identity.

One explanation for the sudden identification of J. Ryan appeared in the *Sunday Times* more than five years later — in December 1966. In a long article on the A6 murder case, the authors, Peter Laurie and Brian Moynahan, included a detailed timetable of events relating to the murder. One item ran as follows:

> 25th SEPTEMBER : 'Dixie' France goes to police with postcard from Hanratty in Ireland. Police watch France's house and tap telephone calls. (*Sunday Times* Magazine, December 18th, 1966.)

Mr Brian Moynahan tells me that the source for this entry was Mrs France herself. In an interview with Mrs France, he explains, she told him and Peter Laurie about the postcard incident, and together they fixed the date as September 25th. Neither journalist could remember how certainly the date was fixed, and Mr Moynahan agrees that Mrs France's memory after so long an interval may not have been perfect.

Certainly, if Charles France did go to the police with a postcard from Hanratty on the 25th, he knew even more about Mr Acott's second suspect than Mr Acott himself. At that time there had been no public mention of Ryan, or of the Vienna Hotel. Nothing had been made public to connect France's friend with the crime. If France did go to Scotland Yard on that day, he must have known something from the inside which connected his friend Jim with the murder, or he must have had some motive for making the connection.

At any rate, the following day, September 26th, Superintendent Acott and Sergeant Oxford visited Mr and Mrs Hanratty in their council home in Sycamore Grove, Kingsbury. 'They sat on the sofa', says Mrs Hanratty, 'and they told us Jimmy was wanted for running cars over to Ireland.' Both parents also remember being asked about a 'friend of Jimmy's called Dixie'. 'I remember thinking through all his girl friends,' says Mrs Hanratty. Both she and her husband thought 'Dixie' was a girl. If Mr Acott did ask for Dixie, it was further evidence that France had visited him the previous day.

Two days later, Mr Hanratty was intercepted on his way back from work by Mr Acott and Mr Oxford who showed him a picture of a friend of Hanratty's called Lanigan. Mr Hanratty said he could not recognize the man. Ryan (Hanratty) was by now Mr Acott's chief suspect, but he wanted to make sure.

On the afternoon of Tuesday, September 26th, he convened a summit meeting of detectives from four counties under Detective Chief Inspector Harry Bowker of Slough Police Station, Detective Superintendent Barron of Bedfordshire, Detective Superintendent Fewtrell of Buckinghamshire and officers from Oxfordshire and Berkshire. The meeting took place at Slough (*Slough Observer*, September 29th, 1961). Its purpose was to re-route the murder inquiry. Some seventy detectives were sent once again over the murder car's route from Dorney to Deadman's Hill, making further inquiries. On Thursday, September 28th, the London *Evening Standard* reported that Mr Acott had that morning again interviewed Valerie Storie:

> Several new lines of inquiry are being followed by detectives, and they want to interview a number of men who may be able to help inquiries. Some of the men are missing from their last-known addresses, and a team of detectives is trying to trace them.

The *Daily Express* and the *Daily Telegraph* narrowed down the number of these suspects to five. There had, they said, been a top-level conference in the office of Sir Joseph Simpson, Metropolitan Commissioner, to trace the movements of these five men.

The hunt for these five men arose from Valerie Storie's information that the man in the car had said he had 'done the lot'. The expression 'done the lot' in prison jargon means 'served a whole sentence without remission'. The man in the car had also said, according to Miss Storie, that he had done 'C.T.' (corrective training). There were, it was discovered, only five men in the country who had recently served an entire sentence of corrective training without remission.

When Acott discovered, on September 28th, that one of these men was James Hanratty, he cast all further doubt to the winds. Hanratty was his man, and Hanratty must be found. Hanratty, too, according to the France postcard and the information from Mr Pratt, was in Ireland.

So the murder hunt, led by Mr Acott and Mr Oxford, moved to Ireland. All air and seaports to Ireland were 'sealed'. Immigration officers and airline officials were warned to keep a watch out for Hanratty, and Mr Acott and Mr Oxford took the first plane to Dublin. As they did so, they issued a description of their new suspect. In spite of his increasing certainty, Mr Acott decided on this occasion to be more cautious than he had been the previous week about issuing his suspect's name.

The description of the 'man police want to help with their inquiries', released in Dublin on September 29th, did not include Hanratty's name or even, at that stage, his alias. He was described as 'a young man of 25, tall, slim with a thin face and rounded cheeks. He has black or brown hair brushed back and wears a dark suit.' (*Daily Worker*, September 30th, 1961.) Strangely, neither this description nor that issued more fully the next day (which described 'a London man born of Irish parents' and left out the expression 'brushed back' for the hair) said anything about the wanted man's eyes. Everything was now concentrated on the search for Hanratty. As for Peter Alphon, he was not relevant any longer. That same morning (September 29th), Alphon faced up to yet another identity parade, this time in Brixton prison, in which two employees of a book wholesale firm, helpfully discovered by police officers, picked him out as having been in the shop at or about the time that Mrs Dalal had been attacked on September 7th. Alphon was taken to Mortlake magistrates' court and immediately given bail of ten pounds in his own recognizance.

The descriptions issued of the new suspect on September 29th provoked considerable activity in the newspaper offices. Naturally, everyone wanted to know who the new suspect was, and the crime correspondents were put to work among their numerous police and underworld contacts to find out.

The biggest and best endowed newspaper crime team was that of the *Daily Express*, whose chief reporter on the A6 case was John King. King, who at the time of writing is in charge of the *Daily Express* Bristol office, recalls that on that Friday evening (September 29th) he found out that the new suspect was James Hanratty, and that his parents lived in Kingsbury. He travelled to north London that evening and at about 8.30 knocked on the door of No. 12 Sycamore Grove. Mr James Hanratty senior was alone that night as his wife and son Michael had gone out to bingo. King told him that his eldest son was wanted for the A6 murder. Mr Hanratty's immediate reaction was to laugh the matter off, but as he reflected on the Superintendent's two previous visits, he realized that the police were serious. After some discussion, Hanratty and King reached an agreement. No money would be paid to the Hanratty family, but King promised to help in every way he could, especially with transport facilities. He also promised to ensure that no other newspaper reporters came near the Hanrattys. The following day, when Sycamore Grove became thick with newspapermen, King and two fellow reporters managed to keep them away. From that day until the end of the trial, *Daily Express* reporters were constantly at the side of the Hanratty family.

Today, John King cannot remember how it was that he was the first to know that J. Ryan, the suspect for the murder, was James Hanratty. He is certain that the information did not come from Scotland Yard. 'This', he explained to me, 'was a loner's murder. The underworld did not want to be disturbed by police inquiries about the murder, and were prepared to give as much information as they could. There was a lot of information circulating around, and I suppose we were lucky in that we found out about Hanratty first.'

Mr Acott, meanwhile, had landed in Dublin and was starting his search for the killer who, he believed, had fled to Eire.

The 'search in Eire' was one of the least distinguished periods of an undistinguished inquiry. During four days' hectic inquiry with the full co-operation of the Gardai, the Irish police, Mr Acott and his friends found two runaway sweethearts in Clonmel, Tipperary, one of whom had been made a ward of court. They also discovered that Hanratty, still using the alias, Ryan, had stayed at Cork and at Limerick some three weeks previously.

While Mr Acott was hurtling through the twenty-six counties, the crime correspondents who followed him took the chance to explain to their readers what was going on. The *Daily Telegraph* of October 2nd started an interesting fiction:

> One of the strangest coincidences known in a murder inquiry led eventually to Eire. Detectives discovered the A6 murderer had 'a double'. The coincidence did not end with physical resemblance. The paths of the murderer and his 'double' crossed. They stayed in similar locations at the same time, although they do not know each other and, it is believed, have never met. The murderer's route was hidden behind inquiries about his double. Now that man has been cleared and eliminated from inquiry ... The murderer has been described as aged 25, 5 ft. 7 ins. tall, slim build with dark hair. His path crossed with a man of this type in the early stages of the inquiry.

This 'double' talk was clearly based on official authority. The *Daily Sketch* the same day reported that: 'Scotland Yard men are having "double" trouble. They have found that not one man but two or more have fitted the Identikit picture and incomplete descriptions they have to work with.'

The crime correspondents responsible for these theories had not seen pictures of the two men they were describing as 'doubles'. Alphon and Hanratty did not resemble each other. It is true that both men's hair was dark, and both men were of slim build but this hardly classified them as 'doubles'. The truth, which the papers and the police were unwilling to spell out, was that the various descriptions of the murderer were so 'incomplete' that detectives in charge of the case had suspected two men who looked entirely different.

Perhaps the most interesting explanation of the switching of suspects came from the *Daily Mirror* on October 4th:

> Alphon matches almost perfectly the Identikit picture of the man police wish to interview in connection with the A6 killing. The eyes, the nose and the hair are almost identical. Last night one of the theories being considered by detectives was that the A6 killer had spotted Alphon and tried to frame him. For the police received information that led them to circulate Alphon's description in connection with the murder ...

It was only after a series of identification parades, and Alphon proving that he was nowhere near the murder scene on the night in question that he was cleared of suspicion.

This is the first and last public indication that 'the A6 killer had spotted Alphon and tried to frame him'. The reason for it was that 'the police received information that led them to circulate Alphon's description in connection with the A6 murder.' Exactly what this information was, no one outside the police and the Home Office knows. But the *Mirror* article was public recognition of the fact that at some stage in the murder inquiry the police had received 'information' indicating that Alphon was the murderer. After the second suspect – James Hanratty – was found, no one again suggested that he had sought to frame Alphon. There was not, it was soon to be discovered, the slightest proof that such a frame-up had been attempted.

The crime correspondents could also explain what Mr Acott was doing in Ireland. 'The Murder Squad', reported the *Daily Mail* on October 2nd, 'are now certain that the killer stayed in London for about two days after shooting Michael Gregsten. He panicked when he heard that Mr Gregsten's companion, Valerie Storie, was still alive and able to talk. He dumped the gun and ammunition on a London bus, and took a plane to Ireland.'

This was nonsense, as Mr Hanratty senior discovered the following day, Tuesday, October 3rd, his birthday. Through the post that morning came an expensive birthday card from his eldest son. The stamp was English, and the postmark London. That morning, Mr Hanratty and his son Michael were driven by John King to Scotland Yard where they handed in the birthday card. 'It is time', said Mr Hanratty to the man who took the card, 'that Acott stopped fooling around in Ireland and came back to London where my son is.'

From Scotland Yard, King drove Mr Hanratty and his son Michael into Soho and Covent Garden in a fruitless search for Jimmy. Michael Hanratty remembers going into the Rehearsal Club, which he knew to be a favourite haunt of his elder brother. He spoke to the girl behind the counter, and explained that his brother was wanted for the A6 murder. The girl advised him to sit down and wait until 'Dixie' France came in.

'I sat down', says Michael, 'and waited. Eventually, France came in. I didn't know him, but I was watching the people coming in. He went up to the bar, and I saw the girl talking to him, and pointing at me, so I knew it must be him. He'd come in for what looked like a long cards session.

'The moment the girl pointed at me, he turned round and suddenly seemed very agitated. Without saying anything to me, he grabbed his coat and left. I caught up with him on the stairs, and explained to him that Jimmy was wanted for the A6 murder. He gave a kind of nervous laugh. "Oh, that's ridiculous," he said. "I haven't seen Jimmy for some days, but I'll soon put this business right, but just now I've got to get back to the wife" – and he almost ran away from me.'

Before leaving the Club, Michael told the girl behind the bar and the doorman to tell Jimmy, if they saw him, that he was wanted for the A6 murder. 'He was so silly,' says Michael, 'I thought he wouldn't give himself up because of his housebreaking.'

While his brother was looking for Hanratty in Soho, Superintendent Acott was returning rather shamefacedly from his 'comb-out' in Ireland. The *Daily Mail* put a brave face on his return: 'The man', it reported on October 5th, 'doubled back on his tracks and slipped through the police net.'

What, in fact, had James Hanratty been doing since the murder? On September 4th he had indeed travelled to Ireland, not to take cover from a possible murder hunt but to get a driver's licence. This mission accomplished, he returned to London about a week later, and took up residence with Mrs Louise Anderson, a middle-aged antique dealer who patronized Hanratty and gave him a lot of money. He proceeded to live a gay existence on the spoils of robberies in Wembley and Edgware. On September 19th, he achieved his life's ambition by buying a car – a Sunbeam Talbot – for which he paid £117 deposit at a garage in Burnt Oak. He took the car to his friends, showed it to the Frances and took Louise Anderson out for rides in it. He had a number of dates with girls, notably with Gladys Deacon and Mary Meaden, whom he took to the Palladium. For most of the time he was wearing the dark chalk-stripe suit he was wearing on the night of the murder.

About three days after buying the car, he met his cousin Eileen Cunningham in the street. He had always been friendly with his cousin, and he stopped to talk to her. She had bad news for him. The police, she said, had been inquiring at his house in connection with housebreaking in Ruislip. This, Hanratty realized, meant that he must have left fingerprints in Ruislip, and that he was now 'on the run' from another five years in prison. As a result, he moved more frequently from night to night—staying at various hotels as well as at Mrs Anderson's.

On September 30th, he broke into two houses in Stanmore and stole a black jacket. For the next four days, he wore the black jacket over the trousers and waistcoat of his chalk-stripe Hepworths suit. On the Monday evening, October 2nd, he went to Ealing to sell a diamond ring he had stolen. He visited Donald Fisher.

'I remember him coming,' says Fisher. 'He was wearing a black jacket over striped pants. He looked like a lawyer. We all went off to Wembley dog races. I remember Hanratty was worried about something, because when we got to Wembley he didn't want to go in the main entrance in case he met his father.'

How Hanratty spent the next few days is not known, but at some time on the evening of Thursday, October 5th, he must have gone to the Rehearsal Club, where he was told he was wanted for the A6 murder. Immediately, he rang his friend Charles France, and blurted out: 'Dixie, Dixie, I am wanted for the A6 murder.' France and his brother-in-law then kept Hanratty talking, asking him to 'calm down' and to 'go to Scotland Yard' while the police, who were in the house, tried to trace the call. 'I was acting on instructions,' explained France later. Hanratty, however, rang off and vanished into the night before the call could be traced.

The following morning he bought most of the newspapers. The *Daily Sketch*, the *Daily Express* and other papers carried reports about a 'mystery woman' who was 'a girl friend of the gunman'. Her name, reported the *Sketch*, was 'Louise'. This convinced Hanratty that the police were on his trail. At about noon he rang Superintendent Acott at Scotland Yard. He told him that he had nothing to do with the murder, but refused to give himself up because he was wanted for housebreaking. He had, he said, just come out from doing three years and if he got caught again he would get five. He then said that he would telephone a newspaper, and would ring again that evening. Almost at once, he rang the *Daily Mirror*. The call was taken by Mr Barrie Harding, then the *Mirror*'s assistant news editor, and the conversation printed in the *Daily Mirror* the following morning went like this:

HANRATTY. I am innocent, but I cannot give myself up to the police. I can prove I was in London on the Monday and I went to Liverpool on the Tuesday morning. The murder was on a Tuesday, wasn't it?

HARDING. Have you got people to give you an alibi?

HANRATTY. Yes I was there doing business with some friends. I can't involve them for various reasons. (*Daily Mirror*, October 7th, 1961.)

That evening, Hanratty went to see *South Pacific* at the Dominion, Tottenham Court Road. At four minutes past eleven, he rang Acott again. Hanratty still insisted he could not give himself up. He gave Acott the address and telephone number of 'Louise' (Mrs Anderson).

Hanratty then went to Portland Place, near Oxford Circus, and broke into a Jaguar. He took the registration number of the dashboard, and bought a key to fit it at a garage in Soho. He then stole the car, drove it through the night to Manchester, and travelled by train to Liverpool. At half past five that evening (October 7th) he rang Acott again from a public call-box in the Exchange district of Liverpool. When his money ran out, Acott ordered the telephone operator to reverse the charges. The two men then had a conversation, which, once again, is a matter of dispute between the two participants.

Hanratty's main purpose in making the call was to tell Acott that he had been to see some people in Liverpool who had refused to back up his alibi for the night of the murder. He told Acott that he had spent the night of the murder 'with three men in Liverpool'. He told him that he had spent the night of August 21st–22nd in the Vienna Hotel, and had the following morning gone to Liverpool, stayed three days with three friends and returned to London on the Friday. Unhappily, however, the three men would not come forward to stand by him as they were fences and didn't want to get into any trouble. Acott begged him to give him the names of the three men, but Hanratty refused.

'No,' said Hanratty (according to a part of Acott's version which Hanratty did not dispute). 'That won't do. They couldn't get mixed up with the police and they don't want to know anything about me or this murder. One of them is wanted on a warrant for non-payment of a fine or something. I've told them I'll pay this for him and give them all some money. I have plenty now, Mr Acott, but they won't listen. They say I embarrass them and they have kicked me out today and told me not to come back again.'

The call ended with Acott asking Hanratty to ring him again if he changed his mind about giving the names of the three men.

Meanwhile, on Friday, October 6th, the same day as Hanratty's telephone calls from Soho, Acott had interviewed Charles France, his wife and daughter at Scotland Yard for what the *Daily Telegraph* (October 7th, 1961) described as 'several hours'. Some time during the interview France *volunteered* the information that his friend Jim Ryan, as he knew him, had once told him that underneath the back seat of a bus was a good place to dispose of valueless jewellery after a robbery.

At that time the only evidence to incriminate Hanratty was the cartridge cases in the Vienna Hotel, and the fact that the murderer said that he had done 'C.T.'. There was no evidence of identification. Hanratty had been behaving normally since the murder and he did not look like the Identikit pictures. France's statement about the back seat of the bus no doubt reassured Acott that he was hunting the right man. France must have known that the gun had been found under the back seat of a bus and that his evidence about Hanratty and the bus could only damage his friend.

The same day – Friday, October 6th – the police went to the address in Sussex Gardens which Hanratty had given Mr Acott and found Louise Anderson. As Hanratty had told Acott, Mrs Anderson had a suitcase of Hanratty's in her flat. In a long interview at Scotland Yard the next morning, Mrs Anderson told detectives about her friendship with Jimmy Ryan which had started about the same time as his friendship with the Frances. She agreed that Hanratty had stayed in her flat, sleeping on two chairs, on several evenings both before and after August 22nd. She had, she said, introduced him to a girl called Mary Meaden.

By now the newspapers were printing detailed descriptions of Hanratty, and from October 8th they printed his alias name, Ryan. There was no press conference at the Yard, no B.B.C. television interview featuring Mr Acott, no commandeering of loudspeakers at dog-tracks as there had been in the Alphon hunt. Instead, the press stuck closely to the pseudonym 'Ginger' Ryan (though they knew he was Hanratty) and all police attention was focused on Liverpool, where Hanratty had telephoned Acott on October 7th. On October 9th and 11th Acott and Oxford had further interviews with

Mr and Mrs Hanratty, who agreed to co-operate as much as they could in tracing their son. By this time, acting on the advice of their doctor, Dr Mond, the Hanrattys had hired a local solicitor, Mr Emmanuel Kleinman, who ran his own practice in Hendon.

What James Hanratty did during the next three days is not clear. On October 9th he went into a florist's shop in the Scotland Road and sent a bunch of carnations to his mother, who had been whisked off to Bedford for that weekend by the *Daily Express*. On the same day, in the same area, he visited a doctor and a hairdresser who bleached his hair. On October 11th, slipping the police net around Liverpool, he drifted to Blackpool, booked a room in a doss-house, and went to the Stevonia café on Central Drive. He was sitting there quietly eating his meal and listening to the juke box when two police officers looked in on a routine call, and saw him. When he came out, they seized him and took him to Blackpool police station. Hanratty protested at first that his name was Peter Bates, but by the time he got to the police station he was expressing his relief that he would now be able to 'clear the whole thing up'. Hanratty claimed later that one of the officers who arrested him, Detective Constable James Williams, made an effort to make him confess, which Mr Williams strongly denied. At any rate, Hanratty ended up by spending the night in Blackpool police station, where he was held on a charge of 'housebreaking in the Metropolitan area'.

At about 2 a.m. the telephone rang in Acott's home with the news that his man was in custody in Blackpool. Acott ordered a car and set off at once with Detective Sergeant Oxford at his side. The Hanrattys' solicitor, Mr Kleinman, had previously been in touch with Mr Acott and requested that he and the Hanratty parents should be kept informed of developments, particularly if Hanratty was found. Mr Acott left for Blackpool without a word to Mr Kleinman.

Acott and Oxford drove through the night, arriving at Blackpool at about 7 a.m. By 7.45 a.m. they were interviewing Hanratty. The interviews which followed formed an important part of the prosecution case, and what was said at them was a matter of considerable dispute between Hanratty and the two police officers at the trial.

The Hanrattys' solicitor was not present. Superintendent Barron of the Bedfordshire police, in whose area the crime had been committed, was not present. Mr Acott asked the questions, James Hanratty answered them and Mr Oxford wrote down the answers.

The notes taken by Oxford, which were presented as crucial prosecution evidence at the trial, were not seen by, nor read to Hanratty at the time, and were not agreed by him to be a correct record of what was said.

The interrogation of suspects by policemen is covered by the Judges' Rules, summarized in the famous legal textbook Archbold. The rules are not mandatory, but failure to observe them is frowned on by the courts, and can lead to a judge's instruction to the jury to disregard the interrogation. Rule 9 appears to be unambiguous:

> Any statement made in accordance with the above rules should, whenever possible, be taken down in writing and signed by the person making it after it has been read to him and he has been invited to make any corrections he may wish.

According to Mr Acott, he started his interview that morning by cautioning Hanratty and warning him that anything he said could be taken down in evidence and used against him. Hanratty replied: 'Fire away. Ask any questions you like.' Acott then asked him questions until about 9.30 a.m. Most of these questions were about Hanratty's movements on the week and night of the murder. There were also questions about the coat which Hanratty was wearing at the time of the murder. After getting his answers Acott returned at 2.15 p.m. and started another interview which went on for only half an hour. Once again, Acott returned to the subject of the alibi in Liverpool, starting with the sentence:

> I can't make it too clear how desperate your position is. I must tell you now. After your leaving Room 24 on 22nd August and before it was occupied again two empty cartridge cases were found at the end of the bed you tell me you slept in that night.

Room 24, however, had been occupied – by Mr Rapur. More important however was Mr Acott's literal interpretation of the code of interrogation which specifically deters the interrogating officer from using pressure of any kind to force a man in custody to disclose his defence.

A little later on, Acott went on: 'I've been pleading with you all day to tell me who the three men are in Liverpool. Your position is more serious than theirs and for your sake I must ask you to tell me who they are.'

How serious, in fact, was Hanratty's position? Two cartridge cases had been found on a chair in a room which he had occupied the night *before* the murder night. Charles France had told police that Hanratty had told him that the back seat of a bus was a good place to dispose of valueless jewellery, and the murder gun had been found under the back seat of a bus. In some aspects Hanratty fitted the description which the murderer gave *of himself* while in the murder car. For instance, his name was Jim and he had 'done the lot' of three years of corrective training. On the other hand, there was no evidence of identification nor any evidence to link Hanratty with Deadman's Hill or with Dorney Reach on the evening of the murder. There was no evidence in Hanratty's character or record to suggest he would commit a crime of this kind. Yet Superintendent Acott still felt it reasonable to tell Hanratty: 'I can't make it too clear how desperate your situation is.'

The next morning Acott and his entourage rose early to accompany Hanratty to Bedford. Superintendent Barron, who had travelled to Blackpool overnight, charged Hanratty with the A6 murder – a technical, holding charge to enable the officers to take their suspect out of the custody of the Blackpool police. As he was preparing to leave the police station, Acott ran into Hanratty's parents who were sitting in the front of the police station, after travelling all night. In a towering rage, Mr Acott refused Mr and Mrs Hanratty permission to see their son. He had, he said, informed their solicitor by phone the previous evening that their son was in custody in Blackpool, but that there was 'no need' for them to visit him there. Hustling the handcuffed Hanratty past his parents, Acott, Barron and Oxford left with their prisoner for Bedford.

The party arrived at Bedford soon after midday. At 4.5 p.m. that day (October 13th), Hanratty stood in an identification parade before four witnesses. Mr John Skillett, who was driving down Eastern Avenue at the same time as the murder car, picked out Hanratty as the man in the car. Mr Edward Blackhall, who accompanied Skillett in the car, picked out someone else. Mr Hirons, the eighty-year-old garage attendant who had filled the murder car with petrol, picked out someone else. Mr Trower, the man who had been standing in Redbridge Lane on the morning after the murder, picked out Hanratty as the driver of the Morris which had flashed past him. The murder charge at Blackpool was not announced to the press, despite these identifications. Yet there was no denying Mr Acott's confidence that he had his man in his grasp.

'A6 MURDER CHARGE IN 24 HOURS' screamed the *Daily Mirror*, the next day (October 14th). 'Detectives investigating the A6 shooting decided last night that a man would be charged with murder in the next 24 hours. He may appear later today at a special sitting of the magistrates' court at Ampthill, Bedfordshire. If a special sitting cannot be arranged, the man will still be charged with murdering Michael Gregsten ... Then the man will be kept in a cell at Ampthill police station to wait for a court hearing on Monday.'

The *Daily Herald* (October 14th) was even more definite: 'A man *will be* charged today with the murder of Michael Gregsten. This dramatic move follows a conference of senior detectives at the murder hunt H.Q. in Bedford yesterday.'

This was all very surprising. The suspect had still to be identified by the only witness to the crime – Valerie Storie.

At a similar stage in the investigation of Alphon three weeks previously, things had looked worse for Alphon than they did for James Hanratty. Alphon had, according to the evidence at the time, been in room 24 of the Vienna Hotel on the night of the murder, and had lied about his alibi. True, Skillett and Trower had picked out Hanratty. But Skillett and Trower had not attended the identity parade on which Peter Alphon had stood three weeks previously. Why, then, were the press so confident that Hanratty would be charged? If Miss Storie failed to identify Hanratty, the case against him would be derisory. How were the Murder Squad so certain on that Friday 13th that their chief witness would not let them down again?

The following (Saturday) morning, thirteen men, twelve of them from a local R.A.F. station, lined up in front of Valerie Storie's bed at Stoke Mandeville Hospital, Aylesbury. She looked up and down the line for some ten minutes before asking them all to say the sentence: 'Be quiet will you, I am thinking.' They all spoke. She looked at them again, and finally spoke Hanratty's number. That evening, at 6.15 p.m., Superintendent Barron formally charged Hanratty with the murder of Michael Gregsten on Deadman's Hill on the morning of August 23rd, 1961. Hanratty replied: 'All right.' Superintendent Acott's seven-week murder hunt was over.

PART TWO

The Case Against James Hanratty

2

Identification: The Three Glimpses

IDENTIFICATION

James Hanratty was charged with the A6 murder on October 14th. On November 22nd, after a number of remands, the prosecution case started in the magistrates' court at Ampthill, Bedfordshire, and lasted until December 5th. The magistrates decided that there was a case to answer, and sent Hanratty for trial at the Old Bailey, London. Hanratty had successfully applied for legal aid and had been interviewed in prison by a thirty-three-year-old 'junior' barrister called Michael Sherrard. Hanratty was immediately impressed by Mr Sherrard, and, at Hanratty's request, Mr Sherrard took over the case as 'leader'.

The prosecution case before the magistrates was presented by Mr Niall MacDermot, who, on December 13th, handed over the papers to a brilliant Queen's Counsel called Graham Swanwick, later Mr Justice Swanwick. On January 2nd, despite powerful complaints from Mr Sherrard, the Recorder at the Old Bailey, Sir Anthony Hawke, re-committed the case to Bedfordshire Assizes. 'I have indisputable authority for saying that there is every likelihood that the trial will come on more quickly at Bedford than here,' he said.

Whether it would be conducted more *fairly* for the defendant was another matter. There was in Bedford an hysteria and local outrage about the crime unequalled anywhere else. The chances of jury prejudice against the accused were considerably higher in Bedford than in London.

On January 14th the charge of murder was reinforced by two further charges – of attempted murder and rape of Valerie Storie. These last two charges were dropped on the opening day of the trial, January 22nd.

The trial lasted for twenty-one full days—the longest murder trial against one defendant in British history. On February 17th, a Saturday, the jury retired. They returned six hours later to ask for clarification on the meaning of the words 'reasonable doubt'. Four hours later still, the jury returned with a sentence of guilty, and Hanratty was sentenced to death. His appeal, on March 12th and 13th, was almost contemptuously dismissed by the Court of Criminal Appeal, and on April 4th he was executed at Bedford.

The prosecution case which the jury accepted was founded on identity. Without the evidence of identity there would have been no case against him. The fact that three people who saw the killer within hours of the killing independently picked Hanratty out of an identity parade was the deciding factor.

(I)   Valerie Storie

Of these identifications, by far the most important was Valerie Storie's. She was the only witness to the crime. As she told the five million viewers of Panorama in the latter's programme on the case on November 7th, 1966: 'I was there. I was on Deadman's Hill. And I *know* it was Hanratty.'

Miss Storie's passionate certainty about the identity of the killer was by a long way the most powerful aspect of the prosecution case. Superintendent Acott, who was in charge of the inquiry, testified to the importance of Valerie Storie's evidence in no uncertain terms: 'I did depend on her', he told the court at Bedford, 'from the day of the murder until today. I stand firm on her.' (Vol. X, p. 26.)

Valerie Storie identified her assailant in three ways: by sight, by voice and by the description which the man gave of himself in the car. Of these, the most important for the court was the identification by sight.

On her own evidence, however, Valerie Storie did not see much, if anything, of her assailant. When she and Michael Gregsten were sitting in the car in the gloom just before dark and there came a tap on the window, she could not see the face of the man who was tapping; as she later told Mr Swanwick:

Q. What could you see?
A. We could see a man standing there—could not see his head—from his shoulders more or less down to his waist. (Vol. II, p. 44.)

I travelled myself to Taplow on August 22nd, 1969, and discovered that by 9.45 p.m. it was almost pitch dark in the cornfield. Of course, the light varies according to the weather, but the probability is that the murderer approached the car in near total darkness.

From the moment the man climbed into the back of the car, Miss Storie and Mr Gregsten were under strict orders not to look at him: 'He told us to face the front, presumably so that we could not see his face, and every time we went to turn he said "face the front".' (Vol. II, p. 45.)

A short time later, still in the cornfield, the man got out with Mr Gregsten to discuss the question of putting Gregsten in the boot:

Q. When he had got out of the car and gone round to the boot with Mike were you able to see his face at all?

A. I could not see his face because he had got a handkerchief or something tied triangular fashion over his nose and mouth, presumably to stop Mike from seeing him.' (Vol. II, p. 48.)

During the entire car journey, Valerie Storie, on her own evidence, was looking to the front. After the car arrived at Deadman's Hill, and after Gregsten had been shot, the murderer ordered Miss Storie to turn round and kiss him. In her statement before the magistrates at Ampthill, Miss Storie said:

While I was facing him, after he had shot Mike and I was still in the front of the car, a car came up from behind and lit up his face. He seemed to be staring through me. Very large icy-blue eyes. This was the only real proper glimpse of him I had. There may have been other cars passed by while I was in the back of the car with him. The only real opportunity was when I was in the front of the car and I was staring him full in the face ... I could see almost the whole of the coloured part of his eye ... The car was coming from behind me, lighting up his face for not many seconds ... When I got in the back of the car, there may have been other cars passing. I think there were some heavy lorries. I only had an opportunity to see a side view, possibly a three quarters view whilst I was in the back when any vehicle went past. I can't really say how many vehicles went past — no more than about 6 or 8 but I didn't really count them. Their headlights would illuminate the man's face for less than 10 seconds.

When he got out of the car, I could only see him in silhouette, at first when he got out with Mike. There was one vehicle went past after he raped me. He was out of the car at this time. I only had a glimpse of him at that time. In any case, I'd got my glasses off. They were in my right coat pocket. I can't see very clearly without them. I am very short-sighted and whilst I can see outlines of objects I can't distinguish them. I had my spectacles on when the car coming from Luton lit up his face.

At the trial, this evidence remained essentially the same. It was always Miss Storie's evidence that the only 'proper glimpse' of the man she had during the whole terrifying experience was when for a few seconds his face was lit in the headlights of a passing car. There were other aspects of the man, of course, which she could see and describe without having seen his face. He was not much taller than she was. He was, she noticed after being forced to kiss him, clean shaven. He was wearing a 'very smart, dark suit' with a white shirt, though she could not remember whether the suit was double- or single-breasted, striped or single-coloured. Yet the man's face, the colour of his eyes, the style and colour of his hair all depended on a few seconds in the light of a passing car while she was being forced to kiss him.

Small wonder, then, that her description of these facial features in the period following the murder was not consistent. Her first description as we have seen was given to the undergraduate John Kerr. According to Miss Storie, she told Kerr that the killer had brown hair and blue eyes. According to Kerr, she told him that he had 'light fairish hair and staring eyes'.

John Kerr insisted from the start that on the back of one of his traffic enumerator forms he had written down the words: 'Valerie Storie, 15 Anthony Way, Slough; staring eyes, light, fairish hair.' He had also noted the car number and her height: 5 ft. 3¼ ins.

After Miss Storie had been taken away in an ambulance, Kerr returned to his work at the R.A.C. box. There, he said in evidence, he was approached by a senior police officer who interviewed him. In the course of the interview he told the officer that he had taken a rough note of what Valerie had said on one of his forms. The police officer had replied: 'I had better have that form.' Kerr handed it to him.

Both at Ampthill and at Bedford, Kerr was quite certain of this incident. After he had told his story at Ampthill the magistrates asked if the form could be produced. The prosecuting counsel, Mr MacDermot, assured them that the form would be produced. There was then a pause and a flurry of conversation between the prosecuting counsel and various police officers. In some embarrassment, Mr MacDermot rose again to tell the court that the form was 'not available'. He could give no explanation as to who had collected the form, where it was, and why it was not available.

At the trial, the prosecution had recovered its composure. Mr Swanwick's reaction to the story of the missing piece of paper was to cast doubt on the credibility of his own witness, Mr Kerr.

'How were you feeling?' Mr Swanwick asked him. When Mr Kerr replied: 'Quite well; as well as one might expect,' Mr Swanwick asked: 'Did you have to consult a doctor?' This line of inquiry was then abandoned at the request of defence counsel, but Mr Swanwick had said enough to suggest to the jury that Mr Kerr was a little overcome by the terrible events on Deadman's Hill; that he was not quite himself as a result, and that he had *imagined* that he had given a piece of paper to a policeman.

Senior police officers gave evidence at the trial to the effect that they had not received anything from Mr Kerr. Police Inspector Edward Milborrow, the first senior officer on the spot at Deadman's Hill, went even further:

Q. Did you receive from Mr Kerr any piece of paper?
A. I did not ...
Q. Did you subsequently carry out extensive enquiries and interview every police officer who had been upon the scene?
A. I did not interview every police officer who had been on the scene but interviewed all the people I knew had been there.
Q. All the people you knew had been on the scene?
A. Yes. I could find no-one who had any information concerning that piece of paper at all.
Q. Did you then go to the county surveyor's office at Bedford?
A. I did. I there made a search.
Q. Did you make a search there and did you find a piece of paper?
A. I did.
Q. Apart from that sheet of paper were you ever able to trace any other sheet of paper?
A. No, I was not. (Vol. III, pp. 48, 49.)

The 'piece of paper' which Police Inspector Milborrow found at the county surveyor's office at Bedford was a form giving instructions for the traffic census, August 21st to August 27th. On the duplicated form was filled in the name and address of Mr J. Kerr, where he was to stand (near Deadman's Hill, 1¼ miles north of Clophill), and by whom transport was to be provided. On the back of this form, half-way down on the left, was written 'BHN 847' (the murder car's number was 847 BHN) and at the bottom was a jumbled set of multiplied figures.

John Kerr agreed that he had had this form on August 23rd. The prosecution then tried to establish that this was the form he thought he had given to a policeman. To Mr Swanwick's chagrin, however, Kerr denied having anything to do with the writing on the back of the form. 'I do not do 4's like that or B's,' he told the court. 'My upward strokes do not taper off like the ones there do.' 'Are you really saying', pressed Swanwick, 'you do not think any of that manuscript is in your handwriting?' 'That is so,' replied Mr Kerr. (Vol. II, p. 32.)

If Mr Kerr did not write the figures on the back of his traffic form, who did? It would seem unlikely that anyone at the county surveyor's office would write down the number of the A6 murder car the wrong way round on the back of one of their forms. It is difficult to imagine any other explanation for the figures on the back of that traffic form than that they were put there in a deliberate attempt to discredit Mr Kerr's own story that he had written the number of the car and the description of the killer on another traffic form, and handed it to a police officer.

Certainly, Mr Kerr's notes about his conversation with Miss Storie would have told the court a great deal about Miss Storie's identification. At the time of the murder, Hanratty's hair was dyed black. The dye, it is true, was wearing a little thin at the edges, but the overall impression was still of predominantly dark hair. It could not possibly have been described as 'light, fairish hair'. If Mr Kerr's insistence that Valerie Storie had thus described her assailant's hair had been backed up by notes made at the time it would have made nonsense of the prosecution's contention that Valerie Storie's identification and description had been consistent throughout.

As we have seen, about an hour after talking to Mr Kerr Miss Storie made a further statement at Bedford General Hospital to Chief

Inspector Whiffen and Woman Inspector Arnett of the Bedfordshire police. No record exists outside the Home Office of that statement, which was not raised at the trial. All we have is the description released to all newspapers and to television that the killer was 'aged about 30, 5 ft. 6 ins., of medium build, wearing a dark suit. He has dark hair, pale face and deep-set brown eyes.' (*Evening News*, August 23rd; all national and provincial newspapers, August 24th.)

It was clearly this description which Miss Storie was working on when she helped Detective Sergeant Mackle to construct an Identi-kit picture of the killer on August 26th and 27th. The Identikit picture which Valerie helped to construct was of a man with medium-dark hair swept right back, and with deep-set dark eyes. As we have seen, the eyes of the suspect changed colour on August 31st, when Valerie Storie, according to the *Daily Express*: 'remembered something more about the killer's appearance. He had "icy-blue saucer-like eyes", she told detectives at her bedside'. (*Daily Express*, September 1st, 1961.)

These 'large, icy-blue, saucer-like eyes' remained in Miss Storie's memory at the hearing and at the trial. 'I describe his eyes', she told the magistrates' court, 'as icy-blue, very large. They merely appeared large to me because they were just staring. Just very large, icy-blue. I could see almost the whole of the coloured part of the eye. *They did not appear to be sunken back*. They looked very cold blue.'

The killer's hair, Miss Storie told the magistrates' court, was 'a medium brown, definitely not a dark brown. It appeared to be swept back without a parting.' At the trial, she qualified this somewhat: 'He had got brown hair, combed back with no parting.' (Vol. III, p. 6, my italics.)

In cross-examination, Mr Sherrard reminded Miss Storie what she had said at the lower court:

Q. You were prepared to say, as I understand it, when you were being asked about it by my friend Mr MacDermot before the Magistrates: 'His hair was a medium brown, definitely not dark brown.' Do you remember saying that?
A. I do not remember saying it …
Q. Would it be an accurate way of describing your recollection of the man's hair to say 'His hair was a medium brown, definitely not dark brown'?
A. (After a pause). I think so. (Vol. III, p. 20.)

Miss Storie's memory of the man who shot her was as follows. If Mr Kerr is to be believed (and Miss Storie denied it at the trial) she told him five hours after the murder that the killer had 'light fairish hair and staring eyes'. A short while later, at Bedford Hospital, she spoke to Chief Inspector Whiffen and Woman Inspector Arnett and immediately afterwards a description was issued to the effect that the killer had dark hair and deep-set brown eyes. Her Identikit picture, drawn up four days later, was of a man with medium dark hair swept back with dark eyes. Her first 'recollection' of large, icy-blue, saucer-like eyes is on August 31st – eight days after the murder. At the hearing she told prosecution counsel that the hair was 'medium brown, definitely not dark brown'. At the trial she told defence counsel that she did not remember saying that at the hearing (although it had been read over to her and signed by her).

Superintendent Acott was quite satisfied that Miss Storie's recollection of her assailant was consistent throughout. He told the Bedford court: 'Her description of the murderer has never changed from the day of the murder until now and I have always regarded it as most reliable.' (Vol. IX, p. 68.)

From the outset, Miss Storie had assured Mr Acott and his colleagues that she would be able to pick her assailant out of an identity parade. These are held in order to protect a police suspect from the bias he suffers if the witness is confronted with one man, and asked: 'Is this the criminal?' The parade is made up of a number of men of roughly the same size and build as the suspect. They stand, with the suspect, in front of the witness, who is then asked to identify the criminal from them, if he can be recognized. There is still, of course, a chance that the police suspect will be selected at random. But the chance is much smaller than in the case of confrontation with one suspect.

Identity parades can only be completely fair if the witness has no idea what the police suspect looks like. If the witness knows that the man the police suspect has brown hair and green eyes, the purpose of the parade is vitiated. It is subject to the same sort of bias as where the witness is confronted by one suspect only. If the witness knows what the man the police suspect looks like, he will, in spite of himself, search the parade for such a man, and, if in doubt, tend to identify him. The less certain the witness in his own mind, the more susceptible he is to bias against the man he thinks is the police suspect.

If an identity parade is held after a police search, when the characteristics of the man the police are looking for are widely circulated to the press, the identification parade is only fair if strenuous efforts are made to ensure that the witness does not know what the suspect looks like.

The Parade at Guy's Hospital

No such precautions were taken before the identification parade at Guy's Hospital on Sunday, September 24th, 1961. Two days earlier, a detailed description had been issued to the press of Peter Alphon, the man police wanted to interview in connection with their inquiries. As we have seen, every aspect of his face and build was closely detailed. If Valerie Storie saw any of these descriptions (as she must have done if she read a newspaper) the identity parade immediately became biased against Alphon.

There is very little information about the men who stood alongside Peter Alphon for that parade, save that they came from the Union Jack Club, and were servicemen, many of them stationed overseas and some of them foreigners.

After looking round the faces for about five minutes, Valerie Storie picked out as her assailant a man who was not Alphon. Who was this man? No one knows, except his companions on the identity parade, Superintendent Acott, his advisers and Home Office officials. The usual practice after identity parades in which someone is mistakenly identified is that the identified man is brought to court so that the jury can test the witness's powers of identification. No such practice was followed in James Hanratty's trial for his life. The man who was picked out by Valerie Storie on September 24th was not produced, and for a description of him the jury were forced to rely on the conflicting evidence of two prosecution witnesses who attended the parade.

The first was Dr Ian Rennie, a doctor at Guy's Hospital. Dr Rennie said that he could not remember exactly what the man picked out at the Guy's parade looked like. 'As far as I can remember', he said, 'he had rather fairish hair and bluish eyes.' (Vol. IV, p. 13.)

The second man was Superintendent Robert Acott. Mr Sherrard's cross-examination of Mr Acott on the question of the identity parade on September 24th, ran as follows:

Q. Is Dr Rennie right when he said that she picked out a fair-haired man on that first parade?

A. I will have to refer to notes.

Q. Can you not remember?

A. I am not going to make a mistake on this point. Would you mind giving me the date?

Q. The 24th.

A. I can give you a full description of the man who was picked out on that parade.

Q. Would you tell us first of all whether he was, as Dr Rennie has told us, a fair-haired man?

A. No. He was not. He had dark, short-cropped hair. Anything else, Sir? I have his full description. I have had this man physically examined. Is there anything else?

Q. Yes. You remember the man who was picked out?

A. Yes, I do ...

Q. Is the man available by any chance?

A. He was some time ago.

Q. Is he available to be brought?

A. He was some time ago, but I cannot say off-hand. (Vol. IX, pp. 68, 69.)

There then followed a discussion as to whether or not Mr Acott should give a full description of the man, since not all of it came from his own observation. Eventually Mr Acott said:

A. I can tell you this from my own knowledge: 5 ft. 9 ins., dark, short-cropped hair, about 27 years of age and he was heavily built.

Q. You and Dr Rennie in a proper light, that is either daylight or decent artificial light, saw the same man, the man she picked out?

A. I can only answer for myself.

The detailed description which Mr Acott had of the man picked out by Miss Storie was never given to the court, nor is this description included in the defence papers. The court never discovered, for instance, what was the colour of his eyes. They knew, however, that although, in her Identikit picture, at the magistrates' hearing and at the trial Miss Storie described her assailant's hair as 'swept back without a parting', on September 24th she picked out a man with dark, short-cropped hair. All the descriptions of the suspect up to that time, many of them based on Miss Storie's word, spoke of a man of medium build. The man she picked out at Guy's, however, was 'heavily built'. Miss Storie herself gave the jury no help at all as to the looks of the man she picked out as the A6 murderer:

MR SHERRARD. On that first parade you surveyed the men paraded before you for something as long as five minutes before saying something or doing something?

A. Yes.

Q. And you then identified a man, as being in your view, the assailant?

A. Yes.

Q. Can you tell us what the man looked like?

A. No. (Vol. III, p. 22.)

Of all the answers given in the trial, that single monosyllable from Miss Storie is perhaps the most extraordinary. For a few seconds in the murder car she gazed into the face of her assailant, lit up by the lights of a passing car. A month later she lay in Guy's Hospital facing a row of men. After five minutes' careful thought she picked out a man as the murderer. Yet neither at the magistrates' hearing nor at the trial could she remember anything about the man she picked out.

The lack of a proper description of the man picked out at the first identity parade is one of the most unhappy gaps in the entire case. Rumour has it that the man was a Spanish sailor. If he was, no doubt his failure to speak English and an alibi in the Mediterranean at the time of the murder enabled Mr Acott to rule him out immediately from his inquiries. That Spanish sailor was a lucky man. The identification of James Hanratty as the killer seven weeks after the murder by Valerie Storie was the most vital evidence in the prosecution case against Hanratty. The Spanish sailor, for a few uncomfortable moments, came perilously close to the gallows after he was identified as Gregsten's murderer by Valerie Storie. Peter Alphon was even luckier. If Valerie Storie had, even by mistake, identified Peter Alphon as the murderer, he would have been charged for the murder, and, with his alibi smashed by Nudds's second statement, almost certainly hanged.

The explanation offered by the prosecution at the trial for Miss Storie's 'mistake' at the first identity parade was twofold. First, they suggested that she was not well enough to take part in the parade. In a curious passage in his evidence, Superintendent Acott said that he personally would have liked to have postponed the identity parade until she was fitter, but Alphon was in his custody and he was forced to get on with it. In fact, as we have seen, Acott wanted to have the parade the day before it was held. (See page 80.) Alphon, moreover, could easily have been held in custody on the Richmond charge, as indeed he was – for five days after the identity parade.

According to the medical evidence, given by Dr Rennie, Miss Storie was perfectly fit to take part in the parade. Her operation had been a minor one. The following day she was fit enough for the long journey to Stoke Mandeville Hospital. At no time since the murder had she suffered any loss of memory.

The second excuse was that Valerie Storie did not ask the men to speak. One of the few consistent aspects of Miss Storie's description of the killer from the outset was that he had a London East End accent and could not properly pronounce the letters 'th'. More than once in the car he had said: 'Be quiet will you, I am finking.' According to her evidence at the trial, she was not aware that she could have asked the men to speak. It was not suggested to her by the police officers at the parade. The prosecution suggested that her failure to ask the men to speak increased the chances of a mistake.

Identity by voice, however, is even less precise than identity by features. There is little a man can do about his size, build and facial features while he is standing on an identity parade. They are immutable. His voice, however, can be changed. Valerie's assailant, standing on an identity parade before her and asked to say what he knew he had said several times in the murder car would almost certainly feign a different voice or accent. If she had asked the men to speak, in short, her fallibility might well have been increased.

The Parade at Stoke Mandeville

Valerie Storie was much better when she was taken to Stoke Mandeville Hospital the day after the Guy's Hospital identity parade. From her remark to the doctor at Stoke Mandeville that the man she had picked out at her first identity parade resembled press photographs of Peter Alphon, it is clear that she was well enough to read the newspapers. If she read about the A6 murder hunt, she would have discovered by October 7th that the police were after a new suspect; and that this suspect had one very distinctive feature.

The *Daily Mail* of October 7th, for instance, had stated: 'Scotland Yard believes that a tattooed man of about 25, *who has dyed his ginger hair black*, can help in their inquiries into the A6 murder.'

This was rapidly taken up: 'She [Louise] was driven to Scotland Yard and questioned about *red-haired* John Ryan, the man every police force in the country has been asked to look for' (*News of the World*, October 8th, 1961); 'He is known as "*Ginger*" Ryan, because of the *colour of his hair, but this may be dyed black now*' (*Observer*, October 8th, 1961); 'He is known to his friends as "*Ginger*" ' (*Daily Mirror*, October 9th, 1961); 'He, the man, is 25, with blue eyes, and *auburn hair dyed black*' (*Daily Mail*, October 9th, 1961); 'Mary [Meaden] said she noticed that Ryan's *hair – which was obviously ginger – had been dyed black*' (*Daily Mirror*, October 11th, 1961, my italics throughout).

On October 12th, all the papers carried the story that the wanted man had gone into a florist's shop in Scotland Road, Liverpool, and from there to a doctor's surgery. The *Daily Sketch* quoted Mrs Ruth Mulloy, who looks after a doctor's surgery in Stanley Road, Liverpool, as saying: 'He had sort of red hair shooting straight up.'

Two days later, Hanratty lined up with twelve other men under the bright lights of the medical inspection room at Stoke Mandeville Hospital, Buckinghamshire. The identity parade had been organized by Detective Superintendent Malcolm Fewtrell, of the Buckinghamshire police, who went to a local air force camp to collect the twelve men, and by Chief Inspector Ballinger, also of the Buckinghamshire police.

According to Mr Kleinman's detailed note of the parade, four of the men had 'mousy' coloured hair, three had fair hair, three had ginger hair, and two had dark hair. They were variably dressed. Hanratty, wearing a green sports coat and fawn trousers provided by his solicitor, stood in the middle of the line at No. 6. The clothes had been found for him at his request. The best way to describe what happened on the parade is to quote from Mr Kleinman, Hanratty's solicitor, who was present and wrote the following note as part of his brief to counsel:

Eight large overhead lights – his dyed hair showed up very badly. She came in through centre door in a bed. Dr Guttman sat next to her. She was in the room some minutes, while officer explained proceedings to her in the presence of the men. She moved up the line twice. Then she asked them to say: 'Be quiet, will you, I am thinking'. Each said it. She moved past them. She moved along the line, again, making third time. Asked to go along line again fourth time. Did so a 5th time. Paused. Did so 6th time. Moved along 7th time. Asked for them to say again: 'Be quiet will you, I'm thinking'. Both spoke in turn on the Inspector's order – he called out their number and they said it. She moved along 8th time as they spoke; came back 9th time. Identified him – No. 6 – after 15 minutes to twenty minutes.

Chief Inspector Ballinger then asked if there were any complaints, and there were none. It is not true, for instance, as stated in a *Sunday Times* Magazine article in December 1966, that Hanratty was the only man on the parade in shirt sleeves. It is true, however, that Hanratty's dyed hair, in Mr Kleinman's words, 'stood out very badly'. A further passage from Mr Kleinman's note on the parade read as follows:

I have in my possession some colour photographs taken by Ronald Gerelli, *Daily Express* photographer. The photographs show that the accused had dyed hair which looked dyed and unnatural, and that any person who knew the accused had dyed his hair could hardly miss picking him out at an identity parade. At the time of the identity parade, it was a vivid tangerine colour resulting from using black dye with other dye (possibly ginger dye), and the accused's appearance was, to say the least, most unnatural.

With regard to the hair, nine days later, that is the following Monday week, 23rd October, the police produced a hair-dresser, Mr W. G. Garner, who examined Hanratty's hair at Ampthill Police Station and snipped off two corners of the colour photographs which he considered most reflected the present colour of his hair. This was done because colour photo-graphs vary due to the length of the exposure of the film. He said the original colour of his hair was light ash blond and it had been dyed very dark – the dye could have been brown or black, poorly bleached out or deducted. He thought the hair had been bleached probably twice. He had signed a statement to this effect.

I mention this hairdresser because the police have not produced him.

A willing testimony to all this comes from Valerie Storie. 'I was', she told the magistrates at Ampthill, 'startled by the most unusual colour of the hair of the accused. I had never seen hair quite that colour before.'

At the trial, Mr Sherrard asked her:

Q. Would I be putting it, possibly colloquially, but accurately, that his head of hair must have stood out like a carrot in a bunch of bananas?

A. That is right. (Vol. III, p. 24.)

The hair of the murderer, it will be remembered, was, according to Miss Storie's evidence at the hearing, 'medium brown, definitely not dark brown'. In Miss Storie's Identikit picture, the killer had hair slicked back, without a parting.

How was Miss Storie able to pick out a man whose hair looked strikingly different to that of the murderer? Could it have been that she had read somewhere, or had been told by someone that the man police were looking for had had his hair dyed – and that the hair-style and colour might be different from those she remembered in the car? If so, her attention would immediately have been directed to the man in the middle, whose hair stood out 'like a carrot in a bunch of bananas'.

The second important point about the parade concerns Hanratty's accent. In a long article on the case in the *Sunday Times* Colour Magazine of December 18th, 1966, Peter Laurie and Brian Moynahan stated: 'Hanratty was almost certainly the only man with a Cockney accent on the parade.'

If this was true, and the authors wrote later that they had got the information from the defence, it was very damaging to Hanratty. Valerie Storie identified Hanratty only after listening to all the men on the parade speak the words: 'Be quiet will you. I am thinking.' If Hanratty was the only man with a Cockney accent, he became instantly and unfairly identifiable as the murderer.

In a letter to the *Sunday Times* a fortnight later, Mr Malcolm Fewtrell, who had found the twelve men for the parade, wrote:

> You imply that those standing with him were local, i.e. Buckinghamshire, men. This was not so. The twelve men ...

orginated from all over the country and it is *almost certain* that some of them were Londoners. (*Sunday Times*, January 1st, 1967. My italics.)

Even Mr Fewtrell could not be sure that any of the twelve had Cockney accents. He had chosen his men conscientiously according to the rules. But the rules said nothing, and still say nothing, to ensure that the men on the identity parade have the same accent as the suspect. They must be of the same height and age group, but not necessarily with the same accent. In Hanratty's case, as it turned out, the accent was crucial.

The last word on the identification parade at Stoke Mandeville must come from Valerie Storie herself in an article she wrote nine months later:

> Suddenly, at the very end of the twenty minutes allowed for the identification parade, I was asked if I recognised anyone. I looked at Hanratty, and said quietly: Number six. In a second, the door of the room had slammed shut behind me as I was quickly wheeled into the corridor. Superintendent Acott gripped my arm and said: 'Well done!'
>
> I knew I had settled my score with Hanratty. (*Today*, June 9th, 1962.)

Valerie Storie's evidence against Hanratty did not stop at identification by sight and sound. Not only had she seen the killer, but she had conversed with him for five hours as the car made its way from Taplow to Deadman's Hill. Her evidence about the killer therefore went beyond mere identification of him in a parade. The killer's description of himself, as retailed by Valerie Storie, seemed to implicate Hanratty less directly but, cumulatively, in a way which did him a lot of damage.

There was, for instance, the killer's description of his criminal experience. 'He said', Valerie Storie told the court, 'that he had never had a chance in life. He said that when he was a child he was locked in the cellar for days on end and only had bread and water to drink. He said that since he was eight he had been to remand homes, Borstal; he had done C.T. and the next thing he would get would be P.D. He said, "I have done the lot". I believe he said he had done five years for housebreaking.'

Some of this fitted Hanratty, and some of it did not. He had done

C.T. (corrective training), but he had never been in a remand home or a Borstal. He had never been locked in a cellar. (There had never been a cellar in any house he had lived in.) He had not been in any institutions as a child. He would not be eligible on his next offence for P.D. (preventive detention) as he was too young. He had done three years, not five, for housebreaking. The expression 'done the lot' is prisoners' slang for serving a full sentence without remission (as Hanratty had done). But to a layman, it means something much more simple. When Valerie Storie was asked what it meant, she said she had: 'presumed that he had done all sorts of crimes and had been imprisoned for them. What he actually meant I don't know.' (Vol. II, p. 50.)

Miss Storie's evidence at the trial differed in a number of important respects from her evidence at the hearing, to the detriment of Hanratty. First there was his driving experience. At the hearing, Miss Storie said: 'He was definitely a back-seat driver and very nervous. We said: "Do you drive?" He said: "Oh, yes," but it still did not make him a better passenger.' At the trial, this had become: 'He said he could drive all sorts of cars.' Hanratty, of course, was a car thief, who could drive all sorts of cars. After the murder and the rape, and after the body of Gregsten had been lifted from the car, Miss Storie said, she begged the man to take the car and go. Yet the murderer, as we have seen, twice asked Miss Storie to show him how to work the gears on an ordinary Morris Minor.

Another part of Valerie Storie's story about the car journey reflected badly on Hanratty. At the hearing, she said, while describing the journey of the murder car:

> We went past the beginning of the Kenton Road in Harrow which I know. We went near Aldenham. He said at one stage: 'Be careful. There are some roadworks round the corner.' We said: 'How do you know? Do you know this area?' He said: 'No, but I know there are some roadworks there.'

This statement was changed crucially at the trial, where she said:

> At one point in our meanderings through the roads, he said: 'Be careful, round the corner there are some roadworks,' and sure enough when we got round the bend there were some roadworks. He then hastily added: 'I do not know this area.' (Vol. II, p. 52.)

The second version, before the jury, left out the question asked by Miss Storie or Gregsten, and made it look as though the killer was afraid he might give himself away with his remark about the roadworks and volunteered the information without being questioned about it. This implicated Hanratty, who lived in Kingsbury and knew the area well. Yet Miss Storie's first version indicated only that the killer knew there were roadworks round the corner — perhaps from a sign saying 'Road Works Ahead'. No evidence was brought by either side as to whether or not there was such a sign, and Miss Storie admitted to Mr Sherrard that she did not notice whether there was or not.

There were other similar differences between Miss Storie's evidence before the magistrates and her evidence at the trial. One important passage of her evidence at Ampthill, signed before the magistrates as a true record of what she said, ran as follows:

> We said that further along was the Bath Road and he said: 'Where does that go to?' We said: 'to Maidenhead or Slough.' At that point he said he didn't want to go to Slough ... When we got to the junction of the A4, he said: 'Where does this road go to?' We said: 'It goes to Maidenhead or Slough.' He said: 'I've had enough of Maidenhead'.

At the trial Miss Storie changed the facts slightly, but importantly:

MISS STORIE. He asked us where the road went to.
Q. Did he mention any road himself?
A. He said: 'Where does that road go to?' and just up the road from where we were was the motorway.
Q. The M4?
A. The M4. He asked where that went to. We said: 'To Reading or to Slough. You cannot get on it from where we are.' He did not seem to understand that he could not get on to that road from where we were. He said that further on was the Bath Road which went either to Maidenhead or to London. He said he did not want to go to London.' (Vol. II, p. 48.)

According to this version, the man in the car made no reference to Maidenhead or Slough, and was clearly not familiar with the area.

In the first version, however, the man said he knew something of the area. He said that he did not want to go to Slough, and had had enough of Maidenhead. Hanratty, of course, had no prior knowledge of Maidenhead or Slough, and the prosecution could find no evidence (for there was none) that he had ever been to Taplow before in his life. No explanation whatever was given by Miss Storie for this vital shift in her evidence:

MR SHERRARD. You will recall that when you were giving your evidence before the Magistrates you gave it in much the way that you have today, and it was taken down at dictation speed. Do you remember?

MISS STORIE. Yes ...

Q. Do you agree that you in fact made no attempt to correct Slough for London or London for Slough or interchange the two?

NO ANSWER (Vol. III, p. 15.)

Another shift in Miss Storie's evidence concerned the killer's watch. On September 20th, about three weeks before Hanratty was charged with the murder, Mrs Gregsten, the widow of the murdered man, visited Valerie Storie in hospital and gave the *Daily Mail* the inside story of the murder. One of the things which Valerie had told her on that occasion was that the killer had a watch and kept looking at it. 'Time', said Mrs Gregsten, 'meant a great deal to him. He kept looking at his watch. Mike and Valerie got the impression that he might have been committing a burglary or something.' (*Daily Mail*, September 22nd, 1961.)

This was repeated by Miss Storie before the magistrates on oath:

We asked him what he wanted. He kept looking at his watch. It was a wrist watch. I can't remember which wrist it was on. I asked him what he wanted. He said: 'There's plenty of time'. We asked what for. He shrugged his shoulders and said 'there's plenty of time'.

This was changed at the trial. Mr Swanwick asked Miss Storie:

Q. Had he got a watch on, do you remember?

A. *He may have — I cannot remember.* (Vol. II, p. 45, my italics.)

The difference, once again, was important. If the killer kept looking at his watch; if 'time meant a great deal to him', he may have been keeping to a prearranged timetable. The chance rapist, who, according to the prosecution, did the murder for sex, was not the sort of man who would keep looking at his watch. If this change in evidence, like the others, was an accident of Miss Storie's memory, it was convenient to the prosecution.

According to Miss Storie, the man said he was hungry, and that he had not eaten for two days. Hanratty had had breakfast that morning at the Vienna Hotel. The man said he had been sleeping rough. Hanratty had spent the night before at the Vienna Hotel, and the night before that at the home of Mrs Anderson. The man said that he knew the Bear Hotel, Maidenhead, and said that the hotel had recently been renovated, which was true. There is no evidence of any kind that Hanratty had ever been to the hotel, or indeed had ever been in Maidenhead in his life. The man had said he was short of money, which Hanratty was not. Finally, Miss Storie had said that the killer was 'not much taller than me'. Miss Storie was 5 ft. 3¼ ins., Hanratty was 5 ft. 8 ins.

When Miss Storie asked the killer his name, he replied after a pause: 'Call me Jim.' Mr Swanwick made a bold effort to convince the jury that this implicated Hanratty, whose Christian name was Jim. One answer to this came from no less a person than Superintendent Acott at the trial, who was asked by Mr Sherrard: 'When the man in the car said, as was alleged, and as I suggest you knew was alleged to have said, "Call me Jim", you are not saying are you that you accept that as necessarily being the name by which the man was known.'

Mr Acott said: 'Not necessarily, Sir, no.' (Vol. XI, p. 27.)

The killer's information about himself, in short, had to be treated with caution. Whether or not he intended to commit murder or rape, he wanted to hide his identity. He had, for instance, worn a handkerchief over his face when he got out of the car with Gregsten. He was unlikely in the circumstances to reel off his name, address and telephone number. Valerie Storie admitted that the killer's assertion that he had been sleeping rough did not fit his immaculate appearance and the recent heavy rain. If he lied about 'sleeping rough' he probably lied about a number of other things, particularly about his name. The evidence of Miss Storie about the man's description of himself should therefore be taken as a guide to genuine identification only where it is based on external evidence. For instance, when the killer spoke about the recent renovation of the Bear Hotel, Maidenhead, it was a fair deduction that he had some knowledge of the Bear Hotel, Maidenhead. Without external corroboration like that, the killer's information about himself was unlikely to be accurate.

There was one other possibility about the man's information

about himself which was not suggested to the court. The killer may well have been giving false information in order to lay a false trail. The fact that the man in the car voluntarily offered information about himself which fitted Hanratty did not necessarily implicate Hanratty. It could also have meant that the man in the car was giving information which he thought fitted Hanratty, so that a trail to Hanratty would be laid to deceive future hunters of the gunman.

(II) John Skillett

Valerie Storie's identification was backed by two further identifications of James Hanratty at an identification parade held at Bedford police station on October 13th. At this parade Hanratty was the only person wearing a dark suit. He complained afterwards that the reports of the case had talked of a man in a dark suit, and that he should have changed his coat. There were nine people on the parade.

The first witness was John Skillett, the engineering foreman who had seen the murder car driving down Eastern Avenue a few hours after the murder, and had caught a glimpse of the man in the car as he pulled level to shout abuse at him at a roundabout. Mr Skillett looked at the men on the parade for about five minutes and then picked out Hanratty.

He was followed immediately by Mr Edward Blackhall, who had been sitting in Mr Skillett's car, in front, on the same morning. He had wound down the window to enable Mr Skillett to shout his abuse, and he had caught a glimpse of the man. He was, in fact, nearer to the man than Mr Skillett. After one minute, Mr Blackhall picked out a dark-haired man next to Hanratty and identified him as the man in the car.

Mr Swanwick, in his summing up speech for the prosecution, tried to distinguish between the views which Mr Blackhall and Mr Skillett had had of the man in the car. Mr Skillett, he said, had had his view of the man's head obscured by the top of the car, and therefore could not see his hair. Mr Blackhall, on the other hand, had seen his hair. Skillett, therefore, was not put off by the tangerine-coloured hair of Hanratty, while Blackhall was.

This effort to explain the contradiction between the two men's identification had been thwarted by Mr Skillett himself. Cross-examined at the magistrates' court, Mr Skillett was quite sure about one thing: 'Neither of the men on either side of the man I picked out *looked anything like him*. If Mr Blackhall picked out someone standing to his left or his right, it would surprise me.'

Yet Blackhall had picked out a man standing next to Hanratty, who, in Skillett's view, did not look anything like him. Blackhall and Skillett saw the same man in the car from almost exactly the same angle, except that Mr Blackhall was closer. Yet they picked out two men who looked quite different to one another. It was only after the magistrates' hearing that Mr Skillett decided that he had not had a proper look at the hair of the man in the car. His sworn deposition at the magistrates' court reads as follows: 'When I saw him in the Morris Minor, his hair was not dark and was not light.'

Cross-examined before the magistrates, Mr Skillett said: 'The man in the Morris Minor had hair about browny colour.'

At the trial, however, Mr Skillett's evidence had changed: 'I could not see it properly, not the colour of his hair ... With the top of the car coming down on the hair you cannot tell the shade of hair.' (Vol. IV, p. 24.)

At the trial, moreover, Mr Skillett was no longer prepared to say what he had said on oath in front of the magistrates – about the men on either side of Hanratty in the parade. 'The first one', he said in answer to Mr Sherrard, 'did not look like him, but the third one, the features were there but it was not right.' (Vol. IV, p. 26.)

Once again, the evidence at Ampthill had changed conveniently to accommodate the prosecution's case.

From the moment Mr Blackhall and Mr Skillett came to the attention of the police as having seen the murder car on the morning after the murder, the police regarded Blackhall as the most reliable witness. This was partly because Blackhall had reported the matter to them; partly because Blackhall, unlike Skillett, had noticed the three red Scotch Tape strips on the back of the car; partly because Skillett, when he saw the murder car, was in a towering rage while Blackhall had remained cool.

When Detective Sergeant Mackle started his work on the Identikit picture of the killer, he interviewed Skillett and Blackhall, but relied to a much greater extent on Blackhall. Skillett admitted that, although he had helped with the Identikit picture, the result was very different from the picture he had devised. The second Identikit picture was devised almost entirely through conversations with Mr

Blackhall. Blackhall composed one of the Identikit pictures, yet he picked out a man who could not possibly have been the murderer, and a man who, in Skillett's original testimony on oath, 'did not look anything like' Hanratty.

Moreover, Mr Blackhall attended the identification parade on which Peter Alphon stood at New Scotland Yard on September 23rd, while Mr Skillett did not. Mr Skillett's absence was important. If the police regarded Mr Skillett as crucial to the case, they would surely have made every effort to ensure that their first suspect was seen by Mr Skillett. Mr Skillett told me, when I interviewed him on August 2nd, 1970, that he had been away on holiday at the time. 'When I came back from my holidays', he said, 'my brother said the police were looking for me to go on an identity parade.' Mr Skillett was not available, and Mr Skillett never had a chance to look at Peter Alphon in an identity parade.

Mr Blackhall, on the other hand, had been to the parade. At the magistrates' court, Mr Blackhall answered questions about that first identity parade as he thought he ought to:

> I appreciate the very serious duty of attending an identity parade [he said], *I recognize that unless I could identify with certainty it would be wrong to identify* anybody on a parade. I did attend an identity parade at New Scotland Yard. I did my best to fulfil my duty. (My italics.)

By the trial, Mr Blackhall had changed his recollection of these matters:

> I was taken from my employment and rushed to Scotland Yard. I was the first one through into the yard. I was given no instructions whatsoever and I just picked out the chap who I thought looked like the chap that was in the car. (Vol. IV, p. 34.)

Today, Blackhall sticks to this second version. His own account of the parade runs as follows:

> We were taken down there on a Saturday afternoon — rushed down there — and I was the first to go in and look at the line. No one told me anything specific — I was just asked to go down and touch anyone I recognized. I walked down the line and there was a fair-haired man in the line who looked something like the man in the car so I touched him. I made to go on down the line, but the policeman stopped me and wheeled me out.

I wasn't even completely clear that I could only touch one man. One of the other witnesses, I think it was the hotel manager, later touched two blokes. They let him do it, but I was wheeled off as soon as I'd touched one.

I remember that Alphon was standing at the end of the line, wearing a navy blazer and an open-necked shirt. I'm sure I would have picked him if I'd gone down to the end of the line. He did look like the man in the car. (Interview, August 2nd, 1970.)

Mr Blackhall thinks today that he was the only witness on that parade who had anything to do with the A6 murder. 'I think all the others were to do with the hotel or the assault on the Richmond woman. Skillett wasn't there, and Trower wasn't there anyway.'

At any rate, Mr Blackhall's failure to identify Hanratty at the Bedford identity parade diminished the effect of Mr Skillett's identification. Mr Skillett today is 'quite satisfied in my own mind' that he picked the man in the car, while Mr Blackhall is adamant that the man in the car was not Hanratty. Blackhall also says that when he and Skillett left the trial on January 25th, 1962, after giving evidence, they walked slowly over to Skillett's car to drive back to London. 'Well,' said Skillett, according to his friend, 'it must have been Hanratty because otherwise the police would never have arrested him.'

(III) James Trower

The next man to walk on to the identification parade was James Trower, the engineering worker who had, he said, seen the murder car in Redbridge Lane on the morning after the murder. Trower walked into the room, took one look and identified Hanratty.

Trower's original story went as follows: At 7 a.m. on August 23rd, 1961, he had gone as was his custom to collect a lorry driver, Mr Paddy Hogan, to give him a lift to work. Trower was then driving a 1952 Humber Super Snipe. Hogan lived at 220 Redbridge Lane, which is about 30 yards short of the turning from Redbridge Lane into Avondale Crescent, where the murder car was abandoned. According to Trower's original story, told at the magistrates' court, he got out of his car, knocked on Hogan's door and stepped back waiting for Hogan to answer. As he did so he heard a grinding of gears, and turned round to see a grey Morris Minor driving past his car. 'It was coming from off Eastern Avenue. It was going at about 25 m.p.h. As the car pulled level with me, the driver looked at me and I looked at him, and it turned left into Avondale Crescent. That would be about 7.8 a.m.'

'I would say', said Mr Trower in cross-examination, 'he was looking at me for 2 or 3 seconds.' Asked what sort of a view he had got of the man in the car, he replied: 'Full face.' During the defence case later on in the trial, the jury asked for further clarification about Trower's positioning in the road when he saw the murder car. Two police officers were then recalled. They had taken pictures of Redbridge Lane and one of them, P.C. Leslie Hanlon, had taken measurements of Mr Trower, his Super Snipe car and the murder car. These measurements showed that it was impossible for Mr Trower, who was five feet ten inches tall, to see the driver of a car looking at him if the Morris was obscured by his own car.

Mr Trower had parked his Super Snipe directly outside Mr Hogan's house, pointing up a slight gradient towards Avondale Crescent. The Morris Minor murder car had come from the same direction and had passed his car as it was standing. On Trower's own evidence he was standing next to his car when the murder car passed him, so he would have had to see over his car to get a full side view of the killer.

Accordingly, Mr Trower was recalled. Under pressure of the facts, his evidence changed. This is how it ended up, in cross-examination:

Q. So that what it comes to is this, that the first you see of the driver is as it [the car] passes the front of the car where you say you were standing?
A. Yes.
Q. And it is then travelling at about 20 miles per hour, you have told us?
A. Yes.
Q. So you would then have had, would you not, as it passed, if it is travelling 30 ft. per second, a rear view thereafter?
A. Pardon?
Q. You would then have had a rear view of the car and the driver after it passed your line of vision?
A. *I would have had a three-quarters view.*
Q. A three-quarters view and then a rear view?
A. Yes. (Vol. XVI, p. 20. My italics.)

In other words, on being recalled, Trower admitted that the first he had seen of the man in the car was 'a three-quarters view'. No one asked Mr Trower how it was that the murderer had *looked at him*; how the two men, according to his original testimony, had looked into each other's eyes for about three seconds. It is difficult to imagine the killer looking *back* to gaze into the eyes of a bystander, especially when the driver was, presumably, anxious not to be seen by anyone.

In November 1966, the B.B.C. Panorama programme, after an interview with Mr Trower, restaged the drive of the car down Redbridge Lane. The viewer saw the same view of the driver which Trower said he saw. All that could be seen of the driver during this restaging was a dull blur.

Immediately after Mr Trower had given evidence for the second time, his friend – a long-distance lorry driver called Paddy Hogan – was called. Hogan was a surprise witness. No statement had been taken from him by the defence before the trial. On the Saturday before giving evidence, however, he had met Trower in Redbridge Lane. Trower was conducting a rehearsal for giving his evidence and was walking up and down the lane, measuring distances. Hogan had a few words with him. A bystander heard the two men talking, and, as a result, Mr Kleinman the defence solicitor was informed that Mr Hogan might have something interesting to say about Trower's evidence.

The following day, a Sunday, Kleinman rushed down to Redbridge and pleaded with Hogan to give evidence for the defence. After a discussion with his wife, Hogan agreed. What he said in court went a long way towards invalidating Trower's identification.

Hogan's story was as follows. He confirmed that Trower was due to pick him up on the relevant morning, but he said that Trower had been late. Hogan himself had gone out on to his doorstep some ten or twenty minutes before Trower arrived, and had seen a Morris Minor come down the road and turn into Avondale Crescent. He had 'glanced up' as the car had passed, and noticed that the car was 'fawn or cream'. Hogan also says that he answered Trower's knock instantly, because he had been waiting for him.

Hogan agreed that the following day policemen had asked them if they had seen anything unusual. He had realized that the car he had seen might have been the murder car but, because he had not even had a glimpse of the driver, he decided to say nothing. Trower had said on the journey that he had been *passed* by a Morris Minor which was being driven as if by a madman, and so they had turned round and made a statement to the police. At no time, said Hogan, did Trower say that he had seen the car from outside Hogan's door, or that he had seen it turn into Avondale Crescent. Hogan therefore assumed that Trower had been passed by the Morris Minor while driving along.

Hogan explained his refusal to make a statement or to challenge Trower's statement until then because his wife had asked him not to get involved. She was having a baby in September. When, however, he had heard Trower's claims in full, and when he had heard from Mr Kleinman that a man's life was at stake, he decided, after a further discussion with his wife, to give evidence for the defence.

Not everything about Hogan's evidence was satisfactory. He was referring to events which had happened several months before. More important, the murder car could not have passed Hogan's door until about ten past seven (Mr Skillett had said that he noticed a clock saying 7.0 a.m. soon after he encountered the murder car) so it could not have been as long as twenty minutes before Trower arrived. There was, however, not the slightest reason why Hogan should have lied, as the prosecuting counsel, Mr Swanwick, suggested. The refutation of Trower's evidence brought for Hogan no personal gain and was offered only at the last moment after several months' reluctance to give evidence at all.

The evidence about identification, which was by a long way the strongest plank in the prosecution's platform, stemmed from three glimpses: Valerie Storie's glimpse in the headlights of a passing car; John Skillett's glimpse, looking across his passenger from his car at the driver of another one which was 'almost stationary'; and James Trower's glimpse at a three-quarters and rear view of a driver whose car drew away at a speed of thirty feet per second. Each of these glimpses lasted between one and three seconds. All three identifications on the basis of these glimpses were diminished in effect and importance by other evidence: Valerie Storie's by the fact that she identified someone else only a month after the murder whose characteristics (dark, close-cropped hair, heavy build) were different to those of Hanratty when she picked him out; John Skillett's by the fact that his car passenger, Edward Blackhall, picked out on different occasions two men, neither of whom was Hanratty, and one of whom according to Mr Skillett 'looked nothing like' Hanratty; Trower's by the evidence of P.C. Hanlon about the size of his car and of his friend Paddy Hogan about the timing of the Morris Minor's arrival at Avondale Crescent.

Summary

British legal history is littered with cases of wrong convictions because of false identification, and for every one such case recorded there are probably twenty which no one hears about. The extent of possible human error was demonstrated most strikingly in the famous case of Adolf Beck in 1896. Beck was spotted one day by a woman in the street who immediately identified him as the man who had defrauded her of jewellery. Fourteen other women, none of whom had made a false identification previously, positively identified Beck as the man who had similarly defrauded them. He was convicted, and served five years in prison. On his release he was again arrested for the same sort of fraud, again identified by a woman, and again imprisoned. Fortunately for him the police then found the man who had committed the frauds. Beck was released, pardoned and paid £5,000 compensation.

The Home Office set up a Committee of Inquiry into the Beck case, which recommended that 'evidence of identity based upon personal impressions is, unless supported by other facts, an unsafe basis for the verdict of the jury.' For nearly seventy years this recommendation has been ignored by policemen, judges and juries. In April 1968, sixty-seven years after the Beck inquiry, the National Council for Civil Liberties sent a dossier of fifteen cases to the Home Secretary in all of which, they claimed, the wrong man had been convicted because of false identification.

The N.C.C.L. dossier followed a spate of identification cases which had been proved to have resulted in false convictions. The cases had provoked a debate in the House of Commons and even an angry leading article in *The Times*. The rules, everyone agreed, should be changed. Many of the cases which had come to light showed that identification was often used as a device to secure a prosecution. Bernard Beatty, for instance, had been sentenced to fifteen years in prison for murder in March 1966 on the basis of the identification of one witness after fifteen other witnesses had failed to identify him.

In another relevant case in November 1967, in Bradford (where four cases of false convictions after mistaken identity were proved in two years), a police officer on traffic duty waved down a van which had failed to stop. The van charged on. The policeman jumped into the car of a Mr Venyige, who was driving past, and gave chase. They caught the van, and the policeman got into it with the driver. After driving for some time, the driver slammed on the brakes, pushed the policeman towards the nearside window, jumped out of the van and ran away.

Mr Venyige told the police that he had got a good look at the van driver through the window of his car when his car had drawn level with the van at some traffic lights. Both he and the policeman later identified a Mr Albert Chapman as the van driver (though Chapman strongly denied it). Chapman was convicted on the basis of this identification and was sentenced to nine months in prison. A prisoner called Roberts, however, read a report of the conviction in the newspapers and confessed. Roberts was convicted, and Chapman was released after seventeen days in prison.

In the same month, in the same city, Patrick Crundall was released while waiting trial for robbing old people in the street. Two of the women who had been robbed picked him out as their assailant from an identification parade, and six other women identified him in the magistrates' court. Four weeks later, the real culprit was caught, and immediately admitted the crimes for which Crundall was standing trial. There was no doubt in Crundall's mind that the identification procedure was farcical and that the witnesses, all of whom suffered from grievances, were more than anxious to co-operate with the police in identifying their suspect.

The cases which came to light in the spring of 1968 showed the extent of the margin of error to which witnesses at identification parades are liable. A young nurse had identified a man of sixty-one as her friend's assailant. The old man, who had never been in trouble with the police before, was charged and committed. He was released only when a twenty-one-year-old labourer, *forty years his junior*, confessed to the attack and was convicted of it. (See, for this and other cases, 'A Case of Mistaken Identity' by James Fox, *Sunday Times* Colour Magazine, November 24th, 1968.)

The *Solicitors' Journal*, commenting on the Crundall case, complained: 'However fairly an identification parade was conducted, witnesses were bound to have the feeling that they should pick someone on the parade.'

In June of 1968 the *Sunday Times* gave a lot of publicity to the case of the Hugman brothers of East London, who had been falsely identified and wrongly arrested for stealing television sets in the City of London.

The row over the Hugman case finally persuaded the Home Office that something had to be done about identification parades. In January 1969, they published Circular 9/1969 setting out new Home Office rules on identification parades. 'Failure to observe the provisions', wrote Philip Allen, the Home Office official who wrote the circular, 'may well result in the judge in his summing up to the jury commenting on the reliability of the evidence obtained.'

The circular's recommendations were only marginally stronger than the section on identity parades in the Consolidated Circular on Crime which they replaced. Section 3 stated: 'If an officer concerned with the case against the suspect is present, he should take no part in conducting the parade.' This was a poor substitute for the ruling demanded by the N.C.C.L. that officers connected with the case *should not be present* at the parade.

There were other aspects of the circular which would have had direct bearing on the Hanratty case. Recommendation 5 ran as follows: 'Witnesses who have previously seen a photograph or description of the suspect should not be led by reason of their recollection of the photograph or description as for instance by being shown a photograph or description before the parade.' This proviso would probably apply to a case where a description of the suspect had been widely circulated in all the press for several days before the identity parade.

Recommendation 8 read: 'The suspect should be placed among persons (if practicable eight or more) who are as far as possible of the same age, height, hair colouring, general appearance, dress ... and position in life [*sic*].' The recommendation made no specific reference to accent, although a further recommendation allows witnesses to ask the identity parade to speak.

Two other recommendations were plainly not followed in Hanratty's identification parades. No. 10 reads: 'The suspect should be allowed to select his own position in the line, and should be expressly asked if he has any objection to the persons present with him or the arrangements made.'

In Hanratty's first identity parade, he objected to being made to wear a dark suit. But he was not asked for his comments until after the parade had been held. No. 11 reads: 'The suspect should be informed that he may alter his position after each witness has left.' Hanratty, in his first identity parade, was not so informed.

Yet the Home Office circular, like so many of its kind, had missed the main point about the weakness of identification in criminal trials. There is no judicial means whereby a witness's accuracy in identification can be tested. Cross-examination cannot possibly indicate whether a particular witness is good or bad at remembering faces. The most positive witness has often the least accurate memory for faces, and the most uncertain witness is often the best identifier. In spite of all this, the 1969 circular still permitted convictions on the basis of identification alone. It provided no real safeguard against the pre-selection of a suspect from outside information or against random identification. There was nothing in the circular which downgraded identification to its proper status.

On November 9th, 1969, a distinguished lawyer gave a talk on the laws of evidence on the B.B.C. At the end of his talk he made a moving plea for a change in the rules of evidence about identification. The speaker was Mr Michael Sherrard, Q.C., one of the most successful lawyers at the bar, haunted still by the ghosts of his past cases.

3

Supporting Evidence

INTRODUCTION

During his argument against the prosecution evidence of identification, Mr Sherrard, in his closing address to the jury, cited the
1949 case of McGrath. In that case, two men were stopped driving
a stolen lorry. After interviewing them both, the police split them
up. One went with one policeman in the police car; the other drove
the lorry with the policeman sitting next to him. As the lorry was
going full speed to the police station, the driver opened the door,
flung himself out, and ran. The policeman narrowly escaped a
serious accident.

An hour later, McGrath was picked up in the area with some
marks on him. He was taken to the police station and immediately
put on an identity parade. Both policemen walked up to him and
picked him out as the man in the lorry. He was tried, convicted and
sent to prison. New evidence then came to light that he could not
have been in the lorry. The Court of Criminal Appeal upheld his
appeal, and he was freed.

Mr Swanwick, in his summing up speech, also made reference to
McGrath's case. 'There was', he said, 'other evidence finally elicited
which pointed away from the evidence of identification and finally
absolved the accused man. My submission here is that the other
evidence supports and reinforces the evidence of identification, so
that the two become stronger, the one relying on the other.'

The 'other evidence' was as follows: first, the cartridge cases
from the murder weapon were found in the Vienna Hotel, in the
room where Hanratty had stayed on the night before the murder;
second, the gun was found under the back seat of a bus on the
evening after the murder, and Hanratty had told a friend that the

back seat of a bus was a good place to hide things; third, Hanratty
had confessed in prison to another prisoner called Langdale;
fourth, the jacket from the suit which Hanratty was wearing at the
time of the murder was missing; fifth, Hanratty's friend, Mrs
Louise Anderson, gave evidence about his character which seemed
to point to his guilt; sixth, the interviews between Hanratty and
Superintendent Acott both on the telephone and at Blackpool
police station, while in no way constituting a confession, were
gravely damaging to Hanratty.

(I) The Cartridge Cases in the Vienna Hotel

The two cartridge cases, later proved beyond doubt to have carried
bullets fired from the murder weapon, were, as we have seen, found
by Mr Crocker and Mrs Galves on a chair in room 24 of the Vienna
Hotel on September 11th, nineteen days after the murder. They
were not buried in the chair, or hidden under it. They were resting
on top of it. One of them was resting so precariously that when Mr
Crocker bent to tear a piece of material from the bottom of the
chair, a cartridge case fell off. The other was then seen instantly by
Mrs Galves.

James Hanratty, on his own admission, had stayed in room 24
on August 21st–22nd, the night before the murder night. On the
night of August 30th, according to the hotel register and to Mrs
Galves's evidence at the magistrates' court and at the trial, Room
24 was occupied by an Indian called Mr Rapur, who did not fit the
description of the murderer.

The prosecution argued that Hanratty had accidentally left the
two cartridge cases in his room before setting off the next morning
with his gun and ammunition.

'These must', said Mr Swanwick in his closing address to the
jury, 'have been left at the Vienna Hotel by the murderer before the
gun was found on the 24th August, because they are identified
beyond dispute as cartridges from the murder gun, and you may
think it is at least highly improbable that anybody would have left
them there after the time at which the gun and bullets, the unfired
bullets, were found on the bus on the 24th August.' (Vol. XVIII,
p. 23.)

There was, however, a considerable time lag between August
22nd, when Hanratty, according to Swanwick, left the cartridge
cases in the hotel and September 11th when they were found. How

was it possible that two cartridge cases could stay for nineteen days on the chair of a hotel room without being noticed or picked up by anyone?

Mrs Snell, the 'wife' of Nudds, told the court at Bedford of a routine which was adhered to in the Vienna Hotel when a guest left a room. She stated (Vol. VIII, p. 8) that the room was properly cleaned, the linen removed from the bed, the furniture dusted, the carpet Hoovered, including the carpet under the chairs, which were moved. Even when a guest did not occupy a room, this routine was undergone twice a week by Mrs Galves and Mrs Snell. Mrs Snell insisted that she had gone through this routine in room 24 after Hanratty left it on August 22nd:

MR SHERRARD. Can you remember whether or not you did anything with regard to a chair in the alcove in that room?
A. Yes. I moved it, so I could get to the other side of the bed to help Mrs Galves.
Q. Did you notice anything unusual with regard to the chair or not?
A. No. (Vol. VII, p. 18.)

The merest tug on the chair by Mr Crocker on September 11th made the cartridge cases fall off. Moving the chair, apparently, had not brought them to Mrs Snell's or Mrs Galves's attention. Moreover the bed *could not have been properly made* without the chair being moved.

Mrs Galves's evidence, on the other hand, was more helpful to the prosecution case. She said that because of understaffing and the slackness which prevailed in the Vienna Hotel, empty rooms were in general not attended to. She said that Mrs Snell had not cleaned room 24 after it had been vacated by Hanratty, but that she, Mrs Galves, had cleaned it without Hoovering or dusting and without moving the chairs. (Mr Crocker also gave evidence to say that the hotel was badly understaffed.) Mrs Galves explained that the Indian gentleman who stayed in room 24 on August 30th, a week after the murder, had occupied the double bed in the middle of the room, and that the cleaning of the room afterwards had not therefore involved moving the chair at the end of the bed occupied by Hanratty. Although she seemed to be uncertain on which chair the cases were found (she thought it was green; Crocker described it as maroon), Mrs Galves's evidence, given in Spanish and passed on to the Court through an interpreter, helped to convince the jury that the two cartridge cases had been sitting on the chair in room 24 unnoticed since Hanratty had accidentally left them there on the morning of August 22nd. Mrs Galves, incidentally, had lost her job at the Vienna Hotel in October, three months before the trial. Under the Aliens Acts, her right to stay in Britain depended on being at work and having a work permit. Despite her lack of work, however, and the fact that it was the end of the holiday season in which the Home Office admits a large number of casual workers for the hotel and tourist industry, Mrs Galves's application to stay in Britain was viewed with uncharacteristic liberalism by the Home Office.

There was however a further difficulty about the prosecution case with regard to the cartridge cases in the Vienna Hotel. Cartridge cases are not bullets. They are only available *after* bullets have been fired. If they were left in the hotel *before* the murder by the murderer, he must have fired the gun *before* the murder. Hanratty could, of course, as was at one stage seriously suggested by the prosecution, have indulged in 'target practice' inside the Vienna Hotel on the evening before the murder. Even in the Vienna Hotel, however, the firing of revolvers in the middle of the night in a silent basement room is likely to attract attention.

If the prosecution was right, Hanratty must have accidentally dropped two cartridge cases which he had had around his person for some time, or he must have fired two shots in the room itself. Both propositions are unlikely. Yet, as Mr Swanwick pointed out, no one except the Indian gentleman had occupied the room from the time Hanratty left. The only evidence that Peter Alphon had been in the room was in the withdrawn second statement of Nudds. The probability is that the prosecution was right when it maintained that no one who could have had anything to do with the murder had slept in the room after Hanratty. Was it right to assume from that, however, that the cartridge cases were left there by the murderer? There is one other alternative. The cases could have been deliberately *planted* in the Vienna Hotel to focus police attention on the room's last occupant. This was an alternative which, unhappily for Hanratty, was never suggested at trial or hearing. Certainly, if anyone had wanted to plant cartridge cases in Room 24, he could easily have done so. It became clear during the evidence about the Vienna Hotel that the doors to most rooms in the hotel, and especially room 24, were not permanently locked. Anyone could have walked into the front door, down to the basement and out again without being noticed. There was also easy access to the room from the garden via low windows, and an easy access to the garden from a public park. Anyone who knew the hotel could have put the cartridge cases there at any time after the murder.

Who knew Hanratty had stayed the night of August 21st–22nd at the Vienna Hotel? In his evidence Hanratty said that he went to the Vienna by accident after applying for a room at the Broadway House Hotel, Dorset Square. If that is right, no one knew of his stay there *before* he went. The only people who knew were told *afterwards*.

One person who knew very soon afterwards that Hanratty had stayed at the Vienna Hotel was Charles 'Dixie' France, in whose house at Swiss Cottage Hanratty stayed both before and after the murder. In evidence at the trial, Charles France told of Hanratty's coming to the France house a few days after the murder.

'I made a remark to him', said France, 'about how he went down the Club on the Monday and with that he said: "Yes, I did not go directly on Monday to Liverpool." With that he pulled out a bill for the Vienna Hotel, and he showed it to my wife. I did not look at it. I was not interested at all. But my wife scrutinised it. I know she was very interested, as a woman would be, and he remarked about how expensive it was to live out.' (Vol. VII, p. 5.) This was confirmed in evidence by Mrs France.

Hanratty, however, gave a different account of this incident to his father and mother when they visited him at Brixton prison before the trial. Hanratty was musing as to the reasons for his friends, the Frances, giving evidence for the prosecution, and he told his parents about how, when he went to see the Frances some three days after the murder, he told them casually that he had spent the previous Monday night at a Paddington hotel. Dixie France immediately showed great interest in this information. When Hanratty told him it cost £1.7s.6d. for bed and breakfast, France expressed disbelief and would not leave him alone until he produced the receipt for the money with the billhead, Vienna Hotel, Sutherland Avenue. After seeing the dated receipt, Mr France left the matter alone. Whichever version is right, Mr France had concrete evidence that Hanratty had stayed that night at the Vienna Hotel.

(II) 'Dixie' France, His Family and the Back Seat of a 36A Bus

Only one aspect of the evidence of Charles France, his wife and his sixteen-year-old daughter Carol bore any significance to the case against Hanratty. During his interviews with the police France volunteered the information that Hanratty had pointed out the back seat of a bus as a good place to hide things under. It was, he said, during a return trip from Hendon Dog Track on August Bank Holiday (August 7th). He told the court at Bedford: 'We waited half an hour for a bus, and an empty bus came along and we went upstairs and as I was going towards the front he called me to the back to sit down in the back seat and his remark was: "This is the only seat that lifts up, and it is a good hiding place", or words similar to that effect.' (Vol. VII, pp. 3, 4.)

This was, of course, damning evidence. It linked Hanratty to the murder weapon. The essence of it was not denied by Hanratty. His version was only marginally different:

> Well, my Lord [he told the trial Court], I remember this matter quite plainly. It was on a Saturday morning. We were going to a betting office at Chalk Farm and we were walking from Swiss Cottage and there were some well-to-do houses on the way to the bus stop where eventually we picked a 31 bus up. On the way to the bus stop, My Lord, we were talking about my screwings and I explained to Mr France how it was done. Eventually, we got to the bus stop — we were still talking about the screwings — and our bus eventually came down the road ... We sat in the back seat, My Lord, and I explained to Mr France that if I had a large amount of jewellery in my pocket I used to sort it out upstairs on the bus. I used to put the good stuff into one pocket, and I explained to Mr France the rubbish I used to put under the back seat, because if I was to put it on the floor people would notice it. That is how the conversation took place. (Vol. XIII, p. 5.)

The difference in detail was important. France's story was about a 'good hiding place'. Hanratty's was about somewhere to get rid of 'rubbish' so that people in the bus would not see a lot of jewellery on the floor and suspect something. When France was challenged on his original story by Sherrard he appeared to concede that Hanratty's version was right:

Q. My instructions are that the question of the back seat of the bus arose in this way. One of the things he said about his business was that he had to be very careful what he carried?

A. That is true, and it was a good hiding place in case he needed to drop anything quickly.

Q. Or if he had got his pockets bulging he would sort out what he used to call, I think, the rubbish and get rid of that—the paste and so on—and keep the other stuff in his pockets.

A. I do not think he could tell the difference between paste and diamonds.

Q. But that is what he said he used to do?

A. If that is what he said he used to do, he must have done it.

Q. Did he say it to you?

A. I cannot recollect.

Q. He may have done?

A. He may have done. (Vol. VII, pp. 13, 14.)

This evidence was important to the prosecution, but it was not as important as distinguished commentators on the case have since pretended. In his short book on the case in 1963, *The A6 Murder: Regina v. James Hanratty: The Semblance of Truth*, the barrister and legal journalist, Louis Blom-Cooper, described the evidence as follows:

> Three highly circumstantial pieces of evidence remained. There was the uncontroverted evidence of Hanratty's stay at the Vienna Hotel in Maida Vale, and the disclosure in a room which he had once occupied of the cartridges from the murder weapon. Coupled with that was the inexplicable conversation Hanratty had with Mr 'Dixie' France to the effect that back seats of London buses were a good place to hide a gun. Then the murder weapon was found in just such a spot! Hardly a coincidence. (p. 19.)

There are in this passage two gross errors of fact. Cartridge *cases*, not cartridges, were found in the Vienna Hotel, and Hanratty's conversation about the back seat of a bus made no reference to a gun. Hanratty, in fact, had argued throughout the trial that he had never in his life had a gun, and no evidence was produced to the contrary.

Hanratty's conversation, according to Mr Blom-Cooper, who had access to a transcript of the trial while writing his book, was 'inexplicable'. Yet both Hanratty and France gave very good reasons in court why the conversation took place. It was the kind of conversation which could very well have taken place at any time between two crooks like Charles France and James Hanratty.

Mr Blom-Cooper's short analysis has served over the last seven years as a textbook for those who have opposed the reopening of the Hanratty case. Most of it deals with legal matters such as the admissibility of circumstantial or hearsay evidence. But Mr Blom-Cooper makes it clear that he thinks that Hanratty was guilty of the crime, and his book helped to convince others of that point of view. It is a pity that Mr Blom-Cooper reached his conclusion.

Soon after Mr Blom-Cooper's book was published a memorandum was presented to the Home Secretary by Mr Fenner Brockway, M.P. for Eton and Slough, presenting fresh evidence and calling for a public inquiry into Hanratty's guilt. The memorandum was greeted with scepticism by the entire press, not least by the *Observer*, one of whose leading articles concluded:

> The memorandum ... contains little of significance that was not known to the authorities at the time of Hanratty's execution ...
> It fails to touch on the *most damning facts* which pointed so convincingly to Hanratty's guilt: the cartridge cases found in the Maida Vale Hotel where Hanratty stayed, and his remark that the best place for hiding a gun was behind the back seat on top of a bus, where the murder weapon was eventually found. Other evidence not elicited at the trial, but which indicated that Hanratty was undoubtedly the killer, was revealed in the recent Penguin book on the trial. (*Observer*, July 14th, 1963 – my italics.)

It was touching that the *Observer* should so prominently advertise the book of their legal correspondent, Mr Louis Blom-Cooper, and support his conclusions on the case even to the extent of repeating a major error of fact upon which they were based.

The discovery of the gun under the back seat of a 36A bus was, in itself, a mystery. The prosecution called two witnesses who had travelled on the bus on the day the gun was found, Mr Arthur Embleton, a driver, and Mr Ernest Brine, a conductor. Both men were in the witness box for a short time, and were examined by junior counsel. The defence had 'no questions' for Mr Brine, and only seven for Mr Embleton. The purpose in calling them, it seemed, was merely to 'prove' the times of the bus's journeys that day.

Mr Brine, however, had had something of interest to say when the gun had been found two days after the murder. The *Evening News* of August 25th, 1961 carried a long article entitled 'Murder On My Route'. In the article, Mr Brine had recalled one of the passengers who had mounted his bus at about 6.30 on the evening of August 24th – about three hours before the gun was found. 'I'll tell you,' he was quoted as saying, 'if there's an identity parade, I'll recognize him again.' He described the man as 'unshaven, eyes fairly deep-set with a staring look about them'. He had 'mousy hair', and was wearing 'brown trousers and a blue jacket'. He had sat on the top of the bus – 'three seats along on the left'.

Whoever this man was, *he could not have been Hanratty*. For Hanratty sent a telegram to the Frances from Liverpool at 7.30 that evening. If Hanratty did put the murder gun on the bus, he could not have done so while Mr Brine was conducting it.

The 36A bus, as we have seen, made two journeys on August 24th. In the early morning it travelled north from Peckham to Kilburn, a journey which took it within a hundred yards of the Vienna Hotel. Mr Embleton was driving it on that morning run, but Mr Brine was not the conductor. When Mr Embleton was asked by Mr Swanwick: 'Did you have a conductor with you?' he replied: 'A woman conductor.' (Vol. IV, p. 24.)

In cross-examination, Mr Embleton was asked:

Q. Is it busy at any stage on your journey from Brockley Rise up to Kilburn or back?
A. The journey itself from the Rye Lane garage from 5.40 was busy as far as Victoria.
Q. And quiet from Victoria to Kilburn?
A. Very quiet. (Vol. IV, p. 49.)

If the gun was put under the seat during this 'very quiet' period, the chances are that the conductress, who must have been interviewed by the police on the same day, would have had something of interest to say. Yet from start to finish of the case, the conductress never appeared. Her statement was not furnished to the defence, nor was she produced at the Bedford identity parades.

The matter could be left there, but for a curious incident in the Court of Criminal Appeal on March 13th, 1962. On that day, the three judges turned down Hanratty's appeal. As they did so, an elderly woman wearing a wide-brimmed straw hat rose in the public gallery and shouted: 'It's not true. He didn't do it!'

The court froze, and everyone turned towards her. The *Daily Mail* report then had her saying: 'Ask ... the conductor of the 36 bus.' (*Daily Mail*, March 14th, 1962.) The *Daily Herald* filled in the crucial dots as follows: 'Ask Mr Brine, the conductor of the 36 bus.' (*Daily Herald*, March 14th, 1962.)

When I interviewed Mr Brine on September 1st, 1970, he told me that he had no idea who the woman was or what motivated her to shout as she had done.

It is at least conceivable that the *Daily Herald* reporter, like the *Mail* reporter, did not hear the name correctly, but assumed that the woman was referring to Mr Brine, since Mr Brine was the only conductor produced by the prosecution at the trial. It is also conceivable that the lady was referring to the conductress on the bus's morning run.

Mr Arthur Embleton, whom I interviewed on September 3rd, 1970, told me that his conductress on that morning was a girl of nineteen or twenty called Pat. She was only working at Rye Lane Garage for a few months, and Mr Embleton cannot, unfortunately, recall her surname or her address at the time. Mr Embleton says he was interviewed at length by the police at the time, but could not remember anything distinctive about the passengers he picked up on the morning of August 24th. London Transport do not keep detailed records of bus routes and conductors for more than two years.

In a letter dated October 7th, 1970, I wrote to the Home Office: 'Could I know the name of the bus conductress on the morning run of the 36A bus on August 24th, 1961?' Back came the reply, on December 18th: 'For the same reasons that we do not normally allow Home Office papers on a recent and controversial capital case to be inspected, we cannot agree to the release of the names of the person to whom you refer.'

The fact that the conversation about the back seat of the bus took place was never denied by Hanratty, although a killer who had put the gun on a bus might well have denied it. The crucial question about this piece of evidence was therefore not: Was it true? but *Why* was it offered by 'Dixie' France who had always, according to the evidence, been on more than friendly terms with the accused?

France said that he had met Hanratty outside the Rehearsal Club late in July of that summer, had taken pity on him, had taken him home and put him up for the night in the sitting-room of his council house. He agreed that Hanratty had always behaved extremely well to his wife and three daughters, aged sixteen, eleven and nine. He had on occasions bought chocolate, flowers and other gifts, and had often given shillings to the children. France assured the court that he knew nothing of Hanratty's housebreakings, and the most he had to do with them was occasionally to advise on the value of goods. According to France, Hanratty had stayed one night when they first met, and had stayed again the following weekend (August 6th and 7th). He had stayed on 'odd days in August' after that. During September they had seen him from time to time, and on odd nights he had stayed with them again.

Throughout the evidence of all three Frances – the eldest daughter, Carol, gave evidence, too – the picture presented was that of a decent respectable council house family, with the father laid low by ill health, who took pity on a young lad just out of prison and put him up from time to time. Not a trace of hostility between France and Hanratty emerged at hearing or trial.

Mrs France was emphatic in praise of the man in the dock:

Q. Your husband said when he was before the magistrates that he gave Jim Ryan's character the highest praise as far as he was concerned.
A. Yes.
Q. Is that right?
A. Yes.
Q. Do you agree with that?
A. Yes.
Q. Did he always behave properly towards you?
A. Yes.
Q. And your daughter?
A. Yes, my three daughters.
Q. He always behaved quite properly?
A. Yes.
Q. What you were good enough to say in the magistrates' court is that he was treated as one of the family. Is that right?
A. Yes, that is true.
Q. 'He got on very well with all of us'?
A. Yes. (Vol. IV, pp. 73, 74.)

1. Michael Gregsten

2. Janet Gregsten and her brother-in-law William Ewer

3. (*left*) Valerie Storie

4. (*below*) The cornfield at Dorney Reach

5. (*right*) The lay-by at the top of Deadman's Hill

6. (*below right*) The scene at Deadman's Hill on the morning of August 23rd.

7 and 8. (*above*) Peter Alphon

9 and 10. (*above right*) James Hanratty

11. (*right*) The Identikit Pictures issued on August 28th, 1961.
The left-hand picture was made up by Valerie Storie;
the right-hand picture by four other witnesses including
Edward Blackhall.

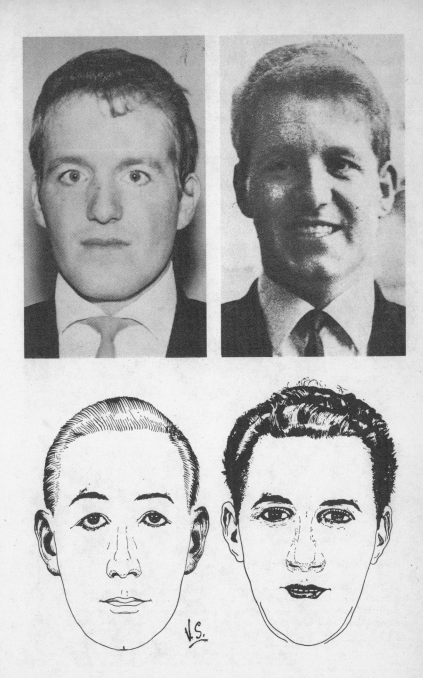

12. (*above left*) Supt Acott and
Supt Barron at Deadman's Hill

13. (*below left*) George William
Nudds

14. (*above right*) Roy Langdale

15. (*below right*) Mrs Louise
Anderson

16. John Skillett, James Trower and Edward Blackhall

17. Mrs Olive Dinwoodie

Carol France, too, had nothing but praise for 'Uncle Jim' as she called Hanratty. He was, she told the magistrates, 'always kind and gentle'.

Hanratty, in his statements to his lawyers before the Bedford trial, indicated that his relationship with Carol was even closer than that:

> I have been to the pictures with Carol France ... Dead sure I took Carol to Battersea Park one Saturday night (in September). I was going to the West End and she asked me to drop her off. (He tried to keep me away from the daughter. He is strict with her.) She was going to Chelsea and I was going to the West End to meet some people ... We had a coffee later. I called another taxi and we went to Battersea Fun Fair — it was about eight o'clock. Took her on all the big stuff — Big Splash — we went on the switchback or Big Dipper, took her on the Big Dipper — rifle range — I know a man there called Taffy who lives in Kingsbury ... we went across to a pub near the embankment and had a kiss and a cuddle on the embankment ... Her father would go potty if he knew.

In other parts of his statement, Hanratty embellished his story of his relationship with Carol France. He told too of his generosity to the Frances who, he said, were very hard up. He said, for instance, that he had given Mrs France fifteen pounds which she said she would use to get a sewing machine out of pawn. In evidence, France agreed that the fifteen pounds was used for this purpose, while Mrs France denied it. Hanratty also said that he had given the Frances rides in his Sunbeam, bought after returning from Ireland. The Frances denied it. Yet the differences between Hanratty's description of his relationship with the Frances, and the Frances' own story were differences of detail. All spoke of a very friendly, almost filial relationship between Hanratty and the Frances. Hanratty, therefore, was surprised and shocked when he heard that France would give evidence for the prosecution.

'Isn't it marvellous,' he wrote to his mother from Bedford prison on October 27th, 'all the friends you get to know and meet and when you get into a bit of trouble they don't seem to want to know you? For instance, I had a very good friend in St John's Wood who is married and has got three children. The police asked me where I had been staying the time before I went to Liverpool. I told them, they went straight round there, had an interview with them; and I found out by my solicitor that they are giving evidence against me to the police. The police have to get a story from somebody, Mum, so they thought they would try there, so whatever Mr France says it will be the truth, I hope.'

This account, of course, was not quite accurate. France had approached the police long before Hanratty had been captured. The police, waiting in France's house, had listened in to Hanratty's desperate call to his friend, which started: 'Dixie, Dixie, I am wanted for the A6 murder.' There is one other mistake in Hanratty's account of greater importance. He did not, in fact, tell the police France's name or address. He referred to them throughout his original conversations with Superintendent Acott as 'friends in St John's Wood'. At one point he explicitly refused to give their names, saying he wanted to protect them. From what did he want to protect them? If France was so respectable, why should not Hanratty immediately tell the police his name?

One reason could well have been that France was involved with Hanratty in some of the latter's thieving in Wembley and Stanmore. France had underworld contacts in Soho and Swiss Cottage and could give advice on how best to get rid of the stuff. France admitted to the court that he would sometimes advise Hanratty about the value of his stolen property. Most probably, he went further and helped Hanratty sell his stuff. For 'Dixie' France was no self-respecting patron. He was down and out in almost every sense. He moved almost constantly in an underworld of petty crooks and receivers. In the summer of 1961, unemployed and hopelessly in debt, he was prepared to do almost anything for money, and must have been greatly interested in the jewellery stolen by Hanratty during August, whose value Hanratty calculated at a thousand pounds.

At the time of the murder, Charles France was unemployed, having been sacked from his job as doorman at the Rehearsal Club. He still spent much of his time at the Rehearsal Club trying to earn a few shillings at rummy, at which he was a master, or in 'marking' in the billiards hall in Great Windmill Street. Three days before the Bedford trial in January 1962, France was admitted to Hammersmith Hospital after being found in a room full of gas. The suicide attempt was not a very determined one, for he was found while still conscious. Four hours after arriving in hospital, France was restrained, again in good time, from jumping out of a high window. Accordingly, he was sent to Horton Mental Hospital near Epsom and treated with electrical convulsion therapy. Mr Blom-Cooper has this to say about France's condition at Horton:

> His depressive state under examination by a consultant psychiatrist revealed that he was worried about the 'great harm' he had done to his family by having introduced Hanratty to his home. It was not quite clear what he meant exactly by this but he undoubtedly felt a genuine resentment at Hanratty's association with his family. He gave one clue of what he meant by saying: 'the b—; it could have been my dear wife and daughter who he killed.' (*The A6 Murder*, p. 127.)

If France did in fact say this while under treatment at Horton, it was a very curious comment. Hanratty had not at that time been convicted of anything. The evidence against him at Ampthill was weak and most correspondents were forecasting an acquittal. Yet France, who had known Hanratty, had liked him and had treated him as one of the family was regarding him as a murderer even before he was convicted!

France gave evidence at Bedford flanked by two nurses from Horton, and in his evidence there is not a trace of the indignation which he is reported to have demonstrated at Horton. Mrs France, on the other hand (despite Louis Blom-Cooper's assurance that 'she did not appear to be greatly disturbed'), collapsed at the sight of Hanratty in the dock and had to be carried from the court. Mrs France had collapsed in the magistrates' court at Ampthill in precisely the same way.

The day after Hanratty's conviction, the *Sunday Pictorial* printed a middle-page spread entitled THE KILLER IN MY HOUSE. Opposite a tranquil family picture, Mr, Mrs and Carol France had, according to the newspaper, each written their little piece about Hanratty — for suitable reward. In this article, again, there was not a trace of hatred or bitterness against Hanratty. 'Dixie' France wrote of Hanratty's gentleness and his 'devotion to his mother'. 'He was', he wrote, 'gay and generous and he loved a joke ... I accepted him as a member of my family.' Similarly Mrs France ('I treated Jimmy as though he were my son') and Carol ('Uncle Jim was a friend') wrote in friendly tones of Hanratty, despite his conviction.

Only later did Mrs France remember an incident which would

have been very important evidence had she remembered it at the trial. Under the heading: THE DAY JAMES HANRATTY NEARLY CONFESSED TO ME, Mrs France remembered Hanratty saying in her house: 'Now I've done something that scares. Something I've never done before and I don't understand. I want to talk to someone. That's why I need a friend.' 'I wonder', Mrs France was quoted as saying, 'if he was trying in a fumbling sort of way to confess to the A6 murder.' At the trial and at the hearing, Mrs France recorded no such damning statement. (*Sunday Pictorial*, March 18th, 1962.)

On March 16th, 1962, 'Dixie' France finally committed suicide.

He went to Acton and rented a room in a Second Avenue doss-house. The landlady found him gassed in his room. He had written long letters to each member of his family in a blue exercise book. At his inquest, held in Ealing on April 5th, the day after Hanratty's execution, the coroner refused 'in the public interest' to allow the letters to be published, but he did say that the letters were written 'in great bitterness and great feeling against Hanratty'.

Mrs France, giving evidence, agreed with the coroner, Mr Harold Broadbridge, that her husband had been under great strain before and since the trial. The trial, she said, 'was the start of all his worrying'. 'I understand', said the coroner, 'that he had received some unpleasant phone calls.' 'Yes,' agreed Mrs France. (*Daily Mirror*, April 6th, 1962.)

All this was very odd indeed. At the trial, France had stressed that his relationship with Hanratty had been of the very best. When he committed suicide only a few days before Hanratty's execution, France's letters, according to the coroner, denounced Hanratty in the most bitter terms. Was this really, as the coroner opined, because of 'the great harm done to you [Mrs France] and your children by Hanratty'? Or was it that Hanratty's plight represented for France his own guilt?

Again, who was making those telephone calls? Who would bother to pester France with bullying and abusive telephone calls, unless it was someone who knew that France's role in the A6 affair was not as mild or as subsidiary as he and his family made out at the trial?

Nor was this the end of the tragedy for the France family. Two months after France's suicide, his daughter Carol was admitted to New End Hospital in Hampstead after taking an overdose of iron tablets.

'I blame the A6 trial', Mrs France told the *Daily Mirror* (May 23rd) 'for what has happened to my daughter ... Cranks make vicious anonymous phone calls ... every time the phone rings, we tremble. We know it's probably another filthy call.'

Still, in May, the phone calls were plaguing the France family. Yet their telephone number was not changed, nor their calls intercepted, nor were the police contacted to deal with the 'cranks'.

Today, the Frances are silent. I spent one long late evening with Mrs France, her two brothers and her youngest daughter in December 1969 discussing various aspects of the case. Beyond stating their conviction that they thought Hanratty guilty, none of them wanted to say anything about the case. The real explanation of their former relationship with James Hanratty, and of Mr France's voluntary, damning circumstantial evidence against a man who counted himself as a friend must remain a mystery. Three things, however, are certain. Very soon after the murder, Charles France discovered that Hanratty had spent the night of August 21st–22nd at the Vienna Hotel. Charles France also knew that Hanratty regarded the back seat of a bus as a good hiding place. And Charles France, for some unexplained reason, worked himself up into a terrible hatred of Hanratty before committing suicide.

(III) The Evidence of Roy Langdale

At the hearing of the case against Hanratty at the magistrates' court at Ampthill between November 22nd and December 5th, 1961, the prosecution admitted that, from first to last, Hanratty had pleaded his innocence of the A6 murder. Apart from a few rather dubious 'verbals' to his arresting officer at Blackpool, everything recorded by the prosecution witnesses at Ampthill about Hanratty's reaction to the charge of murder pointed to an unequivocal denial of guilt. There was not a trace of a confession to anyone. Hanratty's confidence of his innocence was one of the features which made the prosecution case at Ampthill appear so weak. There were optimists among the defence who believed that, in spite of the identifications, the magistrates would find 'no case to answer' against Hanratty, and dismiss the case.

The evidence of Roy William Langdale, introduced after the Ampthill hearing, damaged the consistency of Hanratty's denial of guilt. Langdale was a young man of twenty-four whose adult life had been devoted almost entirely to crime. He had been stealing and assaulting people since he was seventeen, and in those eight years had been convicted twelve times for various offences. In June 1958 he was convicted of assaulting a fellow prisoner in Wormwood Scrubs. He had been sharing a cell with two other prisoners and had tried to persuade one of them, called Dean, to sing 'Jailhouse Rock'. When Dean refused, Langdale bound his legs, threatened him with a knife, and shaved his eyebrows to make him comply. When the authorities discovered Dean's injuries and their causes, Langdale was locked up in solitary confinement until his conviction in June.

In February 1961, Langdale was found guilty at Marylebone magistrates' court of stealing a road fund licence and driving without insurance while disqualified. He was sentenced to six months in prison. The harshness of the sentence was due more to the long string of previous convictions than to the seriousness of the offence.

Langdale came out of prison in the summer of 1961, and immediately started to forge Post Office savings bank books. He had forged some seventeen of these, and obtained £103 in the process, when he and his wife, who was also involved, were arrested and appeared – on November 6th – at Willesden magistrates' court.

By this time, Langdale was a recidivist, and the magistrates at Willesden, after finding both Langdales guilty (as they pleaded), and after putting Mrs Langdale on probation for three years, committed Langdale to the Middlesex Sessions for sentence. His long string of previous offences entitled him to a stiffer sentence than they could award. Forgery carries a penalty of up to nine years' imprisonment, and the Willesden magistrates clearly took the view that Langdale deserved more than the few months in prison to which they were able to sentence him.

Langdale was, accordingly, remanded in Brixton prison, and, after a row with prison officers about his wife's visits, he was put in the hospital block. Also on remand in the hospital block was James Hanratty.

Langdale was taken to Middlesex Sessions on the day – November 22nd – that Hanratty's hearing started at Ampthill. His case did not come up and he spent the day in the cells at the back of the court. When the court adjourned, he and other prisoners got in the van and headed back to Brixton. A junior hospital officer at the prison, Mr Alfred Eatwell, had been seconded from the prison to keep a watch on Langdale.

In the coach on the way back to the prison, Langdale was sitting directly in front of Eatwell. Suddenly, in a loud voice, he started to tell his neighbour about the A6 murder case and about how Hanratty had confessed to him in the exercise yard at Brixton prison. Mr Eatwell, not surprisingly, showed some interest in this account, and reported the matter to his superior officer. The following day he made a statement to the prison governor, who passed it on to Scotland Yard. That was on November 23rd – the second day of the hearing at Ampthill. For some reason, however, the officers in charge of the A6 inquiry were not over-excited by Langdale's revelation that Hanratty had confessed. No one went to interview Langdale that day from Scotland Yard, despite the proceedings at Ampthill.

That same day, Langdale appeared before the judge at Middlesex Quarter Sessions. He had expected to be sentenced to three years in prison. Strangely, however, the prison authorities spoke up for him saying that there was evidence of 'mental instability' (no such evidence was produced). The judge put Langdale on probation for three years – an astonishing sentence in view of Langdale's previous record and the fact that the same sentence had been passed on his wife by the Willesden magistrates who thought it too lenient for Langdale. For once, Mr Langdale seemed to have done something which commended him to the authorities.

Langdale left the court a free man and went home to join his wife. A full week later, Mr Acott and Sergeant Oxford interviewed him at his home. The following day, Langdale made a long statement to Scotland Yard. He had, he said, met Hanratty in the exercise yard at Brixton after the latter had been there about four days:

> We talked to each other. He asked me who I was, what my first name was and what charge I was in for. I told him, and then I asked him who he was and what he was in for. He said: 'I'm James Hanratty, the A6 killer.' I asked him what he thought of the job and what his chances were. Hanratty said: 'It wasn't me – they'll get nothing on me. I've got chances.'

Langdale claimed that during the next three weeks he and Hanratty always walked together in the exercise yard and avoided all contact with other prisoners. In the course of about six days from November 7th, Langdale's statement went on, Hanratty made a series of confessions to the A6 murder:

He came to trust me because I was the only one he'd talk to and he wanted to talk to someone and get this off his chest, and that's when he began to talk to me of the murder. I think he wanted to discuss his case to see if he could find a loophole because he once said to me: 'If I could find a hole in the evidence, the Judge would chuck my case out of court.'

During the last week we were in Brixton he didn't tell me anything really new but he kept going over and over again what he told me about the murder he had committed. Whenever I asked him why he had done it, he always said: 'It was the woman I wanted. I couldn't have done it with him there could I?'

A great deal of Langdale's reports of Hanratty's alleged confession deals with the sexual aspect of the murder, often in the most lurid detail. 'I asked him', said Langdale, 'if he had intercourse with her and if she was all right. He said "Yes, she enjoyed it as much as me".'

Another charming passage read:

He [Hanratty] seems to know the West End very well and when he's not talking about the murder he spends most of his time talking about women and sex. I think he is sex mad ... Hanratty told me on more than one occasion that, even now, whenever he is in his cell, he masturbates when he thinks of how he raped Valerie.

This was very convenient for the prosecution, whose thesis, unsupported by any evidence, was that Hanratty had gone into the car to rape the girl and had murdered Gregsten so that he could get on with the sex. Here was the first evidence that sex was the motive for the murder.

The statement was made on December 1st. The hearing at Ampthill magistrates' court still had four days to run. Yet Langdale was never called at Ampthill. The press was not told of this sensational new development in the case. Nor was the defence. The defence lawyers first heard that this confession was to be part of the prosecution case twelve days before the trial started.

Superintendent Acott was clearly in some doubt as to whether Langdale's statement should be submitted as evidence at all.

Perhaps Acott was disturbed at Langdale's record, and felt that reports of a confession from such a man might rebound against the prosecution. More probably, however, he was worried about the statement because in several instances it was blatantly absurd.

One section of Langdale's statement ran as follows:

> On Sunday afternoon, 12th November 1961, Hanratty told me he'd had a visit from his solicitors and he asked me if I knew anything about blood groups. When I told him I knew there were different groups, he said his group was the same as Gregsten's group and he asked me how therefore could police say whose blood was which. I asked him if he had any cuts or scars and when he said he hadn't I told him it was going to be difficult for him to prove that any blood on his clothes was his. He said: 'I've got a suit in the cleaners with bloodstains on it. If I can prove it was in the cleaners before the A6 murder was committed it would leave me in the clear'. I told him that he would have to get a letter or a bill to prove that the suit was in the cleaners before the murder. He said: 'I might be able to do that and if I can it will leave me in the clear and I'll walk out a a free man'.

James Hanratty knew that at the time of the murder he had two suits. One was a green check suit over which Hanratty thought he had spilt some blood while housebreaking in early August (in fact, there was no blood on it). This suit was put into the Burtol cleaners to be cleaned and tapered on Monday, August 21st—a day and a half *before* the murder. It was not taken out again until September 4th. Evidence for this was given at the magistrates' court by the Burtols staff at the same time as Langdale was reporting the confession to Superintendent Acott. The other suit, the dark Hepworths suit, which Hanratty was wearing at the time of the murder, was put into the cleaners a good three weeks after the murder. The jacket, as we shall discover later, has never been found. But the trousers and waistcoat, discovered by the police, had on them not a trace of blood. The pattern of blood in the car indicated that if the murderer had had blood anywhere on his clothing, it would almost certainly have been on his trousers.

The reported conversation with Hanratty took place, according to Langdale, on November 12th. At that time, Hanratty could not possibly have known about Gregsten's blood group. Why would he say that his blood group was the same as Gregsten's, which anyway was untrue? (Gregsten's blood group was AB; Hanratty's O.)

Hanratty *was* worried about the blood which he thought was on the *green* suit. He told Superintendent Acott in his first interview with him in Blackpool: 'Let me tell you there's blood on the green suit but it's my own blood from a cut on broken glass.' (From Superintendent Acott's evidence in chief, Vol. IX, p. 31.)

No doubt he mentioned this to some of his fellow prisoners at Brixton, pointing out in some relief that the police could make nothing out of the blood on his suit, since the suit was in the cleaners before the murder. Perhaps such a statement became the basis for Langdale's report, but it is certain that Hanratty could not have spoken about the cleaners and the stained suit in the way which Langdale described.

Inconsistencies like these, taken together with the overall unlikeliness of the entire statement, no doubt persuaded Mr Acott to hold his hand. Langdale was told that he might be called as a witness, and was not informed until the week before the trial that he would definitely be called.

As soon as he knew he would be appearing in court, Mr Langdale rang the newspapers telling them of his story and offering it for payment. The *Daily Herald* offered him twenty pounds, but the *Sunday Pictorial* won the auction with an offer of twenty-five pounds, and its issue of January 21st carried a big story about the '24-year-old coalman who has been identified as the mysterious witness who may be called in the A6 murder trial'. Mr Langdale was quoted as saying:

> I arrived home after being away for several weeks. I had hardly joined my wife in my flat when the Superintendent arrived. He talked to me for about an hour; and then he and another officer took me to Scotland Yard where I made a statement. A week later, Supt Acott and the other officer called again. They warned me that I might be required as a witness in the trial.

The *Daily Telegraph* the next day took up the story of the 'surprise witness', and, when the trial started with the opening speech of the prosecution on January 22nd, the *Evening News* and provincial evening papers throughout the country selected Mr Swanwick's reference to Langdale as the main news point. 'A6 STORY OF

CONFESSION' boomed the front-page headline of the *Evening News*. In the minds of the readers of the *Evening News* and most other people the consistency of Hanratty's protestations of innocence had effectively been broken.

In court, however, Langdale was not a convincing witness. He kept forgetting his lines. Mr Sherrard's first question in cross-examination was: 'This is not quite the way you told it all to the police, was it?' To which Langdale replied: 'I am saying as he said it; as he was asking me questions I am saying it. *Do not forget there is a lot of writing there.* I cannot remember every word for every word.' (Vol. VIII, p. 37, my italics.)

Poor Langdale got it wrong from start to finish. In court he said that he had had Hanratty pointed out to him in the prison yard, had approached him and had heard nothing on the first occasion about the murder. In his statement, he had said that Hanratty had told him that he was the A6 murderer at their first meeting. In his evidence about walking and talking with Hanratty in Brixton prison yard, Langdale was tied up in a series of contradictions. In a piece of classic cross-examination, Mr Sherrard forced him to contradict completely an important passage in his original statement to the police. Mr Sherrard was reading Langdale his original statement and checking with him that it was true:

Q. '*All the time I knew Hanratty in Brixton, I never saw him talk to another prisoner.*'
A. *Fair enough, that is correct.*
Q. We shall be hearing a good deal of evidence about this and I must put it to you plainly that the occasions when he spoke to you were very few indeed. Is that right?
A. No. I spoke to him very often.
Q. And that most of the time he walked round with a man called Emery. Do you remember Emery?
A. Yes. I remember Emery.
Q. Did you ever see him talking to Emery?
A. If I was called out on a visit or something like that or I came down the stairs to line up he would be talking to Emery.
Q. He was the man he walked round with – Emery – was he not?
A. I do not know. As I say, I walked with him and maybe one or two days there was a time when other persons walked with him. That just happens.

Q. *Did you ever see him talking to Emery?*
A. *Yes.* (Vol. VIII, p. 48. My italics.)

One more of the many contradictions in Langdale's evidence should be mentioned. In his statement, he had said that on the afternoon of Sunday, November 12th, Hanratty had told him of a visit from his solicitors. As Mr Sherrard pointed out to the court, neither his solicitor nor his barrister had visited Hanratty in Brixton prison until November 18th.

One of the most remarkable aspects of Langdale's evidence is that the important parts of it were not substantiated by a single independent witness. The only supporting witness for the Langdale evidence was Hospital Officer Eatwell who confirmed that he had heard Langdale talking about his conversations with Hanratty in the van back from the Guildhall court to Brixton, and had reported the matter to his superior. Mr Eatwell was asked by Mr Swanwick:

Q. Whilst Hanratty had been on remand in Brixton we have heard he was in the hospital?
A. Yes.
Q. Can you say of your own knowledge with whom he used to exercise?
A. Several.
Q. Yes?
A. I would not know the people he walked round with.
Q. You would not know?
A. No, I could not say.
Q. Of your own knowledge?
A. I could not say, no. (Vol. IX, p. 4.)

This did not help the prosecution very much, and that was all Mr Acott could find to back up Mr Langdale's testimony that he and Hanratty had been on intimate enough terms for Hanratty to confess to the A6 murder. Hanratty was of course very well known in the prison. All the prisoners in the hospital block knew who he was and why he was there. If Hanratty and Langdale had indeed walked round together day in and day out it would surely have been easy to find one prisoner or prison officer to testify accordingly.

The statement of Langdale was served on the defence on January 11th – eleven days before the Bedford trial was due to begin. In some anxiety, Mr Kleinman and Mr Sherrard approached Hanratty in prison and asked him about a man called Langdale. Hanratty said that he remembered no one of that name. While in Brixton, he said, he had walked on exercise with two men – one called David Emery, the other called Blythe. He had, he insisted, never once confessed to the crime nor discussed it in any detail even with Emery or Blythe. It was greatly to the credit of the defence that they were able to produce both Emery and Blythe at the trial.

David Emery had been at Brixton prison on remand on a charge of manslaughter of a prostitute for which he was eventually convicted and sentenced to six years. He told the court that he had exercised with Hanratty from the second exercise – on November 5th – to the last day he (Emery) was there, which was December 19th. Emery categorically refuted Langdale's evidence that Langdale had exercised regularly with Hanratty.

'The only incident I know of Langdale speaking to Hanratty', he told the court, 'was when I made an appearance at the magistrates' court on the 18th November and he spoke to me about that conversation afterwards. That was the only time I can ever remember him speaking to him.'

Mr Swanwick did his best to indicate that Emery, who had a long criminal record (though not as long as Langdale's) was deliberately lying. He could not explain to the court *why* Emery should lie. Unlike Langdale, Emery had nothing to gain or lose by giving evidence in the trial, and did so, not on his own initiative, but only when subpoenaed by the defence. In the course of his cross-examination Mr Swanwick provoked Emery more than he would have liked:

Q. I suggest to you that it was Langdale who walked with Hanratty until he went up for trial and that it was only after that that you got friendly with Hanratty and took Langdale's place: that is the truth, is it not?

A. *Everybody in the prison, including the officers, knew I always walked with Hanratty.* (Vol. XV, pp. 29, 30, my italics.)

Things got even worse for Mr Swanwick when the defence called Nicolai Blythe. Blythe was not a hardened criminal. He had been arrested in October and remanded at Brixton for trial on charges of possessing and trading in cocaine – for which, when he went for trial in December, he was put on probation for two years. Blythe too was certain that Hanratty had exercised 'exclusively with David

Emery, up till the time of Emery's trial, and, obviously, when Emery went up to the magistrates' court for remand. After a month or so I sometimes walked round with them, and when Emery went to trial and was taken away I walked round with Hanratty myself.' (Vol. XV, p. 31.) Blythe told Mr Swanwick that he had never seen Hanratty talking to Langdale. Hanratty himself recognized Langdale when the latter gave evidence, and agreed that he had met him on exercise in Brixton.

'Langdale', he told Mr Swanwick, 'has walked with me on two or three occasions when Emery was not available. Langdale came to me of his own free will; I did not go to him. He come to me and he asked me facts about this case, which hundreds of other people have also asked me. I remember quite clearly and quite plainly him asking me what I was in for, to that effect, and I remember quite plainly I told him that I was a suspect for the A6. That was the only dealings I ever had with that man, and as far as it goes to calling him Roy, I could not — well, when I heard the evidence put forward I could not even remember the man. That is how much I walked with him.' (Vol. XIV, p. 48.)

Although Langdale's evidence played a very important part in the case against Hanratty, almost everyone spoke about it with reservations. In his summing up, the judge asked the jury to consider very carefully the fact that Langdale had told of Hanratty's confession in the full earshot of Hospital Officer Eatwell, clearly wanting it to be heard. Even Mr Swanwick asked the jury to treat Langdale's evidence 'with caution'. The jury no doubt took his advice, especially in view of the evidence of Emery and Blythe. Yet if Langdale's evidence was played down by prosecuting counsel and by the judge, it was treated very seriously by Mr Louis Blom-Cooper when he came to write his Penguin book on the A6 murder.

Mr Blom-Cooper recounted the evidence of Hospital Officer Eatwell about taking Langdale back from the Guildhall court to Brixton prison on the evening of November 22nd. In his evidence, Eatwell talked of 'a conversation' which Langdale had had with another prisoner. He could not, within the rules of hearsay, tell the court what that conversation was, but Mr Blom-Cooper knew through his contacts in the Home Office and regarded it as significant:

Eatwell had heard Langdale telling a fellow accused what he

[Langdale] had heard from Hanratty himself about the A6 killing. In fact he heard the substance of what Langdale gave in evidence as Hanratty's confession to the crime. But there was one piece of evidence which Langdale did not give, probably because he did not remember it: but Eatwell did.

It had *always been assumed* until the opening of the Crown's case at Ampthill on 22nd November that the A6 killer had thumbed a lift from the Morris Minor containing Michael Gregsten and Valerie Storie. The whole of the press referred to this incident and pointed implicitly to the moral that it is always dangerous to give a stranger a lift. *No one knew* that in fact the beginning of the murder trail started in a Buckinghamshire cornfield when the killer surprised his victims as they sat peacefully in a stationary car. But while the press was being told this in the magistrates' court in the small Bedfordshire town of Ampthill, and via the press an enormous reading public, Langdale knew of it from Hanratty's own lips, *the surest possible sign that Hanratty was the killer* unless — and there is nothing to suggest this — Hanratty learnt of this fact from the police investigating the crime. Langdale, not knowing the significance of this fact, repeated the incident as told to him by Hanratty to the fellow accused. Eatwell overheard it and it forms part of his report to the Governor. Apart from the significant item of the way in which the A6 killer came upon his prey, the fact of Langdale's conversation in the prison coach that day in November further reinforces the view that he was telling the truth about Hanratty's confession to him during their peregrinations in the prison yard at Brixton. (*The A6 Murder : Regina v. James Hanratty: The Semblance of Truth* [Penguin, 1963], pp. 101, 102. My italics.)

This was the 'damning piece of evidence' denied to the jury by the rules of hearsay. '*It cannot be doubted*', wrote Blom-Cooper (p. 99), 'that it would have removed any lingering doubts which the jury entertained about Hanratty's guilt ... More important, it was evidence which the Home Secretary had before him when he was considering whether to recommend a reprieve for Hanratty. *It sealed Hanratty's fate* and probably took his case out of that category of cases where there remains a "scintilla of doubt" sufficient to permit the Home Secretary to recommend a reprieve.' (My italics.)

This was an important claim. Blom-Cooper had been talking to people in the Home Office who had been in charge of the case, and he spoke with authority when he wrote that the Langdale/Eatwell incident in the coach was the crucial factor which removed any 'scintilla of doubt' about Hanratty's guilt.

Unfortunately, however, the entire thesis is based on a glaring mistake. Blom-Cooper wrote (and the Home Office apparently believed) that until the opening of the case at Ampthill *no one knew* that the murderer had approached his victims in a Buckinghamshire cornfield, and that therefore the conversation about the cornfield, passed on from Langdale to Eatwell, could only have originated from the killer. In fact, however, for several weeks before the opening of the hearing at Ampthill, it had been common knowledge that the murderer had approached his victims in a cornfield. A passing glance at the newspaper reports of the case would have informed Blom-Cooper and officials at the Home Office that the false story about 'thumbing a lift' was very quickly replaced by the truth about the cornfield.

The story of the 'lift' persevered in the newspapers for only two days after the murder. As early as August 25th, the *Daily Mirror* crime reporter, Tom Tullett, told the paper's thirteen million readers:

> She [Valerie Storie] and Michael were sitting in the car on Dorney Common, Slough, Bucks, discussing the plans for a forthcoming car rally. Suddenly the back door of the car opened and a man got in with a revolver in his hand. He pointed it at the couple, and ordered Michael to drive on.

The next day, August 26th, the *Daily Telegraph* took up the story:

> Superintendent Acott spent several hours yesterday tracing the possible route the murderer insisted on Mr Gregsten taking after holding him up on Tuesday. He ordered photographs to be taken of a cornfield near Dorney Common, near Taplow, Bucks, where it is believed the killer held up the couple. He hopes that Miss Storie will be able to identify the pictures of the cornfield.

The *Daily Herald* of the same day had got hold of the same information: 'He [Acott] identified the spot on a common at

Dorney Reach, near Taplow, Bucks, where the gunman forced his way into the car – a cornfield gateway.'

On Sunday, August 27th, the *People* quoted a farmer's wife, Mrs Nellie Climo, as saying: 'I have told the police about the car I saw here on Tuesday night. It was in the cornfield where I have seen it parked several times before.' The *People* report continued: 'Police are considering the possibility that the man at the Pineapple Inn walked across country to nearby Marsh Lane and found Gregsten's car parked in a cornfield.'

Eight days later, the newspapers' information was even more accurate. An *Evening News* report on September 5th said that police were starting their inquiries at: 'the cornfield entrance at Dorney Common, Taplow, Bucks. It was at this spot that 34-year-old Michael Gregsten sat talking to Valerie Storie in his grey Morris car when a well-groomed gunman, with icy-blue saucer shaped eyes, burst into the back seat with a gun, and snapped: "This is a hold-up. Drive on." '

According to the *Daily Telegraph* of September 12th: 'From 9.30 to 11.30 p.m. ... all three sat in the cornfield near Dorney Reach, near Slough, talking ... After leaving the cornfield ... '

Finally there was the visit by Mrs Gregsten to Valerie Storie's bedside at Guy's Hospital on September 20th. As a result of that visit, Mrs Gregsten was able to tell the six million readers of the *Daily Mail* on September 22nd the exact details of how the murderer, in Mr Blom-Cooper's words, 'came upon his prey':

> Valerie told me what happened. They were parked on the roadside when this man tapped at the car window. Mike, my husband, wound the window half down and the man stuck a gun in and told them: 'Open the door'.

These are only some of the newspaper quotations which can be set against Mr Blom-Cooper's assertion that 'until the opening of the Crown case at Ampthill [November 22nd] ... no one knew that in fact the beginning of the murder trail started in a Buckingham-shire cornfield when the killer surprised his victims ... in a stationary car.' The truth was that anyone who had taken the slightest interest in the case knew all this perfectly well. If Langdale had studied the case with any care at all, he would have known all about the Buckinghamshire cornfield and all about the murderer's approach to the car. So, for that matter, would Hanratty. Even if Langdale, as he and Eatwell insisted was the case, had not been reading the evening newspapers on that first day of the hearing at Ampthill he could have known from at least a dozen other sources about every fact which he retailed in the prison coach that evening.

Mr Blom-Cooper's error was bad enough. His book, and especially the highlighting of the Langdale/Eatwell incident, served to deflect many of the doubters about Hanratty's guilt (myself, incidentally, included). But Mr Blom-Cooper, like any author, is entitled to make mistakes. What is far more serious is his suggestion that the Eatwell/Langdale conversation served to decide the Home Secretary's mind in refusing a reprieve to Hanratty. If a possible scintilla of doubt about Hanratty's guilt was ruled out on the basis of a theory which was patently false, that scintilla is immediately and substantially magnified.

(IV) The Evidence of Louise Anderson

At the time of the A6 murder Mrs Louise Anderson ran a small antique shop in Greek Street, Soho. She met James Hanratty in July 1961, when he walked into the shop asking if she would like to buy some jewellery. The two struck up a relationship. Hanratty called often on Mrs Anderson during the next three months. He stayed several nights in her flat at Cambridge Court, Sussex Gardens, Paddington, sleeping, according to his evidence, and that of Mrs Anderson, on two chairs. In the course of this relationship, Mrs Anderson paid Hanratty a large sum of money estimated by herself to be six hundred pounds. Why should a middle-aged antique dealer pay a twenty-five-year-old housebreaker six hundred pounds over a period of two months?

The obvious answer was given by James Hanratty in his evidence:

Q. Is it right that she gave you various sums of money?
A. That is right, yes.
Q. What for?
A. Well, we used to do business together.
Q. Do you mean you were selling her the proceeds of your thefts?
A. That is right. Well, bits and pieces; what she required. The bigger stuff she did not want, but the smaller stuff she took. For the bigger stuff I had to go to somebody else. (Vol. XIII, p. 6.)

Mrs Anderson, however, who gave evidence for the prosecution, did not agree, though the passage of her evidence which deals with the nature of her relationship with Hanratty makes strange reading. Mr. Sherrard asked her:

Q. You were doing business with him, were you not?
A. Let us put it that I was forced to give him money, and things were left and they were given to Scotland Yard because I was frightened of the man. (Vol. VI, p. 55.)

This 'fright' which Mrs Anderson told the Bedford court she felt for Hanratty appeared to have come on shortly before the Bedford trial. Indeed, Mrs Anderson's attitude to Hanratty started to change from the moment her name was first mentioned in the newspapers.

On October 6th, when Hanratty was on the run, the police came to Mrs Anderson after Hanratty had given her address and telephone number to Mr Acott on the telephone. She was interviewed by Scotland Yard officers for three hours, and Hanratty's suitcase was taken from her flat to the Yard. Mrs Anderson spent that weekend out of London, but on her return she gave an interview to the *Daily Telegraph* about what that paper described as: 'her friendship with a man police wish to interview in case he may be able to assist their inquiries into the A6 murder'. (*Daily Telegraph*, October 10th, 1961.)

The interview probably gives a much fairer picture of Mrs Anderson's attitude to Hanratty than her statements in court and afterwards. It starts with Mrs Anderson describing her first few meetings with Hanratty in which Hanratty tried to sell her various articles:

'I rather liked him' Mrs Anderson went on ... 'He was very pleasant to talk to. I soon discovered that he could not read or write but that didn't matter to me.'

Mrs Anderson said her friendship with the man developed to a stage where he began to call at her flat in Cambridge Court, Sussex Gardens, Paddington. 'We used to sit up very late talking. He used to sleep in the flat on two chairs and covered by some blankets. He never wanted to discuss anything about his family or background ...

'I realised I could very well be his mother, because he was half my age. I deliberately arranged a meeting between him and a girl I know called Mary ... '

Last Friday night Scotland Yard detectives called on her

and questioned her about the man. 'I was astonished when they told me the nature of the inquiries' she said. (*Daily Telegraph*, October 10th, 1961.)

The *Daily Express* of the same day carried an interview with Mrs Anderson and a large photograph of her in her shop. In the interview, Mrs Anderson talked of the meals she had had with 'the man', and how he had proposed marriage to her. The following day the same paper reported that Mrs Anderson had telephoned the man's parents from her antique shop: 'Mrs Anderson told his father: "I wish he would come forward. He has nothing to fear".' (*Daily Express*, October 11th, 1961.)

Mrs Anderson's description of their relationship at that time fitted almost exactly what Hanratty told his lawyers about her. She was buying his goods, and, at the same time, treating him kindly. He, likewise, behaved decently and cheerfully towards her, as he behaved to all his friends and acquaintances.

Most of this description was repeated in Mrs Anderson's evidence for the prosecution before the magistrates at Ampthill. Her evidence at that time was of no significance to the prosecution case. She said that Hanratty had brought a suitcase to her flat after returning from Ireland on September 8th. She confirmed that he had slept in her flat. She said that she had seen Hanratty on the 21st – the day before the murder – which date she promptly changed to the 20th. She confirmed that she had given him money, and that he 'speaks in a high-pitched effeminate voice. He says "finking" instead of "thinking".' Cross-examined at Ampthill, Mrs Anderson agreed that she came across 'lots of people' who say 'f' instead of 'th'. She also said that she had introduced Hanratty to a girl called Mary. 'I thought', she said, 'they were more of an age and might be interested in each other.'

This last point was confirmed by the statement taken by the defence from Mary Meaden a few days after the Ampthill hearing ended, on December 5th, 1961:

During Monday night, the first night I met him, I understood he was staying with friends, he mentioned the address but I can't remember it. On the Tuesday, Wednesday and Thursday and Friday I believe he stayed with Mrs Anderson.
On the Saturday night I stayed with Mrs Anderson but

Jimmy was not there; he rang to say he was too tired and dirty.

Most of Saturday night Mrs Anderson was talking to me, mostly about her financial position. In the course of this she said how short she was and how Jimmy appeared to have plenty and if he was any kind of chap he'd lend her some.

I next saw Jimmy on the Sunday afternoon, it was only for a few minutes and he gave me a present of a compact. He asked to take me out again, I said I was too tired. I went home and later in the evening I rang Mrs Anderson's flat and spoke to 'Jimmy' telling him I was still too tired to go out.

I didn't see or hear from him until the next Wednesday when he rang me at my place of work. He said it was his birthday and would like to take me out. I said I couldn't meet him until 8.30 p.m. He said that was too late and he would meet me on Friday at 7.30 p.m. at the Astoria, Charing Cross Road. He also told me his car would be repaired by then. I knew he had a car as the first time I met him on a Monday I had seen him driving it. It was a Sunbeam Alpine. Mrs Anderson told me that he drove very well and had taken her out to the country in it several times.

Observers at Ampthill could not really appreciate why Mrs Anderson appeared at all. Nothing she said at Ampthill damaged Hanratty in any way. Nevertheless, she was again summoned to appear for the prosecution at the Bedford trial.

On the third day of the trial Superintendent Acott, who was a witness and who had made much of locking himself up in a hotel room during the trial, was approached by Mrs Anderson, who said she had something further to say about James Hanratty. Although he was one of the chief witnesses for the prosecution, Mr Acott, in his capacity as head of the murder inquiry, started interviewing Mrs Anderson. When the prosecution lawyers heard that Acott was taking a statement from Mrs Anderson, they ordered him to stop. An independent lawyer was sent to take the statement which was served on the defence in the middle of the trial.

The statement started as follows:

I have asked to see you this morning because there is something I must tell you before I give evidence in court today. I have been reading the London evening papers this week with the reports of the A6 murder trial and I have been reminded of three incidents which happened while I was in the company of Hanratty and which I had previously forgotten to tell you.

The first of these flashes of memory concerned a 'worn brown leather wallet' which she saw Hanratty looking at one day when searching for a season ticket. What was it that had stirred Mrs Anderson's memory about the brown wallet? Could it have been her reading of the reports of the case that the murderer had taken Michael Gregsten's wallet and that there was some doubt whether this had ever been returned? If this was the reason for telling Mr Acott about the wallet, it served no purpose. For the wallet had, in fact, been found.

Much more serious was the second half of Mrs Anderson's statement. While Superintendent Acott was being interrogated at Ampthill nearly two months before the trial he was asked by Mr Sherrard:

Q. It was alleged that the attacker wore black gloves of nylon texture, but none have been traced to Hanratty?
A. No Sir. (*Bedford Times*, December 8th, 1961.)

Valerie Storie's evidence that the killer wore black gloves had always been inconvenient for the prosecution. All the available evidence, including police statements from Hanratty's family, indicated that Hanratty never wore gloves. He himself had told the Frances, as he told both courts, that he did not wear gloves on his housebreakings, but preferred instead to wipe away his fingerprints with a handkerchief. In this, he was not, apparently, very successful. Detective Sergeant Douglas Elliott of the Ruislip police told the Bedford court that he had taken some fingerprints after a break-in into a house in Ruislip in early April, and into another house in Northwood, Middlesex, in early August. He had sent these prints to the Scotland Yard record office to see if they could be identified, and, by macabre coincidence, on August 22nd (the day before the A6 murder) he had discovered that the fingerprints belonged to James Hanratty. As a result, in early September, Hanratty's description was circulated as that of a man wanted for housebreaking. On these two occasions, and probably on many more, Hanratty's handkerchief had failed to wipe crucial fingerprints from his trail, and Detective Sergeant Elliott's evidence was further confirmation of the fact that he did not wear gloves. This was confirmed even by

Superintendent Acott who said in evidence (Vol. IX, p. 31) that Hanratty had told him, on their first interview in Blackpool, after Hanratty's arrest, 'I never leave my fingerprints. I always rub them off with a handkerchief.'

This hole in the prosecution case was miraculously, if only partially, filled by Mrs Anderson's sudden flash of memory four days before she took the witness stand at Bedford. By coincidence, said Mrs Anderson, she had discovered some four weeks previously that she was missing a pair of black nylon gloves. Moreover, she had lost them over the period when James Hanratty was coming to stay with her, and he had told her that he would never be caught by fingerprints because 'he *always* wore gloves' (my italics).

Mrs Anderson explained that she kept two pairs of black gloves (including the nylon gloves) in a glove box in the hall. They must, she said, have been there all summer because she never wore black gloves in the summer. Then, on a Sunday in December, she decided to wash all her gloves, and, in the course of this thorough operation, she found that her black nylon gloves were missing. What is more, she said, the gloves could be stretched to any size.

Mrs Anderson felt it important to divulge this information not as soon as she had found the gloves missing, but after 'reading the reports of the A6 murder trial'. No doubt she had also read the reports of the A6 hearing at Ampthill in November, in which it was stated again and again that the killer wore black gloves. Why was it that she only remembered about the gloves during the trial at Bedford?

Fortunately for Hanratty, Mrs Anderson was never permitted to tell the court about the loss of these black gloves. The judge, who presided over the case with scrupulous fairness, refused to allow Mr Swanwick to introduce the evidence to the jury. The evidence, he suggested, was 'prejudicial' in the sense that it had no real value or relevance to the case. The period over which Mrs Anderson said she lost the gloves was more than five months. At the same time the evidence could do nothing but damage to Hanratty. Mr Louis Blom-Cooper, in his account, regrets the rejection of this evidence on the grounds that the jury had a right to know of the black gloves. But nowhere does Mr Blom-Cooper question the very curious circumstances in which Mrs Anderson suddenly remembered so crucial an incident.

The return of memory about the gloves was an indication of a sharp change in Mrs Anderson's attitude towards the accused. When first approached by reporters about Hanratty while he was on the run, she had been benign and complimentary about him. She had rung his parents and assured them that he had nothing to fear. At Ampthill her evidence was noncommittal, but in no way damaging or insulting to the accused. At the trial at Bedford, however, she became uncompromisingly hostile to Hanratty.

First of all she said, as she had never said before, that she had seen Hanratty early on the morning of August 22nd – the day before the murder. Secondly she said, as she had never said before, that when she saw him next he had 'very deep scratches' on his face which she thought were 'razor cuts'. Thirdly she said, as she had never said before, that the Hepworths suit, which Hanratty was wearing at the time of the murder, was torn in the lining, in a 'shocking state' and that she had had to repair it. Fourthly she said, as she had never said before, that Hanratty told her of his 'Robin Hood adventures'. While telling the court about these 'adventures' she fumbled, collapsed, and, like Mrs France four days previously, had to be carried from the court.

When she returned to be cross-examined by Mr Sherrard, she tried to retract those of her previous statements which had been helpful or pleasant to Hanratty. She said that she was frightened of the man. She said that her reason for introducing him to Mary Meaden was not, as she stated at the magistrates' court, because the girl was 'more of an age', but because:

> I had been in hospital. I wanted to renew the acquaintance so that she would then stay in my flat and, since I have only one room, a kitchen and a bathroom, then *Mr Hanratty would no longer be able to take possession of my flat.*

Or again:

Q. This man, of whom you were afraid, you introduced to a young friend called Mary Meaden?

A. I have told you that I introduced him to Mary Meaden because I wanted Mary to stay at my flat *so that he would not trespass any longer in my flat, so that I would not be alone with him any longer.* (My italics.)

Mrs Anderson was asked, as she agreed in the magistrates' court, whether there were lots of people in her area who pronounced 'th' as 'f'.

'Yes,' she replied, 'small children, who know no better, like the little children in the restaurant next door to me.'

Upon which an exasperated Mr Sherrard was moved to ask: 'Are you standing there quite deliberately determined to say anything you can to hurt this man?'

To this Mrs Anderson replied, not entirely convincingly: 'How absurd you are.' (Vol. VI, pp. 54–56.)

This was not the end of Mrs Anderson's involvement in the case. Four and a half years after Hanratty was executed, on November 27th, 1966, after public interest in the Hanratty case had been aroused by the B.B.C.'s Panorama programme, the *News of the World* carried a front-page headline entitled: HANRATTY TOLD ME HE WAS A KILLER.

The story underneath the headline was written by '*News of the World* Reporter'. It began:

A former woman friend of James Hanratty has stepped into the current 'was he really innocent?' controversy. She told me: 'There is no question of a miscarriage of justice. He was guilty. A day or so after the murder, he told me he had killed a man. He didn't say it was Gregsten but he said he might as well be hanged for a sheep as a lamb. He was very worried.

'I also know that between the murder and his arrest he had new dentures fitted so that his face was slightly altered and that he dyed his hair.'

In one respect at least this directly contradicted her evidence in the court at Bedford, when she agreed with Mr Sherrard that Hanratty had not behaved like a worried man but was 'cocky' throughout the murder period. No evidence was ever produced of Hanratty having dentures fitted. As for dyeing his hair, Mrs Anderson forgot to point out (and the *News of the World* reporter probably did not remember) that Hanratty had dyed his hair after the murder exactly the same colour as before the murder.

Then there was Hanratty's alleged confession – 'A day or so after the murder he told me that he had killed a man.' Why on earth had Louise Anderson, who had bent over backwards to help police inquiries into the A6 murder, not told of this crucial confession before November 1966? This would have been vital evidence for the prosecution, incomparably more valuable than the 'confession' retailed by Langdale. Mrs Anderson was not anxious to protect Hanratty at his trial. On the contrary, her evidence did him grave damage. Why did she hold back the most damaging aspect of all? And why, if Hanratty had confessed to her, did she say to the press that she was 'astonished' when she heard he was wanted for murder? Why did she ring his father to say he had 'nothing to fear'? Why, finally, if Hanratty did confess to her, did she continue to harbour him, to put him up in her flat, to give him money for his goods, to introduce him to a young girl, and to go for rides in his car?

Mrs Anderson's interview with the *News of the World* was surprising, also, in view of her refusal to take part in the B.B.C.'s Panorama programme earlier the same month. Jo Mennel, the programme's producer, had rung her up and spoken to her about the programme. She talked at length, but pointed out that she was sick in bed and was not very happy about seeing him. Accordingly, Mennel abandoned attempts to show her on the programme.

Nine days after the programme, Robert Pitman of the *Daily Express* launched an hysterical attack on the B.B.C. programme and on the campaign for an A6 inquiry. Pitman wrote that he had had a letter from 'a minor prosecution witness, a sick elderly woman who has been pestered to the point of fear by people who want to question her evidence of more than five years ago.' (*Daily Express*, November 16th, 1966.)

The writer of that letter must have been Mrs Anderson, yet there is no evidence of any kind of her being 'pestered' by anyone, which may be one of the reasons why Pitman did not name or identify her pesterers.

On August 4th, 1970, I went to see Mrs Anderson in her Sussex Gardens flat which she still occupied. I found her living on her own in the most appalling conditions. She had had two strokes in successive years – one in 1968, the other at Christmas 1969, and the whole of her right side was paralysed. Worse still, she could hardly speak. Every word had to be forced out with great effort, and many words she found altogether impossible. She moved round her dark flat with great difficulty. I gathered that she was fed and tended to each day by the home help service but, apart from that, had not seen anyone for eight weeks. She begged me to tell her younger sister in Nottingham that she had moved back to her flat after several months' treatment at Bracknell.

These conditions were hardly perfect for the hostile interview about the A6 murder which I had planned. I spoke to her for a short time about the murder, and she answered my questions almost entirely by signs. She was, I gathered, still certain that Hanratty was the murderer; that she had been forced to pay him money and to put him up in her flat; and had introduced him to Mary Meaden in order to get him off her back. She also agreed that Hanratty had confessed to the murder. I did not, and in the circumstances obviously could not, argue with her.

Two days later, as requested, I rang her sister, a Mrs Olive Edis, in Nottingham and passed on the information about her sister. Mrs Edis, who was very disturbed about her sister's condition, told me that she and her sister had not been on very good terms at the time of the murder, and that she, Mrs Edis, had not taken much interest in it. She had, she said, been astonished to read in the newspapers that Mrs Anderson had given Hanratty six hundred pounds.

'My sister always made out to us that she was hard up,' she said. 'I used to write and ask if she could help with a little money for our mother, who was ill and poor at the time, but we always got replies to the effect that she couldn't make ends meet. I was embarrassed when I read she'd given so much money to Hanratty.'

Mrs Anderson's role in the A6 murder inquiry and trial can be summarized as follows. When first interviewed about Hanratty's involvement in the murder, she reacted in a manner which was entirely friendly to Hanratty. Her friendship with Hanratty was substantiated by Mary Meaden and by James Hanratty himself. As the months went on, however, Mrs Anderson's attitude towards Hanratty hardened. At the trial she had forgotten all the nice things she had said about him, and, more than four years after his death, she 'revealed' for the first time that he had confessed to the murder.

One feature about Mrs Anderson should be borne in mind when considering her evidence and press statements. Without question, she had paid several hundreds of pounds to Hanratty for goods which he had stolen. Mrs Anderson may not have known they were stolen, but her payments to Hanratty must have put her in danger of being charged with receiving stolen goods. In the event, Mrs Anderson was never charged with anything.

(V) The Stanmore Housebreakings and the Missing Jacket

Nothing better demonstrated the nature of the case against Hanratty than the remarkable story of the missing jacket of the chalk-stripe suit which Hanratty was wearing at the time of the murder. What started out as one of the main planks in the prosecution case was very quickly splintered. Instead the 'missing jacket' episode exposed the inadequacy of the police inquiries which were carried out on Hanratty's behalf.

While still on the run, Hanratty had told Mr Acott on the telephone that his luggage was at Mrs Anderson's. The luggage was quickly retrieved. Inside it were a green check suit and the trousers and waistcoat of a black chalk-stripe suit. No jacket was found to the dark suit.

When Hanratty was arrested in Blackpool on October 11th, Messrs Acott and Oxford travelled through the night to interview him there. At once, Hanratty told the police that there was blood on his *green* suit, but that it was his own blood from a cut hand. There was, he said, no blood on the dark suit, which he had worn all through the week of the murder. Acott then asked about the jacket of the dark suit. Oxford's notes of the Blackpool interview record Hanratty as replying:

> I dumped it [the jacket] in Stanmore. I can't give you the exact address. I cut it getting in a window when I was taking the glass out of a bay window about three weeks ago. It was a house on its own in Stanmore. It might have come under Elstree. It was near the Star Garage and a row of shops. There was nothing worth taking in the house, so I took a jacket and wore it because mine was cut on the arm. I was so disgusted that I did the house next door through a window at the back, and got nothing again. I could see they were on holiday. I carried my coat under my arm, and, about 200 yards away, I passed something that looked like a park because it had swings in it for children. I ripped the coat up to make it look worse, and tore out the name tab, so they wouldn't get me back to the screwings. Then I threw the jacket over a hedge near some swings.

Acott said: 'Where exactly were the houses you broke into?' and Hanratty replied: 'You go up Honeypot Lane to a T-junction by the garage and there's a lane which leads off to these two houses which stand in their own ground.'

Soon afterwards, at about 9.30 a.m., Acott and Oxford left Hanratty and started to make inquiries about what he had said. They at once contacted Edgware police station with Hanratty's description of the house and asked for records of housebreaking in the area. At 2.15 p.m. they returned to Hanratty's cell again. Oxford's note of what was said then reads as follows:

ACOTT. We've made enquiries at Stanmore and surrounding districts and we are unable to find any record respecting the housebreakings you mentioned nor to find any trace of your blue jacket.

HANRATTY. No, Mr Acott. That was a lie I told you. I destroyed the jacket.

ACOTT. When and how did you destroy the jacket?

HANRATTY. I can't tell you that. You won't find out.

This was of course extremely damaging to Hanratty. If this record of the conversation was true, Hanratty was admitting to lying about his jacket's whereabouts, and then to destroying it: the implication is that the jacket which he had been wearing at the time of the murder had been disposed of so that it could not be tested for bloodstains or fibres.

Hanratty's account of the conversation was very different. He agreed that Acott had said that there was no trace of housebreakings in the Stanmore area: 'So I insisted there and then that they existed and I turned round and said to Mr Acott: "Have you found my coat?" and his reply was: "Yes".' (Vol. XIII, p. 43.)

If that had been the end of the evidence on the Stanmore house-breakings, it would have been another case of Mr Acott's word against Hanratty's. The jury would probably have believed Mr Acott, and would have gone to their decision in the view that Hanratty's story about the Stanmore housebreakings was a lie to cover the real whereabouts of the offending jacket.

Fortunately for James Hanratty, however, the defence inquiries succeeded where the entire police force failed. All the way through November, as the defence prepared to challenge the Crown case before the magistrates at Ampthill, Hanratty continued to insist that he had dumped the jacket over the hedge after stealing another one in Stanmore. Shortly before the hearing started, he remembered that the name of the house where he had stolen the jacket had been Trethorne, or something like it.

When Mr Acott went into the witness box before the magistrates at Ampthill on December 4th, Mr Sherrard asked him: 'In your inquiries at Stanmore did you come across a house called Trethorne?'

To which Mr Acott replied: 'No.'

As a result of this question, however, Mr Acott sent Sergeant Oxford to Stanmore to find out whether such a house had been robbed. The following day—the last of the hearing—Acott was in the witness box answering questions from Mr Sherrard, when a police officer rushed into the court carrying a note which he passed to Acott in the witness box.

Acott read it carefully and then made a statement: 'I can now tell you something about a house by the name of Trethorne. I have just learned that on the 1st October this year a house named Trevonne of Dennis Lane, Stanmore was broken into, *but no property was stolen. I can only say it was a long way from Honeypot Lane.*' (My italics.)

Were it not for the resource of Hanratty's solicitor, Mr Kleinman, the matter would have rested there. Kleinman telephoned Mr Mills, the householder of Trevonne, that evening. Mills was unco-operative. He had, he said, been told by the police not to say anything to anyone. He really did not want to help at all. Kleinman persisted. A man's life, he said, was at stake. Could Mr Mills be certain that he had not had a jacket stolen when his house had been robbed at the beginning of October? To Mr Kleinman's astonishment, Mr Mills replied that he had already told the police that he had not lost a *sports* jacket. Not a *sports* jacket, insisted Mr Kleinman, desperately clinging to the phone, but a *dark* jacket, perhaps a *black* jacket.

Grumbling, Mr Mills put the phone down and, with Kleinman still holding the line, went upstairs to his wardrobe. There he discovered, to his astonishment, that the black jacket was missing from his morning suit. He only wore his morning suit once or twice a year, and had not noticed the loss. He came down the stairs again and told Kleinman about the jacket. Kleinman told the police, who took a statement, and Mrs Mills duly appeared for the defence at the trial.

The evidence of Mrs Mills and her next-door neighbour, Mr Reginald Powell would not have been available to the defence had they relied on police inquiries. Both witnesses showed that every detail which Hanratty had given about the Stanmore housebreakings was completely true. His description of the route to Dennis Lane was entirely accurate in every way, despite Mr Acott's comment that the burgled house was 'a long way from Honeypot Lane'. The distance from the top of Honeypot Lane to Dennis Lane is about one and a half miles. Hanratty said that he had torn his striped jacket while hanging from some guttering over Mr Powell's house and breaking two top windows. The top windows in Mr Powell's house had in fact been broken. Hanratty said that the electricity had been turned off and that he had lit a coloured candle in the washstand in the bathroom. Mr Powell confirmed that on returning from holiday he had found a coloured candle which had been lit in the washstand. Hanratty said that he had broken in by two ground floor windows in the Mills's house. Mrs Mills confirmed to the court that two of her ground floor windows had been broken. The path at the bottom of Mrs Mills's garden, as Hanratty had described, led to a small recreation ground, where there were some children's swings and a small fence. Mrs Anderson admitted that after October 1st, the day of the break-in, Hanratty had worn the trousers of his striped suit and a black jacket.

The disturbing aspect of Mrs Mills's evidence was its implied comment on the police inquiry into Hanratty's case. Both Mr Powell and Mrs Mills confirmed that soon after the burglary, in about the second week of October, they had received calls from the police asking about a missing jacket.

Mr Powell said that he had returned from holiday on October 6th to find that his house had been burgled, though nothing had been taken. The following day, a Sergeant Collins had made routine inquiries about the housebreaking. Then, on the Wednesday or Thursday after his return from holiday (October 11th or 12th) he had received a telephone call from Edgware C.I.D. His wife answered the phone, and he listened on the extension while the officer asked whether he was missing a sports jacket. His wife had a brief look and replied that there was no sports jacket missing. The following week, Mr Powell said, he got another phone call from the police, again inquiring—this time about a jacket, not a sports jacket. Again he replied 'No'.

Mrs Mills said that on the Sunday when they were burgled she and her husband were visiting friends at Shepperton. About two weeks after the burglary she received a call from Scotland Yard asking if her husband had lost a sports coat. A quick glance through her husband's sports coats was enough for her to answer in the negative and it was not until Mr Kleinman spoke to her husband more than two months later that the jacket was found to be missing.

The police, it is clear, were looking for a jacket. Soon after Hanratty told Acott in Blackpool about the Stanmore house-breakings, the Edgware police rang up Mr Powell and Mrs Mills to ask about a missing jacket. The Stanmore housebreakings *had* been reported to and investigated by the Edgware police. Yet Mr Acott could tell Hanratty, and later tell the magistrates' court under oath, that he had no information whatever about any housebreakings in Edgware at the time Hanratty indicated.

Throughout, both Acott and Oxford sought to put the blame for their mistake about the burglary on the Edgware police. There was, they suggested, something wrong with the records at Edgware. When asked by the Murder Squad to see if there were any housebreakings at the end of September in Stanmore, the Edgware police had, apparently, looked down their list of housebreakings and said 'No'. The burglaries Hanratty had committed were listed under 'house-breaking with intent' not under 'housebreaking', and were therefore, suggested both officers, not regarded as relevant by Edgware C.I.D. In fact, however, the officers at Edgware C.I.D. *had* regarded the Dennis Lane burglaries as relevant, and had rung the occupiers and asked about a missing jacket. Had it not been for the diligence of Mr Kleinman, these police inquiries would not have been available to the jury and Hanratty's story about stealing a jacket at Stanmore would have been dismissed as a wilful lie.

Even so, the jacket was never produced. In spite of the police bungling at Edgware the prosecution was prepared to suggest that the fact that it was missing connected Hanratty with the A6 murder.

'I am suggesting', said Mr Swanwick, while cross-examining Hanratty, 'you took Mr Mills's black jacket because you thought there might be some blood on your striped jacket which might not perhaps come off in the cleaning and that you had better get rid of that striped jacket.'

'Sir,' said Hanratty, answering, 'this is October 1st, this is nearly seven weeks after the crime was committed.'

'But', said Swanwick, 'you realised the police were after you or after a man called Ryan and might be on your track.' (Vol. XIV, pp. 27, 28.)

This was wrong. Hanratty could not have known that the police were looking for him until his brother Michael visited the Rehearsal Club on Tuesday, October 3rd. It was not until October 5th that he rang France in a panic; October 6th that he rang Acott in a panic and, in a panic, rushed to Liverpool. On the night of September 30th – October 1st, however, when he robbed Trevonne, he had no idea that he was wanted for the A6 murder. Whatever else the reason for disposing of his jacket that evening, it could not have been a sudden fear that the jacket he had been wearing for six weeks had blood on it.

There was yet a further point to refute the prosecution's suggestion that Hanratty had disposed of his jacket because he thought it would incriminate him in the A6 murder. According to Valerie Storie's evidence the murderer had helped to drag the body of Gregsten from the car by grabbing hold of his legs. He had then covered the seat and the back of the seat with a rug. The chances were that the murderer's clothes had no blood on them, but the murderer could not be certain. If there was blood on his jacket, there was an even greater chance that there was blood on the trousers. To dispose of one without the other would have been idiotic. As James Hanratty put it to the court: 'Would you keep the trousers? Is it not quite obvious that you get rid of the complete suit? I would not leave the trousers and then get rid of the coat.'

Mrs Mills said in her evidence that the waistcoat and the trousers of the morning suit were left on the hanger. Hanratty, had he wanted to get rid of all the clothes he was wearing at the time of the murder, would surely have taken the whole suit.

What, then, did happen to the striped jacket? It could have made a useful Guy Fawkes garment for the children playing in the Stanmore recreation ground. It could have been picked up by a cleansing department official and thrown away. Or, indeed, Hanratty could have been right about the initial conversation, and the police could have found it. Certainly park officials told the defence that the area had been extensively searched by the Edgware police towards the beginning of October. Whatever happened to the jacket, the least likely proposition of all was that put forward by the police and the prosecution.

(VI) The Acott Interviews

On October 6th, when Hanratty knew he was wanted for the A6 murder, he rang the police to deny any involvement in it. He rang again later that day, and the following day he rang again from Liverpool. Four days later, he was picked up in Blackpool and, on October 12th, Mr Acott and Mr Oxford interviewed him in Blackpool police station. Mr Acott's account of these conversations with Hanratty helped in various important, if minor, ways to substantiate the case against Hanratty.

The content of these conversations was not agreed between the participants. Almost all the incriminating passages in Acott's account of the interviews were denied in court by Hanratty, and the jury were left with a simple choice between the version of a senior police officer and that of the accused. Acott told the court that he took scribbled notes during the telephone conversations with Hanratty, and immediately afterwards wrote a full note. The interviews in Blackpool were taken down by Sergeant Oxford, and agreed between Sergeant Oxford and Mr Acott afterwards. At no time was Hanratty shown a copy of the notes either of his telephone conversations or of the interview notes. At no time was he given the chance to agree that what was written in the notes was a fair account of the conversations. In court several months later he was forced to rely entirely on his memory. So it was that his own initiative in ringing Acott in the first place and his willingness to answer questions in Blackpool told against him.

There was at least one clear indication that Mr Acott's notes were inaccurate. In describing the third telephone call from Liverpool, Acott's notes recorded himself as saying to Hanratty: 'Let me get this clear, Jimmy. Are you telling me that *these three friends of yours in Liverpool* can clear you of my murder by giving you an alibi?' (My italics.) This, according to Acott, followed the first mention by Hanratty of his Liverpool alibi. Unfortunately, however, according to the notes, there is no previous mention by Hanratty of three men.

'Mr Acott,' asked Mr Sherrard, 'would you take all the time you need and that my Lord will permit and tell us where there is any reference to the three friends in Liverpool before that?'

To which Acott, in some embarrassment, admitted: 'I have already noticed this discrepancy.' (Vol. IX, pp. 56, 57.)

It was a mistake, and an important one. Hanratty had argued that he mentioned a Liverpool alibi from the very first telephone call, and Acott insisted that it was not mentioned until the third call. The error in Acott's notes seems to indicate that Hanratty was right and Acott was wrong. At the least, they demonstrate that Acott's notes were fallible documents.

According to Messrs Acott and Oxford the first interview at Blackpool police station took an hour and three quarters. When the interview, as noted by Oxford, was read over in full at a very slow pace in court, it took twenty minutes. This discrepancy of some 500 per cent was explained by Acott by the 'pauses' in the interview, usually attributed to Hanratty and giving the impression that Hanratty had to think out everything carefully before committing himself. At Blackpool Hanratty, according to the police officers' evidence in court, was in a highly nervous state. His eyes, they said, kept popping out of his head. The pulse on his neck stood out. He was very pale. All of which descriptions must have surprised the jury who noticed that Hanratty, even under ruthless cross-examination on trial for his life, answered promptly and often volubly. His face was florid throughout, and he seemed calm.

There were two major and two minor points in the interviews where Hanratty appeared to incriminate himself. The first was reported by Oxford and Acott as follows:

HANRATTY. You won't find my housebreakings, Mr Acott. I never leave my fingerprints. I always rub them off with a handkerchief. [Pause.] I've learnt a lot. I'm a really very clever screwsman. I never make a slip up now. I pick the right places and always take my time. You'll never find my fingerprints now, Mr Acott. [Pause.] I always use a taxi and stay in the best hotels when I'm in the money. I've made over £1,000 in the last two months. I stick to jewellery and keep to one fence who always pays me 30 per cent for my gear. [Pause.] When I came out of Manchester in March I went to see him in Ealing and he gave me £25 to start me up in business. He asked me what I was going to do now. I said: 'I think I'll pack up my jewellery lark', and I asked him to get a shooter to do some stick-ups.

ACOTT. Are you trying to tell me you tried to get a gun from a man in Ealing?

HANRATTY. Yes. He wouldn't play and never got me one. [Pause.] Oh, Mr Acott I've never killed a man in my life.

If indeed the conversation about the gun had come, as this suggests, on Hanratty's initiative, it must have told badly against Hanratty in the minds of the jury. Hanratty's version of this part of the conversation is very different: 'We was half way through the interview and Superintendent Acott put it to me this way. He said: "Jimmy, I have interviewed a man at Ealing called Fisher and he tells me that you have inquired about a gun". This was a very big shock to me at the time. I did not deny it because it was the truth, my Lord. I did not deny it.' (Vol. XIII, p. 42.)

In this version, the Fisher episode came from Acott – not spontaneously from Hanratty as the Acott version suggested. When I interviewed Fisher in June 1970, he told me that he had explained to the police that the conversation about the gun was entirely trivial and meaningless; that he had never got a gun for Hanratty and believed Hanratty had never used one. For these reasons, no doubt, Fisher was not produced to give evidence for the prosecution. Yet if the conversation about the gun was a serious one, why was not Fisher called to substantiate it?

There is even clearer evidence that Hanratty's version of this part of the interview was correct in the defence papers, which include the text of two letters dictated from Bedford prison in the last week in October by Hanratty, both of which were stopped by the police. One letter was to Charles France, the other to Donald Fisher. The latter read:

> Dear Don,
>
>   Mr Acott mentioned to me at Blackpool that I asked you for a gun or did I ever mention buying a gun and you turned round and told him that I enquired about a gun. You know yourself it was only a matter of conversation and you know that if I had had a gun, I would not be in the same line of business as at present. I am worried about this matter and I'd like you to drop me a line and let me know the details.

Acott's version of the conversation about the gun does not mention Fisher by name. According to Acott's evidence, he never asked Hanratty the name of the fence in Ealing and it was never mentioned. Yet here was Hanratty openly addressing a letter to Fisher from prison a fortnight or so after the Blackpool interview in the full knowledge that the letter would be read by the police. If the conversation at Blackpool had gone the way Acott reported, if

Hanratty had foolishly let slip that he had asked about a gun in Ealing without mentioning the fence's name, would he have written a letter to the man in question and given his name to the police for checking? The letter from Bedford is still further proof that it was Acott who raised the subject of Fisher and the gun at the interview.

The second incriminating aspect of the interview concerned Hanratty's reaction to the finding of the cartridge cases at the Vienna Hotel. Acott's version of that passage runs as follows:

ACOTT. I can't make it too clear how desperate your position is. I must tell you now. After your leaving Room 24 on the 22nd August, and before it was occupied again, two empty cartridge cases were found at the end of the bed you tell me you slept in that night.

[Long pause]

HANRATTY. What size were the bullets, Mr Acott?

ACOTT. I can't tell you that.

Hanratty did not deny that he asked about the size of the bullets but his version of the conversation differs in important detail:

He said to me: 'Jimmy, in the alcove where you stayed on 21st August, we found some bullets and a gun.' At this stage I thought the Superintendent was kidding me because I made a remark to this effect. I said: 'You ain't kidding me, Mr Acott, are you?' He said: 'I am not kidding you, Jimmy, this is a very serious business ... ' I said to Superintendent Acott: 'That is the end for me now. I have not had no bullets or any gun at any time,' and at that stage I asked Supt Acott what size the bullets was. I was so excited and depressed with this new evidence that he had sprung on me, I was flabbergasted, and I knew at this stage that matters looked very, very serious against me.' (Vol. XIII, p. 44.)

Acott elicited three other pieces of information which helped to link Hanratty with the killer. Hanratty, he discovered, was a non-smoker. (The murderer had refused cigarettes.) He pronounced 'th' as 'f'. He used the word 'kip'. The third discovery was made as follows. At the end of the first interview, Acott and Oxford indicated that they would leave and return in several hours. 'O.K.,' said Hanratty (according to Acott and Oxford), 'I'll go to kip.' At the end of the second interview Hanratty is reported by Acott to have said: 'All right, Mr Acott, I'm going to have a good kip.'

Q. Why, are you tired, it's only early afternoon?
A. No, I'm not tired but I can always kip at any time, any place.

The murderer, it will be remembered, said on more than one
occasion that he intended to 'kip', and that he could 'kip' anywhere
at any time.

In court, Hanratty denied ever saying anything about sleep:
'If anybody did mention sleep, it was Mr Acott; it was not me.'
(Vol. XIII, p. 43.) Moreover, at least once in Acott's own notes of
Hanratty's conversations, Hanratty uses the word 'sleep'.

The evidence about kipping can be taken together with the
evidence of Police Constable Terence Wilkins of Bedfordshire
police who told the court of a conversation with Hanratty on
October 13th: 'He told me: "Be quiet. I have got a lot of finking to
do"' (Vol. VIII, p. 20) – a statement strikingly similar to that used
by the murderer in the car.

One final point in relation to the confrontation between Acott
and Hanratty at Blackpool is worth mentioning. On the morning
after the interview (October 12th), Superintendent Barron and
Chief Inspector Whiffen came up from Bedford to charge Hanratty
with the murder and take him to Bedford.

'They read the charge to me,' Hanratty told the court. 'They
said: "You will go to Bedford, and you will be put on an I.D.
parade" and I explained to Mr Acott: "Was that fair, putting me on
an I.D. parade with my hair being like this?" His reply was to that
effect: "I did not ask you to get your hair dyed, Jimmy. If you have
got any complaints, you can tell the judge." That was his exact
words … ' (Vol. XIII, p. 45.)

Summary

The prosecution case against James Hanratty was as follows:
that some time before the murder he had, for the first time in his
life, acquired a gun with which he intended to practise stick-ups;
that he had practised with the gun somewhere and had kept empty
cartridge cases on his person; that two of these had dropped on to
the chair in a room where he stayed on the night of August 21st in
the Vienna Hotel; that the next morning he had left the hotel, gone
to Paddington and, again for the first time in his life, taken the train
to the Slough area to reconnoitre for possible future housebreakings;
that evening, wandering about the fields near Dorney Reach, spick

and span in his new Hepworths suit, he had come across a couple in a car and had become obsessed with lust for a girl he could not properly see; that he controlled his uncontrollable lust for five hours while he forced Gregsten to drive across the north-west London suburbs. Finally, he shot the man, raped the girl, shot the girl, drove off to Redbridge, dumped the car and hid up in town for twenty-four hours. Then he hid the gun on a 36A bus, and scuttled to Liverpool to 'fake an alibi' by sending a telegram to the Frances on the Thursday evening. (August 24th).

For the first part of this scenario there was no evidence of any kind: no evidence that Hanratty had bought a gun; no evidence from any of his friends or associates (not even Fisher) that he had ever possessed one or borrowed one or used one in his life; no evidence that he had practised with a gun anywhere at all; no evidence from the people who saw him while he was staying at the Vienna Hotel that he had a gun with him. For his journey from the Vienna Hotel to Paddington we have no evidence save the word of Hanratty himself that he went to Paddington by mistake. Mr Swanwick told the court:

> May I make it plain that there is, as I opened to the jury, *no evidence* – I never opened to the jury that there was any evidence – as to the movements of this witness between the time he left the Vienna Hotel, except his statement that he went to Paddington, and the time when, according to Miss Storie, he happened upon this car at 9.30 in the evening. (Vol. XIV, p. 56, my italics.)

From the multitude of witnesses interviewed by the police about Hanratty's background and housebreaking career, not one could be produced to say that he had ever in his life been to Slough, Taplow or Maidenhead or to contradict his own assertion that he had never been anywhere near any of them. All his housebreakings had been done in the Middlesex boroughs he knew well: Ruislip, Northwood, Wembley, Harrow and Stanmore. There was no evidence of any kind from any of Hanratty's former associates or from anyone who knew him at all that he was the sort of man to lust after a woman to the extent of taking her by violence. Indeed, all the evidence about his behaviour with women was in the other direction. None of the fibres or hairs found in the car fitted and the spermatozoa found in Miss Storie pointed to a secretion of o blood group, which included James Hanratty, Peter Alphon and thirty-six per cent of the British population. There was no evidence of any kind about Hanratty's movements for three days after the murder.

If the man who murdered Gregsten was a sex maniac, he was a very patient one. If the motive for the murder was sex, why force the chief rival to the murderer's purpose, Michael Gregsten, to drive around Buckinghamshire, Middlesex and Bedfordshire for five hours before getting rid of him to possess his lover? Why not leave him in the cornfield and drive off with the woman, or tie him up and put him in the boot, or resort to almost any other action than the five-hour drive upon which the murderer in fact engaged?

The evidence which Mr Swanwick produced to support his curious story fell into three parts. The only evidence immediately and directly linking Hanratty with the crime were the identifications: the 'three glimpses' of the murderer by Valerie Storie, John Skillett and James Trower which enabled them nearly two months later to select a man whose hair at any rate was entirely different to that of the murderer. Doubt was cast on each of these identifications either through inconsistency (as in Miss Storie's case) or, as in the case of Skillett and Trower, through conflict with other witnesses (Blackhall and Hogan).

Secondly, there was the testimony of innumerable police officers, headed by Superintendent Acott and Sergeant Oxford. At the magistrates' hearing, this evidence had concentrated on what then appeared to be Hanratty's 'lies' about his chalk-striped jacket. Only when the defence found that a black coat had been stolen from the house described by Hanratty did this crucial police evidence turn sour and reflect, if anything, in Hanratty's favour. All that was left were the tenuous links in Mr Acott's notes of his conversations and interviews with Hanratty, none of which were checked for accuracy at the time with Hanratty.

Thirdly, there was the evidence of the prison bully and many-times-convicted young coalman, Roy Langdale, that Hanratty had confessed: evidence which was firmly contradicted by other prison companions of Hanratty.

Finally, most important, there was the bulk of what may be called 'circumstantial evidence' which pointed to Hanratty not directly but by coincidence. The evidence included the cartridge cases found in the Vienna Hotel, the testimony of Charles France about the back seat of the bus, the information given about himself by the murderer in the car—his name was Jim, he was a housebreaker, he had 'done the lot'—and, had it been allowed, the testimony of Mrs Anderson about losing her black gloves. There can be little doubt that the eleven-man jury (one of the jurymen had dropped out at an early stage when he became ill at the mention of blood) finally decided that it was this evidence which, taken together, created too many coincidences implicating Hanratty.

All this evidence suggested a masochistic drive towards self-implication. In the car itself, and at Deadman's Hill, the murderer had been scrupulously careful to cover his tracks. There were no fingerprints, no fibres—nothing except spermatozoa to implicate him. Yet before and after the murder, if the prosecution case was right, the murderer left crucial clues all over London. On the night before the murder he had dropped two cartridge cases in his hotel. The day after the murder, he deliberately put the gun where he knew it must be found. Why?

There is one answer which explains the coincidences and the evidence's weaknesses. At the time of the trial no one, least of all Hanratty, had contemplated it, and so it was never suggested to the jury. The gun and the cartridge cases could have been *planted* by people wanting to direct police attention towards Hanratty and away from the real murderer.

The 'supporting evidence' for the case against James Hanratty was supplied by a curious selection of witnesses: Nudds, the recidivist and celebrated prison nark, who lied from the moment the police first started asking questions; Langdale, the younger recidivist who had bullied a fellow prisoner; Charles France, small-time fence and thief, who had run to the police with damning, if circumstantial, evidence against his best friend; Mrs Anderson, the antique dealer from Soho, who escaped inquiry or prosecution following Hanratty's information (and her admission) that he had received six hundred pounds from her in two months in 1961. Similarly, Langdale, who was destined for several years' imprisonment following the Post Office charges he faced in November 1961, found to his surprise that as soon as he told the story of Hanratty's confession, he was treated with delicacy and compassion by the authorities and put on probation. These were the men and women who supplied the 'supporting evidence' of which Mr Swanwick boasted in his final address to the jury.

PART THREE

The Case For James Hanratty

4

The Alibi

The Liverpool Alibi

From the first time that Hanratty talked to Superintendent Acott on the telephone about his whereabouts on August 22nd, 1961, he was adamant that he had been in Liverpool. Whatever changes and lies blurred Hanratty's later evidence about his alibi, he maintained consistently until his death that he had travelled on the morning of August 22nd to Liverpool by train, and had spent the afternoon and early evening there. If he was right, that alone was enough to prove that he did not climb into the murder car at Slough, Buckinghamshire, at 9.30 that evening.

From the early days after his arrest, Hanratty provided evidence for his presence in Liverpool that evening. He described his leaving the Vienna Hotel in the early morning at about 9 a.m. and walking to Paddington (it was, he said in his original statement, 'a lovely morning'). Arriving at Paddington, he realized at once that this was not the station for Liverpool and took a taxi to Euston. After buying a return ticket, he bought some magazines and sat around in the buffet until the next train left for Liverpool.

Hanratty described in very close detail the people who sat with him in his carriage to Liverpool, notably a smartly-dressed man in pin-stripe trousers and gold cuff-links marked with the letter E. The train, he said, had a restaurant. It had, he said originally, left at 10.55 or 11.55 a.m. The leaving times of the trains to Liverpool from Euston on that morning were 10.20, 10.35 and 12.15, arriving at 2.22, 3.25 and 4.45 respectively.

On arrival in Liverpool (in his original statement Hanratty estimated his time of arrival as 'about 3.30'; in court he revised it up to 'between 4.0 and 5.0'), he went for a wash and brush up, and then for a cup of tea in the buffet. He then took his case to a left-luggage office.

The case was valuable to him because it contained the jewellery which he had come to Liverpool to sell, and that is probably why he was able to describe in some detail his encounter at the left-luggage office. The following is the statement he made to his own lawyers during October – before any inquiries had been made into his statement, and before he could possibly know whether or not his statement tallied with the facts:

> After I came out of the buffet, I put my case in the left luggage office. It was my pigskin case. Man there who took it had a *withered or turned hand*, about 5 o'clock. I said to him, how much. He said 1/– ... he asked my name. I said Ryan. He wrote it in the book, gave me bottom half of the receipt, he kept top half ... He put the case on wooden racks on my left ... The man with the *withered hand* took the case. (My italics.)

On leaving the station, the original statement goes on, he started inquiring for Carlton Avenue. A woman told him it was a twopenny bus ride away, up the Scotland Road. He asked two or three other people, and eventually got on to a bus. He got off the bus a few stops from the Scotland Road and went into a sweet shop to make further inquiries. The following is the passage about the sweet shop taken from Hanratty's original statement to his lawyers a few days after his arrest:

> Went into sweetshop and tobacconist. I asked for Carlton Avenue or Tarlton Avenue. She said no Carlton Road around there. Woman and young girl. I had pin-striped suit on. Woman came to the door of the shop and showed me the bus stop which was near it. The sweet shop is in the Scotland Road, opposite a picture house. A woman and young girl there. I asked them the way to Talbot Road, then said Carlton Road. The woman said 'This is Bank Hall, and you have to get on a bus and go into town'. Bank Hall joins Scotland Road. I did not get to Carlton Road. I could not find the street.

Hanratty then explained that he walked back into the town, abandoned his search for his fence and the Carlton Road and went into Lyons for a meal. He came out of Lyons and approached a man on the steps leading up to a billiard hall and tried to sell him a gold watch. The man refused to buy the watch, and tried to prevent him from going up the stairs, saying that the premises were licensed. Eventually Hanratty was allowed up to the toilet, and came down the stairs again.

These incidents were reported by Hanratty to his solicitor, Mr Emmanuel Kleinman, in their first meeting following Hanratty's arrest. Kleinman was impressed with his client. In his first message to counsel on the case he wrote:

> I have now spent several hours with Hanratty. Some 3½ hours on Monday and some 2 or 3 hours on the previous Friday. I have questioned him in as much detail as I could and his answers have always been readily given, and he appears to understand very well what one says to him, and he gives replies quite quickly. He is also prepared to say what he does remember.

The original statement about Liverpool included three encounters which could well be corroborated by the people mentioned: the man with the withered hand in the left-luggage office; the lady and the girl in the sweet shop and the man on the steps to the billiard hall. Unhappily for the defence, however, inquiries about these people were left to the police. And, as in so many instances throughout the conduct of the case, the moment the police started on an investigation connected with Hanratty's defence, the method of their investigation clouded the result in doubt.

Take first the 'man with the withered hand'. Detective Chief Inspector Harold Whiffen of Bedfordshire Constabulary told the court that he had been in charge of conducting Hanratty to the Ampthill courtroom where he was charged four days after his arrest. He was present (for reasons which were not made clear) when Hanratty spoke to his solicitor (for the first time, at length) about his defence. According to Whiffen, Hanratty told his solicitor: 'There is something else to prove that I was in Liverpool because on the 22nd I left my suitcase at Lime Street railway station. A man with a withered *arm* took it and I gave him my name. It was a different man who handed the case over to me.' (My italics.)

If that was what Mr Whiffen heard, his hearing differed sharply from that of Mr Kleinman, Hanratty's solicitor. In the notes of that meeting with Hanratty, and in each of the statements made by Hanratty about the incident in the left-luggage department, Hanratty referred to 'a withered or turned *hand*'.

The difference between the two versions proved to be important. For Mr Whiffen, without, apparently, much regard for the confidentiality of an interview between a prisoner and his lawyer, promptly reported the conversation to his superiors, with the result that the police were the first to start investigating in the left-luggage department of Lime Street station. They found there a regular cloakroom attendant called Peter Usher, two of the fingers from whose left hand were missing. Another British Railways employee called Peter Stringer, who had an artificial arm, worked in the gentlemen's toilet at the station, and was accustomed from time to time to help out in the left-luggage office.

The police discovered that Usher was on duty in the week of the A6 murder from 6 a.m. until 2 p.m. Stringer was on duty from 2 p.m. until 10 p.m., but Stringer told them that it was not his custom to take the names of the people who gave him luggage, and that he usually helped out in the left-luggage office only after 8.30 p.m. The police also discovered that two tickets had been issued for left luggage on August 22nd.

The prosecution (at the trial, though not at the hearing) produced Stringer to say that he could remember nothing of Hanratty, though he was on duty that day. Stringer displayed to the jury an artificial arm, and a gloved hand, and Mr Swanwick, in summing up, asked the jury to accept Stringer as, to quote Inspector Whiffen, 'the man with the withered arm'. The defence meanwhile had interviewed Usher.

From the outset they employed for their inquiries in Liverpool a former officer in the Liverpool police force called Joe Gillbanks. As a policeman, Gillbanks had specialized in crime prevention, and had become an expert in the use of burglar alarms. A few weeks before taking on the case for Hanratty in Liverpool, Gillbanks had left the force and set up on his own with a burglar alarm firm called Burgot. He was not an accredited inquiry agent, but he was recommended to Mr Kleinman partly on the grounds of his contacts in the Liverpool police. He has, incidentally, refused on more than one occasion to talk about the case. I saw him briefly in the offices of Burgot in February 1967, but he refused to answer any questions. 'You can't bring Hanratty back now,' was his only comment.

The first note from Kleinman to Sherrard about the left-luggage office attendant ran as follows:

Gillbanks telephoned again and said he has seen Usher, who remembers Hanratty. He says he did speak about his name being on the ticket, he mentions a name of Ratty, initial N or J, and says Hanratty told him to put his name on the ticket and that he replied: 'What's the difference, you have the number of the ticket.' He did not put the name on. He says the photograph is something like him. He remembers it but he says he was wearing a cap and a blue or dark suit. He says they have discussed it at the cloakroom and it was Tuesday 22, but he says it was probably between 11 and 12.30. This timing seems quite wrong.

The timing was indeed quite 'wrong', but it was the only thing which was seriously 'wrong' with Usher's statement. The conversation about the name rings true to Hanratty's story, especially as the case was full of jewellery and Hanratty would want to make doubly sure about its safety. The name Ratty, with the initial J, must be compared with the name Hanratty says he gave, J. Ryan. Usher identified Hanratty from photographs shown him by the defence and signed a photograph of Hanratty on the back. Lastly, Usher's *hand* was crippled.

I found Mr Usher still at Lime Street left-luggage office in April 1970, and interviewed him in June. The first he had heard of the Hanratty case was when his superior in the office told him that a British Railways Board lawyer was travelling from Euston to interview him on the Hanratty case:

A lot of pressure was put on me not to get involved by the men in the left-luggage office, and when the man came from Euston, I didn't help him very much. Then a senior officer from the Liverpool police came to interview me at Lime Street. He showed me several books of photographs. I picked out five or six photographs of a man who had left his case with me about that time. I asked him 'Am I right?' and he replied: 'We're neutral'. And I said: 'Shouldn't I be going to the trial?' and he said: 'No, we've got the man we want'.

Then the man came from the defence. I picked out the picture again. I'm sure the one I picked was Hanratty. And I told Gillbanks about the man giving his name, and me saying: 'We don't take names'. I had some way then of picking out the date, but, honestly, I don't remember it now. I was very surprised when I wasn't taken to the trial. Stringer had an artificial arm – there was no way of even seeing his hand which was always covered. I'm sure that if I'd gone to the trial I'd have identified Hanratty as the man. I certainly recognized him when his photograph was published in the papers after the trial.

The defence had two main reasons for not calling Usher. They were worried about his performance as a witness, particularly as, according to Gillbanks's reports, Usher was keen to 'get in' on the courtroom scene. More seriously, the times did not fit. Usher's time of duty had stopped long before Hanratty could have got to Liverpool.

But had it? The defence appeared to assume throughout that Hanratty, if he did go to Liverpool on August 22nd, travelled on the train which left Euston at 12.15 p.m., and arrived in Liverpool at 4.45 p.m. This is largely because Hanratty, when dating the time of his train's departure from Euston at '10.55 or 11.55', stated a preference for the latter. There was, however, another fast train leaving Euston for Liverpool that morning – at 10.20 a.m. arriving in Liverpool, Lime Street, eight minutes early, at 2.22 p.m. This train, like the 12.15, was a restaurant-car train. There was also a slow train, leaving at 10.35, which stopped at Crewe, as Hanratty thought his train had done.

Both Hanratty and the Vienna Hotel manager, Nudds, agreed that Hanratty had left the hotel early that morning (Nudds says 8.30; Hanratty about half an hour later). There was then a walk to Paddington (which takes approximately fifteen minutes), and a taxi ride to Euston (eleven minutes). Even accepting Hanratty's time for leaving the hotel, he would still have been at Euston at about 9.35, a good three quarters of an hour before the 10.20 left, and time enough for his two cups of tea at the station. It is hard to see how, on his own timings, he could have missed the 10.20 and the 10.35 and been forced to wait nearly two hours for the 12.15.

If Hanratty did catch the 10.20 at Euston, he would have been at Lime Street before 2.30. Usher would have been due to leave his post in the left-luggage office some thirty minutes before the train came in. The times still did not 'fit', but the margin is much narrower. Usher himself explains that time-keeping was never very exact in the Lime Street left-luggage office. Overtime, sometimes for two hours, sometimes for four hours, sometimes for half an hour, was common.

The Sweet Shop

The second section of Hanratty's Liverpool alibi, consisting of his brief visit to the sweet shop, turned out to be by far the most substantial part of his alibi, if not of the entire case for his defence. The fact that it was not conclusive is, once again, partly due to the fact that inquiries to establish the sweet shop alibi were made in the first instance by the police.

Hanratty says that he told Mr Acott about his visit to the sweet shop in the very first interview in Blackpool. Acott denied this, saying he first heard about the sweet shop from Mr Kleinman. In any event, on October 16th, Acott wrote a letter to the chief of the Liverpool C.I.D., dealing with Hanratty's claims of a Liverpool alibi. The letter's third paragraph read as follows: 'Hanratty says that after he left Lime Street station he called at a sweet shop in Scotland Road, Liverpool, where he asked a woman, who was accompanied by a child, to direct him to Carlton Road or Talbot Road. The purpose of this inquiry by Hanratty is not known.'

The Liverpool C.I.D. responded to this information with alacrity. C.I.D. officers swarmed down the Scotland Road asking at sweet shops if women were serving in August and, if so, whether any of them remembered a young man making inquiries about Carlton or Talbot Road. In all, the police visited twenty-nine sweet shops in Scotland Road, and in all of them except one they met with a negative response.

The exception was No. 408 Scotland Road, a sweet shop not far away from the city centre, owned at that time by Mr David Cowley, a Labour councillor who was later to become Lord Mayor of Liverpool. The police were told that a lady had been serving in the shop on August 22nd. She was not a regular server, but a friend of the family who helped when they were short of staff. Her name was Olive Dinwoodie, and she had been asked to help in the shop during the week of August 21st–27th while Mrs Cowley and her children were on holiday in the country.

Accordingly, the police tracked down Mrs Dinwoodie. To their astonishment, no doubt, she told them that she did indeed remember a young man coming into her shop while she was serving and asking the way to Carlton or Tarleton Road, or something of the kind.

A junior police officer, acting, presumably, on instructions, took Mrs Dinwoodie a single photograph of James Hanratty and asked her whether that was the man who had come into the shop. Mrs Dinwoodie replied immediately that it was the man. From that moment, as a result of police bungling, her identification became suspect. One of the first rules about identification by photograph is that the witness should be shown not *one* photograph to identify, but several, from which to choose one.

In this instance, the prosecution case could not lose by showing Mrs Dinwoodie one picture. If she confirmed the photograph, the prosecution could suggest, as Mr Swanwick did at Hanratty's trial, that the 'one photograph test' was suspect. If she did not confirm the picture, her evidence would immediately have been discredited.

Soon after confirming the one photograph, Mrs Dinwoodie was again shown several photographs, including one of Hanratty different to the one she had confirmed in the first place. Once again, promptly and without any doubt, Mrs Dinwoodie selected the photograph of Hanratty as the man who had come into her shop.

On this, the police started to question Mrs Dinwoodie with great care and in great detail about the incident. Mrs Dinwoodie told them that she had been in the shop for only two days in the month of August. On August 21st, she had been called to the shop by David Cowley, arrived about midday, and stayed there until the shop closed at 6 p.m. in the evening. On the following day she had gone to the shop in the morning and had served all day. In the evening, she had grown ill, and was too ill the following day or any other day that week to serve in the shop. By the time she was well again, Mrs Cowley had returned from holiday. The incident with the man, she made clear, could only have happened on August 21st or 22nd. *There was no other day when the incident could have taken place.*

It was then that the interrogating police mentioned a child. Hanratty, she was told, had mentioned that there was 'a child with her' in the shop. This helped Mrs Dinwoodie to decide that the day on which the incident with the man took place was the Monday — August 21st. For it was on that day that her grandchild, a thirteen-year-old girl called Barbara Ann Ford, had come with her to the shop and stayed with her all day helping her serve. It was the presence of the girl which enabled Mrs Dinwoodie, after some hesitation, to fix the day of the incident as the Monday — and thus, apparently, deprive Hanratty of his alibi.

There is some independent evidence to suggest that in those early days Mrs Dinwoodie was in grave doubt as to the date of the incident. Mr Don Smith, one of Liverpool's most experienced crime reporters, who was working at that time for the *Daily Herald*, heard from a police contact that the Liverpool C.I.D. had found a lady who appeared to substantiate Hanratty's alibi. At once, Smith went to interview Mrs Dinwoodie at her home. He believes he was the first journalist ever to speak to her. 'She told me', he says, 'that she was, at first, fairly sure that the man had come into the shop on the Tuesday, the day of the murder; but that now so many people had been asking so many questions, she wasn't so sure.' (Interview with me, April 7th, 1970.)

The police then contacted the young girl, Mrs Dinwoodie's granddaughter, Barbara Ann Ford. Miss Ford too remembered the man coming in and asking directions. She agreed that she had helped her grandmother serve in the shop on the Monday. But she told the police something else. She had, she said, the following day, Tuesday August 22nd, gone into the centre of Liverpool with her friend, Linda Walton, to buy some dress material. On the way back from town, she and Linda had called in at the shop and stayed in the shop for, she thought, about half an hour. The time, she thought, was about a quarter to five—exactly the time when Hanratty had said he came into the shop. Once again, Barbara Ford decided that the day the man came in was the Monday because she was serving all day in the shop on the Monday, and only went in for half an hour on the Tuesday. Nevertheless the fact remained that she was in the shop on the Tuesday as well as the Monday.

So the police went to interview Linda Walton, who agreed with her friend Barbara. Miss Walton put the time when she and Barbara went into the shop after their shopping expedition as rather earlier than Miss Ford—she suggested 'just after four o'clock'—and also said that they had stayed in the shop for rather longer—about an hour.

The Liverpool C.I.D. inquiries into the sweet-shop incident lasted for a week in which hardly a day went by without police cars arriving at the houses of Mrs Dinwoodie, Mr and Mrs Cowley, Barbara Ford and Linda Walton. The full results of their inquiries were sent to Superintendent Acott in a letter dated October 24th—eight days after Acott's letter had been sent setting out the details of Hanratty's claims.

What was the reaction of Superintendent Acott to this sensational news from Liverpool, which appeared substantially to vindicate Hanratty's Liverpool alibi? He remained silent on the subject. He said not one word to Mr Kleinman or Mr Sherrard about Mrs Dinwoodie's evidence and the police inquiries into it, even though the original information about the 'sweet-shop alibi' had come from Mr Kleinman.

Mr Sherrard, meanwhile, had discovered that there was a sweet-shop minder in Liverpool who might be able to back up Hanratty's alibi. He waited to receive the information from the prosecution, and he waited in vain. The magistrates' court hearing opened on November 22nd and Mr Acott gave evidence for the Crown against Hanratty on December 4th. Nothing in his answers to examination in chief by the Crown counsel at Ampthill let slip what he knew about Mrs Dinwoodie. The following day, Mr Sherrard rose angrily to cross-examine.

Under cross-examination, Superintendent Acott agreed that the police had checked on information given to him by Hanratty's solicitor that Hanratty called at a sweet shop in the Scotland Road area of Liverpool on August 22nd.

'Hanratty', he said, 'has been identified from a photograph by the shopkeeper, Mrs Dinwoodie, as calling there on August 21st or August 22nd.'

> MR SHERRARD. 'When were you proposing to be good enough to tell us, who are defending this man for his life, the result of these police inquiries?'
>
> MR MACDERMOT (Crown Counsel) interrupted to say that he would give the defence the names and addresses of such witnesses as Mrs Dinwoodie at the end of the hearing.
>
> MR SHERRARD. 'A little late, if I may say so.' (*Bedfordshire Times*, December 8th, 1961.)

Having finally obtained the names and addresses from the prosecution, Mr Kleinman and his agent in Liverpool, Mr Gillbanks, set to work. They obtained in the next week (December 9th to 16th) statements from Mrs Dinwoodie, Barbara Ford and Linda Walton. The defence statements, which, unlike the original statements to the police, are now available, showed that there was, as Acott had inferred at Ampthill, still considerable doubt in the minds of all three about the day on which the man had entered the shop.

Mrs Dinwoodie's statement started categorically by fixing the date as the Monday:

> On Monday morning, the 21st August, Mr Cowley sent me a note asking if I was well enough to go to his shop at 12.30 p.m. and, seeing I was not too well, I could bring my grand-daughter Barbara Ann Ford to help me in the shop. She is 13 years of age and was to serve lolly ices to save me running around. On that day, Monday 21st August, just gone 4 o'clock, the *Echo*s had just arrived, I was serving a customer, a man, with some cigarettes, when another man came in, that is the man in the photograph you have now shown me. I could hardly understand him when he asked for directions to Tarle-ton Road. I told him I did not know that road, only Tarleton Street. Several others, customers, came into the shop and I said perhaps they could help him and I went on serving and did not even notice him go out. He was hard to understand, I thought he was Scots or Welsh ...
>
> On Tuesday 22 August, I went to the shop at half past one and John Cowley [brother of David] was there and stayed with me until I left to go home at half past six. I was very sick that day and did not go back to the shop for a fortnight. Barbara was not with me that day at all.

Then, however, came the qualifications:

> *I would not have been able to say whether I saw Hanratty on the Monday or the Tuesday of the week commencing 21st August except that he mentioned my having a girl with me.* I thought he meant the girl was serving with me.
>
> My granddaughter did come back into the shop about 4.45 p.m. She stayed about half an hour. She did not serve on the Tuesday. I am sure the man who came into the shop is the man whose photograph I have signed on the back and dated 16/12/1961.
>
> It must have been the Monday or the Tuesday. It could not have been any other day as I was not in for a fortnight from the Tuesday night having been taken sick.
>
> *If it had not been mentioned to me that a young girl was serving in the shop, I would not have known which day it was.* However, I do remember the man coming in. (My italics.)

Twice in her statement Mrs Dinwoodie makes plain that she fixed the date as the Monday by the information about the child. This information, of course, came from Hanratty. Had it not been for that information, she would have had no other way of telling which day the man — and she was certain the man was Hanratty — had come into her shop. Specifically, what made up her mind was the information that the girl was serving with her. And there *was* a young girl with her, for at least half an hour, at the crucial time on the Tuesday.

Barbara Ford's statement also fixed the day on the Monday, for the same reasons. She remembered the man coming in. 'He spoke in a funny way,' she said. She did not remember the time he came in. 'I have seen photographs by Inspector Parkinson. I did not pick any out.'

Miss Ford was then shown a side-view picture of Hanratty taken in prison, and agreed at once that it was the man who had come into the shop, and signed it. 'I do remember the side-face photograph,' she said, and then, finally and crucially: 'I think it was the Monday because I was serving on the Monday, not the Tuesday.'

All this was thrown into doubt by the description of her visit to the shop by Linda Walton, part of whose short statement read:

> I was in town all day with my friend Barbara Ford. We had been to buy some green dress material and we got back to the shop about four or quarter past. Mrs Dinwoodie was serving. She was by herself. I don't know Mr John Cowley. People were coming in and out of the shop — men and women. Quite a number of men came in, some in groups, some by themselves. Some of the men I knew but others I could not recognise. We stayed a good bit — about an hour I think. She, Barbara, *was standing in front of the counter most of the time with me, but when children wanted serving she went behind the counter to serve them.* (My italics.)

This statement extended the time at which the two young girls were in the shop on the Tuesday, and fixed the time of their first entering the shop as considerably earlier than that fixed by Mrs Dinwoodie and her granddaughter. Above all, it took away the one *criterion* by which Mrs Dinwoodie and Barbara Ford had been able to fix the Monday rather than the Tuesday: the fact that Barbara had been serving on the Monday, not the Tuesday. Linda Walton articulated what must have been obvious: that while Barbara was in the shop in the busy period on that Tuesday evening, she had from time to time volunteered to help her grandmother who was feeling ill. To do so she had gone behind the counter to serve. According to Linda Walton, in short, there were periods on that Tuesday afternoon when Mrs Dinwoodie and her granddaughter were behind the counter together. And the times at which both were behind the counter could well have coincided with the time Hanratty said he went into the shop. During these times several men whom she did not know and could not identify came into the shop. The three statements, taken together, leave no doubt that it could have been the Tuesday when James Hanratty went into the shop to ask the way to Tarleton Road, as he said he had done from the moment of his arrest. And if he did go into that shop between 4 and 5 p.m. it was outside the realms of possibility (as finally even the prosecution conceded) for him to have climbed into the Morris Minor car with Michael Gregsten and Valerie Storie at Dorney Common some four and a half hours later.

There was, however, a further problem to tease Mr Acott and his advisers over that Christmas and New Year as the date set for the Bedford trial—January 22nd—grew closer. Several of the prosecution's own witnesses had already given evidence at Ampthill to the effect that James Hanratty had spent Monday, August 21st, in London. If these witnesses were right, he could not have gone into Mrs Dinwoodie's shop on Monday. If they were wrong, large sections of the prosecution case would be damaged. If Hanratty could be shown at the trial to have been in London on the Monday, then the jury could well conclude that he went into Mrs Dinwoodie's shop in Liverpool on the Tuesday, and thus could not have done the murder.

How do we know that Hanratty was in London on the Monday? There was, first, the documentary evidence. Hanratty had said that he had put his green suit in the cleaners at Burtols in Swiss Cottage on the morning of August 21st, a fact which was confirmed by the Swiss Cottage area supervisor for Burtols, Mr John Wood, who was serving that morning in the shop opposite Mr Ewer's umbrella shop in Swiss Cottage Arcade. Mr Wood gave evidence on oath at Ampthill that he had received the suit on August 21st from a man who gave the name of Ryan, and the address of 72 Boundary Road, London NW8. In his statement to the defence on the subject, Mr

Wood said he did not remember what the man looked like who gave him the suit, but he managed to fix the time when the suit was brought in at 'about 11 a.m.'. There was, of course, documentary proof in Mr Wood's records that the suit was handed in on that day. It was never challenged that the man who handed in the suit was James Hanratty.

At the other end of the day there is Hanratty's signature in the register of the Vienna Hotel, proving that he signed in that night. The hotel manager Nudds reckons that the time of Hanratty's arrival was at about midnight, a time which coincides with Hanratty's own story. Hanratty had arrived at the Vienna Hotel via the Broadway House Hotel, near Baker Street, the 'master' of a group of four hotels including the Vienna. He was seen by the manager of the Broadway House at about 11.30 p.m.

We have seen that there are two fast trains to Liverpool from London in the middle of the day, and trains over such a distance are likely to have been as fast as, if not faster than, cars.

If Hanratty took his suit into the cleaners at about 11 a.m. and arrived at the Broadway House Hotel at 11 p.m., how could he have been at Mrs Dinwoodie's shop at between 4 p.m. and 5 p.m.? He could have dashed from Swiss Cottage to Euston, caught the 12.15 train to Liverpool, which arrived at 4.45. He could then have rushed to Mrs Dinwoodie's shop, dropped in to ask the way to Tarleton Road, and rushed back to Lime Street station to catch the 5.15 train back to London – and the Vienna Hotel by midnight. This was by any standard an unlikely itinerary. Unhappily for the prosecution, others of their own witnesses had been even more specific about Hanratty's movements on that Monday.

Charles France, for instance, one of the prosecution's most crucial witnesses, had told the magistrates:

> He [Hanratty] came back the following day, 21st August, at about 2.30 p.m. My daughter Carol was there. She was lying on the settee nursing her jaw where she had had a tooth out. He stayed until about 6.30 p.m. He had something to eat. He was dressed in a sort of chalk stripe blue suit ... When he left he said he was going to see an old aunt in Liverpool.

Carol France supported her father in every particular, and she could be certain of the date:

I did not see him after that until 21st August. I fix the date because I had just come home from the dentist when Uncle Jim knocked on the door to say he was going to Liverpool. I had had a tooth taken out. Dr Hillman is my dentist. It was a woman who took my tooth out. I got home about 2.30 p.m. The accused came to our house soon after I got in. He stayed until about 7.0 p.m.

To prove the reliability of their witnesses the prosecution had also called a dental surgeon, assisting Dr Hillman, to tell the magistrates: 'On the 21st August last I extracted a tooth from Carol Ann France. I have my record book with me to refresh my memory if necessary. That was at 2 p.m.'

Here was documentary proof to back Carol France's memory of 'Uncle Jim' coming into the house as she lay on the sofa nursing her mouth after losing her tooth. Mrs France, her mother, also remembered the incident: 'He came to our house on Sunday, August 20', she told the court at Ampthill, 'with a suitcase with some washing in it. I washed it for him. *He came back the next day to collect it.* He left my house about 7 p.m.' (My italics.)

To complete this picture, Hanratty in his very earliest statements to the police and to his lawyers had said that he had gone to the Frances' house on the afternoon of August 21st to collect clothes before going to Liverpool, and had left in the early evening. Hanratty's story, told independently of the Frances who refused all contact with the defence from the outset, was backed up in every detail by the three Frances. The dentist's assistant made it clear that the Frances had not got the date wrong. Hanratty had visited them on the afternoon of Monday, August 21st, and therefore could not have gone into Cowley's sweet shop in the Scotland Road, Liverpool, on the same afternoon.

Even this was not all. The magistrates at Ampthill had heard evidence from yet another prosecution witness about Hanratty's movements on August 21st. This witness was the waitress, Ann Price, who worked in the Rehearsal Club and who had been friendly with Hanratty for several weeks before the murder. Miss Price told the court, in cross-examination:

On the 21st August he came to the Rehearsal Club once. Maybe he came twice. I remember then that his hair was black. That was not the usual colour of his hair. I remember remarking that his hair was black, a different colour. He left the Rehearsal Club about 6 or 7 p.m., coming to twilight. About 6 or 7 o'clock. It was beginning to get dark. He would order me a drink, but he would have a Baby Cham if I forced him. He paid with £1 note. He told me that he was going to Liverpool. He came back later that evening, it could have been from 8 o'clock but not later than 9.30 p.m. He may have stayed until about 10 p.m. or just before. He could have been there without my seeing him after the cabaret ... On the 21st August, Jimmy was carrying a leather suitcase.

Against this, must be set Hanratty's own statement to his lawyers, before he or they had any chance to talk to Ann Price:

I went to the Rehearsal Club, I had my striped suit on. I got to the Rehearsal Club about 5.30. I saw Ann Price the coloured girl, bought her a drink and had a chat with her. I think I told her I was going to Liverpool ... she said I looked pale. She also said before this: 'You had your hair dyed.'

The statement then tells of a visit to Hendon dog-track, and a return to Soho to collect a pigskin case full of jewellery from a left-luggage locker in Leicester Square Underground station. He then, according to his statement, went for 'a short time' with a prostitute of whom he was a regular customer and who occupied premises 'in a room over a club and a side road by a public house near the Palace Theatre'. After visiting the prostitute, still carrying his case: 'I went back to the Rehearsal Club to see Ann ... I then called a taxi and went to Baker Street about 11.30.'

These statements were made independently of one another and the coincidence between them can only arise because each is describing what in fact took place on Monday, August 21st. It is inconceivable that both Hanratty and Miss Price could have made up these incidents, or applied them to the wrong day.

There were therefore seven witnesses who had given evidence on oath at Ampthill about Hanratty's movements in London on the Monday, all of which confirmed Hanratty's own statement, made independently of all of them. As even Mr Acott admitted on oath at the magistrates' court: 'It could not have been this man [Hanratty] on the 21st because *we know from the evidence where he was on the 21st.*'

Yet if it was not the 21st when Hanratty went in the shop, it could only have been the 22nd because that was the only other day when Mrs Dinwoodie was serving in the shop. If he did go into that shop on the 22nd, at the time agreed by Hanratty and Mrs Dinwoodie, he had a cast-iron alibi for the A6 murder.

It was a vice out of which, it seemed, the prosecution could not wriggle. Frantic police inquiries were made in connection with the sweet-shop alibi throughout December 1961 and the first three weeks of January 1962. In the course of these inquiries the police unearthed a new witness, Mr Albert Cecil Harding, whose evidence was not served on the defence until after the trial had begun. When Mr Harding stepped into the witness box on the twelfth day of the trial, Mr Sherrard told the judge: 'I have no instructions from Mrs Dinwoodie about this man's evidence, because we did not know about it till this morning.'

Mr Harding was a supervisor in a small delivery firm, and a friend of the Cowleys who owned the sweet shop in the Scotland Road. Every morning and evening on his way to and from work he would call at the sweet shop for cigarettes and occasionally to help with rush-hour serving. In his statement to the police, Mr Harding remembered his visits to the shop on the evenings of the 21st and 22nd of August some five months previously. On the 21st, he said, he had come back from work at about 5.30 to find Mrs Dinwoodie and her granddaughter in the shop; and Mrs Dinwoodie had told him about a man asking for Tarleton Road. On the Tuesday he had gone into the shop at about 7 p.m. and Mrs Dinwoodie was not there. His statement was clearly intended to establish the point that the conversation about Tarleton/Carleton Road took place on the Monday. Mr Harding was able to recall all this detail when he looked at the logs of his delivery journeys. Yet the log books, supplied to the defence with his statement, did not bear him out. On Monday, August 21st, according to his 'daily record of hours and work' he stopped work at 6 p.m. On Tuesday, he stopped work at 5.45 p.m. If his statement was right, this meant that he had gone into the sweet shop on the Monday some thirty minutes before he stopped work, and, on the Tuesday, he had taken over an hour to get from work to the sweet shop, about three minutes' drive away.

Mr Harding was up against Mr Sherrard at his best form in cross-examination, and, as a result, had a very uncomfortable time:

Q. I am going to have one more try. Look at the daily record of hours of work and tell us what the reference to 6 o'clock, 21.8.1961 means?

A. 21.8.61?

Q. I know what that means. What does the 6 o'clock?

A. On the 22nd? [*Sic*]

Q. Yes.

A. Well, it is roughly the time I finished driving, when I reached home.

Q. But I thought you said ...

A. Probably that Monday night I did not put that 6 o'clock in, just put it down as near a time as I could get it. I am not a clock-watcher.

Q. But you were still in the shop till seven?

A. I might have been in the shop after seven. I am not saying it is seven o'clock.

Q. Then what is the use of the 6 o'clock in the column?

A. What I do with my private time is nothing. That is a quarter of an hour slip of the pen, as you might say.

Q. You are not having a slip of the mind are you?

A. No, I am not. My brain is as good as yours. (Vol. XII, pp. 29–30.)

Once again there was this contradiction, so common among prosecution witnesses, between certainty about crucial events (such as the time he went into the sweet shop on the Monday and Tuesday, exactly who was in there at the time, etc., etc.) and vagueness when it came to linking the surrounding circumstances to these events. His entries in the logs, said Mr Harding, which appeared to suggest that he had called in at the sweet shop earlier on the Tuesday than on the Monday, were vague. In this respect he was not a clock-watcher. But when it came to precise details about going into the shop, his memory was absolutely clear and his clock-watching precise.

I interviewed Mr Harding on April 7th, 1970, over a cup of tea in a Liverpool café. He was extremely helpful, although obviously vague about incidents which had taken place eight and a half years previously. He emphasized, however, that he had been able to fix the date of the conversation with Mrs Dinwoodie about the man asking for Tarleton Road by his routine relating to long-distance journeys. He was sure that the conversation could not have taken place on a day he made a long-distance journey because he would have got to the shop later in the day. When I showed him the copies of his log book, however, he agreed that they showed that on that particular Tuesday – August 22nd – when he had made a long-distance journey, he had arrived back at his place of work *earlier* than on the Monday, when he had made 'local calls'.

There was, in short, a similarity between the way in which Mrs Dinwoodie and Mr Harding fixed the Monday as the day on which the event had taken place. Neither could remember off-hand. Both remembered by reference to external evidence. Mrs Dinwoodie remembered because of the information about a child in the shop; Mr Harding remembered because of his routine on long- and short-distance journeys.

Yet both sets of external evidence, tested by the facts, could have proved equally that the events took place on the Tuesday. Barbara Ford *was* in the shop, helping with the serving, at the crucial time on the Tuesday; and Mr Harding's log books showed that it was, if anything, more likely that he had got to the shop in time for the conversation with Mrs Dinwoodie on the Tuesday.

Two days later, Mrs Dinwoodie gave her evidence. She said that Hanratty had come into the sweet shop on the Monday. The prosecution was impaled on the horns of the same dilemma. Their witnesses had made it plain that Hanratty was in London on the Monday. Here was Mrs Dinwoodie saying Hanratty was in the Liverpool sweet shop on the Monday. How, conceivably, could they explain this contradiction to the jury without conceding what was obvious: that Hanratty had gone into the sweet shop on the Tuesday?

The question was dealt with to the best of the prosecution's ability by two answers, contradicting one another, the choice between which was left to the jury. The relevant section of Mr Swanwick's summing up speech to the jury is an excellent example of how a skilful advocate can make a plausible case out of implausible material:

> So that those two conversations, one between Mrs Din-woodie and the person who came into the shop, and the second retailing that conversation to Mr Harding, are clearly proved by every possible means and verified by supporting facts, to

have taken place on the Monday when Mrs Dinwoodie was almost certain it did ...

What does that mean? Either, as the prosecution suggest is the natural and logical meaning of that evidence that it was not the accused who made that enquiry, the real genuine enquiry and not the enquiry he said he made, and that he has gone wrong — *that it was not the accused who made the enquiry at all but a man with doubtless some resemblance to him and that that is a bit of alibi which he has managed to buy*: or — this is less likely but I must cover the possibilities — the second, though less likely possibility, though it is, I suppose a possibility, is that the Frances are wrong in saying that the accused was with them on the afternoon of the 21st, despite the evidence of Carol having her tooth out, which she undoubtedly did on that day — yes, it was that day, toothache on the Saturday — and the Frances are wrong about that, and, if they are wrong about that, it is possible I suppose, that Hanratty could have gone to Liverpool on the Monday and have caught the 5 o'clock train back, arrived at Euston at 9.10 and have gone to the Broadway Hotel, near Baker Street, which would not be very far from Euston, and could have been sent from there to the Vienna Hotel, where beyond any doubt he certainly spent the night of the 21st. I put that possibility, *but by far the greater possibility is that it was not Hanratty at all.* (Vol. XIX, pp. 12–13, my italics.)

Even Mr Swanwick was half-hearted in suggesting that Hanratty had walked into Mrs Dinwoodie's shop on the Monday. He agreed that the possibility that 'the Frances were wrong' was remote. Nor did he mention all his other witnesses, Mr Wood and Miss Price in particular, who were also wrong if Hanratty had been in Liverpool on the Monday.

Rather than attack his own witnesses, Mr Swanwick preferred another explanation for the Dinwoodie incident. The man who went into the shop, he suggested, *was not Hanratty at all.* It was another man, from whom Hanratty had *bought the information.* This explanation needs to be spelt out carefully, as Mr Swanwick did not do. It is that Hanratty, as soon as he discovers that he is wanted for the murder, travels to Liverpool to buy an alibi; that one man there who looks like Hanratty says to him: 'Yes, I remember that I went into a sweet shop in the Scotland Road and asked the way to Tarleton Road. A lady was in there with a child. She told me to go back into town. You can pretend that man was you. It will help your alibi.' For which information Hanratty pays cash. When finally caught by the police, he uses the sweet-shop story to bolster his Liverpool alibi.

The story has an aura of absurdity about it. First, Hanratty had a reason, which he gave, for asking for Tarleton Road, or Carleton Road. Several months previously, he told the court, while still in prison, he had met a man who said he was a receiver and who gave a Liverpool address—which he remembered as Talbot, Tarleton or Carlton Road. He wanted to sell this man his stolen jewellery. Secondly, there was the identification of Mrs Dinwoodie and her granddaughter, Barbara. Mrs Dinwoodie identified a picture of Hanratty as the man who had come into her shop.

In any event, was it really conceivable that, six weeks after the event, so skeletal a story would have been offered up as alibi material for a man wanted for murder? What possible chance was there that a sweet-shop server, who, for all anyone knew, served regularly in the shop, would remember a date of so small and trivial an incident? Finally, if Mr Swanwick's view of what happened was accurate, the alibi was, in fact, completely worthless. For the sweet-shop incident, Mr Swanwick insisted, took place on the Monday. It was therefore useless as an alibi. Yet Hanratty, according to Mr Swanwick, was prepared to pay good money for an 'alibi' in a sweet shop which could almost certainly not be stood up, and, if it was stood up, would be proved to be false. The standard response of any prosecution presented in court with a cast-iron alibi is to make the charge: 'It was bought.' In the case of James Hanratty and Mrs Dinwoodie the charge was rather less credible than usual.

Even in the scrupulously fair summing up of Mr Justice Gorman, there was a note of incredulity about Mr Swanwick's submission:

It is suggested that this is an invented or bought enquiry. You have to consider the position and you have to determine what view you form, because the prosecution has not hesitated to say —and I make no comment; I make no complaint—that this alibi at Liverpool was the result of a journey made to Liverpool at some time by this man, seeking to buy an alibi with the £250 which he is supposed to have told Dixie that he had in the railway embankment. That was put to him as a suggestion. Now it merits very anxious consideration. (Vol. XX, p. 61.)

The Man on the Steps of the Billiard Hall

After he left Mrs Dinwoodie's shop, Hanratty's story went on, he travelled back to town, and, after a few more desultory inquiries about Carleton Road, decided to give up the search and went for a cup of tea and a meal in Lyons next door to Lime Street station. After tea, he made a languid attempt to sell his gold wristwatch:

> I went to a Billiard Hall across road – I wanted to raise money. I only had £8 or £9 on me, to me that is not a lot of money – I had watch just over fortnight. I stole it. Man at door who owns the place. He is always there in Lime Street, he stands on steps. I said to him, would you be interested in buying a gold watch. He said No. I went up the stairs towards the Hall. He said, don't go up there; these are licensed premises. I said, what difference does that make. He said, it makes a lot of difference. I don't want you to go upstairs with it.

Inquiries were made by the defence in Liverpool of billiard hall proprietors around Lime Street, and a Mr Kempt, the proprietor of Reynolds Billiard Hall in Lime Street (which has since been demolished) agreed at once that one evening the previous summer he had gone down, as was his practice, to stand on the steps of his billiard hall, when a man had come up offering to sell a gold wristwatch. He had refused, and had stopped the man from going to the hall because, he said, it was licensed premises. Kempt also told the court that he had started his holiday on August 26th. The incident took place before the 26th, but he could not pinpoint the day of this encounter nor identify the young man who approached him, save that he was about five feet tall, in his middle twenties. Finally, Kempt said that the time when he was accustomed to stand on the steps was between 6 and 7 in the evening – the billiard hall's slack period.

Up to this point, each part of Hanratty's story appeared to be sound and substantiated: substantiated by the evidence of the Frances, Ann Price and Mrs Anderson about his intentions of going to Liverpool: substantiated by Usher and Kempt; but substantiated above all by Mrs Dinwoodie and the story of the sweet shop. From the moment Mrs Dinwoodie and Kempt appeared in court, opinion in the courtroom moved strongly in favour of the innocence of the accused. The desperation of the prosecution in relation to this part of Hanratty's defence is demonstrated by the late, panic serving of Mr Harding's evidence. Had the only alibi witnesses and evidence been those concerning the period up to 6.30 p.m. on August 21st, Hanratty's case would have appeared almost impregnable.

At the last moment, however, seven days after the trial was started, the confidence of the defence in their ability to substantiate their client's alibi for the murder received a severe jolt from an unexpected quarter – James Hanratty himself.

The Rhyl Alibi

As we have seen, almost as soon as he knew he was wanted for the A6 murder, James Hanratty telephoned Superintendent Acott at Scotland Yard to protest his innocence. He phoned him in the morning and in the evening of Friday, October 6th from call-boxes in Soho. On the night of October 6th–7th he travelled by stolen Jaguar to Manchester and thence by train to Liverpool. He rang Acott from Liverpool again on the Saturday.

There is a dispute between Hanratty and Acott as to the mention of an alibi in these conversations. Hanratty says that in the very first conversation he told Acott that he had spent the night of Tuesday 22nd in Liverpool with three men, and that in the second conversation he told Acott that he would go to Liverpool to see if his friends would stand alibi for him. Acott's version, on the other hand, stresses that no mention was made of any Liverpool alibi before Hanratty phoned from Liverpool on October 7th.

There is however a very important piece of evidence, which for some reason was not produced in court, which substantiates Hanratty's version and discredits Acott's. In the first phone conversation Hanratty told Acott that he would be telephoning a daily newspaper. Almost at once, he rang the *Daily Mirror*, much to the delight of that newspaper which ran the phone conversation as their lead story in all editions on October 7th. A section of the conversation which Hanratty had with Barrie Harding, assistant news editor of the *Mirror*, is extremely important:

HANRATTY. I can prove I was in London on the Monday and *I went to Liverpool on the Tuesday morning*. The murder was on a Tuesday, wasn't it?

HARDING. Have you people to give you an alibi?

HANRATTY. Yes. I was there doing business with some friends. I can't involve them for various reasons. (My italics.)

If Hanratty told that to the *Daily Mirror*, it is a fair guess that, in spite of Acott's denials, he told it to Acott. The chances are that it was in the second conversation, shortly before stealing the Jaguar for his trip to the north-west, that Hanratty first told Acott of 'three men' with whom he had spent the murder night.

At any rate, in his conversation with Acott on the following day, when he was in Liverpool, the 'three men' are established in the conversation. Hanratty told Acott that he had seen the three men, but they had refused to stand alibi for him. He therefore intended to stay on the run.

Four days later he was arrested in Blackpool and interviewed by Acott there. Acott pressed him again and again to reveal the names of the three men he said he stayed with on the murder night. Hanratty refused. 'How can I tell you who they are?' he asked. 'They all have records, and one of them is wanted by the police.' When Acott came back in the afternoon and explained the seriousness of the case against him, Hanratty did volunteer some information about the three men: 'The flat was in the Bull Ring off Scotland Road. It's in the middle of a bomb site and slum area. There's a woman in the flat with two children, a boy and a girl. I *think* I went on Tuesday, but I can't tell you the address.'

Q. You think you went there on Tuesday? Now you're not sure which day?

A. No. I'm not sure, but I still think it was on Tuesday.

Q. What else can you tell me about the three men?

A. Well, I met two in Liverpool about four years ago, when I was on Y.P. [Young Prisoners].

Much to Acott's irritation, Hanratty persistently refused to give the names of the three men, but he did, later, tell his solicitor that one of the men had a warrant outstanding against him for non-payment of a hire purchase instalment on a television set.

The Liverpool police, meanwhile, had undertaken a thorough search in and around the Scotland Road area among people who may have known Hanratty after the latter's telephone call from Liverpool. On October 16th, Detective Chief Inspector T. M. Elliott of the

Liverpool C.I.D. set in train further exhaustive inquiries after receiving a letter from Superintendent Acott about the three men. The Bull Ring area was scoured for any flat fitting Hanratty's description. In one, three brothers were found with criminal records but they denied all knowledge of Hanratty and did not fit the description he had given.

Meanwhile Hanratty's solicitor, after two preliminary interviews with his client, had been quick to spot the weakness in the defence case. In his first brief to counsel to appear for Hanratty on remand on October 23rd, Mr Kleinman wrote:

> The difficulty with this case is that although Hanratty pleads an alibi, he refuses to disclose the names and addresses of his four chief witnesses with whom he said he was staying during the period the murder was committed and during which he alleges he was at Liverpool ... However, he gives sound reasons for withholding information as regards to these witnesses, although not such good reasons as would lead a man to endanger his life on a capital charge. *They might, however, be quite good enough reasons for a criminal who is convinced of his innocence, and the fact that the case against him cannot be established.* (My italics.)

As the weeks went on, however, and the hard information failed to materialize, the defence lawyers became worried. In his advice on evidence, dated December 11th, 1961, Mr Sherrard wrote to Mr Kleinman:

> It seems to me to be very important indeed to establish that there were in fact three men in Liverpool of the kind described by Hanratty. I can but advise that it is vital to trace them or at least prove cogent evidence of their existence ... It might be helpful if photographs of the area could be provided ... From a tactical point of view it might be as well to see whether permission could be obtained (in conjunction with the D.P.P.) from the Prison Commissioners for Hanratty under guard to be taken to Liverpool with Mr Kleinman in order that he should lead us to the place where he says he stayed ...

Further on, Sherrard mentions one of the names vaguely mentioned by Hanratty as one of the three men:

If at all possible steps should be taken to interview a man called McNally or MacNally with whom the defendant was in Walton Prison, Liverpool. I feel that from this man we might obtain a 'lead' which will be helpful in finding the three men with whom Hanratty says he stayed.

On January 7th, Sherrard again wrote a detailed 'advice on evidence' to Kleinman, and although Mrs Dinwoodie had turned up by then, he was still unhappy about the alibi: 'In my view, it is still vital to obtain from Hanratty the details relating to the men with whom he stayed which will enable us to trace them. McNally appears to have been one of the men involved ... '

The next day, Sherrard went to Brixton prison for another long interview with Hanratty in which, again, he pressed for details about the three men in Liverpool. Hanratty was a little more specific, but not much more helpful:

Terry McNally was one of the people I stayed with in Liverpool. The same one I did time with. The flat is right opposite the flower shop in the Scotland Road. There is a red phone box opposite the flower shop on the right hand side. The flat is between the flower shop and the Post Office on the opposite side of the road. It's on the second floor with a green door. The wife's name is Lil. I don't know John's surname ... McNally took me there. I went to Liverpool in June or July – met McNally and he took me to meet them.

Mr Gillbanks, working in Liverpool for the defence, found Terence Francis McNally, who admitted to knowing Hanratty, but was decidedly unhelpful about him. 'If Hanratty does not open up, why should I,' he said in the curt statement which Gillbanks obtained. Gillbanks checked the twenty-three blocks of tenements opposite the flower shop in the Scotland Road. One block did have balconies and green doors, but after what seems to have been a thorough check, none of the occupants answered to Hanratty's description. 'Gillbanks', wrote Kleinman to Sherrard on January 17th, 'thinks we should again endeavour to have Hanratty go to Liverpool to point out the flat. He thinks there will be grave difficulty otherwise.'

Accordingly, on January 17th, with the trial only five days away, Sherrard and Kleinman travelled to Bedford prison to interview their client. Sherrard once again questioned him, perhaps a little more desperately than previously, about the three men. Much of the alibi, he assured his client, could be sustained. Mrs Dinwoodie, Usher, Robert Kempt – all seemed to back up what he said. Yet the case against him was a powerful one. Valerie Storie's identification would carry much weight. Could he not now, in his own best interests, tell his lawyers about the flat and the three men?

Then Sherrard added a final warning to impress upon his client the importance of the situation. 'If the judge directs you to be taken to Liverpool, and you don't take us to them', he said (according to Kleinman's notes), 'you will be lost.'

The notes went on:

> He realises this. He says: 'I have been there on two or three occasions. I can go right there. Two bedrooms and a little kitchenette and living room. I slept in the living room. John took the jewellery the first evening, the Tuesday. McNally and John went out to get rid of the stuff.'

But the letter which arrived at Kleinman's office the next day from Gillbanks in Liverpool brought bad news. A subpoena had been served on McNally, who was very angry. He now insisted that he had not met Hanratty since leaving Lewes prison four years earlier. 'He does not frequent the Scotland Road area of the City,' Gillbanks's letter ran, 'has no relations or associates in the district, and does not sleep away from home ... During the week commencing the 21st August he was employed (at Dunlop Rubber, Speke) on the 7 a.m. to 3 p.m. duty and did not miss work.'

'I have now', Gillbanks's letter went on, 'made exhaustive inquiries in ALL those tenements and I am satisfied that there is no family living in any of them which would fit the description supplied ... I feel confident that had any family as described been living in the area ... I would have discovered them.'

McNally's change of tone on being issued with his subpoena and Gillbanks's blank in the Scotland Road tenements meant, in effect, that Hanratty's stated alibi for the night of August 22nd–23rd, the murder night, was unlikely to stand up in court. This was not a simple matter of a man 'not remembering' his whereabouts. He had given enough clues for the men to be found. Yet not only the defence but also the police had combed all the areas and all the tenement blocks he had mentioned without finding a flat, family or person similar to his description.

The trial started on January 22nd, and still the main part of Hanratty's alibi, pieced together from several interviews, was based on the 'three men in Liverpool' story. The narrative, in the final collated statement which Mr Sherrard had before him in his brief from Kleinman, read:

> During the three days I was in Liverpool I stayed with McNally in a block of flats known as the Bull Ring or the Gardens in Scotland Road, or a road just off it, Skellone Road. McNally lives there with a married couple. It is a second floor flat, and I think there is an entrance in the Scotland Road. I have been there before, it has a balcony with a green door ...

On the Tuesday evening, his statement went on, he had been to see *The Guns of Navarone* at the cinema. On Wednesday he had hung around waiting for McNally to sell his goods. On Thursday he had gone to a fun fair in New Brighton, and had tried to get into a boxing title fight, involving a coloured man. On Thursday evening, McNally sold the stuff and Hanratty left the flat. He sent a telegram to Charles France and took the night train back to London.

For this statement the only corroboration was that *The Guns of Navarone* was showing in Liverpool (on a four-month run); that there was a boxing match between Howard Winstone and a coloured boxer on the Thursday evening; and that Hanratty did send the telegram to France on the Thursday evening. As Mr Sherrard pondered over these papers before the trial began, he must have reflected on one glaring inconsistency: from arrival in Liverpool until the conversation with Kempt, his client's story was admirably supported by independent evidence; *after* the conversation with Kempt, however, the story was completely uncorroborated. Whatever the explanation for this contradiction it could not have been that Hanratty had done the A6 murder. For the Dinwoodie/Kempt evidence, if it did support Hanratty's story, proved that he could not have been in Slough at 9.30 when he was in Liverpool four hours earlier.

The trial opened on Monday, January 22nd. The first day was taken up almost entirely with Mr Swanwick's opening speech for the prosecution which made much of the 'unsubstantiated' alibi of the three men in Liverpool. The following day, Tuesday 23rd, Valerie Storie gave her categorical assurance that Hanratty was the man on Deadman's Hill. As the prosecution case unfolded, Hanratty became increasingly worried. He trembled at the prospect of facing the court and prosecution counsel with an alibi which was demonstrably weak.

Each day, Mr Sherrard and Mr Kleinman had a conference with their client in the Bedford cells. At one of these conferences in the first week of the trial, either on the Tuesday (23rd), Wednesday (24th) or Thursday (25th), Hanratty first mentioned to his counsel that the story of the three men was a fabrication; and that he had spent the murder night at Rhyl, which is some forty miles from Liverpool.

This was information which Mr Sherrard did not expect, and did not relish. He had been pressing his client to reveal the names of the three men in Liverpool. He had tried to persuade Hanratty to break faith with his criminal friends and reveal their names to save his life. When Hanratty suddenly revealed that the whole story was a pack of lies, Mr Sherrard was placed in an intolerable situation. An alibi which could not be substantiated was bad enough; a changed alibi was a great deal worse. How, Mr Sherrard asked in exasperation, could he be expected to convince the jury of anything his client said if the crucial part of his story—the 'three men' alibi—was admitted to be a lie?

Hanratty, however, by now thoroughly frightened by the way the case was going against him, was determined. He would not give evidence, he said, unless he could tell the truth. His only hope against the brilliance of Mr Swanwick and the lies which he believed had been told against him by people like Charles France, was to stick to what he knew were the facts. These facts, taken down on the backs of envelopes by his bemused counsel and solicitor, were as follows.

He had, he said, left home during the week his parents were on holiday in mid-July, 1961, and had fallen quickly among his old associates on the London burglary network. On July 23rd he had stolen a car and driven with an accomplice to the Midlands. In Shrewsbury the car had had a puncture. A policeman had approached and asked Hanratty for a licence, which he did not have. Abandoning his friend to the policeman, Hanratty had run away and hitched a lift to Cardiff. After a night and a day in Cardiff, he had hitched a lift back north and eventually, exhausted and totally destitute, he had arrived in the seaside resort of Rhyl on Tuesday, July 25th.

He had wandered to the fairground and explained his plight to a friendly worker on the dodgem cars, who had persuaded the fair-ground manager, Mr Webber, to 'give him a start' on the cars. He handed in a national insurance card which he had obtained in Cardiff, and which bore the name Hanratty.

After several hours' work, the fairground worker, whom Hanratty remembered as 'John', had asked him to stay the night at his house and Hanratty agreed. He had spent the night in 'John's' council house and, next morning, 'John' had lent him a pair of shoes, since his own were run down. 'John' had gone ahead to the fairground, but Hanratty had not followed him. Instead, he had hitched a lift out of Rhyl and travelled to Liverpool and thence, eventually, to London. During the conversation with 'John' the night before, the subject of stolen goods had come up, and 'John' had said he knew people in Rhyl who might be able to get rid of stolen goods at a good price.

A month later, Hanratty had, as he had always maintained, travelled to Liverpool on the morning of Tuesday, August 22nd. He had gone into the sweet shop and talked to the man on the billiard hall steps. Then, however, he had decided to abandon his search for his contact in Liverpool and travel instead to Rhyl to see if 'John' could help him sell his goods. He had caught a bus in the late even-ing, arriving in Rhyl as it was getting dark. After some trouble, he had found a boarding house which put him up for two nights. The boarding house backed on to the station. It was a terraced house with no front garden, and he had paid twenty-five shillings for two nights' stay. A landlady had taken the money, but he had not signed the register.

The next morning he had gone to look for 'John'. He could not remember how to find 'John's council house. He went to the fair-ground and the cafés where he had eaten in July, but could not find 'John' anywhere. He spent that night (23rd–24th) in Rhyl and returned to Liverpool the next day at about midday. He had gone to the fun fair, to the boxing stadium, sent the telegram to France and returned to London by the night train.

When he heard he was wanted for the A6 murder he wanted above all to convince the police that he could not have done the murder, and to do so without giving himself up or falling into the hands of the police. He tried to think of people whom he could per-suade to ring Scotland Yard and assure police officers that he, Hanratty, had been nowhere near Taplow the previous August

22nd. Desperately, he realized that there was no one in Rhyl on whom he could rely to get in touch with the police on his behalf. In some panic, he decided to appeal to some of his burglar friends in Liverpool to 'stand alibi' for him. Although he knew that none of his acquaintances in Liverpool were aware of his visit to the city on August 22nd, he still reckoned that 'thieves' honour' lubricated with some generous bribes would prove more reliable than a landlady in Rhyl whose name he did not know and whose address he could not remember.

He rang Acott and the *Daily Mirror* to say that he had been in Liverpool with friends on the night of the murder. He then stole a car and travelled to Liverpool via Manchester to confront some of his friends. The people he approached in Liverpool (whoever they were, and McNally may well have been one of them) told him, not surprisingly, that they did not want to get mixed up with the police, still less to offer the police false evidence in a murder case, even for the payment of the £250 Hanratty was offering them. Kindly, but firmly, they sent him away, and Hanratty wandered off to New Brighton, to Preston and eventually to Blackpool, where he was arrested.

Once arrested, his problem was compounded. Either he stuck to a story which he knew could not be substantiated; or he told a new, true story which might not be substantiated. Confident of his innocence, Hanratty told Sherrard, he decided to continue with the false story. The more he continued with it, the deeper he was committed to it. Yet, in spite of the damage done to his case by the previous lies, he could not contemplate going into the witness box in front of Swanwick and telling a story which he knew to be false. He therefore insisted, if he was to give evidence, that he told the Rhyl story to the court.

There was one alternative open to Mr Sherrard: not to call Hanratty at all. If Hanratty was not called, the alibi would be discussed only in terms of the inquiries into the 'three men' alibi. It would still be open to the jury to believe that there might have been three men in Liverpool, despite the police inquiries. On the other hand, the disadvantages of not calling Hanratty were obvious. It would look as though the defence had something of importance to hide. Mr Sherrard always believed that one of the main proofs of Hanratty's innocence was his client's attitude and bearing, which he wanted the jury to see.

Immediately, Mr Kleinman telephoned Mr Gillbanks in Liverpool with the story about the Rhyl alibi and Gillbanks left at once for Rhyl. He contacted an old acquaintance of Liverpool police days, Mr Frank Evans, who lived on his police retirement pension with his sister in Rhyl. Together the two men set about making inquiries about Hanratty's Rhyl alibi.

The first document mentioning the Rhyl alibi in the defence papers is one of the many hurried scrawls written, literally on the back of an envelope, by someone in Mr Kleinman's office. It is dated January 26th — that is the Friday of the first week of the trial: 'Gillbanks phoned ... have traced people H. stayed with in Rhyl. He stayed with man referred to as John, who is in fact Terry Evans and who has an old taxi. H. stayed overnight and stole a pair of shoes. Evans has never seen him since.'

There are several more notes fixing the date of Hanratty's stay with Terry Evans at 'about July 27th', and saying that it can be checked exactly with the insurance card. There is then a line, and the following notes at the bottom of the page: 'There is such a cafe as described ... Hundreds of bed and breakfast houses which back on railway station which have no front gardens. John tight curly hair with a tattoo on his forehead ... T. Evans put him up for the night, and took him to the fairground the next day.'

So at least part of Hanratty's story was right. Gillbanks was instructed urgently to continue with his searches, while Sherrard increased pressure on Hanratty for more details on Rhyl. Three days later, on January 29th, Sherrard impressed upon Hanratty the dangers of changing his alibi.

Hanratty was adamant. Even though at that time there seemed no hope of an alibi witness from Rhyl, he insisted on sticking to the Rhyl story. Sherrard then asked Hanratty to sign a statement making it plain that the decision was, in the last resort, Hanratty's and Hanratty's alone. The statement is dated 5 p.m. (about half an hour after the trial proceedings for that day had finished) on January 29th, 1962, and reads as follows:

> I have been advised in great detail as to the importance of my being absolutely truthful about my alibi story. The statement I made to Mr Kleinman in which I explained about going from Liverpool to Rhyl on August 22, 1961 is true. I hereby instruct my solicitor and counsel to proceed on the basis of the true story

about Rhyl. Please try to find the landlady in the house there. This has been read to me: I fully understand it and hereby sign to this effect.

(Signed) JAMES HANRATTY

There then follow a series of hurried notes as Hanratty tried to remember more about the house he stayed in in Rhyl. The landlady, according to the notes, was 'about fifty, like my mother'. There were 'two tables in the back where I had breakfast', and 'a green bath in the attic'.

The notes end with descriptions of how to get to the house: 'There was a picture house on the main road going towards a bridge. It was one of the turnings on the right going towards a concrete bridge (hump-backed) with a rail.' There is then a map drawn from Hanratty's description, and pointing the way to the house in which he had stayed.

The information was sent at once to Gillbanks. But things still seemed hopeless. One of the chief difficulties was that there was no way of publicizing a photograph of Hanratty. The rules of contempt of court forbade the publication of a photograph of the accused until after the trial.

To help Gillbanks in his inquiries, therefore, Mr Sherrard asked the judge, as the court opened on Monday February 5th, for special dispensation to take a photograph of Hanratty. The dispensation was granted and the photographs were taken on the steps of the courtroom by the River Ouse. They were sent off to Gillbanks, who started to hawk them round landladies in Rhyl.

As Hanratty climbed into the witness box on Wednesday, February 7th, their inquiries had still proved fruitless. Hanratty's evidence in chief about Rhyl was given before his agents in Rhyl had found anyone to substantiate it. The section of the transcript dealing with his original answers on where he spent the night in Rhyl is worth quoting at length:

A. I enquired on five or six occasions to get bed and breakfast in the area. As being August time, I found it very hard, but eventually I come to a small private house with a sign Bed and Breakfast.
Q. Tell us everything about it that you can remember.
A. Well, it was dark at this time my Lord and I had travelled in and

out through other streets. I knocked at this door eventually, and a woman answered the door.

Q. Whaṭ did she look like?

A. Well, she was middle-aged, about fifty, average built. She wore glasses and had greyish hair; I remember quite plainly in the morning, leaving the premises, there was a coat rack.

Q. Where?

A. In the hall.

Q. What sort of coat rack?

A. It was a coat rack that you hang like your overcoat or raincoat or hat or something to that effect, with a mirror ... It was a big article. It was on the right hand side coming in the door ...

Q. Did you notice anything else which was a little bit unusual in that house somewhere?

A. Yes, I did my Lord.

Q. What was it?

A. In the hallway, I did not notice it in the evening but being day-break, in the morning eventually, after having breakfast I noticed there was a plant, a green plant in a bowl in the hall.

Q. Was there anything else that you noticed in that house in any other room of the house you went to? Did you notice something?

A. There was a green bath.

Q. A green bath?

A. I remember the green bath quite plainly.

Q. Can you remember whereabouts in the house the green bath was ... ?

A. In the top part of the house, I would say the attic; in the top part. It might not be the attic, but that is the ...

Q. Can you remember how much you were required to pay or how much you paid at this particular house?

A. I paid 25/- for two nights, that is 12/6 a night.

Q. Was there any register or book to sign?

A. No. There was no register or book to sign.

Q. Can you recall anything about any trains in relation to that house?

A. Well, it was dark when I eventually entered the house, and I did not draw the curtains because it was a back room. I did not bother to draw the curtains. I could hear trains shunting, but I could not see them the following morning when I woke up.

Q. But you could hear them?

A. I could hear them quite plainly. (Vol. XIII, pp. 14, 15, 16.)

That same afternoon, Hanratty faced the full onslaught of Mr Swanwick, who, pooh-poohing the Rhyl story, asked for more information about the boarding house. 'Well,' answered Hanratty, 'I remember there was no front garden to this house. In the morning I looked out of the window and found a small courtyard.'

Q. Is that at the front or the back?
A. That is at the back, Sir. (Vol. XIII, p. 55.)

If Hanratty was inventing the Rhyl boarding house, as Mr Swanwick suggested, he was taking formidable risks with the details of his description. He had no idea whether or not anyone had been found by the defence agents who fitted his description.

Astonishingly, however, on that same Wednesday the defence agents struck gold in Rhyl. Gillbanks and Terry Evans, who had offered his help, were knocking on doors of boarding houses close to the station, and were making progress down Kinmel Street, which runs parallel to the railway station. The question at every door was the same: Do you have a green bath in your attic?

At No. 19 Kinmel Street, a boarding house called Ingledene, Gillbanks and Evans were stopped short. Yes, the landlady replied, there was a green bath in her attic. Terry Evans takes up the story:

> We showed her the photograph of Hanratty. We didn't tell her it was Hanratty – or anything to do with the murder trial. We just said: 'Did you have a young man like this come to stay with you last summer?' She agreed at once that she'd seen the fellow before, and after a conversation with her daughter, she confirmed that a young man like that had come to her door, and that they'd put him up for two nights. (My interview with Evans, April 8th, 1970.)

Gillbanks telephoned this information straight to Kleinman's office – a conversation which is recorded on yet another little note. It is dated February 7th, 1962, and headed, *Mr Gillbanks*:

> The landlady has not previously been interviewed by the police. Neither have Evans or Webber.
>
> There is a cafe known as Dixie's ... The boarding house has a bath – all green. It is not boxed in. The only window is a skylight. There is a bed in the bathroom. H. might have been put in the bathroom if they were pushed for accommodation.

The landlady has seen the photograph and seems to recognise the man. She has fair hair, not grey. She does not always wear glasses, but she does wear them. Light-rimmed glasses. She is rather small. No more than 5′ 2″. She is 58 years old, but looks young for her age.
The photograph is familiar to her.

She can't be certain when, and in which room, Hanratty stayed. She said it might have been the attic bedroom since, during the latter part of August 1961, she did take a number of people for bed and breakfast. H. might have been one of them.

She has a feeling that she does know the young man.

She has a book for visitors, but says that she does not bother with bed and breakfast visitors (Gillbanks says she does not bother at all but wants to keep up appearances).

She will be as helpful as she can as she wants justice done.

The landlady, Mrs Grace Jones, then looked at her books and decided, without prompting from Evans or Gillbanks, that the young man had visited her house in the week of August 19th–26th the previous summer. At once, Gillbanks borrowed a car and the very next morning, Thursday February 8th, he, Evans and Mrs Jones drove to Bedford.

They arrived as Hanratty was finishing his long two-day session in the box, to be followed there by Mrs Dinwoodie. The court then rose for the evening, but not before the defence had informed the prosecution that they had found Mrs Jones, and that she would be giving evidence the following day.

Both Evans and Mrs Jones gave evidence on the Friday morning. In Terry Evans, the defence had an excellent witness. Evans had taken a liking to Hanratty when the latter had stayed in his house the previous summer, and was convinced from the outset, as he is convinced today, that Hanratty could not have committed the A6 murder.

In cross-examination, the prosecution tried to establish two main points from Evans: first, that his house resembled the boarding house described by Hanratty, and that the latter was remembering details of Evans's house when describing the boarding house. Secondly, that Hanratty had no reason to visit Evans with stolen jewellery.

Evans mocked the first prosecution suggestion. The bath in his council house, he said, was not green but blue. There was no attic. There was no coat rack – just hooks in the hall. When Mr Swanwick suggested that the grey-haired landlady in Hanratty's story could have been Evans's mother, Evans replied that his mother never came to his house at night, and had never met Hanratty. As for the trains, Evans doubted whether they could be heard from his house.

On the second point, there was an important question which still worries Evans today:

Q. Had Hanratty any reason at all to think you would be the sort of person who would be interested in disposing of stolen property? A. No, I should not think so.

In several interviews with me and with others, Evans has expressed his concern about this answer, and has explained how he tried, without success, to make a further statement to the court putting it right. While it was true, he explains, that Hanratty had no reason to think that Evans *himself* might dispose of stolen property, he had every reason to believe that Evans could *put him in touch* with people in Rhyl who dealt in stolen property. In the course of the long conversation which he, Hanratty and three other friends had that night in July, Evans, who deals in scrap metal, had talked about the market for stolen goods in Rhyl. Thus, while his answer to Swanwick was strictly correct, the main point confirming Hanratty's story was not presented to the jury.

As Evans put it himself on the B.B.C.'s Panorama programme in November 1966:

All they allow you to say in these courts is yes or no. What I wanted to say was that the evening he stayed in my house, I was talking with Hanratty and three other chaps about everyday affairs, what we do and what we don't do, and I did tell him, because I did know a chap, I told him at the time that I knew a fellow who would buy stolen property. I wouldn't say so in the courts; I couldn't say what I wanted to say. I had to say yes or no. I had to say No because I wouldn't buy stolen property myself. But I did know a chap who would buy it.

There was yet another, even more crucial, fact which was not extracted from Evans by either counsel, largely because, with so little time to spare it had been impossible for Mr Kleinman to interview him properly. Evans agreed that he drove a black taxi. But he was not asked why the black taxi was not seen by Hanratty near the fairground in the place where it had been kept in July.

Hanratty had said that he had gone to the fairground to look for the taxi, but could not find it. Why? If asked, Evans would have answered that on the weekend of August 19th–20th, he stopped working at the café by the fairground, and no longer drove his taxi up to the front from that day. Up to that weekend the taxi was in its usual place on the front. After August 20th, Evans kept it at home.

Evans was followed into the witness box by Mr Webber, the fairground manager, who testified that Hanratty had worked there for an evening on July 25th, 1961. Webber was then followed by the landlady, Mrs Jones, whose evidence dominated the rest of the defence case.

Mrs Jones can have had no idea of the ordeal which was in store for her when she agreed to travel to Bedford. On Thursday (February 8th) she had sat all afternoon in the court foyer. At about 11 a.m. on the following morning, she took the witness stand for the first time.

At first, when she was examined by Mr Sherrard, things were easy. She described her house, all the details of which fitted Hanratty's description: the trains could be heard but not seen; there was a plant and a coat rack in the hall; the rate for a night's stay was twelve-and-six. Then she identified Hanratty:

Q. Do you see anyone in court who you think you can recognize, so far as that photograph is concerned, first of all? Look right round the court.
A. There he is, there [witness points to dock].
Q. Where did you see him, do you think?
A. Well, I feel as if I have seen him at our house.
Q. Can you tell my Lord and the jury which month it was you think that this happened, that you saw him in your house?
A. Well, it was between the week of 19th August to the 26th August.
Q. Which year?
A. Last year. (Vol. XV, p. 16.)

At the end of her short examination by Mr Sherrard, Mr Swanwick asked if he could postpone his examination until after lunch. As Mrs Jones came out of the courtroom, she met Terry Evans, whom she had met on the way down from Rhyl. The judge had told her not to talk to anyone about the case, but she was lonely and welcomed Mr Evans with a smile. Terry Evans asked her if she had recognized Hanratty in the court. The conversation was repeated the following Monday in court by Terry Evans, who insisted on giving it in full:

A. When Mrs Jones came out of the back room, I asked her if she recognized Mr Hanratty and she said: 'I am almost sure.' So I said, 'Well, I suppose the reason you might not have recognized him straight away was the colour of his hair.' So then I asked Mrs Jones what was the colour of his hair when she was supposed to have known him and Mrs Jones said it was dark brown.

Q. Is that all?

A. No. So I said, 'Well it is most probably right, because his hair was dark brown.' (Vol. XVI, p. 6.)

On returning to give evidence after lunch, Mrs Jones was severely rebuked for speaking to Terry Evans. Before long she was in a state of near collapse. From the outset, Mr Swanwick set out to discredit Mrs Jones, and show her up in the unlikely colours of liar and publicity hound. 'A little publicity for Ingledene would not come amiss, would it?' asked Mr Swanwick. Mrs Jones replied: 'Oh, I do not want publicity for Ingledene.' Mrs Jones had recognized the man in the photograph before the A6 murder or the Bedford court was ever mentioned. The suggestion that she travelled to Bedford in order to get publicity for her boarding house was absurd. But Mr Swanwick could improve even on that.

Mrs Jones told him that she kept two books, one a record of visitors, and one in which visitors could sign if they wanted to. Referring to this second, small book, Mr Swanwick asked:

Q. Have you brought that one with you?

A. No.

Q. Why not?

A. Well, I didn't think it had anything to do with visitors ...

Three sentences later, Mr Swanwick produced the book from his desk and showed it to Mrs Jones, asking, 'Is that your visitors' book, which you did not bring?'

Mrs Jones answered: 'Yes, that is it.'

This was too much for the judge, who exploded in some anger:

MR JUSTICE GORMAN. I thought you asked this lady if she had brought it.

MR SWANWICK. I did my Lord.

MR JUSTICE GORMAN. But you had it.

MR SWANWICK. My Lord, this was obtained after this lady ...

MR JUSTICE GORMAN. But you asked this lady if she had brought it and all the time you had it.

MR SWANWICK. I did my Lord.

MR JUSTICE GORMAN. So she could not very well have brought it. (Vol. XV, p. 40.)

Mr Swanwick continued questioning Mrs Jones about her two books in order to show that, from the books, Hanratty could well have visited the boarding house any week *after* August 26th. One of the visitors' books had been broken. The pages were loose, and Mrs Jones shuffled helplessly through them under the stern eye of Mr Swanwick. Once, Mr Swanwick went too far:

Q. It would not be quite right, would it, to say that when you were shown the photograph, you recognized it?

A. Well, no.

Mr Swanwick should have left it there, but he was too eager for overkill:

Q. It would not. Then why did you say it in answer to my learned friend when you were asked?

A. Well, *he had different colour hair to begin with.*

Q. What?

A. *If he had had dark brown hair, I would have known him straightaway.* (My italics.)

Still Mr Swanwick could not leave the point:

Q. Why did you say this morning in court, when you were first asked about being shown the photograph and asked about when you were first shown the photograph — why did you say: 'I recognize him' when in fact what happened was that you said you could not remember whether you had seen the person or not.

A. No, I got muddled — the hair. *He had not got that coloured hair when he was in our house.* (Vol. XV, p. 46, my italics.)

Thanks to Mr Swanwick's enthusiasm the jury now knew that

the man who had been in Mrs Jones's house looked like the accused with dark hair – or, in other words, looked exactly like Hanratty looked at the time of the A6 murder.

Under pressure of cross-examination, Mrs Jones agreed that she could not be certain of the week in which the young man had come to her door. But her ordeal was not over yet. Over the weekend the police raided Ingledene again and found yet another book, which had not been mentioned in the courtroom. The book gave details of the people staying in the hotel during the murder week, and also disclosed that there were two more rooms to let – rooms not mentioned in the other books. When Mrs Jones reappeared for further cross-examination on the Monday, February 12th, she was confronted with the fact, which she admitted, that she had lied about her books, claiming there were only two. There then followed a long period of cross-examination in which Mr Swanwick sought to 'fill' the boarding house in the week of August 19th–26th the previous year.

The book disclosed that there were, in all, six bedrooms in the boarding house, four of which were to let. Four of these bedrooms were on the first floor, Nos. 1, 2, 4 and 6. Nos. 3 and 5 were on the second floor. No. 2 was occupied by Mr and Mrs Jones, and, in high season when all the other rooms were full, their son Gwyn doubled with them. No. 5 was usually occupied by Mrs Jones's daughter, Brenda Harris, then in her mid-thirties. The books showed that three of the other rooms were filled, and the prosecution called three witnesses in rebuttal of Mrs Jones's evidence.

Mr Thomas Williams, a welder from Denton, Manchester, was a regular visitor to Ingledene in the summer, and from August 19th–26th he had stayed there with his wife and seven-year-old daughter. They had occupied the room above the dining room in the front of the house – No. 6. Mr Williams told the court that in the large room behind him on the first floor there was a large family (mother, father and three children); in a room upstairs there was a Yorkshire couple and an elderly lady (the mother of one of the couple). Apart from that, he could not place the residents in the rooms. He could not say whether the large family and the Yorkshire couple were there all the time he was there and he agreed with Mr Sherrard that 'there were some cancellations and plenty of comings and goings at the house' while he was there. Mr Williams said he had not seen Hanratty in the house during that week.

Mr Douglas Such, an electrician from Studley in Warwickshire, said that he, his wife and his three-year-old son had been in Ingledene from Saturday August 19th to the morning of Wednesday August 23rd, when they had left. He, too, after momentary hesitation, decided in court that he had not seen Hanratty at Ingledene. Mr Such gave a detailed description of who was sitting at the breakfast table on the 'first day' he was there (the Sunday), and he too agreed that there were a number of cancellations and comings and goings over the weekend. He too mentioned a Yorkshire couple and an elderly lady, who, he was sure, had been in the boarding house all the time that he had been there. Mr Such was not so sure about the large family (mother, father, three children) which he also mentioned:

Q. Was the Yorkshire couple there all the time that you were there?
A. Yes.
Q. And the couple with the three or four children or the two or three children?
A. *I cannot be absolutely sure about that.*
Q. Have you any recollection? Can you help us about that? I know it is difficult.
A. I would not like to give an opinion. (Vol. XVII, p. 8, my italics.)

Mr Swanwick was anxious for a commitment here. He knew that if the large family had left before Mr Such left, it would not have been there when Hanratty said he was there. Mr Such also said he had not seen Hanratty in the house, though he had left on the morning after Hanratty said he arrived.

The most impressive witness from the prosecution point of view was Mr Joseph Sayle, a National Union of Railwaymen official from Liverpool, who had been in Rhyl on a recruitment drive on the relevant week and had stayed at Ingledene from August 21st to 24th, in room No. 4, the small front room on the first floor. Mr Sayle had not seen Hanratty, though his memory of the other Ingledene guests was vague. He too remembered the Yorkshire couple with the elderly lady who had been there throughout his stay. He also remembered that 'The family on the left, close to the wall, was a family of a man and wife and I think two children.' Those were also there throughout his stay, 'as far as I can remember'.

Mr Williams and Mr Such mentioned a large family, but neither could be certain that this family was in the house for either of the two crucial nights. Mr Sayle did not remember a large family. He remembered a family with ('I think') two children, which could well have been the Williamses with one child. The situation was as follows:

Room 1. Mr and Mrs Such and son (for the Tuesday night).
Room 2. Mr and Mrs Jones and son (Tuesday and Wednesday nights).
Room 3. The Yorkshire couple plus mother (both nights).
Room 4. Mr Sayle (both nights).
Room 5. Brenda Harris, and, possibly, a friend called Joan who used to double up with Brenda on dance nights in Rhyl.
Room 6. Mr and Mrs Williams and daughter (both nights).

This was the very satisfactory case for the prosecution which was put by Mr Swanwick to Mrs Jones to show that James Hanratty could not have stayed in Ingledene on the nights he said he did. Mrs Jones, however, had an answer for it:

Q. All I am asking you at the moment is was there more than one single gentleman that week? According to what you have told us already, there would not be room for more than one?
A. There would have been room for one in that attic if Joan slept with my daughter.
Q. In the attic; that means in the bathroom.
A. Yes.
Q. You told us that the bathroom was kept only for the family?
A. Yes, but there are some — they come to the door and they cannot get anywhere and we show them the bathroom and say: 'We have only the bathroom to let'; we show it to them, and, if they agree to take it, well it is up to them to take it. We do not press them to take it. (Vol. XVI, pp. 51, 52.)

Mr Swanwick quickly veered off the question of the bathroom, and did not mention it again until his summing up. No doubt the question was nagging his mind, for he exaggerated what he had proved in the section on the boarding house:

Large front room, the Williams; small front room, No. 4, Mr Sayle; large room behind the Williams, a man and wife and three or four children of whom at least two of the witnesses spoke ... Then there is the large back room past the toilet, the

Such family. That is the first floor filled. One room upstairs is occupied by the Yorkshire couple and their mother, whom at least two of the witnesses remember, leaving for Mr and Mrs Jones, the daughter and the son, nothing on the first floor and on the second floor one bedroom and the bed in the bathroom. (Vol. XIX, p. 7.)

This was wrong. The large family with three or four children had been mentioned by only two witnesses, both of whom were vague as to what nights it had stayed. No members of the large family were produced in court. Mr Such specifically refused to say that the large family had been there throughout the time he was there—and he left on the Wednesday. Mr Swanwick, once more, had indulged in overkill. It was fair to include the Yorkshire couple, as all the witnesses had remembered them as staying there throughout, but unfair to include the large family. Without the large family, however, Mr Swanwick was left with the nagging possibility that, in spite of all the witnesses, Hanratty could have stayed in the bed next to the green bath in the attic.

There were a number of features which appeared to support the thesis that if Hanratty did stay in Mrs Jones's house, he stayed at least one night in the attic with the green bath. The room with the green bath was (and is) marked PRIVATE. Mr Williams, who had visited Ingledene for week-long stays at least twice before 1961, said in evidence that he had never seen the green bath in the attic. Neither had the other guests. The bath is not visible from the outside of the room even if the door is open. Mrs Jones was, in the first instance, embarrassed about the fact that the bed was there at all:

Q. Has the bathroom got anything in it besides a bath?
A. Do I have to answer that?
Q. Well, I hope you will, Madam.
MR JUSTICE GORMAN. Yes, you must answer.
A. Well, there is a bed in—there is a bed in the room. (Vol. XV, p. 38.)

Mrs Jones's shyness was not surprising. The regulations about hotels and boarding houses do not normally allow guests to sleep in bathrooms. This was, no doubt, why the room was marked Private, and why anyone who slept in it was not registered. It was why guests in the bathroom were given breakfast in the back room, and asked to make themselves scarce of the other customers, especially the regular guests.

Then there was the description which Mrs Jones had given of the circumstances in which the bathroom would be offered to guests: when they came in desperation, perhaps late at night, looking for somewhere to spend the night without much hope of finding anywhere else. These were circumstances which exactly fitted those given by Hanratty.

Finally, perhaps most convincingly, there is the critical telephone call from Gillbanks to the defence, on February 7th, recording the first impressions of Mrs Jones. 'She can't be certain when, and in which room, Hanratty stayed. *She said it might have been the attic bedroom* since, during the latter part of August 1961, she did take a number of people for bed and breakfast.' (My italics.)

There remains, however, one major difficulty. Hanratty himself did not say he slept in the same room as the bath. The section of his evidence relating to the room he slept in reads as follows:

Q. Can you remember where you slept there, if you slept there that night?

A. Yes, I can remember quite plain.

Q. Where was the room? How did you get to the room?

A. I went up a flight of stairs and it was on the second floor and it was a back room.

Q. When you say 'the second floor' tell my Lord and the jury how many flights of stairs, if any, you go up. If you cannot remember, then say so.

A. I am not quite sure because I have been in so many boarding houses and you get confused with – I do not want to make such a serious ...

Q. That is quite right.

(A little later.)

HANRATTY. Well it was dark when I eventually entered the house and I did not draw the curtains because it was a back room. I did not bother to draw the curtains. (Vol. XIII, pp. 15, 16.)

There were no curtains in the attic bedroom. The only other description given by Hanratty of the room was to his lawyers before the trial. In the initial scribbled notes of Hanratty's first statement about the Rhyl boarding house, there occurs the sentence: 'In bedroom was a small sink.' There was, however, no sink in the attic bedroom. Even accepting Hanratty's own doubt about detail, and his references to all the other hotels he had stayed in, this does throw some doubt on the suggestion that Hanratty slept in the attic bedroom.

There is, however, a clue to another possibility. In the lawyer's notes, scribbled on a rough piece of paper while Hanratty talked in his cell about his visit to Rhyl, there occurs this passage: 'Left little leather hyde case. Landlady about 50 like my mother. I was wearing the double-breasted striped suit. Said could I leave my case, I will pick it up later.'

If Hanratty booked in at Ingledene and settled down for the night, why would he leave his case? If he had booked in and gone out for a drink or a meal, why would he say he would 'pick the case up later'? One explanation would be as follows: On arrival at Mrs Jones's he was told that the only room available that night was the attic (or even a sofa in one of the ground-floor rooms) but that, due to Mr Such's cancellation, there was a room for the following night. Hanratty then asked if he could leave his case while he searched for something better, and, after a fruitless search in the surrounding streets, he returned, slept in the attic or on a sofa; and the next day, he took Mr Such's room (No. 1) when the latter left early in the morning. His description of the room he stayed in fits Mr Such's room almost exactly.

There are, in short, three alternatives, none of which are excluded by the evidence produced at the trial and since. First, Hanratty could have stayed two nights in the attic bedroom with the green bath. Secondly, he could have stayed in Brenda Harris's room (Brenda Harris, as was the family's custom in the high season, having moved into the attic). Thirdly, he could have spent one night in the attic, or on a sofa, and the second night in No. 1.

When I interviewed Mrs Jones and Mrs Harris in April 1970, they seemed sure that the man they thought was Hanratty had stayed in the attic bedroom. They did say that Mr and Mrs Jones would not have slept downstairs, but they did not deny that from time to time other members of the family would sleep downstairs, especially Mrs Jones's son Gwyn. Mr Thomas Williams, who still lives in West Park Avenue, Denton, Manchester, thinks that there was someone sleeping downstairs when the house became full during the week he stayed there.

Having 'proved' without the necessary proof that Hanratty could not have stayed in Ingledene that night, Mr Swanwick went on to make a number of points to indicate that Hanratty could not have been in the boarding house. First, he said, Hanratty could not describe any of the other guests, although he must, if he had stayed there, have had breakfast with them. Secondly, he had described a breakfast-room with two tables, while the main breakfast-room had five tables. Thirdly, he had had 'neither sight nor sound' of children.

There were proved to be only two children staying in Ingledene on August 21st and 22nd – Mr and Mrs Such's little boy, and Mr and Mrs Williams's seven-year-old daughter. The Suches left on the morning after Hanratty arrived.

On Hanratty's own testimony, he spent only one full day in Rhyl. The rules of the boarding house insist that guests leave the rooms by day, returning only at night. The only time when Hanratty could have seen the other guests was at breakfast, and, as we shall see later, there is evidence that he did not have breakfast in the main dining-room.

Finally, the people in the boarding house most likely to have seen Hanratty, if he did stay in the attic, were not the Williamses who stayed on the floor below, or Mr Sayle, who, on his own admission, was out on union business from dawn to dusk, but the Yorkshire couple on the upper floor, who were not produced.

There was one further point upon which Mr Swanwick stumbled, not so much through his own enthusiasm as through the hurry with which inquiries, including prosecution inquiries, had to be made:

> Most significant of all, three doors away, just three doors away, from this boarding house at which he arrived at night, or when it was dark, there is a betting shop, which had been there since July, with a jockey and whip sign outside it illuminated at night. Does he [Hanratty] really suggest to you, and can you really believe, that somebody who had stayed in that boarding house for two nights would not have been able to say: 'Ah, now there is one thing I can remember: the jockey and whip sign illuminated outside'? (Vol. XIX, p. 4.)

It was true that the betting shop had been opened in July. But the sign was not there when the betting shop opened. It was put up several weeks after the shop was opened. When I interviewed the shop manager, Mr Raymond Corbett, in April 1970, he told me, 'The shop opened in mid-July. I took over from my father on August 4th. The sign went up some weeks after I arrived. It must have gone up some time near the time Hanratty says he was here. I've often wondered if the sign *was* up at that time, but I haven't been able to find out.'

Not a trace of this doubt is reflected by Mr Swanwick, who implied but did not prove that the sign was up on August 22nd.

There is no doubt that a long and considered view of Mrs Jones's evidence in connection with Hanratty's, particularly if her own suggestion that Hanratty might have stayed in the bathroom was taken seriously, hardly led to the conclusion drawn by Mr Swanwick that 'the alibi is proved false and another lie is nailed'. Yet the jury reached that conclusion, partly because Mrs Jones's evidence was unsupported, partly because of her wretched performance with her books, partly because of Hanratty's change of alibi, partly because of the appearance of three guests in the boarding house in the same week who were adamant that they had not seen Hanratty there. Almost all of these objections to Mrs Jones's original statements could have been avoided if the defence had had time to validate Hanratty's Rhyl statement and had not been forced to rely on resources of inquiry miserably smaller than the prosecution (which had every policeman in the country at its beck and call). The Rhyl alibi was supported at the trial only by Mrs Jones whom the prosecution managed to discredit. As was rapidly becoming clear, a few weeks of inquiry would have produced several other witnesses at least as credible, if not more so, than Mrs Jones. Even before the trial had ended, the suggestion that Hanratty was in Rhyl had provoked a spontaneous reaction among several Rhyl citizens.

Coming home from work on the evening of Wednesday, February 7th, Mrs Margaret Walker, who lives in the narrow South Kinmel Street, which runs off Kinmel Street, saw a small crowd gathered in Kinmel Street. Mrs Jones, she understood, was going to Bedford to give evidence at the A6 trial. The reason was that she had put up a young man who looked like a photograph of James Hanratty for two nights last August. Much against the wishes of her husband, who begged her not to get involved, Mrs Walker went the next day to Rhyl police station and made a statement.

Two days later, the police station at Abergele, a small town near

Rhyl, received a telephone call from a chicken farmer of Kinmel Bay, near Rhyl, called Trevor Dutton. They went to his home and took a statement, which, like Mrs Walker's, is not available. At least six other people made voluntary statements to the Rhyl police during the next few days which had some relevance to Hanratty's claims of an alibi. In one way or another, these names were handed over to the defence. There is no way of telling how long a gap there was between the making of the statements and their transmission to the defence representatives, but, because of the pressure on the defence at Bedford, not all of them were followed up.

While Mr Gillbanks was away at the trial at Bedford his assistant, Mr Frank Evans, managed to get round to see many of these witnesses, including Mrs Walker, but for one reason or another, chief among which was that the trial had only a few days to run, he did not influence the defence to call them at the trial. Mrs Walker remembers asking if she would be needed at the trial, and being told: 'Oh, no, I don't think that will be necessary.' I interviewed Mr Frank Evans in his home in Rhyl on February 1st, 1967. He described to me some of his interviews at the time, and I quoted him in the 'Mandrake' column of the *Sunday Telegraph* (where I was then working):

'We went to see three girls up the road who had met Hanratty in a cafe. They spoke very well of him' says Evans.

'Then there was an old lady in River Street. She seemed fairly clear about the date when Hanratty called at her house looking for digs, but her son kept telling her that she couldn't be certain, and she didn't want to be involved. We saw some other landladies and a landlord of a pub.

'Most of them said that they had made a statement to the police and they didn't want to say any more.

'I can't remember very much about it, now, but I do remember that almost everyone we saw said they'd seen the man on a Tuesday, Tuesday, Tuesday — it was always a Tuesday. The trouble was we couldn't find anyone definitely who could remember *which* Tuesday.'

Evans remembered that he and Gillbanks had seen Mrs Walker separately towards the end of the trial, but he thinks that she was not completely clear about the date of the man's visit. (*Sunday Telegraph*, February 5th, 1967.)

All this took place, as far as the public or the jury were concerned, in conditions of almost total secrecy and frantic haste. While trying to conduct the case for the defence in court throughout the day, Mr Sherrard and Mr Kleinman had to interpret the telephone calls from Evans and Gillbanks at Rhyl and decide whether or not to call new witnesses to establish the Rhyl alibi. It was an intolerable situation for any lawyer, and Mr Sherrard eventually decided that the alibi would have to stand or fall on the evidence of Mrs Jones and of Terry Evans.

After Mrs Jones and Terry Evans had given evidence, and probably after Mr Sherrard had finished his closing speech for the defence, news of yet another witness substantiating the Rhyl alibi filtered through.

On the Sunday before the trial ended (February 11th) the Sunday newspapers carried large pictures of Mrs Jones. These pictures attracted the attention of a taxi driver in Staines called Christopher Larman.

Mr Larman was lodging at that time in the house of Mr and Mrs Jack Dyos of Beehive Road, Staines. Mr Dyos, whom I interviewed in September 1968, recalls how Mr Larman immediately started talking about the picture in the *Sunday Times* of Mrs Jones and how the young man now standing trial may well have been a young man he had met in Rhyl the previous August.

So worried was he about this that he went the following day – Monday, February 12th – to the Staines police station and made a statement to Detective Inspector Robert Fields, then chief of Staines C.I.D. I interviewed Mr Fields on September 25th, 1968, when he was head of security at Shepperton film studios at Chertsey. He told me: 'I realized the urgency of the matter because the trial was on, so the following day I sent a message by telephone to Superintendent Acott at Bedford saying that the statement had been made to me.'

Mr Fields of course cannot remember what time of day he sent the urgent message to Mr Acott at Bedford. But it almost certainly arrived too late. For at about 11 that Tuesday morning, Mr Sherrard rose to sum up his case for the defence. He was followed by Mr Swanwick's final speech, the long summing up by the judge and, finally, the verdict. There is nothing in the defence papers to indicate when Mr Acott or his representative gave Mr Larman's name to the defence, or whether there was time, even at that late stage, to consider bending the trial rules to call Mr Larman to the witness box. The only reference to Larman in the papers is a signed statement he made to Mr Michael Oliver of Smellie and Co., a firm of inquiry agents in London employed by the defence after the trial to follow up information which came to their attention. Larman's statement to Oliver is dated February 21st – the Wednesday after the trial ended. Christopher Larman, whom I interviewed on September 21st, 1968, says that he was summoned to the Strand offices of Smellie and Co., where he was shown a sheaf of a dozen photographs, from which he immediately picked out one of Hanratty. (This did not prove very much, since Hanratty's picture by that time had been sprinkled all over the press, though on seeing Hanratty's picture in the papers, Mr Karman was all the more certain that he had seen him in Rhyl.)

The statement which Mr Larman gave Mr Oliver read as follows:

On Sunday, 18th February, 1962, I saw photographs of James Hanratty, and I immediately remembered that I had seen him before and also the occasion where and when I had.

It was on the 22nd August 1961, at the junction of Kemmel [the usual pronunciation of Kinmel] Street, Rhyl and Bodford [presumably Bodfor] Street, Rhyl, at about 7.30 p.m., that this man stopped me and asked me where he could obtain bed and breakfast. I took him by the arm, and turned him round and directed him to the Windsor Hotel, which we could see from where we were standing, telling him that a guest house right opposite to this hotel would be able to help. It was, in fact, the guest house owned and run by Mrs Jones of Kemmel Street, Rhyl.

He left me and went off in the direction I had pointed. I particularly remember this man because of his hair which was most outstanding being bronze and dark in parts. He was a shade taller than me, about 5 ft. 7 ins., dressed in a dark suit, neat and tidy. He spoke with a London accent.

Mr Larman was able to identify the date of this encounter as August 22nd, 1961, for on that evening he was on a round of Rhyl public houses bidding goodbye to friends in Rhyl before leaving the town the following day. The previous day, he remembered, he had drawn money from a Post Office savings bank for the purpose of the pub crawl, and the Post Office savings book with the relevant entry was made available to Mr Oliver.

To reassure himself that he was not wrong in the matter, Larman made notes in an old 1960 diary at the time, which he kept. On the flyleaf of the diary are written the following notes:

Left Perry Jones, Ltd, Towers Estate, Vale Road, Rhyl on 23rd June, 1961.
Restarted work at H. Davies, Crescent Road, Rhyl, on June 28, 1961.
Left H. Davies on August Saturday 19th, 1961.
Left for London on August 23rd, 1961.
Restarted work on cab for Coop and Sons on August 29, 1961

This certainty about dates and the description of the young man's hair added up to substantial support for Hanratty's story, more of which poured into Mr Kleinman's office after the trial.

As far as the general public were concerned, however, the only witness for Hanratty's alibi was still Mrs Jones, The only indication that there were stirrings in Rhyl and elsewhere of more people who might substantiate the alibi was a short article in the *Daily Sketch* on the Monday morning after the (Saturday) conviction:

RING THIS NUMBER

A Rhyl householder who saw the first published pictures of James Hanratty in yesterday's newspaper has offered evidence which might support the condemned man's alibi. Defence solicitor, Mr Emmanuel Kleinman, when told by the *Daily Sketch* of the offer last night, said: 'Immediate steps will be taken to verify the information.' (*Daily Sketch*, February 19th.)

The *Daily Sketch* reporter had telephoned the defence with the news from Rhyl which he had uncovered, and, although it was a Sunday, Mr Kleinman rang Gillbanks and asked him to follow the information through. The 'Rhyl householder' in the story was Mrs Margaret Walker, and Gillbanks travelled hotfoot to Rhyl to speak to her again. The next day, Monday, February 19th, he was able to write again to Kleinman enclosing statements from Mrs Walker and from a householder in the same street, a Mrs Ivy Vincent. Mrs Walker's statement read, in full:

I am a married woman and reside with my husband and

18. Carol France and Mrs Charlotte France

19. Charles (Dixie) France

20. (*above left*) Michael Sherrard
(right) outside the Bedford Court

21. (*left*) Detective Supt
Douglas Nimmo

22. (*above right*) Terry Evans

23. (*right*) Mrs Grace Jones

24. (*above*) The sweet shop in Scotland Road, Liverpool

25. (*left*) Ingledene, Kinmel Street, Rhyl

26. (*above right*) Mrs Betty Davies

27. (*right*) Charles Jones

28. (*above far right*) Mrs Ivy Vincent

29. (*far right*) Christopher Larman

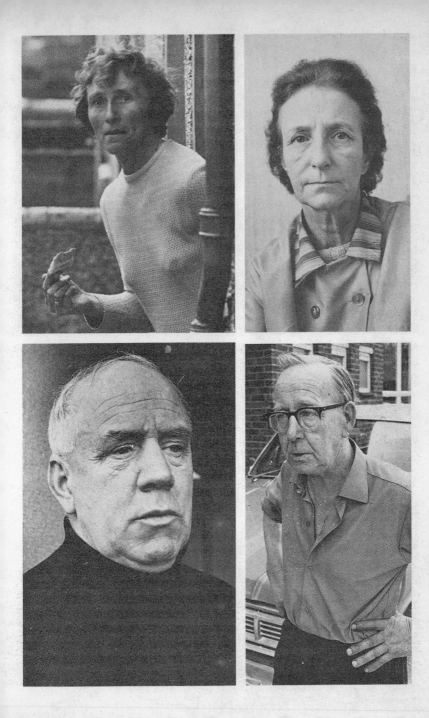

30. (*above*) A6 Committee's delegation to
Rhyl, May 1968
Front: Michael Hanratty, Mr and Mrs
Hanratty
Back: Trevor Dutton, Author, Jean
Justice, Jeremy Fox

31. (*left*) Mr Hanratty outside the House
of Commons

32. (*above right*) Michael Fogarty-Waul

33. (*right*) Jean Justice

34. James Hanratty

35. Peter Alphon with his mother

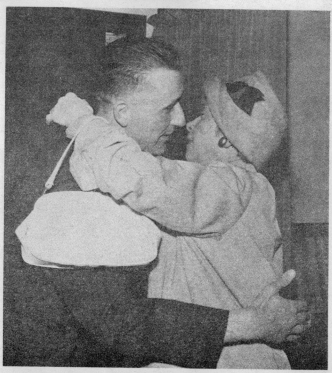

family at 12 South Kinmel Street, Rhyl. The third week in August last, on the Tuesday evening about half past seven, I was standing at my front gate when a young man came up the street. He asked me if I could put him up for a couple of nights for Bed and Breakfast. I told him I could not and sent him over to No. 23 to see if he could be put up there.

The man was about 24/27 years, neatly dressed in a dark suit, his hair was dark and brushed back, but there was something not quite natural about it, as though it was streaky or tacky. I have seen photographs of James Hanratty in the weekend papers and they are very much like the young man, but I don't want to commit myself.

The photographs you have shown me are very like the man who called here, but the hair was dark. Mind, I couldn't swear it was him.

It was definitely the Tuesday before 25th August because I had some personal news of something that was to happen on the Friday. It did happen, and I don't want to say what it was.

(signed) MARGARET WALKER

The second statement was from Mrs Ivy Vincent, who lived with her family at No. 23 South Kinmel Street, Rhyl:

I remember about the third week in August Mrs Walker was talking to a young man at her gate. He went from her to another door and then came to me. He asked if I had any vacancies, and I said, No, I was sorry. He wanted bed and breakfast for two nights. I told him to go further up and if he was not successful to try the houses in Kinmel Street at the back of me. I have seen the pictures of James Hanratty in the *Sunday Pictorial* and I seem to recognise his face.

Hanratty, it will be remembered, had said in evidence that he had made several inquiries at houses before he had managed to get put up at the boarding house in which he said he stayed. These statements, particularly Mrs Walker's, seemed to back up his statement. Mrs Walker was unsure about identification (hardly the reaction of a woman who was making up a cock-and-bull story for publicity) but her reason for being unsure was the same as Mrs Jones's in the Bedford courtroom: the colour of the man's hair. 'The photographs', she said, 'are very like the man who called here, *but his hair was dark.*' (My italics.)

The most important aspect of Mrs Walker's statement was her certainty about the date. She was *certain* about the date because of a disaster in her family which was to occur on August 25th, a Friday, a disaster which did in the event take place, and she remembered the evening very well as being the Tuesday before that Friday — the Tuesday of the A6 murder — because her son always visited her on Tuesdays. On this occasion she had been discussing the family tragedy with her son, and had just bidden her son goodbye when the young man had appeared.

Finally, there was Mrs Walker's description of the young man's hair — 'not quite natural, as though it was streaky or tacky'. Hanratty's hair, it will be remembered, had been dyed dark on August 5th, and on August 26th, the Saturday, he had had it dyed again because the dye was beginning to wear off. Mrs Walker's description of the young man's hair, given six months after the event, exactly fitted the state of Hanratty's hair on the evening of the A6 murder.

On February 22nd, Kleinman wrote again to Gillbanks. 'We feel that no stone should be left unturned and Mr Sherrard feels it would be worthwhile for you to return to Rhyl to ascertain whether any other persons may have seen our client on the 22/23 August, possibly people on Amusement Arcades, any personnel at the Coach Terminus or the barbers where Hanratty said he had a shave.' Kleinman also asked Gillbanks to visit Mrs Walker and Mrs Vincent again and ask them a number of other details about the young man.

Gillbanks had no luck at the amusement arcades, the barbers, or the coach terminus. Neither housewife could provide any more hard information about the young man. There was, however, one interesting point about time. 'Mrs Walker', wrote Gillbanks in his letter dated February 25th, 'fixes the time owing to her domestic arrangements and *because it was getting dark and the street lamps were lit*.' (My italics.) Sunset in August 1961 in Rhyl, as Gillbanks's letter also stated, was shortly after 8.30 p.m.

Unknown to Gillbanks, however, the publication of Hanratty's photograph in the press had had further repercussions in Rhyl. Terry Evans was approached, twice in the week following the publication, by two people in Rhyl who said that a young man who looked very like Hanratty had been asking for him (Evans) the previous summer. The first was a Mr Ernie Gordon who was then the manager of Dixie's café near the fairground – the café where Evans and Hanratty had eaten meals the previous July, and where Hanratty said in court he had asked for Terry Evans on August 23rd. 'That fellow', said Gordon to Evans (according to Evans) 'was looking for you last summer.' Similarly, a newspaper seller called Charlie Jones, sometimes known as Charlie White, who has a stall outside the bus station in the centre of the town, approached Evans with the information that he had spoken to a young man who had asked for 'John' on the fairground some time the previous August.

There was one other important reaction to the publication of Hanratty's photograph. A young actor called Michael Da Costa was sitting in the turkish baths in Russell Square reading his Sunday papers when suddenly he exclaimed to everyone there that he had seen the man's face before. He could not, he said, remember where, but two days later he read a cutting in one of the papers about Hanratty's claim to have travelled on the day before the murder from Euston to Liverpool; checking his diary, Da Costa discovered that he had travelled from Euston to Northampton to visit his mother on the morning of August 22nd, and he then remembered that he had seen a man looking exactly like Hanratty at Euston station that morning. He phoned the defence, and on February 20th he made a statement to Mr Oliver.

'I clearly remembered', he said, 'that I had seen Hanratty on Euston station on that date [August 22nd] either at the paper stall or in the refreshment buffet off the main hall. I distinctly remember him, as, being an actor myself, I noticed his hair looked dyed and I thought it was a wig. Also at the time I was in a part that portrayed just what this man looked like, and because of this I took particular note of him.'

Da Costa made a further, more detailed statement to the defence on February 26th, which contained a number of details about the man's clothing which did not fit Hanratty's (for instance, he said his jacket was single-breasted, while Hanratty's was double-breasted). But the second statement made it clear that he was not sure on detail: 'I know I know his face ... I'm worried about going to court. I remember faces but not details.' The second statement also made it clear that Mr Da Costa was very anxious to avoid publicity in the case.

By March 1st, Mr Kleinman had prepared his brief for Mr

Sherrard to appear on behalf of Hanratty on his appeal. The brief included the statements of Mrs Walker, Mrs Vincent, Mr Larman and the two statements of Mr Da Costa. A tantalizing decision now confronted Mr Sherrard: should he seek powers to introduce these witnesses as fresh evidence before the Court of Criminal Appeal?

There can be no doubt that both lawyers seriously considered the question of producing the new witnesses at the Court of Appeal. On March 10th – two days before the appeal was heard – Hanratty wrote to his mother from Bedford prison:

Dear Mum,

Thank you for your lovely letter which I received today. It cheered me up a great deal and I'm looking forward to the appeal ... I am a little bit concerned in the way that this appeal will be carried out and I feel if a mistake is made on my behalf presented by Mr Sherrard it would make matters very difficult for me. I am very worried at this stage, as Mr Kleinman says he is calling further witnesses and I do not know what really lies behind this case, but they have great faith as well as myself and that is all that matters ...

The appeal was heard on March 12th and 13th. No application was made by the defence to submit to the Court any of the new statements which they had acquired about Hanratty's claimed alibi at Rhyl. Mr Sherrard relied entirely on submissions that the judge had misdirected the jury. Mr Justice Gorman's summing up, however, despite minor errors of emphasis and one or two small errors of fact, was a masterpiece of impartiality. Lord Parker took only twenty-five minutes to dismiss Mr Sherrard's submissions and the execution date for Hanratty was set for April 4th.

The following day, Mr Kleinman spoke to the press:

Mr Kleinman said yesterday that fresh evidence had arisen since Hanratty's trial. 'We have taken', he said, 'some statements which we could not very well put before the Court of Criminal Appeal. It is information which we, as defence lawyers, feel the Home Secretary should have before considering a reprieve.' (*Daily Telegraph*, March 15th, 1962.)

On March 15th, Mr Kleinman wrote a letter to Mr R. A. Butler, the Home Secretary: 'I am advised to place before you for your consideration all statements which were taken since the hearing of the above's trial at Bedford together with the relevant correspondence.'

The statements, all of which the Home Secretary had in his possession some three weeks before Hanratty was executed, included those of Mrs Walker, Mrs Vincent and Mr Larman. In those three weeks no inquiry was made by policemen or Home Office personnel of these three people to see whether their testimony could substantiate the alibi. In Fenton Bresler's book, *Reprieve,** a detailed study of the Home Secretary's prerogative to reprieve a prisoner condemned to death, the author concluded that the Home Secretary rarely if ever takes new evidence into account when reaching his decision about a reprieve.

The question therefore remains: why was the new evidence not referred by the defence to the Court of Criminal Appeal? We have one answer from Mr Kleinman himself, in a letter to the *Sunday Times* some six and a half years later:

> While they doubtless acted in good faith, the statements of the persons quoted ... were not consistent with the evidence Hanratty gave on oath at his trial.
>
> Quite apart from inconsistencies as to identification and detail (as well as some mutually contradictory features) there was no point in seeking to rely on the evidence of Mr Larman, Mrs Walker and Mrs Vincent, because their statements (even without the test of cross-examination), did not match Hanratty's evidence on the crucial issue of time. He could not have spoken to any of these people at 7.30 p.m. because his evidence on oath was that he did not leave Liverpool by coach for Rhyl until about 7.30 p.m. and that when he arrived in Rhyl it was late evening and dark. It was, of course, not dark at Rhyl at 7.30 p.m. That the statements in other respects did not find support from Hanratty himself added substantially to the difficulties. (*Sunday Times*, September 30th, 1968.)

The impression is given by Mr Kleinman's letter that the times of these encounters are remembered and recorded accurately. In fact, *all* the witnesses, especially Hanratty, are vague about the time in their statements. Mrs Walker says it was 'about half past seven', Mr Larman says 'about 7.30', and Mrs Vincent does not mention the time at all.

Hanratty's version is even vaguer:

* Harrap, 1965.

MR SWANWICK. Do you remember how you got from Liverpool to Rhyl?

A. Yes, by coach.

Q. Do you remember what coach?

A. Yes, I caught it in the station at the back of Lime Street — at the side of Lime Street, not at the back ...

Q. Was it a single decker or a double-decker?

A. It was a double-decker bus.

Q. What time would this be?

A. This would be *about half past seven. It might not be the exact time.* (Vol. XIII, p. 61, my italics.)

When Mr Swanwick asked him about his arrival in Rhyl, Hanratty categorically refused even to guess at the time:

Q. You told us that when you arrived in Rhyl it was dark; is that right?

A. No, I did not say that.

Q. What did you say?

A. I said it got dark towards the evening.

Q. What time did you arrive in Rhyl?

A. I am not sure. It was August time. It don't get dark till late.

Q. What sort of time would you put it? I will help you by telling you that according to my diary the sun set at Liverpool at 8.30.

A. What, in August?

Q. At that time, 21st August. [*Sic.*]

A. Would it?

Q. Can you give us any idea of the time you got to Rhyl?

A. Off-hand I cannot. *If I was to say a time it would not be fair, because you would cross-examine me, and I am not sure of the exact time.*

Q. I only want an approximate time if you can give it.

A. I could not, *because I did not time it.* (Vol. XIV, p. 11, my italics.)

'I did not time it'! That, surely, is the best reply to the complaint that the difference between Hanratty's rough guess at the time his bus left Liverpool and Mrs Walker's and Mr Larman's rough guesses at the time they met him was enough to annul the extraordinary coincidences between Hanratty's story and those of Mrs Walker and Mr Larman.

But there was a further point to show that Mrs Walker's estimate

of time must, on her own account, have been marginally wrong.
Mrs Walker, it will be remembered, had been asked by Mr Gillbanks what had helped her to fix the time of the encounter, and she
had replied (according to Gillbanks's letter published above) that
she had fixed the time: 'because it was getting dark and the street
lamps were lit'.

As Mr Kleinman himself points out, 'it was not dark at Rhyl at
7.30 p.m.', so Mrs Walker must have been wrong about the time.
And the encounter, from her own statement about the streetlights,
must have taken place an hour (or more) later — at exactly the time
when Hanratty, according to his statement, was wandering around
Rhyl looking for lodgings.

Of course there were minor and marginal differences of detail
between the statements and Hanratty's. But the major factors were
strikingly similar:

	Mrs Walker	Mrs Vincent	Mr Larman
Hair	'his hair was dark and brushed back, but there was something not quite natural about it, as though it was streaky or tacky.'	'his hair was straight back.'	'his hair was most outstanding being bronze and dark in parts.'
Age	24/27 years	23/27 years	(no estimate)
Clothes	'neatly dressed in a dark suit.'	'had a dark suit and was neat and tidy.'	'dressed in a dark suit, neat and tidy.'
Height	(no estimate)	'taller than me [5′ 2″].'	'about 5′ 7″.'

The marginal differences in the statements have to be measured
against the coincidence that three eminently respectable witnesses
had volunteered information which appeared in all major aspects to
substantiate Hanratty's story about his journey to Rhyl.

What therefore was the real reason why Mr Kleinman and Mr
Sherrard, after several days' anxious indecision, decided that it
would do their client more harm than good if the witnesses appeared

(as they could have done) before the Court of Criminal Appeal? Most probably, the deciding factor was the performance of Mrs Jones in the witness box at Bedford. On the face of it, Mrs Jones, before she appeared in the witness box, had seemed an excellent defence witness, and Mr Sherrard had watched in horror as she was gradually demolished by Mr Swanwick; while the boarding house was gradually 'filled' with people who said they had never seen Hanratty, and while, after exposures of bad book-keeping and contradiction of detail, Mrs Jones had withdrawn her assertion about the date when the young man had stayed in her house.

It was an example of how statements taken out of court by sympathetic inquiry agents can change in a courtroom. It was at any rate arguable that Mrs Jones's performance in the witness box, through no fault of her own, did Hanratty more damage than if she had never appeared. The thought must have occurred to Mr Sherrard: if that could happen to Mrs Jones, whose evidence was supported by external facts about her boarding house, by how much more could Mr Swanwick at the Court of Criminal Appeal have reduced to shreds the evidence of Mrs Walker, Mrs Vincent and Mr Larman? At any rate, for whatever reason, no new witnesses were introduced at the Appeal Court and the press, notably the *Daily Sketch* whose reporters knew all about Mrs Walker and Mrs Vincent, kept silent. When Mr Larman telephoned the *Daily Mirror* two days before Hanratty's execution in a desperate attempt to save his life, he was given a polite brush-off. The result was that for four and a half years no one except the lawyers, the Home Secretary and a handful of newspaper reporters knew anything about any of the three witnesses.

During those years there was considerable interest in the A6 murder case. On August 2nd, 1963, there was an adjournment debate in the House of Commons after a detailed memorandum providing further proof to establish Hanratty's innocence had been presented to the Home Secretary. The debate was opened by Mr Fenner Brockway, who told the House: 'At the trial, Hanratty disastrously attempted to present a phoney alibi. He is dead *and there is no evidence on that matter*.' (My italics.) In each of the years 1963, 1964 and 1965 full-scale books were written about the case – *The A6 Murder: Regina v. James Hanratty: The Semblance of Truth* by Louis Blom-Cooper (Penguin, 1963), *Murder versus Murder* by Jean Justice (Olympia Press, Paris, 1964) and *Deadman's Hill: Was*

Hanratty Guilty? by Lord Russell of Liverpool (Secker and War-burg, 1965). Blom-Cooper, without adding anything new from Liverpool or Rhyl, concluded that the Rhyl alibi was 'palpably false'. Justice's and Russell's books were pleas for Hanratty's innocence, yet neither author uncovered anything about Rhyl save the evidence which had been revealed at the trial. Mrs Walker, Mrs Vincent, Mr Larman and Mr Dutton were names not known to any student of the Hanratty case throughout all those years.

On August 4th, 1966, however, Lord Russell initiated a House of Lords debate on the A6 murder. The following month, *Queen* magazine published an article written by me naming Peter Alphon as the murderer, and the interest of the communications industry in the Hanratty case was once again aroused. In October, the B.B.C. current affairs programme Panorama, under the new and vigorous editorship of Jeremy Isaacs, started to prepare a full-length (fifty-minute) programme on the case.

On October 23rd I travelled with Jo Mennel, the programme's producer, to Liverpool and Rhyl to make initial inquiries into the alibi. After a short interview with Mrs Dinwoodie in Liverpool, we drove to Rhyl and spoke to Mrs Jones (who was, she said, 'more certain now' that Hanratty had stayed in her house on the relevant Tuesday), and to Terry Evans. Terry Evans told us how Charlie Jones the newspaper seller had approached him after Hanratty's conviction and told him that 'that man was looking for you last summer.' Evans also promised to search out those people in Rhyl who knew something about the case, and we returned to London.

A week later, Mennel went back to Rhyl, this time with John Morgan, the programme's reporter, and a film crew. They filmed an interview with Mrs Jones and with Terry Evans, and talked to some of the people whom Evans had rounded up for them. Evans, how-ever, had an apology. Despite considerable efforts, he told them, he had been unable to find the newspaper seller, Charlie Jones. Jones, he said, was not selling papers any more, and no one knew where he lived.

Some ten minutes later, Charlie Jones walked into the café where the reporters and Evans were sitting. Evans leapt up, and approached him. 'Charlie,' he said, 'tell them about what you told me last summer about Hanratty.'

Jones told them, first across the table, and then, almost immedi-ately, outside on camera. One Tuesday evening late in August 1961, he said, a young man had got off a bus from Liverpool and had asked for a man by his christian name. Jones asked for more details. He works at the fairground, said the young man. Jones pointed him in the direction of the fairground and watched him walk away to it. When Hanratty's picture dominated the Sunday newspapers on February 18th, 1962, he had met Evans in the street and mentioned to him, in passing: 'That fellow was looking for you last summer.'

Remembering Evans's involvement in the trial, he had put two and two together and reckoned that this was the man. After a brief discussion, however, both Jones and Evans had agreed that Hanratty had been convicted and there was no point in raising the matter with the local police.

Here was a new alibi witness who was also sure, on television at any rate, that the day on which he had met this man was on the Tuesday of the fourth week in August, 1961.

The programme provoked more comment and criticism than a Panorama programme had done for years. The views of the critics were mixed, but one newspaper, the *Sunday Telegraph*, was incensed at what their leader, the following Sunday (November 13th) described as 'Trial by Television'. One of their most experienced reporters, Mr R. Barry O'Brien, had been sent to Rhyl to interview the newspaper seller.

O'Brien spent two days in Rhyl, and at least four hours with Charlie Jones. His story was printed on the front page of the *Sunday Telegraph* and was entitled PAPER SELLER DISCLAIMS TV ALIBI FOR HANRATTY. It quoted Jones as saying: 'I cannot really remember when I saw Hanratty. It is no good saying I can.'

This was a fair point. Jones's attempts to fix the exact date of his encounter with the man at the bus station had been so inadequate that the Panorama editors, ill-advisedly, had cut them out of the programme. But O'Brien went on to argue that the encounter probably took place when Hanratty first went to Rhyl – on Tuesday, July 25th – and got a job on the fairground.

To prove this, Mr O'Brien started by misquoting the transcript of the programme. 'Mr Jones said on the programme', he wrote, 'that Hanratty came off the bus around 7 p.m.' (The bus from Liverpool did not arrive until 8.19 p.m.)

In fact, the transcript of the programme records Jones as saying: 'He came off the bus at around 7 o'clock, *or eight o'clock*.' (My italics.)

O'Brien's second point was this. Jones told him that he met the man off the bus while waiting to sell papers after the 6 p.m. performance of the circus. The circus at Rhyl had two performances for the first two weeks in August, while for the last two weeks there was one performance only.

When I saw Jones some eighteen months later, he denied being specific about the circus. 'I just said I was waiting until after the circus,' he said. 'How could I have known what performance it was?' At any rate, the encounter could well have taken place while he was waiting for the hour-long performance of the 7.30 circus to finish.

Yet O'Brien's article ignored the one feature of Jones's story which had brought him to the attention of Panorama in the first place, and which proved beyond doubt that the encounter could not have taken place when Hanratty first went to Rhyl – in July. The man, said Jones, *had asked for a man by his christian name, who worked in the fairground.* When Hanratty went to Rhyl in July, he did not know Terry Evans – or anyone else who worked on the fairground. Indeed he did not know anyone in Rhyl, since he had never been there in his life. The fact that the man asked for a fairground worker by his christian name is clear proof that, if the man was Hanratty, it must have taken place after Hanratty's first visit to Rhyl in July.

The *Sunday Telegraph* story created enough of a journalistic flurry for most national newspaper editors to send reporters from Manchester to Rhyl to see Charlie Jones. These included a reporter from the *Daily Telegraph* sent to cash in on his sister paper's 'scoop'. When the journalists arrived in Rhyl, however, they were confronted with further information which appeared to conflict with Charlie Jones's disclaimer. An enterprising freelance journalist from Llandudno called Derek Bellis had been making inquiries in and around Kinmel Street. He had discovered that Mrs Walker and Mrs Vincent had made relevant statements to the police at the time of the trial. This information he passed on to two newspapers, the *Daily Mail* and the *Daily Telegraph*. 'Three More Saw Hanratty in Rhyl' was the headline of the inside-page story of the *Daily Telegraph* of Monday, November 14th. Not only did the newspaper report that Mrs Walker had seen a young man asking for lodgings on Tuesday, August 22nd, and that Mrs Vincent had corroborated this, but it produced a new witness, hitherto unheard of in the story: 'Mrs

Brenda Harris, daughter of Mrs Grace Jones, said she remembered a young man wearing a dark suit, staying at her house for two days.' (*Daily Telegraph*, November 14th, 1966.)

Mrs Harris lived in the boarding house at 19 Kinmel Street, helping her mother with the meals and housework. It was Mrs Harris who, according to Terry Evans, had agreed with her mother that the photograph of Hanratty resembled the face of the man who had stayed in their house the previous summer. She had not been taken to the Bedford trial largely because her evidence was a duplicate of Mrs Jones's. Her appearance in the story at this late stage was, however, important. It proved that Mrs Jones's story was not a figment of her imagination, but was supported by other members of her household.

The disclosure of these three witnesses, though poorly treated by the press, greatly increased the case for a public inquiry into the case. A detailed article in the *Sunday Times* colour supplement by Peter Laurie and Brian Moynahan gave considerable space to the statements of Mrs Walker and Mrs Vincent. I wrote a two-page article in *Private Eye* of November 25th, 1966, entitled 'Hanratty and the Rhyl Alibi', quoting at length from Mrs Walker in Ryhl, and from Mrs Vincent.

On January 30th, 1967, Mr Roy Jenkins, the Home Secretary, decided that there was a case to answer. In a written House of Commons answer, he announced his decision to set up a secret police investigation into Hanratty's alibi under Detective Chief Superintendent Douglas Nimmo, head of the Manchester C.I.D.

Mr Nimmo went to Rhyl on February 9th, 1967, and stayed there until the 15th. In those six days he interviewed a number of witnesses, none of whom were legally represented. No one was present at the interviews as an independent observer.

One of the most unsatisfactory aspects of secret investigation by the police is that there are no rules about the way in which the inquiry is conducted. Most people, approached by police officers who are conducting an inquiry, will not hesitate to co-operate without insisting on an observer. In such circumstances, there is no one except the person interviewed to retail what was said at the interview.

Some time between February 16th and March 23rd, Mr Nimmo wrote his report and presented it to the Home Secretary. Its results were publicized, not by official statement, but by 'inspired leaks' by the Home Office.

On March 23rd most newspapers reported noncommittally that the Nimmo Report had been handed in to the Home Secretary. But Percy Hoskins of the *Daily Express* had more information:

> The claim that James Hanratty, executed in April 1962 for the A6 murder, was in Rhyl on the night of the murder has not been substantiated. This, *I understand*, is the final conclusion of the 250,000-word dossier handed to the Home Office yesterday. It is based on a seven-week investigation made in the North Wales seaside town by Detective Chief Superintendent Nimmo, head of Manchester C.I.D. It will be closely studied by Mr Roy Jenkins, the Home Secretary, and a statement will be made to the Commons after the Easter recess. It is unlikely to lead to any further inquiry. (My italics.)

The *Daily Sketch* headline read: HANRATTY'S A6 ALIBI WAS FALSE, JENKINS TOLD IN POLICE PROBE. *'It is believed'*, wrote the *Sketch* correspondent, 'that police think the story was false.' (My italics.)

Over the weeks that followed, the A6 murder hit the headlines again and again, but the newspapers assumed that the Nimmo Inquiry had disproved Hanratty's Rhyl alibi. On May 14th the *Observer* declared: 'A recent police inquiry, ordered by the Home Office, failed to substantiate a claim that Hanratty was in Rhyl at the time of the murder ...'

A week later (May 21st), the *Sunday Telegraph* crime correspondent agreed: 'I understand the Nimmo inquiry finds there is no proof of an alibi. A similar inquiry ordered in secret by Sir Joseph Simpson, the Commissioner of the Metropolitan Police, reached the same conclusion earlier, *I can disclose*.' (My italics.)

On the same day, Ken Gardner of the *People* wrote: 'The Nimmo Report has not yet been published. But *I can reveal* that the inquiry proves that Hanratty's alibi was false.' (My italics.)

Half the national press had uncovered the conclusion of an unpublished police investigation! The speed and accuracy with which the press could acquire secret conclusions which suited the authorities was matched only by the inscrutability of the Home Office when it came to revealing the reasons for those conclusions and the methods by which they were reached.

The Rhyl alibi, it seemed, had been discounted once more, but throughout the Parliamentary session following the Easter recess,

Jenkins remained silent. Despite all the leaks, he could not reach a decision on the A6 case.

Mr and Mrs James Hanratty watched these developments with a mixture of anger and alarm. They had assumed that the disclosure of the new witnesses would bring about the public inquiry into their son's guilt for which they had been pressing for so long. Now, everything seemed to be lost in smear and innuendo. Not for the first time, they decided to take matters into their own hands.

Without seeking the help of any of the members of the A6 Murder Committee, they got into a car owned by a friend, and drove, with their son Michael at the wheel, to Rhyl. They visited Mrs Jones, Mrs Harris, Mrs Walker and Mrs Vincent and appealed to them to tell all they knew. As a result they took statements which added a great deal to the already substantial case for their son's Rhyl alibi.

Mrs Walker's statement reiterated what she had already said in her four previous statements, and added something else which seemed at the time of less significance. 'The man', she said, 'was carrying no luggage.' At first sight, this would seem to conflict with Hanratty's story, since he had brought his jewellery from Liverpool in his leather case. But it is worth recalling his note in the cells about 'leaving his case' at Mrs Jones's and saying he would 'pick it up later'. If he did leave the case there, he could well have popped round the corner to Mrs Walker's to see if he could get something better than Mrs Jones could offer, in which case he would have had no luggage. Secondly, the Hanrattys noticed that Mrs Walker had an Alsatian, and Mr Hanratty remembered his son telling him at Bedford that one of the women he had approached for lodgings had a 'large dog with her'.

Mrs Vincent's statement ran as follows:

When I opened the door, this young man was standing there. He asked me if I could put him up for a couple of nights, and he pointed to Mrs Walker's house and said that the lady over there had sent him to me. I told him I could not put him up. He then asked me to recommend him to anyone else. I told him to go into Kinmel Street. He hesitated and I told him that this (my house) was in South Kinmel Street. The man from Bedford showed me two photographs and I picked out from these two the young man who had asked me if he could stay a few nights. He was identified as James Hanratty.

Yet the most important of the three statements was the one taken from Mrs Brenda Harris, daughter of the Ingledene landlady, Mrs Jones:

> I have already made a statement to Mr Nimmo stating that all the bedrooms were occupied during the week 19th to 26th August 1961 by guests. The only room we had a vacant bed in was in the attic, which contains a green bath. We offered this to a young man about 25 years of age with dark hair, who I feel sure was James Hanratty. The reason why the guests in the dining room never saw him was because he had breakfast in our general room. That's how he knew the back yard was tiled.

The prosecution case against Mrs Jones's evidence at the trial was based, it will be remembered, on the following points:
1. Owing to the chaos of her books, the date when the young man stayed was entirely a matter for Mrs Jones's memory, which was suspect.
2. All the guest rooms were full that week.
3. Three guests who had been in the hotel that week said they had not seen Hanratty.
4. The breakfast-room contained five tables, while Hanratty said the room where he had breakfast contained two.

Mrs Harris's statement helped to answer all these points. It gave support to Mrs Jones's memory of the date. It showed that the room offered to the young man was not a guest room. It stated that Hanratty had been given breakfast in the family room at the back of the ground floor which had two tables in it.

The reference to the back yard arose not out of anything which happened at the trial but out of Hanratty's further detailed description of the house to his parents both during and after the trial.

People meet each other in bed-and-breakfast boarding houses either at breakfast, or at high tea or by chance bumping into each other on the stairs. Guests are expected to leave the boarding house (or stay in their rooms) during the day. There is no general lounge or television room at Ingledene. If Hanratty ate breakfast in the back room, there is no reason why anyone should have seen him. The attic with the green bath was not an official room, and was not registered as a bedroom as required by the legislation controlling boarding houses. This is why from the outset Mrs Jones was reluctant to talk about the bed in the attic bathroom.

The three statements taken by the Hanrattys, and their implications were published in a long article in the *Sunday Times* on June 11th, 1967. Mr and Mrs Hanratty wrote on June 27th asking for an interview with the Home Secretary, and were eventually seen by senior Home Office officials. Shortly after the interview – on July 12th – the Home Secretary decided to send Chief Superintendent Nimmo *again* to Rhyl to investigate the alibi claims.

This extraordinary decision was greeted with scant publicity (two paragraphs in the *Daily Express*, one paragraph in the *Sun*, for instance). According to the *Daily Express* Mr Nimmo had spent seven weeks on the Rhyl inquiry, including a week in Rhyl interviewing all the relevant witnesses. He had written a 250,000-word report (about the size of three standard novels). Among the people he had interviewed were Mrs Walker, Mrs Vincent and Mrs Harris. Yet after the Hanrattys had taken statements from these three same people, Mr Nimmo was dispatched once more to Rhyl to plough in the same furrow.

Why? None of the newspapers could explain. The *Daily Express* reported:

> Detective Chief Superintendent Nimmo, head of Manchester C.I.D., is to make a second inquiry into the claim that James Hanratty did not commit the A6 murder for which he was hanged. Supt. Nimmo will investigate again an alibi which he said after the first investigation could not be substantiated.
> (*Daily Express*, July 13th, 1967.)

When I rang the Home Office on behalf of the *Sunday Times*, I was told: 'The new visit is based on alleged new material not available at the time of the first inquiries.'

The statements of Mrs Walker and Mrs Vincent as taken by Mr and Mrs Hanratty were exactly the same as those in the possession of the Home Office since 1962 which Mr Nimmo must have seen. Similarly, Mr Nimmo had interviewed Mrs Harris. The only recognizable reason why Mr Jenkins should have sent Mr Nimmo back to Rhyl was that the statements in the *Sunday Times* appeared to conflict with the first Nimmo report.

On Mr Nimmo's second visit during the third week of July,

things were not as easy for him as before. Lord Russell of Liverpool advised the key witnesses not to give evidence before Nimmo without legal representatives, and accordingly when Nimmo approached them about an interview in Rhyl police station, he was turned away. 'I told him', says Mrs Walker cheerfully, 'that he wasn't even coming in the gate.'

Eventually an agreement was struck between Lord Russell and the Home Office that the witnesses would make statements to Mr Nimmo in front of legal representatives. Interviews then took place with lawyers present, including Mr Barney Berkson, a solicitor from Birkenhead who had acted in the past for Lord Russell. All the efforts made to shake Mrs Walker were, says Mr Berkson, futile. She remained certain that she had seen a young man looking very much like Hanratty asking for two nights' board and lodging in the late evening of August 22nd, 1961.

Mr Nimmo then prepared his second report (there is, unhappily, no information from Mr Percy Hoskins as to how long this one was) which was submitted to the Home Office at the end of July. On July 30th, Lord Russell held a press conference in Rhyl in which he summarized the witnesses' statements as they were made before Nimmo, and in which he also produced incontrovertible evidence (on the basis of what had been said by police officers to Mrs Walker) that his telephone conversations with Mrs Walker had been overheard and recorded by the police.

Mr Jenkins studied the second Nimmo report with some care, although by all accounts it differed only marginally from the first. For three months the Home Office was silent. Then, suddenly, Miss Joan Lestor, Labour M.P. for Eton and Slough, put down a written question on the case to Mr Jenkins.

Miss Lestor had become involved in the case in the autumn of 1966 after being approached by Mr Tony Mason, a freelance journalist from Slough, who was one of the first journalists alerted after the murder. At the outset, Miss Lestor's enthusiasm knew no bounds. She was, she assured the Hanratty parents, absolutely convinced of the boy's innocence, and would 'stop at nothing' to get an inquiry. After one or two interviews with Mr Jenkins, however, Miss Lestor's enthusiasm began to wane. In conversation about the case she became more guarded. Her decision to put down a written question indicated, in effect, that she had given up the fight for an inquiry. Written questions in the House of Commons are answered with written replies, and are subject to no supplementaries. It is a device for obtaining non-controversial information; or, occasionally, a method by which Ministers make minor announcements. The question from Miss Lestor, which was answered on November 1st, 1967, was, however, extremely controversial. She asked 'the Secretary of State for the Home Department whether he now intends to hold a public inquiry into the conviction of James Hanratty'. This had been the subject of two police investigations, not to mention two major television programmes and several substantial newspaper articles.

The section of Mr Jenkins's reply which dealt with the Rhyl alibi read as follows:

Material has been submitted about Hanratty's claim that he was in Rhyl on 22nd and 23rd August, 1961, the date on which the murder took place. At my request, Detective Chief Superintendent Nimmo of the Manchester City Police who had not previously any connection with the case, has made detailed and exhaustive investigations covering all possible lines of inquiry into the alibi.

This alibi was also an issue at the trial. It turned largely on identification (as did the case against Hanratty at the trial), and retrospective statements about identification cannot easily be given greater weight than those made with fresh recollection at the time of the trial, over five years ago. These difficulties could be set aside only if Mr Nimmo's investigation had turned up some new evidence of substance which raised material doubts about the original statements.

Mr Nimmo's thorough investigations have not had that result. He has found nothing to strengthen the evidence called at the trial on Hanratty's behalf and no further evidence which, if put before the jury, might have influenced the verdict. The only witness who now appears to give direct confirmation of the alibi is a lady who claims she saw Hanratty in Rhyl for a few minutes on the evening of August 22, 1961. But the defence, after interviewing her at the trial, decided not to call her as a witness; after the trial, she was shown photographs of Hanratty by the defence and made a statement in which she declined to give a definite identification. When she was seen by Mr Nimmo, she at first maintained that she had given a definite identification to the defence in 1962. Mr Nimmo's conclusion (with which I agree) is that her firm identification of Hanratty is of recent origin and is in all the circumstances unreliable. None of the other witnesses claims a positive identification relating to a particular date.

The statement contains nothing about any of the Rhyl witnesses except Mrs Walker; nothing about the evidence of Mrs Harris, which had provided clear answers to the prosecution's refutation of Mrs Jones's evidence at the trial; nothing about the fact that, according to Mrs Harris, James Hanratty slept in the attic with the green bath; nothing about the evidence of Gwyn Jones, Mrs Jones's son, who had told Superintendent Nimmo that he remembered seeing a young man like Hanratty at about the relevant time. The young man had stayed in his house for two nights and had asked him about the availability of girls. In spite of all these statements, and without even mentioning them in his answer, Mr Jenkins was satisfied that Mr Nimmo had 'found nothing to strengthen the evidence called at the trial on Hanratty's behalf'. Similarly, there is no mention of the fact that Mrs Walker's evidence was directly and substantially supported by Mrs Vincent, who saw the young man in question only seconds after he had come to her house from Mrs Walker's.

After ignoring all this evidence and all these statements Mr Jenkins then battled with the statements of Mrs Walker. He ruled her out on two grounds. First, the defence had not called her at the trial, after interviewing her. Secondly, when shown photographs after the trial she had not made a definite identification, and that her identification of Hanratty was therefore 'of recent origin'.

At the time of Jenkins's statement Mrs Walker's original statement to Gillbanks on February 19th, 1962 was not available to anyone outside the Home Office (except, of course, Mr Nimmo). Much to the Home Office's irritation, it has now become available, and it compares badly with the bowdlerized version of it presented to the House of Commons by Mr Jenkins.

As we have seen, the interview of Mrs Walker during the trial had been conducted as the defence counsel in Bedford was starting his final summing-up speech to the jury. It was almost impossible at that stage for Mr Sherrard to call Mrs Walker to the trial. As soon as she was shown pictures of Hanratty, Mrs Walker agreed that they closely resembled the man who came to her door. Her actual words were:

> I have seen photographs of James Hanratty in the week-end papers, and they are very much like the young man, but I don't want to commit myself. The photographs you have shown me are very like the man who called here, *but the hair was dark*. Mind, I couldn't swear it was him. (My italics.)

This can, no doubt, be dismissed as 'not a definite identification'. In reality it is crucially significant; the difference in hair colour could have been more than enough to restrain Mrs Walker from definite commitment. Yet in the House of Commons, Mr Jenkins inferred that Mrs Walker was vague six years before about the identification, but was now certain. In fact, Mrs Walker has stuck to exactly the same story from first to last.

Nor did the Jenkins statement, or decision, change Mrs Walker's mind. *The Times* of November 3rd reported: 'Mrs Margaret Walker, of South Kinmel Street, Rhyl, today reiterated her claim that James Hanratty called at her house on the night of the A6 murder.'

The Home Office came in for further criticism on the Frost programme on November 15th, when Lord Russell outlined in detail the case for the alibi, and Mr Barney Berkson, the Birkenhead solicitor, reiterated his belief that Mrs Walker and Mrs Vincent were effectively substantiating the alibi when they gave evidence the second time before Superintendent Nimmo. A vote of the audience at the Frost programme after the show was almost unanimous for Hanratty's innocence.

Yet the lack of Parliamentary interest in the case continued to confound the parents of James Hanratty and their small band of supporters. Early in 1968, the A6 Murder Committee, attended for the last time by Lord and Lady Russell who left soon afterwards to take up permanent residence in France, decided to organize yet another journey to Rhyl the following May, in an attempt to discover more evidence to substantiate the alibi.

The Committee therefore took a half-page advertisement in the *Rhyl Journal* on May 22nd, 1968, headed CAN YOU HELP MR AND MRS HANRATTY CLEAR THEIR SON'S NAME? The advertisement appealed to anyone in Rhyl who felt they had evidence about the

Hanratty case to come and see the Hanrattys who would be staying the weekend in the Westminster Hotel, Rhyl.

Six members of the Committee duly travelled to Rhyl on Friday, May 24th: Mr and Mrs Hanratty and their second son, Michael, Mr Jeremy Fox, Mr Jean Justice and myself. During the evenings of 24th and 25th we visited the witnesses who had already come forward: Mr Charles Jones the newspaper seller, who insisted that he still believed that he had seen Hanratty outside the bus station in Rhyl in August 1961, Mr and Mrs Jones, their son Gwyn and Terry Evans.

On the Saturday evening, we received a message advising us to visit Mr and Mrs Noel Davies, who were living at 19 South Kinmel Street, Rhyl. Mr and Mrs Hanratty and I duly went down to the house, where Mrs Davies was alone. After some persuasion, Mrs Davies agreed that she too had been visited by a young man in late August who was looking for rooms. At the time, she had been living next door to Mrs Jones—at 21 Kinmel Street. The following day, we returned to the house and took detailed statements from Mrs Davies, her husband and her mother, which read as follows:

STATEMENT BY MRS BETTY DAVIES, 33, of 19 South Kinmel Street, Rhyl. May 26, 1968

In the summer of 1961, I was living at 21 Kinmel Street, Rhyl. During the season we took guests in for bed and breakfast. On July 20, I gave birth to a baby girl in Chatsworth House, Prestatyn. The baby was ill, and stayed in Chatsworth House, when I returned home on Friday, July 28th. This was the busy part of the season and the house was full of guests.

My baby died on July 31st and was buried on August 3rd. The house remained full for some time afterwards, but towards the end of August, as the end of the season approached, the guests began to leave.

One evening late in August—I cannot remember the exact date—I was alone in the house with my small daughter. It was late in the evening, growing dark. The bell rang and I answered the door. A young man was standing on the pavement outside. I'd say he was in his twenties. He had dark hair and was softly-spoken.

He asked if I could take him in for bed and breakfast. I did not like the look of him, especially as he had no luggage. I said we couldn't take him in, and suggested he tried further down the street. I went through the house into my mother's house which backed on mine. I told her that a young man had come to the door and that I didn't take him in. When my husband returned soon afterwards, I told him the same.

Some months later, a man came to the door and said he was acting on behalf of a firm of solicitors in London. He asked if there was a green bath in the attic. We said we hadn't, and he went away. About the same time, a uniformed policeman called to show me an outline sketch of a man, and asked if I recognized it. I said I couldn't, and he went away.

I have read and talked about the Hanratty case since, and I believe that the man who called at my house in late August, 1961, could have been James Hanratty. I am therefore making this statement in response to an appeal from Mr and Mrs Hanratty.

STATEMENT BY MRS MARGARET DAVIES, 61, of 27 South Kinmel Street, Rhyl. May 26th, 1968.

In the summer of 1961, I was living in South Kinmel Street, and my son and daughter-in-law, Betty Davies, had a baby in July, which died on July 31. For several days after she came out of hospital, her house was full of guests and I did the cooking there. By the third week of August, the guests had gone. One evening in the third or fourth week in August, I was sitting in my house and was visited by Mrs Margaret Walker, of 12 South Kinmel Street. Among other things, Mrs Walker told me that a man had come to her house looking for digs, but that she had no room for him. While Mrs Walker was in my house, my daughter-in-law ran into my house through the back door. She stood in the doorway of the lounge and said that a young man had called to ask for digs, and that she had told him to try further down the street. I had told her beforehand not to take any man into the house if he was on his own.

I cannot myself remember the exact date when this incident took place, but Mrs Walker remembers the date exactly because of a family matter which was settled on August 25th. She knows the day when the young man visited her house was the Tuesday before the 25th. On the day when she visited my house, and when we were interrupted by my daughter-in-law, she was talking to me about the same family matter, which was to be settled that week.

STATEMENT BY MR NOEL DAVIES, of
19 South Kinmel Street, Rhyl. May 26, 1968.

In the summer of 1961, I was living in 21 Kinmel Street, Rhyl, and was working on renewing the drains at the Catholic Church, Wellington Road, Rhyl. My wife had a baby on July 20th, which died on July 31st. For some time after the baby died, my wife was not well and the house was full of guests. I would return home from work about 5.0 o'clock in the evening, and help with the housework. I would wash up the tea things, and peel potatoes and lay tables for the following day. While the busy season was on, I didn't get out for a drink until after 9.30 in the evening. If anyone came to the door, I would answer it.

As the season came to an end, and things became easier in the house, I would go out for a drink earlier in the evening, returning regularly at 9.30 to 10.00 p.m. in time to help with the night-time cups of tea for the guests. One evening in late August, I returned home about this time, and my wife told me that a man had come to the door asking for bed and breakfast, and that she had turned him away. I had suggested to her some time before that if a man came alone to the house, she should turn him away.

I cannot remember the exact date of this incident, but it must have been in late August, because in early August I was in the house every night until about 9.30, and would have answered the door.

There is, of course, no definite identification in any of these statements and none of the three people can remember exact dates. A reasonable member of any jury, however, would not find it easy to dismiss the statements out of hand because they are linked so closely to the statements of Mrs Walker, Mrs Vincent and Mrs Jones. Mrs Davies's statement fixes the date of the visit of the young man by an event which any mother is certain to remember most vividly — the birth and death eleven days later of a baby girl. Because the baby was ill, Mrs Davies stayed at the nursing home in Prestatyn until July 28th.

It has been suggested that Hanratty's search for lodgings in the Kinmel Street/South Kinmel Street area, and his eventual stay at Mrs Jones's boarding house, could have taken place on Hanratty's previous visit to Rhyl, after he had stayed one night at Terry Evans's on July 25th. Mrs Davies disposes once and for all of that theory. It is clear that she was visited by the same young man who visited Mrs Walker and Mrs Vincent. These meetings could not have taken place on July 25th because Mrs Davies was in Chatsworth House Nursing Home, Prestatyn, from July 20th to July 28th.

Returning to the hotel on the Saturday evening, the Hanrattys were greeted by an even more remarkable development. Mr Trevor Dutton, the poulterer from Kinmel Bay, had arrived at the hotel after reading the *Rhyl Journal* advertisement, and he had a curious story to tell us.

During Hanratty's trial he had read in the reports that Hanratty had been trying to sell a gold watch in Liverpool. He also read that Hanratty had travelled from Liverpool to Rhyl. He then remembered that, in the previous August, he had travelled on one of his rare visits to Rhyl to visit the barber and to put some money in the bank. In Rhyl High Street, outside Burtons, he had been approached by a young man in a two-toned, dark grey and light grey suit who had offered to sell him a gold watch.

Mr Dutton was in Rhyl when he read this report, and he travelled back to his home in Kinmel Bay wondering whether he ought to report the incident to the police. What decided him to do so was a glance at his bank deposit book which reminded him that the date on which he had visited Rhyl the previous summer to put money in the bank was August 23rd, the day of the A6 murder. There can have been no mistake about it, for there were only two deposits for the entire year — the other in the spring. So Mr Dutton phoned the police at Abergele and made as detailed a statement as he could to the police. He could not identify the man, he said, but the coincidence about the watch and the date prompted him to make a statement. Mr Dutton is well known in the Kinmel Bay area as a man of unimpeachable integrity. Throughout his dealings with us that night, as he wrote out his statement and signed it, he stressed that he was most anxious to avoid publicity.

Between making his statement to the police in February 1962 and repeating it to us in May 1968, Mr Dutton had not heard a word about the Hanratty case. His statement is in the police files on the case at Scotland Yard, and must therefore have been read by Chief Superintendent Nimmo when he conducted his inquiry into the Rhyl alibi. *Yet Nimmo never contacted Dutton or made any attempt to interview him.* What Mr Jenkins called 'thorough and exhaustive inquiries' by Mr Nimmo did not stretch even to an interview with a man who had at the time of the trial exposed a very remarkable coincidence in relation to Hanratty's alleged alibi.

The only reference in the defence papers to Mr Dutton is his name and address scrawled on the back of an envelope. A clerk at Hanratty's solicitor's office had taken a message from the prosecution to the effect that 'these names may be of interest to you', and Dutton's name was one of two written down. No one in the defence felt it necessary (or, more likely, had the time) to interview Dutton either before or after the trial.

Yet Dutton's evidence *was* important. It provided yet another link in a chain of events which corresponded closely to Hanratty's story, and provided documentary evidence as to the date.

On the Sunday of our visit to Rhyl (May 26th, 1968) we held a press conference, attended by representatives from most national newspapers. The revelations about Mrs Davies and Mr Dutton, taken in the context of all the other Rhyl evidence, were given wide publicity, especially in northern editions. The following Wednesday, Mr and Mrs Hanratty went to the Home Office with the statements of the Davies family, of Mr Gwyn Jones and of Mr Dutton, plus a letter again demanding a public inquiry.

These representations went unanswered for three and a half months – which is a long delay even for the Home Office. On September 10th Mr and Mrs Hanratty received a letter from Mr I. M. Burns, Private Secretary to the Home Secretary, assuring them that the five statements they had submitted had 'received the most careful and thorough examination'.

'Mrs Davies' statement', the letter went on, 'claims no more than that a man who called at her house one evening late in August 1961 could have been your son; and her husband and mother-in-law, who did not see the caller, simply confirm that they were informed of the visit at the time.'

This is only half of the truth. The importance of the three Davies statements is that they confirm and extend the firm testimony of Mrs Walker.

But it is in relation to the Dutton statement that the Home Office reply is at its most tortuous: 'The statement made by Mr Dutton ... refers to an attempt by a man to sell him a gold watch in Rhyl High Street on 23rd August, 1961; but your son's evidence at the trial did not include any reference to an attempt to sell a gold watch in Rhyl ... '

It is strictly true that Hanratty did not say anything at the trial about attempting to sell a gold watch in Rhyl. He did, however, say that he had gone to Liverpool in an attempt to sell jewellery and a gold watch; that in Liverpool he had tried unsuccessfully to sell a gold watch to a man on the stairs of a billiard hall; and that, immediately afterwards, he had travelled to Rhyl in an attempt to find Terry Evans who, he hoped, would be able to help him sell his jewellery. He had a full day in Rhyl with nothing to do, and it is a fair guess that he had a shot at selling his gold watch there (perhaps successfully). That is certainly the view taken by Mr Dutton, and that was the reason he made his statement to the police.

No sooner had the Home Office letter been received, however, than the Hanratty parents and their supporters received even more startling evidence that their son's Rhyl alibi could be substantiated.

By the middle of September, Mr Kleinman, James Hanratty's solicitor, had handed over all the papers concerning his former client's defence to another solicitor acting for Mr and Mrs Hanratty. Among the papers were the statements made to the defence in February 1962 by the various Rhyl witnesses in relation to the Rhyl alibi: Mrs Walker's statement, quoted at length above; and Mrs Vincent's statement. But the statement which immediately attracted attention was that of Mr Christopher Larman, the former building worker at Rhyl, who had stated at the time of the trial that he had seen Hanratty in Kinmel Street, Rhyl. Until that evening in September 1968 Mr Larman's statement had not been made public.

One man who had read it was Chief Superintendent Douglas Nimmo, who had available to him the Home Office Hanratty papers, which included a copy of the statement Christopher Larman had made soon after Hanratty's conviction in 1962. No doubt, he formed the view that no inquiry into the alibi would be complete without speaking to Mr Larman.

Accordingly, Mr Nimmo and/or his representatives traced Mr Larman to a house in Ranelagh Road, Southall, and made inquiries there from Mr Larman's brother-in-law, Mr William Marshall. Mr Marshall informed them that Mr Larman was in Australia, and that was the end of the matter. Mr Larman received a letter in Australia from his brother-in-law to the effect that a man had called in an inquiry about Hanratty, but Mr Larman was not contacted by letter or in person by anyone connected with the British police, or by Mr Nimmo. Between making his statement to an inquiry agent for the defence in 1962 and speaking to Jean Justice and me in Southall in September 1968, Mr Larman had never been contacted about his evidence.

Is Mr Larman or his evidence mentioned in the Nimmo Report to the Home Secretary? In his reply to Miss Lestor's written question in the House of Commons, Mr Jenkins stated: 'The only witness [from Rhyl] who now appears to give direct confirmation of the alibi is a lady ... ', and again: 'None of the other [Rhyl]witnesses [apart from Mrs Walker] claims a positive identification relating to a particular date.'

Both these statements were inaccurate. Mr Larman's statement gave 'direct confirmation of an alibi' and claimed a 'positive identification relating to a particular date'. Either Mr Jenkins knew of the Larman statement, in which case he manifestly misled the House, or he did not know of it, in which case he was inadequately briefed. Either way, Mr Nimmo's failure to contact Mr Larman or Mr Dutton throws some doubt on Mr Jenkins's assurance to the Commons that: 'Detective Chief Superintendent Nimmo ... has made detailed and exhaustive investigations *covering all possible lines of inquiry into the alibi.*' (My italics.)

The Larman revelations were published in great detail across half a page of the *Sunday Times* on September 29th, 1968. Jenkins's statement to the Commons was openly challenged. The reaction, however, was minimal. There was no statement from the Home Office, largely because there was no demand for one in Parliament. Six days after the publication of the article I received a letter from Miss Joan Lestor, Hanratty's former champion in the House of Commons, whose question the previous year had been answered, it was now clear, with a mixture of half-truth and misrepresentation. Miss Lestor wrote charmingly to compliment me on a book I had written three years earlier on immigration and race. Her letter started with a brief reference to the A6 case: 'First of all may I congratulate you on your latest A6 effort. I very much doubt, however, that we will get any further on that for some considerable time – if at all.'

As though to vindicate her own gloomy predictions, Miss Lestor did not put down any further questions relating to the Hanratty case, and more than a year passed before any further evidence about the alibi came to light. In December 1969, I wrote letters to the *Rhyl Journal* and the *Liverpool Daily Post*, saying that I was writing a book about the Hanratty case and was anxious to interview anyone who had made a statement to the police at the time.

The letters were published in both papers on December 10th, 1969 (the letter in the *Rhyl Journal* was given much prominence), and two days later I received a letter from a Mr Robert H. Fish of Llysfaen Avenue, Kinmel Bay, saying that he had given information to the police about Hanratty's alibi at the time of his trial.

I interviewed Mr Fish in his home on Tuesday April 7th, 1970. In August 1961, he said, he was living in River Street, Rhyl. One evening he remembered directing a man who was looking for lodgings. The man was standing on the corner of River Street and Aquarium Street. He was unsure of the date except that it was in August. When Hanratty's picture appeared in the papers after his trial, Fish went at once to the Rhyl police station to make a statement. He is still convinced that the picture in the paper was that of the man he directed. He asked the police to pass his name on to the defence.

Mr Fish's statement is a vague one. There is no positive identification, and he is uncertain about the date. But there are several aspects of it which are of interest. River Street is a long way from Kinmel Street. It runs well to the west of the town centre at right angles to the promenade. Curiously, though, there is another reference to River Street in connection with the alibi. Mr Frank Evans, the former police officer who had conducted inquiries on Hanratty's behalf in Rhyl, had spoken of 'an old lady in River Street' who had said categorically that a man looking like Hanratty had come to her door looking for lodgings on the vital date. She had, said Evans, only been dissuaded from coming forward by her son. I have made considerable, unsuccessful attempts to find this old lady (in May 1968, three of us knocked up every house in River Street). But the coincidence between Mr Evans and Mr Fish's references to River Street is a surprising one.

Secondly, the Rhyl police did *not* give Mr Fish's name to the defence, either at the time or later. The defence never heard of his evidence. Thirdly, Mr Fish was interviewed by Mr Nimmo, which shows that he did make a statement to the police at the time. It also shows that his evidence must, according to Nimmo, have been of some importance, since Mr Nimmo made no effort at all to get hold of at least one man who made a statement about the alibi (Mr Dutton).

While it does not in itself give a great deal of substance to the Hanratty alibi, Mr Fish's experience tells us something about the way in which the police and the authorities acted in relation to this alibi inquiry. The instinct of any individual who feels he has something to say about a criminal case is to make a statement to the police. Due to the fuss and hurry with which the defence was forced to conduct these Rhyl inquiries there is in the defence papers no list of the people their agents interviewed, nor of the people in Rhyl who had made statements to the police. There may well yet be up to a dozen people in Rhyl who voluntarily made statements to the police at the time of the trial or afterwards, and were since told by the police not to get involved any further. Mr Henry Parry, for instance, the landlord of the Windsor Hotel (immediately opposite Mrs Jones's house), tells inquirers that he has made a statement on the Hanratty case to the police and does not wish to take it any further. There are certainly other people in Rhyl who have something to say on this case, but who, for one reason or another, do not want to be involved. One such is Ernie Gordon, who, at the time of the murder, was running the Donald Duck Café, called Dixie's, near the fairground: Gordon's evidence would be crucial to any inquiry, but when he was questioned about it by Panorama reporters in 1966, he mumbled about 'not getting involved' and denied everything.

In the certainty that not all the available evidence has been uncovered, the case for Hanratty's Rhyl alibi can be summarized thus:

Hanratty said at his trial that he travelled from Liverpool to Rhyl by bus on the evening of Tuesday August 22nd, 1961, carrying jewellery, including a gold watch, which he hoped to sell through Terry Evans, whom he had met before. He did not know Evans's name, but knew him as John. His only method of identifying him was by an old black taxi which Evans used to keep parked near the fairground.

After arriving in Rhyl, he 'enquired on five or six occasions to get bed and breakfast in the area'. He was not successful until he came across a small boarding house, terraced, with no front garden, where a middle-aged lady took him in for two nights and charged him 25/–, without making him sign anything. He remembers that the house had a green plant in the hallway, a tiled yard at the back, a green bath in the attic and you could hear the trains without seeing them. He had breakfast in a room with two tables.

He stayed the following day in Rhyl, looking unsuccessfully for Evans, and on the Thursday departed for Liverpool.

During his stay at Rhyl he was wearing the double-breasted dark suit with the chalk stripe. His auburn hair was dyed dark, but the dye was beginning to wear off.

The following facts have now been established:

Terry Evans, with whom Hanratty stayed in July, moved his taxi from its usual parking place near the circus on the weekend of August 19th–20th.

On an evening late in August Charlie Jones the newspaper seller directed a young man in a dark suit along the front towards the fairground. The young man, who had just got off a bus, asked for a man who worked on the fairground. But he knew only his christian name.

Just as it was getting dark, on the evening of August 22nd, 1961, Mr Christopher Larman directed a young man in a dark suit with hair 'bronze and dark in parts' down Kinmel Street towards Mrs Jones's house. Mr Larman later identified the man from photographs as Hanratty.

At the same time of the same day, a young man dressed in a dark suit, with dark hair which looked 'streaky, or tacky' came to Mrs Walker's front door in South Kinmel Street and asked for lodgings for the night. He went over the road and asked the same of Mrs Vincent at No. 23. Again he was turned away.

On the same day, a young man called round the corner at Mrs Davies's house and asked for lodgings. Mrs Davies did not take him in.

On or about the same day, Mrs Grace Jones, who lived next door to Mrs Davies, took in a young man for two nights at her boarding house. The house had a green plant in the hallway, a tiled back yard, a green bath in the attic. The trains could be heard, but not seen from any of its rooms. The price charged for two nights' stay was 25/–. The young man did not sign the register. He stayed for two nights. The room in which he had breakfast had two tables. From photographs and in court Mrs Jones identified the young man as James Hanratty.

On the morning of August 23rd, Mr Dutton was approached in Rhyl High Street by a young man wearing a two-toned dark suit with a light grey stripe who offered him for sale a gold watch.

Almost all of these facts have been made public since the trial. Even the most faithful believer in coincidences would find it difficult to agree with Mr Jenkins's contention to the House of Commons (November 1st, 1967) that there is 'no further evidence which, if put before the jury, might have influenced the verdict'.

The fundamental question which dogs all discussion of the alibi, therefore, still remains properly to be answered: Why did Hanratty from the outset not mention the Rhyl alibi? If he was indeed, as so much of the evidence seems to suggest, asleep at 19 Kinmel Street, Rhyl, while Valerie Storie and Michael Gregsten were being shot on Deadman's Hill, why did he not tell Superintendent Acott so on the first occasion when he rang him up?

The change of alibi left Hanratty open to the charge, remorselessly repeated by Mr Swanwick, that he had invented the alibi at the last moment in the hope that attention would be distracted from his manifestly false alibi with 'the three men' in Liverpool.

'The hallmark of a false alibi is one that is set up at the last moment,' said Mr Swanwick. (Vol. XIII, p. 54.) It cannot be checked by the prosecution and it may be possible to substantiate by rather less powerful evidence than an alibi which the prosecution has had time to check.

This is partly true, but the advantages of a changed, last-minute alibi for the accused, are, as Mr Sherrard was the first to realize, outweighed by the disadvantages. If a man changes his alibi in the middle of a trial, he at once loses credibility. It looks as if he is bending his story according to the circumstances of the trial. This is why Sherrard warned Hanratty again and again of the danger in changing the alibi story, and, eventually, made his client sign a statement taking full responsibility for the change.

But why did Hanratty not talk of Rhyl from the outset? Why, when he knew he was wanted for the A6 murder, did he not go to Rhyl to check on the boarding house in which he said he stayed? Here is his own answer:

MR SWANWICK. Why did you never go back [to Rhyl] to try to pinpoint it [the boarding house]?

A. Because at this stage when I spoke to Mr Acott over the phone I know I had already told Mr Acott a lie about Liverpool and it was quite obvious to me inside that I never committed this crime and I had nothing at all to fear. But—let me finish—as this case eventually went along I got so frightened with the evidence what was being brought forward to me, with the lies and such things as what has happened in this witness box—well, it is disgraceful to talk about them. But I am just trying to suggest at this stage when I spoke to Mr Acott I did not fear any danger, because I knew in my heart and soul I did not commit this crime.

Q. But you had from 7th to 11th of October, and you were in Liverpool or Blackpool—in that area—when you could have gone along and tried to find this boarding house, and if you had found it all your troubles would have been over, would they not?

A. Yes, in that sense, yes, but in the state I was in at that time I was very depressed and with the tension in the papers, it is very hard to say how your mind will react at that stage. I was a wanted man by Mr Acott. He wanted me to interview me. It was in the papers and the police wanted to interview me. I could not go and knock at houses in Rhyl and ask if I stayed there on 23rd and 22nd August. I was a wanted man. I had to check and those houses I had to go to.' (Vol. XIV, p. 9.)

One sentence recurs throughout this and other explanations: 'I was a wanted man.' Hanratty, it will be remembered, had spent most of his adult life in prison. He knew that he was wanted for housebreaking and he knew too that, if caught by the police, he would have no defence to the housebreaking charges. Capture by the police would land him in jail for at least five years for housebreaking.

Anyone in Hanratty's position, therefore, guilty *or* innocent of the A6 murder, would have been guided by one overriding preoccupation—to avoid falling into the custody of the police. He knew that to substantiate the Rhyl alibi would mean travelling to Rhyl, finding the name of the boarding house and the people who ran it and finding someone who could speak up for him to the police so that he could avoid going to them himself. This, he reckoned, was impossible. He therefore decided to tell a false story about Liverpool, and try to persuade one of his criminal friends in Liverpool, for payment of a large sum of money, to ring the police and substantiate the false alibi. This was the only method Hanratty could devise which would get the police off his back, without giving himself up and being charged with housebreaking.

Why, then, did he not tell the truth after his arrest? His explanation is that he was scared to admit his earlier lies. Yet there is another explanation which is partly supported by the evidence of some close relatives who visited Hanratty in the cells before the trial. Hanratty was wanted for housebreaking. If he had immediately been cleared of the murder, he would have been charged at once with housebreaking, and would have started, inevitably, a long prison term. If he was innocent of the murder, his main motive was to avoid this prison sentence. He was also enraged at the police behaviour and the pestering of his family. There was without doubt strong motivation for Hanratty to 'lead the police a dance'; to protract the case until the publicity would make it more difficult for the police to charge him with housebreaking. There were also, as he might have calculated from the outset, big financial rewards to be made out of acquittal in a murder case. Hanratty had signed a contract shortly before his trial in which the *Daily Express* offered him five thousand pounds for his exclusive story in the event of his acquittal. Certainty of acquittal of the murder, in short, coupled with the fear of a prison sentence for housebreaking could well have caused Hanratty to deceive the police with a bogus alibi story.

In the 1963 Commons debate on the case, Mr Niall MacDermot, Q.C., made the general point:

> One may ask, why should he construct a false alibi at all? But I think the answer to that is simple. He could not count on alibi evidence in the sense of having someone to call to testify where he was at the time of the trial. A person of low intelligence finding himself in that situation, knowing himself unlikely to be believed, particularly when he had a criminal record, would tend to construct a false alibi if he can get people to come in and support it ... (Hansard, August 2nd, 1963, col. 819.)

But, whatever the explanation for the 'three men in Liverpool story' the change to the Rhyl story points not to Hanratty's guilt, but to his innocence.

Let us assume for the moment that Hanratty was guilty. He

phones Acott with a false alibi in Liverpool, travels there to get someone to back it up, fails, and is eventually arrested in Blackpool. There he continues with the false story, all the time protesting his innocence. He insists that he cannot give the names of the three men for two reasons: first, they are wanted men, and would be betrayed by his information; secondly, because they were wanted men, they would deny everything even if found. At one stage Hanratty admitted openly to Sherrard: 'I do not want you to find them' (the three men). By a fantastic miracle, Mrs Dinwoodie identifies him and helps to substantiate his alibi in Liverpool. By a miracle, a respectable witness appears to give credence to his lies.

If he was guilty, if he had never been to Rhyl on August 22nd, he was best advised to continue with his story. He could have pleaded in court as follows: 'I did not do this crime. I do not have to prove where I was. I have told you where I was, but I am not prepared to betray my friends to prove it. At any rate, here is Mrs Dinwoodie's evidence to prove I am telling the truth.' If he was guilty, that was by far the best defence he could offer. If he was guilty, if he had not been to the boarding house in Rhyl, it was reckless folly to invent a cock-and-bull story about Rhyl at the last moment, thus sacrificing any credibility he may have had in connection with the Liverpool alibi. The chances of any corroboration for a vague and unlikely story about Rhyl were minimal, while the chances that his story could be proved untrue (especially if he had stayed at Ingledene on some other date) were very high indeed.

All the pressures on Hanratty were against changing his alibi. Obstinately, however, and independently, he insisted on telling the Rhyl story in court. The only credible explanation for thus ignoring the advice of his lawyers was the one he gave in court: namely, that he had in fact been to Rhyl, had hoped to avoid arrest in the first instance by telling a lie, had compounded the lie rather than change his story — and then, at the last minute, faced with a gruelling cross-examination, had plumped, too late, for the truth.

5

Crook, not Murderer

James Hanratty: 'A bit of a Crook, but not a Murderer'

Only four of the twenty-one volumes of the transcript of the Bedford trial proceedings are devoted to evidence in defence of James Hanratty. At least one of these is taken up with evidence about the alibi (Mrs Dinwoodie, Mrs Jones, Terry Evans, Mr Kempt, Mr Webber). There are three witnesses about the jacket and the Stanmore housebreakings, and two more to refute the 'confession' to Roy Langdale. Evidence was also heard from two women, Mrs Audrey Willis and Mrs Meike Dalal, who were assaulted within a fortnight of the A6 murder; from a bus inspector about hiding things under bus back seats; and from Mary Meaden, Hanratty's ex-girlfriend. The bulk of the defence evidence came from James Hanratty himself.

Apart from the alibi, the most powerful card in Mr Sherrard's pack was his client. The more the jury saw of Hanratty, Sherrard felt, the less would they believe that this petty thief could possibly have performed such a ruthless murder.

The British public have one picture of Hanratty, which is not the same as that presented to those who attended the Bedford trial, nor to those who knew him. The picture was inspired by a journalistic passion for sensation. From the moment of his arrest in October, 1961, crime reporters throughout the country busied themselves preparing 'background stories' about James Hanratty. They collected two sorts of stories—one to be presented if Hanratty was guilty, and another if he was freed. Because of the rules of contempt of court, the stories were held back until after the trial.

On February 18th and 19th, the two days after the verdict, Hanratty became for the British people 'a monster' (*The People*).

The *News of the World* (February 18th) ran a hair-raising feature entitled 'The Evil Mind of James Hanratty'. The *Sunday Pictorial* which had 'bought' the France family, ran a centre-page feature about them entitled 'The Killer in My House.' The *Daily Express* did not spare the gory details about the 'killer'.

Making James Hanratty into a monster was a difficult job even for the crime correspondents, but, with maximum assistance from the police and prison officers, they managed it reasonably well. Little was written of Hanratty's childhood, perhaps because he grew up in a secure, cheerful and generous working-class family. Much was made of a minor accident during a bombing raid in the war, in which Hanratty fell over in his garden. Much, too, was written of his slowness at school, though no paper quoted the sisters at St James's School in Burnt Oak, who would have testified that Hanratty, if slow at his studies, was a willing and popular member of the school community. The suggestion by a doctor to Mr and Mrs Hanratty after a standard medical test when Hanratty was eleven that he should go to a special school was translated by the press into a 'recommendation'.

James Hanratty left school at fifteen, and started work alongside his father in the local council cleansing department. During his six months there he had to go into Wembley Hospital for a week to have his leg and head treated after a fall off his bicycle. This episode was exaggerated by the press far beyond its real importance.

Then, suddenly and without explanation, Hanratty left home and travelled to Brighton where he and his family had been on holiday during his childhood. He worked for a while delivering logs. He did not contact his family, who searched for him hopelessly throughout London. One evening he was found lying in the street, unconscious from fatigue. He was taken to the Royal Sussex Hospital, and from there to St Francis Hospital, Haywards Heath. The doctors there suspected some kind of brain damage, and operated on his brain. No damage was found, and a perplexed doctor, without explaining the term or the diagnosis, certified him as a 'mental defective'.

The diagnosis came as manna from heaven to the liberal newspapers whose legal correspondents, while not prepared to contemplate the possibility that the British courts could condemn an innocent man to death, were very happy with the suggestion that Hanratty was not in charge of his own mind, and therefore, although he did the murder, should not hang. Many lawyers, on publication of the 'new facts' from St Francis Hospital, Haywards Heath, breathed a sigh of relief and started to criticize the defence for not pleading 'diminished responsibility'.

'Diminished responsibility' was a defence recently introduced into British law, available to killers who admitted killing, but who were not in possession of their senses when the crime was committed. The court, if satisfied with this plea, could bring in a verdict of manslaughter rather than murder, and the prisoner would be condemned to life imprisonment.

The evidence about Hanratty's mental condition, therefore, provided an opportunity for liberal lawyers and journalists to ignore the real facts about Hanratty and plead for his reprieve on the grounds that he was a 'mental defective'.

On March 18th the *Observer*'s front page headline read: HANRATTY WAS A MENTAL CASE, BUTLER IS TOLD. The unexplained diagnosis of the doctor in Haywards Heath ten years previously was offered as evidence. The doctor himself was in Australia, and was not contacted to expand on his two-word summary. The *Observer* and other newspapers, however, managed to substantiate it with rumour. 'There have been suggestions', wrote the *Observer*'s Staff Reporter, 'in reports of prison psychiatrists, who have seen Hanratty during his periods of detention in prison in recent years, that Hanratty is a psychopath.' (*Observer*, March 18th, 1962.)

The journalistic significance of the rumour was instantly clear. A psychopath had done the murder, and Hanratty, the journalists discovered, was a psychopath. Mr Louis Blom-Cooper in his book states correctly that once, in 1958, Hanratty had tried to smuggle a shirt out of a prison laundry and that he 'always wore well-cut suits and dressed neatly'. From evidence like this, Mr Blom-Cooper had no difficulty in classifying Hanratty as an 'inadequate psychopath'.

The main evidence of Hanratty's 'psychopathy' was gleaned by the journalists from prison records. Even here, there was some difficulty. In Hanratty's first two prison sentences, he had earned the maximum remission. The *Sunday Telegraph* discovered that in the second spell he had been 'disciplined' for misbehaviour, a fate no doubt encountered by most other prisoners imprisoned for the same period.

During his three years' corrective training, however, he had not earned any remission. He had tried to escape from Maidstone prison, and, still trying to escape, he was shunted from Camp Hill prison in the Isle of Wight to Strangeways prison in Manchester and finally to Durham prison. Even so, try as they could, the newspapers could find for Hanratty no greater crimes in prison than attempting escape, 'spitting', 'insulting' warders, and becoming a rather unsuccessful 'tobacco baron'.

The Home Office had, in fact, been worried about Hanratty's mental state from the moment of his arrest, and had commissioned Mr Rhys J. Oliver, the medical officer at Bedford prison, to examine and observe Hanratty before and during the magistrates' hearing. Mr Oliver's report was submitted on December 7th, 1961, and told more of the truth about James Hanratty than all the newspaper accounts put together:

> *H.M. Prison*
> *7th December,* 1961

Name of Prisoner   James Hanratty
Date of Committal   16th October 1961
Committing Court   Ampthill Magistrates Court.

Sir,
The mental condition of the above prisoner is as follows:
   There is no family history of mental illness.
   When first received into our custody on October 16th he was composed, coherent, and able to give a clear account of his previous life.
   He said his general health had been quite good until he fell off a bicycle at the age of 15 years. In this accident he broke a leg and was treated at Wembley Hospital, mainly as an out-patient. After recovery from this fracture, about 3 months after the accident, he began to get headaches, depression, and lack of concentration. He says he left home during a period of amnesia, and was in Brighton, where he had a job selling logs, when he suddenly collapsed and was taken to hospital (Royal Sussex) where he began to get severe head pains, and was transferred to a Mental Hospital (Haywards Heath). An X-ray of the skull taken at the Royal Sussex Hospital was normal. An E.E.G. was within normal limits.
   The day after his admission to Haywards Heath a craniotomy was performed. There was no evidence of any cerebral lesion to be found, and the wound was closed without drainage and healed by first intention.

No abnormalities were found in any other investigations, such as blood, urine, etc.

In an interview with the parents some three days later, an interesting point was that a patient at the Royal Sussex told the father that the boy had spoken quite intelligently to him during the period he was supposed to be semi-comatose and unable to recognize his father.

In subsequent interviews here Hanratty said he could not read or write, yet he purchased newspapers and apparently read them, and wrote a letter to his parents in quite good handwriting, having some assistance with spelling from my hospital officer.

I have never at any time found any psychiatric traits calling for treatment, and he has been quiet and amenable, eating well, and sleeping well until the last few days of the hearing in the Magistrates' Court, when he began to get a bit worried about the case.

He is, in my opinion, quite fit to plead, he knows the difference between right and wrong, and must be held responsible for his actions.

I am Sir,

> Your obedient Servant
> Sgd. RHYS J. OLIVER
> Medical Officer.

The 'monster' depicted by the newspapers should also be compared with the evidence which had come out in court. The France family testified that he had always been kind and decent to them. The defence called Mary Meaden, a former girlfriend of Hanratty, who said that Hanratty's behaviour had always been impeccable. Apart from Mrs Anderson's dubious testimony there was and is no evidence from anyone who knew him that he had the remotest inclination towards violence or sexual savagery. For six months the entire resources of the British police force were at Mr Acott's disposal in his search for clues about James Hanratty. Almost everyone who knew Hanratty must have been closely interviewed. Yet Mr Acott could not find one case of violence or sexual assault.

James Hanratty's was not, of course, a shiningly attractive personality. He was vain, irritating and unstable, often thoughtless in his instability. He enjoyed the wretched company of the London underworld. Of the ten years of his life after leaving school, only four were spent out of prison, and his spells in prison inevitably hardened him. But throughout he remained essentially gentle and harmless.

Mr Acott also admitted that from the moment of his arrest Hanratty had protested his innocence of the crime. The best evidence of Hanratty's own attitude is in the letters which he wrote to his family during his six months' imprisonment following his arrest. Most of these were dictated to warders, and I have not altered the spelling in any way. His first letter was to his mother only three days after his arrest:

Dear Mum,

Just a few lines to let you know I am keeping my head up and not worrying. They are treating me very well considering the circumstances.

I have just written to the solicitor, and he knows everything that there is to know, and as soon as he produces the evidence it will be a shut and closed case.

I don't want to talk about this matter no more because I know how you worry, and there is nothing to worry about.

Well, mum, things was going very good for me until I went to Ireland. I had a marvellous time and met some very nice people. It was a big surprise to me when I heard the police wanted to interview me, but now they have interviewed me they are making a big mistake. Well, mum, they had to charge someone, but by the time they have finished with me, they will wish it hadn't have been me.

In the second week in November, Hanratty was visited by his cousin Eileen Cunningham. According to Miss Cunningham, the visit was a cheerful one in which both Hanratty and his cousin discussed his inevitable release. On November 16th, Hanratty wrote to his Aunt Anne, Eileen's mother:

I must say I was very pleased to see Eileen on Tuesday. She cheered me up a great deal and when you see her I would like you to thank her for me. Though we never had long together it made my mind more at ease. Well, Auntie, I bet when you got to hear about this trouble, it was a great shock to you, but you know that I couldn't do a terrible thing, like that. Though I am a bit of a crook, I wouldn't hurt a mouse.

Five days later he wrote again to his mother:

By the time you receive this letter I will be in court, but I thought I would drop you a line to let you know I shall probably be staying there for a short while. I don't want you to worry too much about me. I know you can't help worrying to a certain extent, now that things have straightened out, they might look bad at the moment but please do not worry too much ... I gather from the papers Mr Acock has found some more witnesses against me. This is going to be a very long case, and the papers ar'nt doing me any justice but you and I know that it is not in me to commit such an awful offence.

On November 25th, in the middle of the hearing at Ampthill, he wrote:

Dear Mum,
                    Just a few lines in answer to your kind and welcome letter which I received on Friday. I was very pleased to hear from you and hope that you have got rid of your cold by now. Well mum I know it must be bad for you and dad just now, but I want you to have faith in me mum.

If I had done this terrible thing I would have took my own life weeks ago. As you know I love you and Dad very much. Though I left home I was thinking of you all the time, and I am not saying that just because I am in trouble. I want you to explain to Dad that what he heard the other day was not true. What Mr Acot said about the interview at Blackpool I am going to speak up for myself when the time comes because if I don't Mr Acot will do all he can to convict me. He had made one mistake already and he has made others.

But I have got faith in my defence re Mr Kleinman and Mr Sherrard. They are both very intelligent men, and without any doubt they know that I am innocent. They won't say much to you about the case but I know more than anyone else. And when the time comes I want you and Dad to be present at the big Court, so that you can hear this ridiculous charge. As I said before, please have faith in me. I will soon straighten this terrible thing out.

On November 30th, the Hanratty parents received a short note from Bedford prison about their future visit, which ended: 'We will soon straighten it out.' At Christmas, he sent his mother three pounds 'to buy yourself a bunch of flowers'.

Four days before the Bedford trial (January 18th), Hanratty wrote to his brother Peter:

Dear Peter,

Just a few lines to let you know I'm keeping well and in the best of health, it will not be long now, before I see you, its been a very long time Pete but the end is drawing near. Its been real nice to have Mum, Dad and Mick at my side all the time. I don't know what I would have done without them.

Well I know its up to me to make it up to them when I come home, as I haven't been much of a son in the past but I have really learnt my lesson after this lot! Its surprising what the law can do to a innocent man. They can turn him inside out in no time but me being used to the game they did not find it so easy Pete.

Well Pete, dad told me that you and Lindsay have broken up I thought you two were a good match but you know your own mind, I thought I was going to be best man there, but a good looking lad like you should not have to be without a girl for long, you take after your Big Brother. Tell Richard to keep the old spirit up I hear he is doing fine at the factory, if there is anything he wants in the wardrobe help himself. It won't be long now before we are all together again so until then all the best.

Throughout the trial Hanratty did not write to his parents or his family, partly because he was able to see them more often in the cells of the Bedford court. On Wednesday, February 7th he climbed into the witness box, and started to answer questions. He was in the box for the whole of that day and almost all the next. From Wednesday afternoon to Thursday afternoon he was subjected to the most rigorous cross-examination on every aspect of the case by Mr Swanwick.

No one in the court then, and no one reading the two volumes of transcript today, can argue that Hanratty answered like a mental defective or a psychopath. On the contrary, the most striking aspects of Hanratty's response are consistency and coherence. Mr Blom-Cooper and other legal experts were shocked that from time to time Hanratty was rude to Mr Swanwick. For instance, the latter's first question was: 'Hanratty, do you always hold your right eyebrow higher than your left?' To which Hanratty answered, after a moment's hesitation: 'I do not know, Sir, because I cannot see it.' Again, when Mr Swanwick asked whether he could have got back from Mrs Dinwoodie's shop on Monday, August 21st, in time to book in at the Vienna Hotel, Hanratty answered in exasperation: 'How about Mrs France? I did not leave them until seven o'clock. I thought you had more intelligence.'

For this impertinence, Hanratty was rebuked by the judge, and posthumously by Mr Louis Blom-Cooper who quotes both the answers as proof of Hanratty's instability. In fact, however, both replies were justified. The question about the eyebrow was one of the tricks in which court lawyers indulge to 'throw' a witness at the start of a cross-examination. Even Mr Acott had rejected any suggestion that one of Hanratty's eyebrows was higher or bushier than the other. Mr Swanwick's silly question got a silly answer, and deserved it. In the second case, Hanratty was quite right. Mr Swanwick's own witnesses had testified against what he was suggesting to Hanratty, and the latter had every reason to reply in irritation. The lawyer's first two rules of court procedure—a barrister can be as offensive as he likes to a witness; and a witness must always be submissive and courteous to a barrister—were for two fleeting moments broken by a man who was on trial for his life.

Any section of that long cross-examination could be quoted to prove that Hanratty's answers were not those of a mental defective. A good example was a section dealing with the contention that Hanratty was a stick-up man:

Q. If you are a stick-up man, there is a chance that the person you are sticking up will see you, is there not?

A. There is, yes.

Q. And anything that you can do to alter your normal appearance would be a good thing, would it not?

A. It would, yes, I will be quite frank.

Q. One of the easiest ways of altering your appearance is to alter the way you do your hair?

A. Yes, I will be quite frank, it is.

Q. I suggest to you that you had decided to become a stick-up man, and you had brushed your hair back?

A. Can I answer that question?

Q. Yes.

A. If I was a stick-up man, I would not bother dyeing my hair. I would have a mask of some kind, because it is not your hair you have to worry about, it is your face. If I was a stick-up man, I would have to be face to face with somebody, and it is quite obvious to a man who has had experience over the years of what I have had with housebreaking, etc., it is quite obvious a man about to do a stick-up would not have his hair dyed; he would have a mask of some kind. And if you are suggesting that I have done stick-ups, well, I must put it to you that you are wrong.

Q. I am not suggesting you had done any stick-ups until the 22nd August.

A. You are wrong. I have done no stick-ups. I have owned no gun.

Q. I am not suggesting you did any afterwards either. I am suggesting that this was your ambition and you had just got this gun. That you went to the Vienna Hotel to play with it like a new toy, and you went out to use it for the first time on August 22nd; and that after the murder you abandoned it on the bus. Do you follow?

A. Sir, are you trying to suggest to the court that I went out on the 22nd August to do a stick-up with a gun? Is that what you are trying to say?

Q. Indeed I am.

A. Well, is it not quite obvious if I did that I would not be looking for a car in a cornfield, as you put it to the court. I will be looking for some cash, a bank, a shop, something to that effect. I would not be looking for a car in a cornfield for some cash for a stick-up. (Vol. XIV, p. 37.)

So it went on—a rasping duel between the brains of Mr Swanwick, trained at Winchester, University College, Oxford and the Inner Temple, and the untrained wits of James Hanratty. No one can say that Swanwick came off the best. All his questions were answered directly. There was from Hanratty no evasion and no sign at any stage of break-down. When asked about his trade, he asked for no pity:

Q. I am right in saying that you have been a professional housebreaker since you were sixteen?

A. That is quite correct.

Q. Breaking regularly into other people's houses, which you describe as your business?

A. That is quite correct.

Q. Taking their goods with no conscience and no regrets?

A. Yes, I agree.

Q. Is that right?

A. Yes.

Q. Selling them for what you can get to your clients?

A. That is correct, yes.

Q. No regard, of course, to the sentimental value of anything which you took?

A. No.

Q. No feelings towards the house owners who had come back and found their premises broken into and their goods missing?

A. Sir, I must put this point quite clear. I ain't a man the court approved of as of good character, but I am not a murderer. This is a murder trial, not a housebreaking trial. (Vol. XIV, pp. 50, 51.)

And again:

Q. It may be that the predominant motive was that you wanted the girl; it may be that you wanted to practise a stick-up; it may be that you did not mind the money and the car?

A. I had all the money I wanted. I give Mrs France £15 that day. If I wanted a woman I could have gone in the West End and had a woman for a fortnight. If I wanted a woman I could get one for a fortnight.

Q. But is not the difference this, that then you would not have had the thrill of holding them up with a gun?

A. The man who committed this is a maniac and a savage. I know what you have proved here. I am not a man the court can approve of, but I am not a maniac of any kind. I can prove it with my past girl friends. I am a decent — I cannot say honest — but I try to live a good and respectable life except for my housebreakings. (Vol. XIV, p. 57.)

There were other aspects of Hanratty's behaviour in court which impressed those who saw him. When Valerie Storie identified him, and indeed throughout her evidence, he sat impassively, his face a mixture of puzzlement and concern. When Mrs Jones, from Rhyl, stepped into the witness box his mother noticed that his nose began to bleed — as it always did, she recalls, when he became excited.

The jury pondered their verdict for ten hours. According to normal court practice, they were refused a transcript of the trial, though they asked for one. The verdict came as a shock to almost everyone in the court, including, many thought, the judge, who hesitated for a long time before sentencing Hanratty to death. Hanratty was utterly broken by the verdict, and, for the first time since the start of the trial, collapsed against the front of the dock. 'I am not – innocent. I am innocent, my Lord,' he mumbled incoherently, 'and I will appeal. That is all I have to say at this stage.'

The state of shock continued in the cells for several days after the verdict. His parents did not get a letter for more than a week after the verdict, and Hanratty asked that they should not visit him. His first letter after the verdict was dictated on February 28th:

Dear Mum,

       Just a few lines to let you know I am keeping up my spirit and I want you to know that I will be going to court on the 12th March once again. I only hope that this time it's carried out a little bit fairer than the previous trial that I had. I saw Mr Sherrard and Mr Kleinman on Sunday. They cheered me up a great deal. Everyone is trying to do their best for me. They are giving me every assistance and help possible.

Well, Mum, there is not a lot of news I can give you at this stage, I am glad that you understand about the visiting as you know how upset I get but when I go to London I will arrange to have a visit for you and Dad. I will be wearing that nice white shirt that you bought me for Christmas. I'm looking forward to this date as the days are quite long at the present in here. Well, Mum, give my love to Dad and the boys and tell them they are in my thoughts all the time and also give my love to Auntie Anne and Mrs McGee. With that I will say good night and God bless you all from your loving son.

Again, on March 2nd he wrote:

Dear Mum,

       Just a few lines in answer to your kind and welcome letter which I received the other day. I was very pleased to hear that you were all in good health and spirits at home.

Things are just the same here. I am over the shock now and I am patiently waiting for my appeal, which you already know is the 12th March and I will be looking forward to seeing you then. I have had one or two letters from different people all expressing their faith in me and the outcome of the appeal. All I ask is when I go to the court that I be given a fair trial and I feel this time the circumstances are different. I have great faith in Mr Sherrard, he said to me 'The guilty will be punished and the innocent set free'.

It is clear to thousands of people not only in here that the jury had made a terrible mistake.

Well Mum we do not want to talk too much about this I am writing to let you know how I feel.

I can't say at this stage that I am feeling happy, but I am keeping my spirits up and that is what really counts.

You will no doubt wonder what I do during the day, well I play cards, draughts and listen to my wireless.

I must say that the Staff has done everything in their power to make things as pleasant as possible in the circumstances here.

With that Mum give my love to Dad and the rest of the family.

Goodnight, God Bless you all.

With the failure of his appeal, however, on March 13th, the world again collapsed around him. His letters home, to every close member of the family, increased in number and intensity. In between March 17th and his execution two and a half weeks later, he wrote his parents eight letters, his brother Michael three, his other (younger) brothers one and his Aunt Anne, one. The next three letters tell their own story:

Dear Mum and Dad,

Just a few lines in answer to your kind and most welcome letter. Well, Mum and Dad, I feel sure things will still go in my favour. I was very disappointed last week but I have got over that now, I won't allow myself to get upset any more but it is very hard to do so, it has been a terrible strain to us all.

I recieved a letter from my solicitor, he seems to be working very hard doing what he can and I feel quite sure and I said this last week and I say it again, that somebody somewhere knows the truth and will come forward. Mum I never knew that it would end like this, what have I done to deserve this, only you and Dad with your faith in me keeps me going, or I do not know what would happen, no-one can imagine what it is like to experience something like this, I wake up every morning and it seems like a dream and I pray that one morning I will awake and it will not be a dream any longer.

I hope you will understand why I haven't asked you and Dad to visit me, because I love you so much and it is too much of a strain for me seeing you under these circumstances. I have just been visited by the R.C. Priest, and we had a nice little talk together, he has informed me that he has been in contact with my solicitor, and has got up a petition in Bedford for me, so he has great faith in me and so have a great many more people. I am now going to write to Mr Butler the Home Secretary hoping he will consider my case carefully and come to a favourable decision. I am afraid I will have to close now, but I will write again to you in the week Mum, give my love to Dad and all at home, and all those kind people who are trying to help. God bless you all, From your loving son.

Dear Mum and Dad,

Just a few lines in answer to your kind and welcome letter which I recieved this morning.

I have just been visited by three men from the Home Office about the inquiries into this case. I was interviewed by them for over two hours and I have to go back and see them in the morning, they asked me certain questions referring to the case, they brought up all my past history and asked me questions referring to my childhood. They are only doing this as they have their duty to carry out, it is just a formality which happens to everybody who is in my position at the present.

I will be glad when this has all been straightened out, because as I sat there I thought I was back in court again, having questions put to me, I would like you to ring Mr Kleinman and tell him what I have just told you. And I am sure that he will want to know about this and that will save me writing to him.

Well with that Mum I shall not talk about the case anymore as it has been on our mind for too long and there are much nicer things to talk about.

How are you and Dad keeping, I hope you are both in good

health as with this weather which we are having now there are plenty of colds about.

Well I often sit back and just wait for some good news to come referring to my case, and I know as soon as it comes to your knowledge you will inform me straight away, as the Governor has stopped my papers as the news that was being published in them was causing me some disturbance, as it is bad enough being in here without reading articles which upset you and make things much worse for yourself.

I didn't know about Mr France until I read it in your letter as I am away from the other fellow men and the officers that are present with me are not allowed to discuss the matters that refer to my case. So I will have to rely on you to inform me in your letters what is happening in my interest. I hope I am not upsetting you by writing this letter as I feel it isn't a cheering letter to send you, but I want you to help me in this way, so the next letter which you will receive from me I will make sure that it will be put in a different way, I am a little bit anxious about my concern and I would never have learnt about Mr France if you had not told me, so please forgive me for not writing such a pleasant letter this time. Put that matter to Mr Kleinman for me please.

I will close now and write soon. Give my love to all the Family.

Dear Mum,

Just a few lines in answer to your kind and welcome letter which I received this morning and I hope you have received the one I sent you yesterday. Well I said yesterday that I would write you a nice letter today and not talk about the case. Well Mum there isn't a lot I can say as not much happens each day but yesterday was a bit of a strain. I had a nice hair cut a couple of days ago and after washing my hair regular in here my hair is nearly back to its normal colour, though falling out. Its enough to make any man's fall out what I have been through. Last night I had a very nice half hour listening to the football match between Spurs and Benfica. I don't know what I would do without my little wireless as it helps to pass away days, as you know I don't care much for reading. I've wrote a lot of letters this last week to different people I don't think

I mentioned it in my letter to you yesterday but I wrote Sister Catherine a letter and one to the Pope in Rome. I sent it by air mail as I feel it would reach there much quicker this way. I hope to get a reply next week. I got a letter from Sister Catherine with yours this morning, it was a very nice letter and she is going to help me all she can. So with that Mum keep your chin up, give my love to all the family and all those kind people who are helping me. I'm going to write to Mrs McGee tomorrow as I'm sure that you have discussed the case with her but I will write and give her my opinion of the case tomorrow.

I won't be writing again till the weekend but you will be in my thoughts all the time. Give my love to Dad and tell him to keep up the old spirit, if any news of interest comes to you will you let me know. So until the weekend Mum, try not to worry too much.

There was one slender hope left: the petition for his reprieve. On March 24th, eleven days before his execution, he wrote a long rambling letter:

Dear Mum and Dad,

Just a few lines to your kind and welcome letter which I received on Saturday. I was very pleased to hear that everything is going alright and that you and Dad are keeping up that old spirit, and that is all I ask is that you keep up the old spirit and leave the rest to me. The cook is just coming in with my dinner Mum and I must say it is a very nice one, but not as appetising as yours. Well I have received some very nice letters these last few days, and I will be glad when it is time for me to get this lot off my mind, as my petition has been received by the Home Secretary and it won't be long now. He can only come to one decision so don't worry, I know it is a big strain for you and the family.

You asked me about Dad and Micky coming to visit me, I don't want you to think for one minute that I am being selfish, but I feel Mum that I am not doing it for myself, as it would be just as hard for me as it would be for Dad. There is nothing more I would want than to see you, Dad and the family, it is too much for me, it doesn't matter how much I try I still get upset in the circumstances. I know you and Dad will try to cheer me up, and you want to come to assure me that you are doing everything possible to help me.

I wrote to Mrs McGee and also Auntie Annie and Sister Catherine so I keep my mind occupied. I have still got my little wireless and I spend many an hour listening to the programmes, I miss my papers but the Governor has only done it for my own good as there was far too much scandle, and I hope when you read the Sunday papers that they didn't upset you. You always get that in a case of this kind and I feel there would be a lot of people will have a lot of sympathy towards her, but really speaking all the pain and suffering she has been through, I am going through a sight more pain and difficulties in a different way.

So please Mum don't let anything upset you because there is everything to look forward to, and I am sure that the Home Secretary will be reaching my case this week-end, and I am expecting my answer to my petition at the end of next week. So with that Mum there will be such a splash one of these mornings and we will all be together again. I will have to close now, God Bless you all.

Three days later he wrote to his brother Michael, handing over his car. As the execution date approached, the prison restrictions on letter-writing were lifted even further, and the warders at Bedford prison, who behaved throughout this episode with notable compassion, allowed Hanratty's letters to grow longer. On March 28th and again on April 1st he wrote to his mother with the same mixture of forced cheerfulness and insistence on his innocence. Increasingly, too, he began to write about the people responsible for the crime:

Dear Mum,

Before I go any further I would like to wish you a very happy birthday and also a very enjoyable Mother's day. I have bought you a nice box of chocolates for Sunday so you can sit down and relax and enjoy them. I know your birthday is sometime next week, so I have taken the opportunity of sending the card with the chocolates and I hope you will like them. I know that Dad and the boys will make things nice and easy for you on Sunday, and I will be thinking of you.

It has been brought to my notice that you and Dad have

been working so hard and that you have put your petitions through to the Home Secretary and I would like to say this. I am so pleased with the way you have shown your courage up all through this case. I would like to thank you once more for all that you have done for me, and I'm sure no one could have done more than you and Dad. I know that you have had faith in me from the beginning and that knowledge has helped me to keep my spirits up.

I feel that without any doubt that one day my name will be cleared without any doubt. With that knowledge there is no need for you and Dad to be ashamed of any gossip or any remarks of any sort. When eventually the truth does come to light people will regret the remarks they have made against me. I have sat here for the last three weeks and I still can't imagine that this is really true. I pray at nights that I will wake up one day and find that it is all over. When I lay here at nights hour upon hour, night after night, hoping and knowing somewhere the person knows what I am going through. People today don't seem to have any conscience at all.

So Mum keep that old chin up and say that little prayer, I'm sure between the two of us our prayers will be answered.

Well, Mum I'm trying my best to cheer you up with this letter so I will talk a little bit about myself and that will take our minds off other things.

This afternoon I sat listening to the radio and I wondered to myself if you had had a shilling each way on your old favourite Lester Piggott. While I was waiting for the race to start myself and the two officers took two horses each out of 30 odd runners and we had a bar of chocolate on the result. The one who had the winner, or the nearest to the winner, won the chocolate, and I bet you can guess who won it. Out of my two horses I took Blast which wasn't placed. But my second horse which was Robson's Choice was second. If you didn't hear the race it was the Lincolnshire Handicap.

Well Mum I will have to close now. I gave your regards to Father Hulme and he was very pleased. Give my love to Dad and to Mick, Pete and Ritch and tell them all I can think of no finer place to be than at home with you all. From your loving son.

Dear Mum,

        Thank you for your very kind and very welcome letter. I only hope that Dad and the boys are giving you a nice treat to-day as you know what to-day is don't you? Well I will be thinking of you this afternoon sitting back in your arm-chair reading the Sunday paper, and eating your chocolates. I know Dad hasn't got much of a sweet tooth, but I'm sure he will join you in eating these chocolates. Well Mum I'm doing as you said. I'm trying my utmost to keep myself together, and this is the first time in my life that I have acted like a man. I will do so until my name is cleared. I have only kept myself together knowing that I had you and Dad with me all the way and that I was innocent.

I am glad you liked your card Mum. The wireless is on and I am listening to family favourites now and I can just imagine you and Aunty Annie getting the dinner ready. The two officers who are with me now, when they were off duty, they went to the Bingo – the first night they had ever been – and they won £13 between them. The other two on the morning shift they also won £10 between them and they both shared the same as the other two. So they are very pleased with themselves. They don't come from Bedford. They are special Staff from other Prisons.

I feel Mum that they won't be with me much longer and they will be going home to their wives and children. I get on well with the six of them. Father Hulme comes in and sees me every evening, and I say my few prayers. We have a little talk about the daily happenings and he cheers me up a lot.

I have improved my game of draughts and I keep the officers on their toes and alert at all times. They call me 'King of the Draught Board'. Well Mum I hope you and Dad are keeping your spirits up and not worrying too much. No matter what happens we know that the country has made a terrible mistake. There is nothing that we can do. There is only one person who can help us now and I'm sure that he will. Give my love to Aunty Annie and also Mrs McGee. I'm sure that they understand the details of this case. If I was given the opportunity whilst the trial was on to explain in more detail I'm sure that the verdict would have been different. As you know, when I went into the witness box, I went in there for one purpose only.

That was to be asked questions and to be insulted. Mum I wish you had really been there and seen and heard the way this case was put to me. I was in the witness box 10 hours and I answered every question truthfully and correctly but it was a waste of time because they had already made their minds up. I knew in my own mind that was going to happen before I ever went to Bedford, and I prayed at night that my case would be dealt with in London. Never mind Mum it will work out right in the end. I know it will. Just have that little bit of faith that you have had all the way Mum and Dad. Goodbye and God Bless you all. From your loving son.

On March 28th, Mr Hanratty senior handed in to the Home Office a petition with the names of more than 90,000 British citizens calling for a reprieve for their son. On Sunday April 1st Mr R. A. Butler went to church near his home at Greenstead Green in Essex and read the lesson about the reprieve given to Barabbas by the Roman authorities in Judaea shortly before the crucifixion of Christ. Reporters gathered outside the church were anxious to discover whether any decision had been made about Hanratty's reprieve. They got no answer, and deduced that Mr Butler had been seeking guidance from the Almighty about his awful decision.

The decision had, however, been made. On the Monday morning, April 2nd, the Hanrattys received a letter from the Home Office dated the previous Friday, informing them that the Home Secretary 'has been unable to find any sufficient ground to justify him in recommending Her Majesty to interfere with the due course of the law'.

As soon as this news was conveyed to him, Hanratty dictated a letter to his father in the condemned cell at Bedford:

Dear Dad,
            I am very sorry that things have turned out like this, but I know that you have got the courage and strength to bring back the family good name, and you have been such a good father to us all, I know that you will take extra care of Mum.

I can't say how sorry I am that this has turned out this way, but that was not my fault, it was the fault of others. I am writing this letter, knowing this is my only chance to thank you and Mum for all that you have done for me. And the only way I can pay my respect to you and the family is to show what kind of man I really am, though I am about to take the punishment for some one else's crime, I will face it like a man, and show both courage and strength, and try to make you proud of your son.

Thank you Dad for your two wonderfull visits, your courage was really wonderfull, and I will never forget the way you controlled yourself, you can't really understand just how much that really meant to me. The time is nearly here, and I will be thinking of you. And only hope I can be as much a man as you are. God Bless you all. Your ever loving Son.

Mr Louis Blom-Cooper, in his book about the A6 murder, cites this letter to substantiate his view that Hanratty may have committed the murder in concert with others.

'There is', he writes, 'in the contents of the letters a hint that, although the A6 killing may have been a crime for which he alone could be adjudged criminally responsible, yet at the same time he was not alone in setting in motion the train of events which led to the murder on Deadman's Hill.' (*The A6 Murder: Regina v. James Hanratty: The Semblance of Truth*, pp. 131, 132.)

This was a very damaging inference. Like the evidence of Langdale it punctured Hanratty's consistent and public declarations of his innocence. It was offered without detailed quotation from the letters, and had not the slightest shred of justification. Hanratty had written: 'I am about to take the punishment for someone else's crime'. Mr Blom-Cooper concluded from this that he felt that 'he alone could be adjudged criminally responsible' – an act of semantic contortion astonishing even for a barrister-at-law. If Mr Blom-Cooper had quoted at length from all or any of Hanratty's last letters his readers would have seen that Hanratty's protestation of innocence was consistent throughout, and grew more urgent as his execution became inevitable. There is not one line, not one sentence which could possibly be interpreted as a confession.

There is a further point, conveniently forgotten by Mr Blom-Cooper, which underwrote this consistency. As we have seen, Hanratty referred more than once to the Catholic priests who visited him in prison. Anxious that the young man should confess his sins on earth before facing his Maker, the priests pressed him, within the confidence of the confessional, to tell them the whole truth about the murder.

On March 17th, Father John Hughes of the Church of the Holy

Child Jesus in Bedford, was so impressed by Hanratty's denials of guilt that he decided on his own initiative, and contrary to all the practice of his Church, to approach the newspapers. The *Sunday Express* of March 18th carried the priest's expressed conviction that James Hanratty was innocent of the A6 murder.

There was still a fortnight to go before the execution date, and it could be argued that Hanratty was lying to the priest in the hope that a reprieve might still be granted. Such an objection does not apply to two other priests who saw Hanratty regularly after the reprieve had been refused. Both priests, Father Hulme from Bedford and Father Keogh, who had met Hanratty in Brixton, told Hanratty's parents after the execution (and repeated to Fenner Brockway before the House of Commons debate in 1963) that Hanratty, far from confessing to the murder, had protested his innocence to the very end.

On the evening of April 3rd, the eve of his execution, Hanratty wrote for the last time to his parents:

Dear Mum and Dad,

I am finding this letter very hard to put together. But I am going to try very hard to do everything I can to help you to recover from the terrible shock caused by all this. I am sorry I have caused you this terrible strain, both you and Dad and all the family.

You have all been so brave all the way in the case, and to show my gratitude to you all, I am going to face up to it, and am going to be a son that you and Dad can be proud of. I have not been much of a son to you in the past but Mum what I am about to say to you, comes from the bottom of my heart. I have always loved you and Dad and all of my family and I don't think that there is a son anywhere in the world that loves his Mum and Dad as much as I do at this stage. Though I will never see you again, through the fault of others, I will know in my own mind, as my love for you is very strong, your love for me will be just as strong. I was very pleased in the way you and Dad had great courage on your visit to me. It must have been a great strain on both of you.

As I tried my utmost best to keep hold of myself, where I failed, you showed your courage in every way, and you only done it for me. I am sitting here Mum and you have been on my mind all evening. But I will be glad when morning does come.

Before I close I must say that everybody here has been so kind to me, and they have all shown their gratitude towards me. In every little way, I still find it very hard to believe what is about to happen but Mum, I promise you that I will face it like a man, and I am sure that it is the way you and Dad would want it, and I hope that this will open the eyes of many people.

And what I have said before, will one day be proved to the world. Well Mum, though I have been in trouble at certain times in my life, it was only my own fault to blame, from the family I come from there was no need for me to turn to crime, every man makes mistakes sometime or other in his life. And my bad mistake was dog racing, I feel thats what really put me on the road to crime. If I had any will power to stop, I would not have been away from home so much, as a man has everything he needs in our home.

Many a man would be glad to have the home you and Dad gave to me, but it was my own fault for not taking it, and if I had taken it, and stayed at home, my life might have been different. Because I would have had every chance in the world to settle down and lead a good clean and honest life.

You know I am not very good at putting these letters together and I am trying my utmost, I only hope there is nothing I have forgot to say, but before I close Mum, the time is getting near and when it comes I will be thinking of you and Dad, and that will give me lots of courage and strength. And my mortal sins have been forgiven.

I was visited by Father Keogh from Brixton he came to give me that extra little bit of courage, he is a fine gentleman, and I am going to see him any hour now. And I am going to ask him to visit you, so as you can see for yourself what kind of a person he really is. He stayed with me with Father Hulme on Tuesday from 6 p.m. till 10 p.m. We joked together and had a long talk. I shall not see them again until Wed. morning, and they will also help me to keep my courage and spirits up, but I would do it on the courage alone that you and Dad have shown so Mum and Dad until we meet again you will all ways be in my thoughts. So God Bless you all. From your ever loving son Jim.

In the early hours of the morning of April 4th he wrote finally to his brother Michael, and asked for a solemn commitment:

Dear Mike,

          Well Mick I am going to do my best to face the morning with courage and strength and I am sure God will give me the courage to do so.

    Mick now you are the eldest in the family I am counting on you to look after the family and I know that I could not count on any body better than yourself. Mick we always got on well together and we had many good times together over the years. But I am going to ask you to do me a small favour, that is I would like you to try and clear my name, of this crime. Someone, somewhere is responsible for this crime and one day they will venture again and then the truth will come out, and then Mick that will be the chance for you to step in. I feel the police will try to hush it all up if they get the chance. So Mick I am counting on you to keep your eyes on the papers. Well Mick with that as time is drawing near, it is almost daylight, so please look after Mum and Dad for me, as you just could not wish to have better parents that the ones you have got. I only wish I could have the chance all over again. But never mind, Mick as I don't know what I have done to deserve this. But Mick, that's fate for you. Thanks for all the trouble you have been to, I can assure you that you have not been wasting your time, as it will all help to bring out the truth in the end, and Mick don't let anyone say a bad word about me. I feel I will have to say goodbye for now. Give my best wishes to Mum and Dad and all the family. Your loving brother, Jim.

P.S. I hope you will like the car as it is one which I am sure you will like, I wish I had paid the full amount and had given it to you as a gift before now. But please Mick remember it is a very fast car, and whatever you do take care when you drive it. With a car of this standard it is very powerful. I know you are a very good driver and know that you will take care of it, and I hope you really enjoy it for many years to come. Keep smiling Mick. Jim.

A few hours later James Hanratty walked with dignity to his death. The majesty of the British legal system had exacted retribution in its traditional way. It was left to others, rather less well-equipped, to seek the truth about the A6 murder.

PART FOUR

Peter Louis Alphon

6

The Confessions of Peter Alphon

When Peter Alphon left Mortlake magistrates' court on October 3rd, 1961, he was, officially at any rate, regarded as entirely innocent of the A6 murder and the assault on Mrs Dalal.

He was free – but his character had been grievously libelled by the publicity which had linked his name with the A6 murder. For several days the previous month, his name had dominated the front pages of newspapers. He was wanted for the A6 murder, and, moreover, was the first suspect. Even when caught and 'cleared' through Miss Storie's failure to identify him, he was held in prison on the Dalal assault charge for four days. Bail was refused until, in a series of identification parades, he was picked out by witnesses from a firm supplying almanacs near Leicester Square who said he had been in their shop at the time of the Dalal assault. These witnesses were found and delivered by the police. Nevertheless Alphon, if he was blameless, had been cruelly treated.

As John Gordon of the *Sunday Express* put it:

> It seems to me that Scotland Yard should have a little firmer foundation on which to make public allegations as serious as those in both cases involving Alphon before it subjects any citizen to such an ordeal. (*Sunday Express*, October 8th, 1961.)

Alphon's ordeal was softened no doubt by the payment of one thousand pounds by the *Daily Express* for his exclusive story, published on October 4th. But he was obviously determined to clear his name once and for all, and exact damages from the authorities for the anguish they had caused him. He had, after all, only one, very minor, previous criminal conviction (for taking and driving away a motor cycle in 1953). He had been to a public school (Mercers)

303

which he had left early at fifteen. He had spent most of his time since then, barring a short period in the R.A.F., staying with his parents or in cheap hotels and, above all, reading. In fifteen years he had read massively. He had studied in great depth astrology and theosophy (which aims at direct communication between God and the soul). He had become interested in witchcraft and black magic. In politics he was a Fascist, and a great admirer of Hitler. He had never held down a consistent job. From time to time he would work as an almanac salesman, or, less frequently, as a barman in public houses in the West End. When asked for an occupation by police during his first answers to questions in August 1961, he replied that he was 'a student'. He was a keen gambler – particularly on the dogs. He was a loner, relying very much on his own company and his own resources, and keeping, to all outward appearances at any rate, within the confines of the law.

No one was surprised, then, when, on November 6th, 1961, Peter Alphon took out a writ against Superintendent Robert Acott alleging defamation of character and wrongful imprisonment. The writ claimed that in naming Alphon in his murder-hunt appeal on September 22nd, Acott had implied that Alphon had something to do with the murder; and that by holding him on the Richmond charge without checking the almanac suppliers' alibi, Alphon had been wrongfully imprisoned. Alphon's tough-minded solicitor, Mr H. McDougal, was confident of success on the action, especially on the wrongful imprisonment charge, for which legal aid was available.

A number of other writs were also taken out – against the *Daily Mirror* for printing Acott's appeal on September 23rd; against the *Daily Mail* for an article published the same day about Alphon's background, which was highly uncomplimentary. Mr McDougal was very confident of a 'satisfactory settlement' of these actions, also.

Peter Alphon was not a witness at the A6 hearing at Ampthill or at the Bedford trial. His name came up only in passing at Ampthill, when the Vienna Hotel manager Nudds told the court of his second statement, since withdrawn, which had implicated Alphon. Superintendent Acott also told the court that he had put out a murder hunt for Alphon after Nudds's second statement, but had eliminated him after his inquiries.

At the trial, in his cross-examination of Mr Acott, Mr Sherrard dwelt at much greater length on Nudds's second statement and the murder hunt for Alphon. In re-examination of the Superintendent, therefore, Mr Swanwick felt it necessary to clear up the Alphon business once and for all:

MR ACOTT. I can think of a good many points, concrete points, which certainly put together, plus my feeling, eliminated him.

MR SWANWICK. In case there might be any suggestion that he is still responsible will you give my Lord the main points?

MR ACOTT. First, he was not Jim or James; he was Peter. He was 29; our suspect was in his mid-twenties. I beg your pardon he [Alphon] was 31. He was 5 ft. 9 ins. Our suspect was 5 ft. 6 ins. He has hazel eyes; our suspect had large, saucer-like blue eyes. He pronounced the diphthong 'th' correctly; our suspect could not. Our suspect had an East London accent; Alphon did not and was well-spoken. The suspect was described as an uneducated man; Alphon was distinctly educated.

Our suspect had been described by Miss Storie as hesitant and claiming time for thinking; I found not the slightest hesitancy in Alphon who readily and immediately answered all my questions. The suspect had used the word 'kip'; Alphon never used the word 'kip'.

The suspect had shown great desire to stop and sleep somewhere; despite the fact that Alphon had been up all the previous day and I had kept him up all night with this interview, followed by the identification parade, the medical tests, laboratory tests, never in my presence did he show any tendency to sleep ...

He volunteered himself for identification tests, medical tests, laboratory tests, and was pleased when I arranged them.

My enquiries showed that he had not driven a motor car but had a good many years before had some little experience with a motor cycle.

Our suspect again by Miss Valerie Storie was described as immaculate; Alphon was shabbily dressed in a blazer and old grey flannel trousers. (Vol. XI, pp. 48–49.)

At least two of these reasons given for eliminating Alphon could have been applied to Hanratty. Hanratty's height was 5 ft. 8 ins., just one inch shorter than Alphon and two inches taller than 'our suspect'. And Hanratty, like Alphon, had immediately agreed to all blood and laboratory tests.

Secondly, many of the points given for eliminating Alphon were known to the police before the murder hunt for Alphon was started. Alphon's christian name, his height, the colour of his eyes, his dress, his education and reading habits had been included in Scotland Yard's official description of Alphon as the man they wanted to interview. If these were all points which 'eliminated' Alphon from Mr Acott's inquiries, why did they bother to put out the most explicit and extensive murder hunt for him?

We shall discover later in this chapter that Alphon, when excited, slips naturally into a Cockney, or at any rate an 'uneducated' London accent, that he often mispronounces 'th' as 'f', that he is, almost always, hesitant in his manner, and that he has car-driving experience.

All Acott's thirteen 'points of elimination' were based on Valerie Storie's description of the man in the car; and most of them were based on the murderer's description of himself to Miss Storie. As an experienced policeman, Mr Acott must have realized that a man climbing into the back of a car with a gun would be unlikely immediately to tell his victims his name, address and telephone number. More probably, he would *disguise* his real identity, give a false name, use a false accent, provide for himself a false background. Of course, if the same man was being investigated by police for the crime, he would seek to present himself as *differently* as possible from the man in the car. That is why Acott originally ignored the marginal differences between Alphon and 'our suspect' which he told the Bedford court were the reasons for eliminating him.

Finally, most important, the long list of 'eliminators' left unanswered one crucial question. *Where* was Alphon on the night of the murder? If Acott had been able to answer this question, there would have been not thirteen points, but one. 'I can prove', Acott would have told the court, 'that Alphon was at such and such a place on the night of the murder,' and if he had *proved* it, that would have been the end of any suspicion against Alphon for all time.

Acott provided no such alibi, *because he could not prove one.* He knew that the alibi given by Alphon four days after the murder to the Finsbury Park police could not be established. He knew that Alphon had not been with his mother on the evening of August 22nd. He had made sure of that in the long interview with Mr and Mrs Alphon on the afternoon before the hunt for Alphon was launched. The Superintendent knew too that Nudds's third statement that Alphon had been in the Vienna Hotel on the murder night was, like all Nudds's evidence, highly unreliable. So, Mr

Acott carefully avoided providing Alphon with an alibi for the night of the murder.

Acott's ineffectual dismissal of Alphon was heard with great interest by Mr Jean Justice who had watched the trial from the public gallery.

Jean Justice, the eldest son of a prominent Belgian diplomat, had spent his childhood in Ireland and, with his parents, in different parts of the world, mainly in Eastern Europe and the Middle East. He resisted throughout his father's pressures to 'get on with it', and preferred to paint and listen to music rather than study. At eighteen, he had worked for a short time with a shipping firm in Antwerp, and had gone from there for a year at Louvain University. To his father's fury, he refused, out of political conviction, to serve military service in Belgium, and in 1951, when he was twenty-one, he went to St Catherine's College, Oxford. He failed his exams, and banned from Belgium, he bought a farm in Devon with a friend.

In 1956 he sold the farm and bought a short lease on a down-at-heel block in Half Moon Street, off Piccadilly, London. In the same year, he met Jeremy Fox, a barrister. The two men were drawn together by each other's loneliness and became close friends. Fox moved into No. 26 Half Moon Street, and the two men bought a cottage in Sussex and started to dabble together, with some success, in property speculation.

Throughout the late 1950s, Justice effectively became an alcoholic. In the summer of 1961, Fox took him on a trip round Europe, and, when they returned, Justice determined to try to discipline himself against drink. To do so, he took a menial job at a firm of Hammersmith solicitors. For several months he served writs and took statements, like any articled clerk.

Justice was fascinated by the law, and carried his fascination to excess. In 1960, he was determined to attend the Lonsdale/Gee spy trial, to which only members of the Bar were admitted. He persuaded Fox to lend him his barrister's wig and gown, and confidently presented himself at the trial. He was, however, discovered and unveiled, to the delight of the newspapers and to the chagrin of Fox, who nearly got sacked from Lincoln's Inn.

Soon after returning from Europe, in October 1961, he read in the papers that the Crown were to deploy some eighty witnesses at the A6 trial. He was employing a chauffeur at that time—a former minicab driver called Gordon Perkins, who had driven him down to his Sussex cottage one weekend, and had agreed to become his chauffeur for eight pounds a week. Perkins persuaded Justice to go to the Ampthill hearing of the A6 case, and drove him there almost daily. Justice remembers being dubious about Hanratty's guilt, even at the hearing. Returning from Ampthill, he persuaded a sceptical Fox to accompany him on inquiries on behalf of Hanratty. The two men went night after night in December 1961, including even New Year's Eve, to the Rehearsal Club in Archer Street. They saw Charles France, but did not interview him. They also saw Ann Price, who told them that she did not believe Hanratty was guilty.

They got involved in a rather purposeless chase of a young man who went under the pseudonym of Jimmy James and who had been detained during the inquiries about the murder without having anything to do with it. They also met Lennie Fields, later to be jailed in connection with the Great Train Robbery of 1963, who told them that Hanratty had been pestering him and his girlfriend all summer with a gold watch he was trying to sell.

By the beginning of the trial on January 22nd, Fox had become interested enough in the case to drive Justice to Bedford for almost every day of the trial. As Justice listened sceptically to Acott's 'thirteen points' eliminating Alphon from his inquiries, he determined to see Alphon. That evening, he persuaded Jeremy Fox to find Alphon's address from the writ which Alphon had issued against Acott. Alphon's address on the writ was given as the Ariel Hotel, on the Bath Road just outside London Airport. Justice rang the hotel and eventually spoke to Alphon at 1 a.m. on Friday, February 9th. Pretending that he wanted to take a photograph, Justice asked if the two men could meet, and Alphon agreed a meeting at the offices of his solicitor, Mr McDougal. At McDougal's offices the following day, Justice and his brother Frank were told that Alphon had changed his mind and would not see them. A visit to the Ariel Hotel that evening, and a search lasting well into the night, costing a considerable sum in tips, proved fruitless.

On the evening of Sunday, February 11th, Justice went again to the Ariel Hotel, and spoke to Alphon by telephone from the reception desk. Finally, with much reluctance, Alphon agreed to meet him and before long the two men were walking towards a pub on the Bath Road where they talked for two hours.

From the start, they took a liking to each other. Alphon enjoyed the ponderous cross-examination to which he was subjected, and

Justice in turn enjoyed the charm and courtesy of his companion. That night, and on their next meeting, Alphon remained polite, but Justice discovered a little about his companion's Fascist views and contempt for immorality and homosexuality which contrasted with Justice's leftish, more permissive approach. Alphon's father, Justice discovered, who had retired the previous year from Scotland Yard, gave his son a small allowance. Alphon was devoted to his mother, though not on good terms with his father. About the A6 murder, Alphon professed only academic interest. He explained that he had been wrongly arrested by the police, and said, laughing: 'They can't pin it on me now.' He would not offer a view about whether or not Hanratty was guilty.

Two days later, Justice again met Alphon in the foyer of the Ariel Hotel, and again the two men talked for several hours in the Bath Road pub. Justice noticed on this occasion that Alphon had travelled to London and back that day by hired car, and had plenty of money when he needed it. The Ariel Hotel is not inexpensive and Alphon had been staying there almost permanently since the previous November. That evening, the two men travelled to London, and Justice and Fox gave Alphon dinner at the Ox on the Roof restaurant in Chelsea. Fox, too, took an instant liking to his friend's quiet companion.

From the restaurant the three men went back to Half Moon Street to talk and play gramophone records. 'I was convinced at the time that he had had nothing to do with the murder', says Justice, 'but I felt he could tell us something about it.' Alphon left on very good terms with his new friends, who gave him their telephone number.

On Friday 16th, the day before the verdict in the Bedford trial, Alphon checked out of the Ariel Hotel, leaving no forwarding address. Over the weekend following the verdict and sentence at Bedford, Justice and Fox heard nothing from him. On the Monday (19th) Alphon rang to say that he had moved to the (also not inexpensive) Regent Palace Hotel in Soho and asked them round for a drink that evening.

The following day – Tuesday, February 20th – the evening papers carried the news that Mr McDougal, Alphon's solicitor, had been bombarded with obscene and threatening phone calls. Fox and Justice went to Scotland Yard to make statements about the telephone calls, since the caller had said that his name was 'Jeremy' and 'Mr Fox'. Both said that they had nothing to do with the phone calls and Justice added that he did not think Alphon was responsible either.

That same Tuesday, Jean Justice and his brother Frank went to see Alphon at the Regent Palace Hotel, and Alphon proudly showed them a surrealistic drawing. At first sight, the drawing is nothing but a series of criss-crossed lines in dark purple and other colours. It is only when the drawing is held level with the eyes that words, hand-printed in long spider-like lettering, stand out from the maze of lines.

On one side is written: PETER MCDOUGAL. (Alphon had booked into the Regent Palace Hotel under the pseudonym of Peter McDougal.)

On the other side is the single word: MURDERER.

At the bottom, written in black outside the pattern, is: BEDFORD.

The words gave Justice quite a shock, and he determined to get hold of the document. He noticed, however, that Alphon was not at all keen on parting with it.

On Sunday February 25th Justice and Fox went to the Regent Palace Hotel and Alphon showed Fox the drawing for the first time. While Fox was looking at it Justice seized it and quickly left the room. He then did everything possible to use the drawing to James Hanratty's advantage. On February 27th, he and Fox went to Scotland Yard. The following is the description of that encounter as recalled by Fox in a statement to the defence two days later (March 1st):

About 11.15 a.m. we were shown into a room and a few minutes later Inspector Webster came in, accompanied by Chief Superintendent Kennedy (then head of the Murder Squad). Kennedy said: 'Where is the famous drawing or photograph that you have to show me?' Mr Justice said, opening the envelope: 'The original is with my solicitor. He would not let me part with it, but he has given me a photostat to give you.' He handed him the photograph and Kennedy looked at it from several angles. Mr Justice said: 'Do you see what it is? Can you make it out?' He said: 'Yes, I see it at once.' He handed it back to Mr Justice very abruptly, and then said: 'This is a lot of balls. Get out of here, you two men. You're on the fringe of interfering with the course of justice!'

The two men had better luck when they visited Christmas Humphries, Q.C. with the drawing and asked his opinion of it. Humphries answered that the drawing might in the circumstances be regarded as a confession and advised them to hand it over to the defence with a view to it going to the Court of Appeal. The drawing was given to the defence, but was not presented to the Court of Appeal. It was sent with other papers to the Home Secretary, together with the petition for the reprieve.

After a week's silence, however, Alphon rang Justice again and their meetings started once more. Very quickly, the two men, with nothing to do all day, each with enough money to indulge themselves almost at will, grew very close indeed. 'I used', writes Justice, 'to meet him at one o'clock in the Kings Arms in Shepherd Market. He would be sitting there on his own, reading the *Greyhound News*. He would invariably buy me a large Amontillado. Then, hands clasped in token of the deep bond between us, we would talk.' (*Murder versus Murder*, p. 15.)

In the evenings, Justice continues, 'Night after night in my flat at Half Moon Street, Peter and I would listen to pop records, drink Guinness and go over the details of the A6 murder.'

Justice goes on to write very honestly about his relationship with Alphon over March, April and May of that year:

> If Peter Alphon had not been powerfully attracted to me, he would never have confessed verbally or written the confession notes that reveal him as the A6 murderer. Quite unpredictably, the man whom I was leading on in the hope of extracting information from him gradually came to feel more than mere friendship for me ...
>
> It was after I became aware of Peter's passionate regard for me that I began to see how much I could undermine his defences. Just as a man will tell the woman he loves secrets he has never revealed to anyone else, so Peter might be persuaded to let me share some of the dark memories that I could plainly see were disturbing him from time to time. If I allowed him to think that I was wholly in his power, his 'little girl' as he sometimes called me, then he might foolishly assume that he could confide in me without fear of betrayal. All I had to do was to convince him that I was as infatuated as he was. (Op. cit., pp. 98, 99.)

None of this was fantasy. The deep affection which Alphon had for Justice is on record on scores of feet of tape, covering scores of conversations between the two men, many of them recorded without Alphon's knowledge. In one of the tapes, Alphon says to Justice: 'All my life, I have seen people happy together, and wondered what it was all about. I never understood what it meant until I met you.' There is no doubt that over those three months, in a state of considerable emotional disturbance, Alphon came to rely on Justice as he had never before relied on a friend.

Where Justice's official version may stray a little is in his own attitude to Alphon. For there is no doubt at all that Justice felt a considerable affection for Alphon. As Justice put it to me: 'I felt: here is a man who is really, genuinely fond of me. I was flattered by having such a friend.'

In the loneliness and disorder of his own life, Justice took to Alphon almost as strongly as Alphon to Justice. 'I was', said Justice, 'like a double agent: giving and taking so much I didn't know all the time which side I was on.' He drove the friendship forward and exaggerated his own feelings in order to find the truth about the A6 murder. Quite soon, he became convinced that Alphon was the A6 murderer.

During the first fortnight in March the two men saw each other constantly. Throughout this period, Alphon was reserved and cautious in any discussion about the murder. Nevertheless, Justice noticed that Alphon became more nervous and hysterical as the day fixed for Hanratty's execution grew closer. On March 13th, the Court of Criminal Appeal dismissed Hanratty's appeal, and Alphon wrote at once to the *Daily Express* calling for a reprieve.

'Former A6 murder suspect Peter Louis Alphon said yesterday he will support any approach for a reprieve for James Hanratty, the convicted killer,' reported the *Daily Express* of March 15th. 'Mr Alphon, aged 31, said: "I've studied the case very closely, and I believe Hanratty was innocent. There has been so much confusion and doubt in this extraordinary case that I'm prepared to do all in my power to seek a reprieve." ' The following day, March 16th, Charles France, the crucial prosecution witness against Hanratty, committed suicide by gassing himself in a room in an Acton doss-house. For several days before his suicide he and his family had been the victims of a sustained campaign of abusive and threatening telephone calls. 'If Hanratty dies, you die!' was the theme of the caller.

On the morning of March 17th, Justice rang Alphon with the news of France's suicide. 'That's made my day,' replied Alphon with undisguised satisfaction. He was in high spirits at the White City and at the Ox on the Roof restaurant that evening, and did not leave Half Moon Street for the Regent Palace until very late—about six in the morning.

Returning to the hotel that Sunday morning, he was involved in 'an incident' in which a chambermaid had, apparently, fainted in a room close to Alphon's. About an hour later, he was arrested outside the hotel, in Glasshouse Street, and charged with disorderly conduct. The next day, Monday March 19th, he appeared at Bow Street magistrates' court and was remanded on bail. On March 27th he appeared again. The prosecution story was as follows: Mr Cyril Potter, the inquiries superintendent at the hotel, said he was called to a room early in the morning in which two or three people were trying to treat a chambermaid who appeared to have collapsed. Peter Alphon was also in the room. He was, according to Mr Potter, shouting: 'Send the police; send an ambulance!' Alphon then, again according to Mr Potter, went back to his room two doors away. 'I told Alphon to leave,' said Mr Potter. 'He said, "I'm fucking well going. But you don't know who I am." '

Constable Charles Collins then took up the story. He said he had come with a fellow policeman to the hotel in response to a telephone call from Alphon alleging larceny. When the policemen arrived, they found Alphon in a telephone kiosk in the ground floor of the hotel. He was speaking, apparently, to Scotland Yard, and saying: 'Let me speak to Acott. Not there? Well, get him then! You know who this is, don't you?' He then appeared to get on to his solicitor, and shouted: 'Not talking sense? How can I? I am in a telephone box being beaten up by two policemen.' This seemed very odd, said the constable, because 'we had not spoken to Alphon nor been within striking distance of him.'

Alphon had then been bundled out of the hotel and arrested. He was shouting: 'You cannot do this to me! I will sue you and Acott! My name is Alphon! You will pay for this!'

All this was reported fully in the newspapers of March 29th (the headline in the *Daily Mirror* was ALPHON, A MAID AND RUMPUS AT HOTEL). Strangely, however, and much to the disgruntlement of the magistrate, Sir Robert Blundell, the police asked for an adjournment of the case. The case was adjourned until April 3rd (the day before Hanratty's execution). On this occasion a doctor who had examined Alphon at about 10 a.m. on the morning of the incident testified that Alphon had had 'no alcohol for at least five or six hours'. This corresponded with the evidence of another doctor at the former proceedings who had said that though Alphon's breath smelled of drink there were 'no other signs of drunkenness'. (That doctor incidentally also testified that Alphon, while being examined, had said: 'We can sell this to the *News of the World* for £500 and make a good thing.')

Sir Robert Blundell was nonplussed. He dismissed the charge, but he also dismissed Alphon's claim for costs, with a rebuke: 'I have to decide whether your completely lunatic and unstable disorder was brought on by drink,' he said. 'I cannot say that this is so. You have only yourself to blame in finding yourself where you are, and you have no complaint against anybody.' (*Evening Standard*, April 3rd, 1962.)

The court, of course, could not decide what *had* 'brought on' Alphon's 'completely lunatic and unstable disorder'. Certainly there was nothing in Alphon's past record to suggest that this behaviour was typical of him.

Two days after the 'rumpus' at the Regent Palace, Justice, Fox and Alphon went for dinner at the Hindshead Hotel in Bray. On the way out, they stopped at the Old Station Inn, Taplow, where Michael Gregsten had had his last drink. Alphon went out of his way to tell his companions that this was *not* the pub where the couple had been. Alphon and Fox left the pub first and Justice quickly asked the proprietress, Mrs Mary Lanz, if she had seen either of the two men before. Mrs Lanz confirmed then, and agrees today, that Alphon ('the one with the Guinness') had been into her pub on more than one occasion the previous summer.

After dinner in Bray, the three returned via the village of Dorney Reach and Justice made a remark about the cornfield. Jeremy Fox was driving. Suddenly he heard one of his two companions shout 'stop' and he turned into a field by the side of the road.

Fox got out of the car, and went for a walk. Alphon slid into the driver's seat and started up the car. Justice, gripped by a wild fear, ran to a cottage by the side of the field, woke up the startled inhabitants and gabbled out an incoherent story. The good farmer and his wife calmed him down and accompanied him back to the car. Fox returned and the three drove back to London. The following day, officers from the Burnham police station told the farmer that the man with Justice and Fox could not have been Alphon since he was in jail awaiting trial on the Regent Palace charge. In fact, of course, Alphon had been granted bail.

When I interviewed Mrs Nellie Climo, the farmer's wife who lives next door to the field where the murderer came upon Michael Gregsten's car on the evening before the murder, she confirmed that it was her house which Justice had knocked up that night. 'My husband nearly got the shotgun to him,' she confessed, ruefully. Justice's histrionics on that occasion ensured that Mr Climo and his wife saw the car parked in the same field where Gregsten's car had been parked the previous August.

In his memorandum to the Home Secretary about this incident, submitted a year later, Jeremy Fox admitted that he was not sure whether the order to stop came from Justice or from Alphon. Several years later, however, Fox wrote an explanatory letter to the then Home Secretary, Mr Roy Jenkins. The letter is dated August 8th, 1966:

> Perhaps I should first say something about the cornfield incident. As I stated before, I do not know whether it was Mr Justice or Alphon who asked me to stop the car when it reached the cornfield. I am as sure as it is possible to be however that Mr Justice had never been to the cornfield before and did not know where it was, so that it would be a great coincidence if it was in fact Mr Justice who asked me to stop there.

The cornfield had, of course, been discussed in detail at the trial, but its exact whereabouts had been pinpointed on maps which were available only to the jury and the relevant witnesses and lawyers. No precise map had been published in the newspapers. There are several fields adjacent to each other in the Dorney Reach area which fit the descriptions given in court. Justice says he had never been to Dorney Reach or Marsh Lane in his life before. Marsh Lane was not lit at night. Yet somehow Jeremy Fox's car ended up in the same cornfield. Perhaps understandably, although the visit to the cornfield, like the McDougal drawing, was not in itself conclusive of anything, Justice became convinced from that night that Peter Alphon was the murderer of Michael Gregsten.

For a week after the incident, the two men avoided each other. By now Hanratty's appeal had been abruptly dismissed by the Court of Appeal, and Hanratty was languishing in the condemned cell. In the last week of Hanratty's life, however, Justice and Alphon saw each other as regularly as before. By this time, Justice and his brother Frank believed that they were dealing with the A6 murderer, while Fox remained sceptical. On the other hand, as the date of the execution approached, Alphon began to behave in an increasingly reckless and hysterical manner.

On April 2nd, however, Alphon was away all day, saying he had a job to do. His absence was important in the light of a very curious incident which took place on that day in the village of Old Knebworth in Hertfordshire.

On the morning of August 24th the previous year, the day after the A6 murder, a housewife called Mrs Audrey Willis opened the back door of her house in Old Knebworth to a man wearing what she described as 'a grey raincoat with epaulettes, dark trousers and brown shoes'. The man was 'about thirty', with 'a long, thin face' and 'deep-set eyes', which she thought were brown, and 'a pale, sallow complexion'. The man asked for her husband and, when she said her husband was out, produced a short, black revolver from his pocket. He asked for money and she gave him four pound notes. He then asked for a glass of milk and something to eat. She gave him the milk, which he drank, and a packet of biscuits which he put in his pocket. He also asked her to take off her shoes, which she did. He then told her to accompany him to the back door, which she did, and he ran off.

The incident was given wide publicity in the newspapers of August 25th, whose correspondents linked it with the A6 murder hunt. Mrs Willis was called by the defence at the trial, and the quotations above are taken from her evidence. She was asked whether James Hanratty was the man who had held her up and she replied that he was not. Her examination ended there.

An even more remarkable coincidence did not come out in court. On April 2nd, 1962, two days before the execution, Mrs Willis was visited again by a man with a gun who went through a very similar rigmarole. This incident was mentioned only briefly by the press. 'I am certain', Mrs Willis told the *Daily Herald* (April 3rd, 1962), 'that it was the same man.'

The coincidence of the two visits—one on the day after the murder, the other two days before Hanratty's execution—needs to be set against the fact that Peter Alphon broke his routine and left his friends in London on April 2nd, saying he 'had a job to do'. Throughout that time Alphon was in almost permanent anguish about the forthcoming execution of Hanratty. Like France's suicide, the second confrontation with Mrs Willis was precisely the sort of incident which might have given the authorities cause to think again about a reprieve.

On the evening before the execution Alphon came to Justice's flat at about 6.30 p.m. Justice had by this time contacted Fenner Brockway, the M.P. for Slough, who had shown considerable interest in the case. Brockway had alerted Scotland Yard that Alphon might that night be persuaded to say something in public or in writing which could be cause enough to stop the execution. While Alphon was in Justice's house at Half Moon Street, a Scotland Yard policeman and an official from the Home Office called. Justice answered the door to tell them that Alphon was upstairs. He had not said anything yet. 'Keep him there,' Justice remembers them saying. 'We'll come back.' The officers never returned.

Justice, his brother and Alphon went to the Mayfair Hotel for dinner, where Alphon behaved very strangely, saying he felt the floor was going from under him. They then went to Soho for a few drinks and returned to Half Moon Street. 'I told him', says Justice, 'that if he wanted my friendship, he had to save Hanratty. Frank and I tried everything we knew to get him to give himself up, to go to the police station, to put something in writing. He didn't do it, and so the man was hanged.'

From the execution onwards, Justice continued in his determination to prove that Alphon was responsible. The two men saw each other constantly, not only in London but also in the Sussex cottage which Justice and Fox had bought. Gradually, Alphon began to make more specific references to the murder. On one occasion, sitting in the Barrington, Alphon remarked: 'If I'd known you a year ago, this terrible murder would never have happened.'

From the second week in May, Justice consistently and subtly pressed for some definite proof of Alphon's part in the murder, which he promised would be kept confidential between them. Finally on May 15th in the Imperial Hotel, Russell Square, Alphon handed over several pages of handwritten notes which appeared to be the base of a detailed confession. In full the notes read as follows:

1. Obtaining the gun. Reasons for this. Name of person George.
2. Frame-up in Vienna. How I knew Nudds. Reasons for this frame. Altering the register. (Alibi with my mother.) Planting cases in Room 24 when R. was out. Asking Nudds if Ryan had left.
3. Slough. Had gun but hoping not to commit murder at that time but well in mood for it. The dogs. Bookmaker who might know me. Going out after Mentals Only Hope. Walking out into the country. Stopped at pub opposite Old Station Inn. On to Marsh Lane. Couple in car fitted my mood and my main plan.
4. From the moment I went in imitated working class person with voice and background although I never met Ryan. But a lot of what I said which could be interpreted as Ryan's hatred of ordinary middle class people stemmed from my heart and was my own hatred of them.
5. I played with them as cat and mouse – but all the time I was tense and being an extrovert I showed it and exaggerated and a lot of nervousness was communicated to them.
6. When I killed him and she said 'Oh, you swine, you bastard, you've shot him,' I felt the need to give her some explanation and I said, 'He shouldn't have tried to turn the tables on me.' She said, 'He wasn't, you swine. You are mad.' I said, 'He moved too quickly.'

I knew I must kill her but first I might as well rape her. I felt tense and overwrought and I felt that even fleeting love would help me.

She said, 'Do what you like now. Nothing matters any more.' We went in the back of the car. She was crying and sobbing all the time but relaxed when we had intercourse.

In the end she said, 'What are you going to do?' I said, 'I must kill you now. It is either your life or mine and I have a messianic mission.' She said, 'Please don't hurt me! I'll do anything for you and won't give you away.' It was then that I said, 'One day you will see me on an identification parade but you will not identify. Remember and listen to me now, Valerie, and one day I will come back for you and we will be happy together.' She swore she would not identify me. I knew all along that I would have to kill her but felt touched by her repeated assurances that she would not identify. I said 'Goodbye,

Valerie. You will stay here.' But as I walked away I turned and shot her (?) times. She fell and lay on the ground. I went over and fired more shots into her. She lay absolutely still. I believed she was dead.

7. Meeting the drivers on the road. Driving badly.

8. Meeting my friend at Southend. Disposal of gun.

9. All my interviews with police (Finsbury Park and Acott) can be found from my papers with McDougal.

10. If they had been other sort of people I wouldn't have killed him.

11. When I reproached them on their illicit love, Gregsten said, 'That is nothing to do with you.' I became heated and said that everything which happened was my business. That I could see civilization slipping into vice and decadence. He laughed and this antagonised me more. As I spoke with them more and more his mentality emerged and I came to detest and despise him and knew he would be no loss to the world.

1. Car passed. Lights lit up face 20 minutes after Gregsten's death.

2. I arrived in car about 9.30.

3. Left about 11.30.

4. Drove to lay-by by roundabout route.

5. I said, 'Shut up. I'm thinking my plan out.'

6. Fired about ten times at her.

7. Drove off about 3.0.

8. Raped Valerie about 20 minutes after Gregsten's death.

9. Fired shots at Gregsten at point-blank range.

10. Said, 'Kiss me' before raping her when she was in front seat.

11. ·38 Enfield revolver.

12. Past attempt at cornfield.

The notes outlined no motive for the murder. Their author, it was clear, was an hysterical puritan, outraged by 'illicit' sexual behaviour. There is some suggestion of foresight of the crime in the statement: 'hoping not to commit murder at that time, but well in mood for it.' After coming out of the pub opposite the Old Station Inn, say the notes, 'Couple in car fitted my mood and my main plan.' What main plan? Was the plan inspired by a general desire for revenge against society? Anyway, how did the planner know that this couple were behaving 'immorally'? How did he know that they were not married? How did he know that they were engaging in 'illicit love' about which he says he reproached them?

Yet, if there is no motive for a crime there is for the first time in the history of the case the suggestion that Hanratty was framed for the murder. The cartridge cases, say the notes, were *planted* in Room 24. In the car, Alphon says: 'I imitated working class person with voice and background although I never met Ryan. But a lot of what I said which could be interpreted as Ryan's hatred of ordinary middle class people stemmed from my heart and was my own hatred of them.' In other words, in the car he was purposely imitating Hanratty so that his words could be interpreted as Hanratty's.

There is only one genuine clue and that so slender as to be (at that stage) worse than useless. 'Meeting my friend at Southend', wrote Alphon, and then, immediately, in the same paragraph and on the same point, 'disposal of gun'. For the first time in his relationship with Justice, Alphon admitted here that there was someone else involved in the murder plan.

But the confession notes, as Alphon and Justice both knew, could hardly be regarded as important new evidence. They could easily be written off as a faked scenario for a book or a play. Justice felt, however, that the confession notes represented a major victory, and he kept up the pressure.

Throughout May, June and July, Justice, certain now that Alphon was the murderer, always met him in public or made sure that there was someone else at Half Moon Street during Alphon's frequent visits. From time to time, Justice had to summon police officers from West End Central Police Station to remove Alphon from his flat in the early hours of the morning. Jeremy Fox, on the other hand, remained sceptical for several months.

'In the early stages of my connection with the case', Fox wrote to the Home Secretary four years later, 'I did not really believe it was possible that Alphon with whom I was associating daily could in fact be the murderer.' Fox remained unconvinced until July 1962 when he said, casually, to Alphon: 'You know, Mrs Hanratty feels pretty badly about her son being hanged for a murder he did not commit.' 'He made no verbal reply', wrote Fox in his letter, 'but I do not think I have ever seen such a terrible look of anguish come over anyone's face as came over his at that remark.'

Justice, however, was frightened, and Alphon knew it and played upon it. 'If he wasn't the type of man he had been, I wonder how

far I'd have got with my vindication of Hanratty,' says Justice today.
'He laid down all the rules of my life: what I did, whom I saw,
almost what I read. Suddenly, I was desperately trying to get rid of
him. I flirted with danger, and then I wanted to get away from it.'

In July, Justice fled to Vienna. From his hotel, every evening, he
rang Alphon who was staying at his cottage in Sussex. Alphon was
infuriated by Justice's absence and started to bombard Justice's
hotel with threatening telegrams. One such read: 'En Route to
Vienna with Enfield: A Friend.'

Justice panicked. He tried to buy a revolver at a Vienna gunsmiths',
and was directed to the police station to get a licence. A police officer
rang Scotland Yard, and, before he knew where he was, Justice was
bundled into a Vienna mental hospital, where he was detained
against his will. The British Consul in Vienna, Mr Waddell,
signed a note consenting to the detention. Justice was detained there
for five days, and only managed to get out when friends noticed his
absence, travelled to Vienna and, after creating a furore at the
consulate, had him released.

By the third week in August, Justice had had enough, and on the
first anniversary of the murder, August 22nd, 1962, he decided not
to see Alphon again. He had kept in touch with Scotland Yard and
was regarded there as a major menace. On the morning of August
22nd, when Justice and Superintendent Kennedy spoke to each
other again, Kennedy was near the end of his tether. 'If you don't
stop this business of the A6', shouted Kennedy, 'loonybins for you.'
'I take the hint,' replied Justice, who used the police warning as an
excuse finally to break off his relationship with Alphon.

That same morning—August 22nd—Alphon travelled to the
Kingsbury home of James Hanratty for a curious encounter.

'He came in at about half past twelve,' says Mr Hanratty. 'Just
knocked at the door and we let him in. He sat down, and started to
talk about Jimmy. He said he didn't think they'd ever get enough
evidence to hang him and he wanted to write a book about the whole
business.

'Then he took his cheque book out of his pocket and asked if he
could compensate me for what had happened to my son. I really
saw red then, and so did Peter [Peter Hanratty, another son] who
was with us at the time. We made it clear that if he didn't leave at
once, he would be in trouble. So he left.'

The next day, Justice met Alphon in the Barrington Club in

Piccadilly to tell him that they could not meet again. 'I blamed the police,' says Justice. Alphon was furious. He said he would not let Justice out of his sight, and, when Justice left the club, Alphon followed. He followed him to the Ritz where Justice was meeting the Hanratty parents for a discussion about the previous day's events. Mrs Hanratty arrived at the hotel first and walked in to find the two Justice brothers in furious argument with Alphon. Mrs Hanratty insisted that they leave at once to meet her husband as arranged at Green Park station, and the four of them moved off. At Green Park station a brawl took place in which, according to Mrs Hanratty, she was struck in the face and held round the neck by Alphon. Eventually, Alphon ran off and vanished into a taxi.

The names of witnesses of the incident were taken at the time, and Justice and the Hanrattys pressed for a prosecution for assault. When the authorities refused to act, they took out a private prosecution. A summons against Alphon was granted, but not served. Only after questions and letters from Fenner Brockway, M.P., and an unashamed piece of trickery by Justice, who arranged a meeting with Alphon in the Grosvenor Hotel, was the summons served – in the Grosvenor. Alphon was eventually tried at Bow Street court on October 27th. Mrs Hanratty gave evidence about the attack on her, and Justice tried to produce the confession notes in court. The magistrate decided that his mind 'was not entirely free from doubt', and Alphon was acquitted.

After the Green Park incident, Justice went on holiday with Fox. While on holiday, he wrote an undertaking to the police that he would never seen Alphon again. Apart from the meeting in the Grosvenor Hotel, arranged so that the Bow Street summons could be served, this undertaking has been kept. Justice has seen Alphon on a number of occasions since – in court and outside his house at Brighton. But the two men have never met since October 1962. Their relationship, however, continued – on the telephone. Justice explained to Alphon that the police had barred any physical meeting between them, but that they could not object to telephone calls.

Throughout the summer of 1962, Justice had had meetings in the House of Commons with Fenner Brockway and, usually, the general secretary of the National Council for Civil Liberties, Mr Martin Ennals. Also present on some occasions was Mr Tony Mason, the Slough journalist. At one of these meetings, Justice announced that he would not see Alphon again but would probably speak to him on the phone, and Ennals suggested that a tape-recorder be fitted to Justice's telephone. Justice took up the suggestion, and as a result the continuing relationship is on record. Several dozen conversations between the two men in the seven months following October 1962 were tape-recorded.

It is plain from the outset that Alphon did not know that the conversations were being recorded. He often asks if Justice is alone, and, on more than one occasion, refuses to believe that he is. Once, clutching his battery-operated tape-recorder, Justice was forced out into the cold to speak to Alphon from a public call-box.

The bulk of the conversations consists of chatter about politics and about each other's day-to-day problems. Alphon's affection for Justice comes over again and again. In their first conversation, in October, Alphon complained bitterly about the cutting off of the relationship the previous summer, and wept. A few weeks later, he said:

> I've never worked, so you're not dealing with Frank or Fox. Don't think that I don't understand things because I do. But unfortunately I think I'm a little bit kinky, and if you say that you love me, that's all that counts. I'm going to tell you something and I really mean it. If I ever found out that you were lying I wouldn't do anything. To be quite frank with you, I wouldn't think you were worth the trouble. That's what I think ... You'd be a dead loss. (Quoted in *Le Crime de la Route A6*, pp. 198, 199.)

The A6 murder arises in the conversations from time to time, although Alphon is obviously unhappy about talking about it at any length. Usually it crops up in an aside, or to illustrate something else: 'There's only one man that means anything in the world to me and that was Hitler, and they crucified him. When you say that Hitler lived again in the cornfield that night, that was one thing we had in common.'

As Justice continued his stubborn persecution, Alphon, who knew after the Bow Street case in October 1962 that Justice would not hesitate to take his confessions to the authorities, was susceptible to uncontrollable rages:

ALPHON. You are an evil person. What you do to people is evil.
JUSTICE. What you have done to Gregsten ...

A. What I have done to Gregsten is one thing. Two rights don't make a wrong. What you are doing is evil. I'm a human being, you know.

J. What was Gregsten?

A. Hume was a murderer, but he didn't go through what I'm going through. I'm telling you, Justice, I have stood just as much as I can stand. People will know one day just how tolerant I've been. But there's a limit to my tolerance.

Later in the same conversation Justice asked: 'Why did you tell me you did the murder?'

Alphon answered: 'I'm not concerned with that. If I am a murderer, I am still a human being. If I do a cold-blooded murder like that, I should have sympathy and affection.' (*Murder versus Murder*, p. 145.)

Only very occasionally did Alphon allow himself to be drawn into any detailed account of the murder night. An exception comes in another extract:

A. I don't think talking makes things clear. Hitler talked a lot before the war, but no one took any notice of him till he struck; then they did not know what to do.

J. Like in the car, you mean?

A. Yes, that's right. I will just tell you one thing. No, I had better not.

J. About the car?

A. Yes. Anyway I can tell you Gregsten did not take any notice at all. Did not take any notice at all of talk. You know what happened to him. It is not easy to terrorize anyone by talk, you know. Don't think it was all terror in the car because it wasn't.

J. I quite agree.

A. It *was* after the shot was fired – but not before. He was quite cocky.

J. Who?

A. Gregsten. (Quoted in House of Commons Hansard, August 2nd, 1963, Col. 806.)

In January 1963 Alphon started demanding money from Justice with threats of violence. Eventually, Justice agreed to put money in an envelope in Alphon's bank in the Strand. An empty envelope was deposited (and the police tipped off), but never collected.

Justice was not the only person whom Alphon telephoned during those months. The Hanratty family were persecuted by silent and anonymous phone calls. Mrs Hanratty remembers one night in particular when the phone rang late and she called out to her sons asking if they were expecting a call. When she picked up the phone, a voice said: 'I am the A6 killer, Mrs Hanratty. And I'm coming to get you.'

One night in May, Alphon rang the Hanrattys again, and engaged in a long conversation with the father. The police were contacted from a neighbour's house, and two squad cars arrived. The police listened to about three hours of Alphon's chat to Mr Hanratty, which included a clear confession to the A6 murder. They traced the call-box where Alphon was, and stopped him, but no charges were made. On the following day, on police advice, the Hanrattys changed their telephone number.

There was one aspect of the conversation which disturbed Alphon more than Mr Hanratty. As they discussed the case, Mr Hanratty let slip that he had heard Alphon say something on one of Justice's tapes. There was a long silence. 'I didn't know the bastard was taping me,' said Alphon softly, and in sudden rage let out a stream of abuse against Justice.

The revelation that his conversations with Justice were recorded for posterity came as a great shock to Alphon. It was proof of what Alphon had always feared: that Justice's friendship was a front for a plot to discover the truth about the A6 murder. Alphon's call to Justice immediately following the revelation about the tape-recording is therefore the most interesting of all in this period. It is the first conversation between the two men for almost two months. The date is May 17th, 1963:

A. I have got a mission. Don't forget that. Something you haven't got. That's the gulf between us. You are just living for yourself, aren't you. I have got my mission, messianic mission and I am going to fulfil it. I am not going to let anyone stand in the way of it. I thought I'd have had a few friends on the way; unfortunately, I can see that I haven't. When anyone has a mission, they don't have any friends. You just thought I was a murderer.

J. Why did you tell me?

A. Why are you trying to persecute me for it? Is not the crime enough?

J. I agree. I am ashamed of my conduct. I'm paying for it. You shouldn't have told me.

A. You asked me, you asked me out of curiosity in the beginning ... This affair came about to glorify me. I have only been dragged in the mud. I could deny the voice or anything ...

(*and, a bit later*)

J. Why did you tell me you did the murder?

A. What's that got to do with it? I told you the truth. You told me a fucking pack of lies didn't you? Why shouldn't I tell you? You were my friend. People don't do what you did. There are murders going on all over the world. I didn't expect your reaction to be what it was.

This deep resentment at Justice's infidelity is the theme of many other conversations in this period. Yet for all his apparent recklessness, Alphon had not given much away. Even though he did not know he was being taped originally, he had dealt with the murder only in passing and only with such details that were known at the trial. Even if his confessions to the murder sounded convincing there was no hard evidence to back them up. Above all, Alphon still refrained from giving any motive for the crime or any detailed explanation as to how it was that he happened to be in Marsh Lane on August 22nd, 1961. There is nothing of a motive in those early tapes but vague references to his contempt for 'illicit love' and to his 'messianic mission' to stamp it out.

There is, however, even in those early tapes, some indication that Alphon was in touch with other people who knew about the crime, and were in part responsible for it. In the first conversation ever to be taped, Alphon shouted: 'You betrayed my confidence! You have got to be put away. Don't you understand? I really believe it. *Everyone believes it here. They all* believe it. They think I should come over and kill you.' (My italics.)

Very much in the same vein, a month later:

A. My friend says: Get rid of that fucking man before he puts you inside, and by God I will.

J. Why?

A. Because you're unreliable and you're dangerous.

On another occasion, he said: 'You get your little Hanrattys and find out who really hanged him. They think it was me. *I can tell you two other people … that had as much to do with it as me.*'

But the clearest indication that someone else was involved in Alphon's version of the crime came in December, soon after he had been arrested by railway police at King's Cross and charged with stealing three pounds from a Hungarian lady called Mrs Fedzuk. Alphon was disturbed by the charge, for which the evidence was less than satisfactory, and spent many hours ridiculing the British legal system. Behind the ridicule lay a threat:

> If I'm convicted for this, and I don't for one moment expect that I shall be, I am going abroad, and I'm going to tell the truth in a world press conference and I'm going to shame British justice in the eyes of the world. And I will give them one important bit of proof—something you haven't discovered—*which will involve someone else*, and that will be the absolute finish of them after what they've done to me. You tell your friends in the police when I go abroad and I tell the TRUTH [shouted] British justice will never raise its head again. You tell your friends that. You will have won, dear. If that's what you wanted, to vindicate Hanratty, you'll have won. But if you want any glory for yourself, you may be sure that you won't get any from me. Because I'll leave your name right out. When I'm far away, then I'll tell the real truth. You tell your friends in the police that. Put the word around. *It will involve someone else.* Someone else. (Quoted in *Le Crime de la Route A6*, pp. 202, 203, my italics.)

In the conversation on May 17th, Alphon repeated the pledge: 'I did say I would go abroad and tell the truth if convicted on the Fedzuk case—I will one day. I will get my case against Acott first.'

On January 21st, 1963, despite contradictions in the prosecution case, Alphon was convicted and fined twenty-five pounds on the Fedzuk case. But his visit abroad to tell 'the truth' and 'to involve someone else' had to wait for four more years.

In the early spring of 1963, Jean Justice, Jeremy Fox and Tony Mason set to work on a detailed memorandum to the Home Secretary on the A6 murder. The memorandum contained the drawing, the confession notes and a complete transcript of all the telephone conversations between October 1962 and May 1963.

It also included the text of the statement which Justice and Fox had taken in March 1962 from a man called Michael Fogarty-Waul, who, at the time of the murder, had been living in a caravan in Pecks Farm, a field off Marsh Lane. Mr Fogarty-Waul told them that on a Tuesday the previous summer he had met a man at Slough dog races who had asked him for a lift. He had dropped the man at a hotel in Slough. About three weeks later, late at night, he was driving down the A4 when he came to the turning to Marsh Lane. On the corner was the man whom he had met at the Slough races. The man accepted a lift down Marsh Lane, and when they arrived at Pecks Farm said he was going to Maidenhead. 'You've come on the wrong road,' said Fogarty-Waul, 'you should have kept straight along the one you were on.'

'Oh, that's all right,' said the man, 'I can find my way across the fields.' He left the car in Marsh Lane and wandered off. Fogarty-Waul remembers thinking this was rather odd, as he had never seen the man in the area before.

Two days after the murder, police officers interviewed him in their routine inquiries in the area. Had he seen any strangers in the area recently? they asked. Mr Fogarty-Waul then told them of the man to whom he had given a lift at midnight a week or two before the murder. Several months later, on the night of February 27th–28th, 1962, ten days after Hanratty had been found guilty at Bedford, Mr Fogarty-Waul went fishing in the river at the bottom of the field where Michael Gregsten and Miss Storie had been held up. At about 1 a.m. he returned with his catch to his car parked in Marsh Lane outside the field. As he came up to his car, he noticed a man near it, who seemed to be touching the car. Thinking it was a friend, he shouted jovially at the man, who looked up quickly and ran away. Fogarty-Waul gave chase but the man doubled back from the field, cleared the hedge and ran off in the direction of the M4.

Mr Fogarty-Waul immediately remembered the incident which he had reported to the police. He was certain that the man by his car was the same man he had given a lift to the previous summer. He drove at once to Burnham police station and reported the incident. 'It's the same man as I told you about last summer,' said Fogarty-Waul. 'He was trying to get in my car. If it is the man, he's probably come to get rid of me.' To which, he remembers, one of the policemen replied: 'That'll upset the apple cart.'

There was, explained the police, no transport to give hunt for the man. The van outside, they explained, was 'immobile'. And, anyway, anything to do with the A6 case was a matter for the police in Slough, not Burnham. So Mr Fogarty-Waul drove to Slough police station, reported the incident and went as instructed to wait by his caravan. Half an hour later a van, which Fogarty-Waul thought was very similar to the 'immobile' van at Burnham, came down the road with two police officers in it. Fogarty-Waul pointed out where the man had run. The police car drove off, only to return after travelling about a hundred yards. 'We can't find him,' said one of the officers. 'But we can let the dogs out.' 'What for?' asked Mr Fogarty-Waul, in exasperation, 'For a piss?'

Then Fogarty-Waul drew the attention of the officers to the fingerprints on the car. The car was dusty and the handmarks on the side showed up clearly. 'You could take these prints at least,' said Fogarty-Waul. 'They might help you find the man.'

Upon which one police officer took off one of his big leather gloves, and looked up at the sky. 'It's a bad night for fingerprints,' he said, and wiped the handmarks off the car. Mr Fogarty-Waul returned to Slough police station after his interview with Justice and Fox some weeks later, and was told that the two officers in question were no longer there. One had left the force. The other had been transferred, they knew not where.

Mr Fogarty-Waul told Justice and Fox that the man at the car was, he was sure, the same man he had given a lift to in Marsh Lane a week or two before the murder. 'He had the same kind of walk,' he said. Fogarty-Waul was shown pictures of Alphon in the *Daily Telegraph* and agreed that the man bore a strong resemblance to the man to whom he had given a lift. He also said that his passenger had looked like the actor Sidney Tafler.

In July 1963, the memorandum was handed to Fenner Brockway who sent it to the Home Secretary and 'booked' an adjournment debate on the case for August 2nd, shortly before the House rose for the summer recess. Before the debate, Brockway and his supporters conducted a well-organized propaganda campaign. More than a hundred M.P.s signed his petition to the Home Secretary calling for an inquiry into the case. The signatories included M.P.s from all parties, and several Labour front-benchers including Mr Roy Jenkins. Every M.P. was sent a copy of the memorandum and several M.P.s informed themselves of the details of the case.

Brockway opened the debate by reading the confession notes. He then dealt briefly with Mr Acott's reasons for eliminating Alphon which he had given at the trial. The tape-recordings between Alphon and Justice, said Brockway, proved several of these 'eliminating' points to be wholly invalid. In the first place, there were a number of occasions in the tapes when Alphon, nervous or excited, pronounced the diphthong 'th' as 'f'. In the second, there were also a number of occasions when Alphon spoke in a Cockney accent. Two of Mr Acott's more telling points had, he said, been destroyed by the tapes.

Brockway repeated many of the arguments used at the trial which pointed to Hanratty's innocence, and ended by reading at length from the transcript of the tape-recordings.

Five back-benchers spoke in the debate: two Conservative, three Labour. All of them spoke in favour of an inquiry. Mr Peter Kirk, Tory M.P. for Gravesend, who later became a minister in the 1970 Conservative Government, said: 'I am convinced that if this evidence had been before the jury, they would not have convicted Hanratty.'

Mr Eric Fletcher, later Deputy Speaker of the House of Commons, spoke of 'a very serious situation: my Hon. Friend [Brockway] has been at pains to collect a great deal of evidence which tends to show two things: first, that Mr Hanratty was innocent of a murder for which he has been hanged; second, that another gentleman, Mr X, although at one time arrested by the police, is now at large and has confessed to the murder.'

Mr Donald Johnson, Tory M.P. for Carlisle, appealed to his Home Secretary: 'I feel that my Right Hon. Friend will create public confidence in justice, in his administration and in his office if he accedes to the request which has been made to him today.'

Mr Niall MacDermot, later to become a minister in the 1964–6 Labour Government and a Queen's Counsel, explained that one of the reasons at the time of the trial why he thought Hanratty would be convicted was his mis-pronunciation of the diphthong 'th'. This had been shown to be shared with 'Mr X' (Alphon) and this caused him to hesitate.

Finally, Mr Chuter Ede, Home Secretary in the post-war Labour Government, who had signed the death warrant for Timothy Evans, attacked the notion that the British legal system was infallible, and called for an inquiry.

Two of the speakers singled out the statement of Mr Fogarty-Waul. Mr Kirk told the House:

> I find that [the statement of Fogarty-Waul] a very convincing statement, and I should like to have Mr Fogarty-Waul's evidence tested by inquiry, by examination and, if necessary, by cross-examination to ascertain whether it is true.

Mr Fletcher said:

> I was impressed also by a reading of the evidence given by Mr Fogarty-Waul. It seems to me very odd that this Mr Fogarty-Waul did not come forward to give evidence at Hanratty's trial. He is obviously in a position to give most valuable information, and I should have thought that it was important at any inquiry to test his evidence. (Hansard, August 2nd, 1963.)

The debate was answered by Mr Henry Brooke, Home Secretary. He started by casting doubt on all confessions made after a murder. The Home Office, he said, had received two anonymous confessions, apart from Alphon's, to the A6 murder. After filling in the background to the case, Brooke turned to the memorandum. In the first place, he said, the journey by Fox, Justice and Alphon to the cornfield was suspicious because one of the men had expressed an interest in seeing the cornfield. The car, therefore, had been driven through Dorney Reach for that purpose and Mr Fox had not been sure who had given the order to stop. (No names were mentioned throughout the debate. Justice was 'the businessman'; Alphon, 'Mr X'; Fox, 'the barrister'.)

After dealing rather peremptorily with Justice's visit to Vienna, and indulging in some old-fashioned smear ('Both Mr X and the businessman are people of precarious mental balance and there is evidence of the businessman being a heavy drinker'), Brooke turned his attention to the confession notes.

At once, he produced a powerful argument against the credibility of the notes:

> The confession suggested that on the night of the murder, Mr X attended the greyhound races at Slough until after a dog named 'Mentals Only Hope' had run. He then walked out in the country, stopped at a public house at Taplow and walked from there to the cornfield where Mr Gregsten and Miss Storie

were sitting in their car. In fact, the murderer surprised them there at about 9.30 p.m.

Yet, according to Mr X's account, he did not leave the Slough stadium until about 9.5 p.m., a gap of 25 minutes. It is about six miles from Slough stadium to the public house at Taplow, and it is another mile and a half from the public house to the cornfield. (Ibid.)

It was, undoubtedly, impossible for Alphon to have left the stadium after 'Mentals Only Hope' had run, and arrive at the cornfield in time by walking. On the other hand, the subject of 'Mentals Only Hope' had come up often in conversation between Alphon and the two Justice brothers on their many visits to the White City. The name attracted all three men, and, on one occasion, Justice, studying the dog's past form, exclaimed that 'Mentals Only Hope' had run at Slough on the murder night, and joked that Alphon must have lost money on the dog before leaving to do the murder. There is some evidence, in short, that the 'Mentals Only Hope' incident was suggested to Alphon – but its obvious absurdity is enough to cast considerable doubt on the detail of Alphon's confession then and later.

Brooke's second point against the confession had less substance:

At the time of the murder, Mr X could not drive a car. He had never held anything more than a provisional driving licence, and that was a number of years before. He had held no driving licence. He had no driving licence at the time. It is quite inconceivable that Mr X could have been the man who drove the car that night after the murder from seven miles south of Bedford until the car was seen in Ilford some hours later. (Ibid.)

This must be one of the major non-sequiturs of that month's House of Commons debates. Alphon, said Brooke, could not drive, because he did not have a driving licence – a fact which Mr Brooke repeated three times in three sentences. If he did not have a driving licence, argued Brooke, he could not *conceivably* have driven from Bedford to Ilford.

What about Hanratty? 'There is of course', said Brooke, 'no question about Hanratty's ability to drive a car.' Of course not. Hanratty was a car thief who had driven cars of every kind and had owned a Sunbeam Talbot. But Mr Brooke forgot to tell the House that at the time of the murder Hanratty did not have a driving licence, and indeed, like Alphon, 'had never held anything more than a provisional driving licence'. On Mr Brooke's own logic, Hanratty, who had no driving licence, could not have driven from Bedford to Ilford.

The man in the car on Deadman's Hill had asked Valerie Storie twice to show him how to use the gears of a standard Morris Minor. He had also asked how to start the car. He had seemed unaccustomed to cars. But he had driven the car off towards Luton.

One man who has closer experience of Alphon's driving than Henry Brooke is Mr Gordon Perkins, who had acted in the spring and summer of 1962 as Jean Justice's chauffeur. Mr Perkins tells me the following story:

> One night Peter [Alphon] and I went to hire a car to drive down to Fox's cottage in the country – Laudate.
>
> We hired a Vauxhall Victor with the gear stick on the steering column. Alphon tried to hire it in his own name but the company refused him because he didn't have a driving licence. From the moment we set out, Alphon kept asking if he could drive the car himself. I said No. It was a hired car and it wouldn't be insured if he drove. We got out at a pub and Alphon kept trying to get me sloshed. He succeeded in the end – at a steak house in Kingston-on-Thames. I was very drunk indeed and I flung him the keys and told him to drive. He started the car all right, selected first gear and drove off. But he drove recklessly, fast and without complete control of the steering wheel, and he never dipped his lights. I kept telling him to turn left to try to slow him down, but it didn't work very well. Finally he did turn left, stopped, and I plucked the keys out of the ignition. I was frightened. We had driven about twenty miles I suppose, for about three quarters of an hour. The car wasn't damaged, but I kept thinking it might be.

That sort of driving is far more consistent with the driving experience of the man on Deadman's Hill than that of Hanratty. In his confession notes, Alphon had written: 'Meeting the drivers on the road. Driving badly.' But at any rate, despite his lack of a driving licence, Alphon could drive, and could have driven a car from Bedford to Ilford.

One final point about the driving of the car indicates that the murderer was not a perfect driver. When the car was inspected in Ilford one of its bumpers was buckled and there was a dent in the back. Valerie Storie told the court that these marks were not on the car when it left Deadman's Hill.

Henry Brooke then proceeded to his most startling revelation. Three times he told the House that Alphon had 'a complete alibi' for the murder.

'It is', he said, '*beyond challenge* that Mr X was occupying a room at the Vienna Hotel in London at the time of the murder and therefore could not have been at Dorney Reach or Deadman's Hill.' (My italics.)

This was too much for Mr Brockway who interrupted: 'Was that not on the evidence of Nudds, who has himself admitted that he is a liar?'

Mr Brooke replied: 'The main thing about the evidence of Nudds is that he made three statements and he gave evidence after. The jury accepted, and I have no reason whatever to doubt, that the first and third statements were true and that the second statement, which he admitted was a fabrication, was untrue. There is also evidence from the hotel register and so forth, very convincing evidence.'

There is of course no way of knowing whether the jury accepted any part of Nudds's evidence. The probability is that they rejected all of it. The man had been proved a liar and a 'grass'. The evidence from the hotel register, as Brooke must have known, proved nothing, except that Alphon signed it. It did not implicate Hanratty, and it did not eliminate Alphon. The register by itself does not prove that Alphon stayed all the murder night in the Vienna Hotel.

If it was 'beyond challenge' that Alphon had stayed the night of August 22nd in the Vienna Hotel, why did Superintendent Acott not say so at Hanratty's trial when asked why he eliminated Alphon from his inquiries?

Brooke's fourth point was that Alphon did not mispronounce 'th' and did not speak with a Cockney accent. He explained the passages in the tapes where 'th' was mispronounced by Alphon by saying that Alphon was pretending to be the killer. Yet the passages in which the accent and the 'th' change are not consistent. They are random, and they correspond to Alphon's changes of mood.

Fifthly, Brooke argued that 'none of the witnesses' picked out Alphon at the identity parades. He did not say who these witnesses were. One of them was Mr Edward Blackhall, who failed also to pick out Hanratty. Mr John Skillett and Mr James Trower – both of whom did pick out Hanratty – did not attend Alphon's identity parade. Mrs Dalal, the Richmond housewife, *did* identify Alphon as her assailant. Apart from Miss Storie, there is no way of knowing who the other witnesses were.

Sixthly, Brooke contended that there was nothing in the confession notes which could not have been garnered from a close study of the trial. Although the verifiable facts could have been gleaned from a close study of the trial, there were parts of Alphon's notes, such as 'meeting my friend at Southend' in connection with 'disposal of gun', and a 'past attempt at cornfield', which told a completely different story to that which emerged at the trial.

Finally, Brooke pointed out that the tapes suggested that the murderer knew Miss Storie, and that there was no evidence that this was so, or that Alphon knew Miss Storie. In fact, however, the passage in the tapes suggested rather that Alphon knew *of* Miss Storie and her relationship – a fact for which a great deal of evidence was shortly to come to light.

After speculating, without evidence and inaccurately, on the motives for the confession ('the businessman is a wealthy man. He [Alphon] may have felt that in some way or other he could obtain money from the businessman through this behaviour'), Brooke launched into his peroration:

> If I thought that there was anything in the memorandum I have received, I would not hesitate to appoint a public inquiry. Indeed, I go further than that. If I thought that on any reasonable view there could be anything in it, I would welcome an independent investigation, but I suggest that we must keep a sense of balance and proportion in these matters. I must tell the House that I have found nothing to cause me to doubt in any way that, after a full trial in which every point in Hanratty's defence was carefully examined, Hanratty was rightly convicted ... I cannot agree to reopen the case because I believe that it is impossible that Mr X [Alphon] could have done it. (Ibid.)

That evening Fenner Brockway appeared on Independent Television News. One of the tapes was played over, and Brockway was asked: 'Who do you think did the murder?' He answered: 'I think Mr X did it.'

On August 14th, twelve days later, a writ for libel was issued by Peter Alphon against Fenner Brockway and against I.T.N. In the interim, Alphon had given an interview to the *Daily Sketch*, announcing in a huge headline: 'I AM MR X.'

The argument behind the writ was that the pseudonym Mr X no longer masked the identity of Peter Alphon. Brockway's speech in the Commons had made it as clear as possible short of stating his name that Mr X was Peter Alphon. The statement on television, therefore, 'I think Mr X did it,' was a clear libel on Alphon. The argument carried a great deal of force, and Galbraith and Best, Alphon's solicitors, issued a confident statement to the press:

> Our client is determined to clear his name of the charges brought against him by Mr Brockway. Since Mr Brockway is so anxious for an inquiry, Mr Alphon has taken this action in the hope that the whole of Mr Brockway's allegations will now be examined and pronounced on by a judge and jury.

The writ had its desired effect. Brockway was warned by his legal advisers to 'keep off' the A6 while the libel case was pending. (I.T.N. received the same instructions.) Mr Gerald (later Lord) Gardiner was briefed to appear for Brockway, and Brockway kept quiet. 'I should never have agreed to their terms,' he says today. 'I was frightened and I should not have been.'

Somehow, however, the writs against Brockway and I.T.N. have gone the same way as the writs Alphon took out against Superintendent Acott, the *Daily Mirror* and the *Daily Mail*—into obsolescence.

Peter Alphon was not the only one to be outraged at the Brockway debate. On August 4th, two days after the debate, the *News of the World*, a newspaper which throughout the case has never failed to argue Hanratty's guilt, printed an article entitled: 'Mr X's Confession is just plain Rot'. Its author, Charles Sandell, wrote:

> He [Alphon] certainly did not commit the A6 murder. He was questioned at the time and had a waterproof alibi.
>
> I remember discussing the case with him in a Fleet Street pub, and he told me he was at a greyhound meeting on the night of the murder. (*News of the World*, August 4th, 1963.)

Another experienced journalist to mock the Alphon confessions was Peter Duffy, Chief Crime Reporter of the *Daily Sketch*, who, as soon as he saw Brockway's memorandum, published a long article entitled: 'Guilty, I Say'. Mr Duffy wrote: 'I know the man named in the report as having confessed. He is a publicity-seeking dreamer, who did not commit the A6 murder.'

Mr Duffy listed a number of the memorandum's claims and coupled them with 'facts' of his own, including an alibi for Alphon.

Claim: There is supporting evidence that this man was near the cornfield on the night of the murder.

Fact: The Yard have evidence that on the night of the murder this man was miles away, engaged in his job as door-to-door salesman. (*Daily Sketch*, July 11th, 1963.)

According to Mr Brooke, Alphon had 'a complete alibi'—in the Vienna Hotel; Mr Sandell was able to provide him with 'a water-proof alibi' at a greyhound track while Mr Duffy had him selling almanacs.

For several months after the Commons debate, there was little or no contact between Justice and Alphon. In November and December 1963, the telephone calls started again. At first, Alphon was cold and distant, recalling the 'betrayal' of Justice in taping his conversations and handing them over to the Home Secretary. As the conversations went on, however, Alphon seemed to get used to the tape-recorder and to talk more freely. In one mocking extract he tore Henry Brooke's Commons speech to ribbons, laughing at the alibi which Brooke had so conveniently found for him. 'I would rather', he said, 'have Brooke than Nudds as an alibi witness.'

Then, on Wednesday, March 18th, 1964, there took place a recorded conversation between the two men which far surpassed any of the previous conversations in importance. Up to that time, Alphon had not given the name of anyone else who was involved in the murder. He had spoken vaguely of 'someone else' and 'my friend', but the identity of this person and the role which he or she played in the murder was never outlined or even hinted at. Until March 1964, Alphon's confessions had referred only to a generalized campaign against 'illicit love' as the motivation for the murder. Even Justice was not convinced of any planned motive for the crime. In his book, *Murder versus Murder*, which he was completing at that time, Justice wrote that the A6 murder was a 'sex crime' and stated 'my firm opinion that sex, not robbery, was the root cause of the A6 tragedy'. (*Murder versus Murder*, pp. 54, 55.)

Speculation, in other circles, however, had been rife that there may well have been other people who sent the murderer to the cornfield. In his book, Mr Louis Blom-Cooper had asked:

> Is it altogether fantastic to wonder whether Hanratty was in some way *sent* to the cornfield in Buckinghamshire with a gun in his hand? Let us suppose that Gregsten's conduct was such that someone might go to the lengths of trying to scare him. No physical harm might have been intended ... *The A6 Murder*, p. 41.)

Peter Alphon had, however, hardly hinted at a 'prime mover' who had sent him to the field.

Then, suddenly, in his conversation with Justice in March 1964, Alphon named the man who, he said, had inspired the events which led up to the murder. He has named this man since on a number of occasions.

I shall refer to this man as Mr X, or X. X had shown more than ordinary interest in the A6 case. He had regularly attended the trial at Bedford, and had listened to the Commons debate on the case from the public gallery.

The circumstances leading up to Alphon's naming of Mr X were as follows. As early as the autumn of 1962, Jean Justice had visited Mr X and discussed the murder with him. Justice and X had become acquainted and met often. Some days before the March 18th phone call, Alphon heard that Justice and X were meeting. He rang Justice in the afternoon of the 18th to warn him that he would ring again in the evening and that he would then 'capitulate' and 'tell everything'. He rang promptly that evening, more disturbed and worried than usual, and told Justice to put his tape-recorder on. 'If you didn't tape this one,' he said, 'you'd be the biggest fool in existence.' And then, immediately, he started to talk about 'my friend':

A. I think my friend is a little more dangerous than yours if you could call him a friend. But I don't think you could call him one any longer because he doesn't cough up.

J. Well, who is your friend? Have I met him personally?

A. I think you have. Yes, personally. You know who I bloody well mean. Don't you?

J. How do I know who you mean?

A. First of all I want your assurance that you are not trying to trap me.

J. I'm not trying to trap you. I give you my word.

A. I don't want a squad of police outside this phone box. Before you go on—you accepted the call—I wanted to speak to you ... I'm frightened. I'm very frightened because it's me that is in danger more than you.

After repeating that he was frightened, and fencing for several more minutes, Alphon referred to the confession notes which Justice had got from him nearly two years previously:

A. That is just rubbish, isn't it? What you have got is a lot of rubbish. *I think you ought to look for a more mundane motive in that murder.* You have mentioned someone before haven't you.
J. Who?
A. You have mentioned somebody before. I'm not prepared to men-tion—well I will mention him.
J. Well, mention him.
A. X! [the name shouted out] ... That's who I say.
J. Why is he dangerous?
A. He is going to kill me.
J. What?
A. He is going to kill me.
J. Why?
A. He is going to try. But I don't think he will. And I think you are in with him. I wouldn't be a bit surprised if you are in with him.
J. Well on that score I'm afraid I'm going to put down the phone if you go on like that.
A. You are. So you are in with him. So you are in with him are you? I thought that. That is what I thought.
J. How dare you.
A. You are in with him. Now look I want you to give him a message from me. I want you to give him a message.
J. I don't know what—you rang me up to say that you were going to capitulate which had nothing to do with anyone else. Well if he is so dangerous will you tell me why?
A. I want you to give him a message if you are in with him. No. I'm not a copper's nark and I'm not going to go to the police. I've never done that. That is why I was entrusted with the job in the first place because they knew that I wouldn't go. And I was there to separate a couple of people, you understand, in the car. And I gave them five hours to do it ... If you put a strong man in. Somebody who is willing to go in with a gun and see that

justice is done ... I gone in and I've given him every chance—
five hours—that was the motive! I'm telling you. That is why it
took five hours. Five fucking hours it took. Do you understand
that. You've got your motive.

Throughout the tape, Alphon seemed desperate to discover
whether X had told Justice anything which would indicate that X
was out to split on Alphon and turn him over to the authorities,
probably with Justice's help:

A. The thing is, did he tell you anything? Did he nark at all? Did he
tell you anything?
J. *I'm* asking *you* a question.
A. (*desperately*). Did he tell you anything? I'm asking you. I'm sure
you can tell me something. What are you trying to do? What are
you trying to do? Did he tell you anything? It's only after you
saw him that all this came up. Did he tell you anything? After
you saw him, did he tell you anything? After you saw that man.

Justice then manages to calm Alphon by asking some questions
about the murder. But Alphon returns to his panic questioning soon
afterwards:

A. Did he tell you anything? That man. That's all I want to know. I
want to know whether he squealed. Did he say anything to you?
J. Oh, I see what you mean. No.
A. Did he say anything?
J. NO! [shouted]
A. If I knew—that's the point. I would never squeal him. I'm not a
copper's nark for all you said, you know. Never, never not that.
I could never go to the police. Because if I knew that he said
that I had had a reason. If only I knew that he had said
something.

A little later, another thought struck Alphon:

A. I want to know about our friend. Has he bought—no, I don't
think he could buy you. Have you bought him, or has one of you
bought one another or what? Are you in with one another? Are
you in together? Well, of course, if you are, then one of you is
going to go. And I think it will be him.
    I can get him. You can tell him that I can fucking well get him
myself. I can come along and do that. I know what he's trying to

do ... But are you in with him? That's what I want to know. I'm more worried about the psychological thing.

Yet another more pecuniary aspect of Mr X also worried Alphon:

A. And when people refuse to pile it up. I'm not referring to you, though you have. But other people do as well. And they try and put the finger on you as well and hope to get away with it. People want their cake and eat it. And they are behind the murder. 'Our friend' I am alluding to. And then they don't pile up. Don't pile up any longer. And they go and squeal as I think he squealed to you, and said everything. But that's when the whole thing came out after that. Then they tried to fucking well cut me up at King's Cross on my own territory. They tried to do me up as well. And he's still living in luxury. I don't like that.

Jean Justice, after assuring Alphon that X had not squealed and that he (Justice) and X were not 'in it together' started to ask questions about the murder. For the first time in the history of these conversations, he started to get sustained and intelligible answers:

J. Whose intention is what I'm getting at?
A. I would have thought the intention was with the person who thought about it in the first place. It's a philosophical matter. I would have thought that. The intention was if you can get a strong-willed enough person in the car with a gun. If he had gone out and gone away and said: 'Well, goodbye, I'm going back to my wife and two children, and leave you to Valerie and goodbye, I won't see her again' — it would have been all right. I would have thought he might have done that. But he didn't. So what do you mean — whose intention? Everyone's intention. It's my intention. All right, it's mine. I take the onus of responsibility.
J. But how did you come across them?
A. I take the onus of responsibility on that.
J. But you were briefed as to where they were and who they were and where they went to — obviously.
A. Obviously.
J. I mean, you didn't come across them by accident.
A. No, I didn't come across them by accident. I've just told you, haven't I? I take the onus of responsibility for that. I'll take it on my shoulders. But I don't have to take it. But the moral

burden for what's happened and for what's happened since remains on someone else's shoulders – or does it?

Justice then asked about payment for the crime:

J. Right, how much?
A. What – money you mean?
J. There must have been some incentive.
A. At the start?
J. Yes.
A. You wouldn't believe me.
J. Yes, I would.
A. Well, it would have to be four figures.
J. It would have to be four figures – yes?
A. Five thousand.
J. Yes.
A. Do you believe that?
J. Well, if it's five hundred or five thousand it's the same.
A. Well, it wouldn't be five hundred.

As the conversation went on, Alphon began to talk more freely about the murder:

J. I am sorry for Hanratty.
A. Well, so am I ...
J. Well, you could have saved him ...
A. I wasn't prepared to do that. I'm not a copper's nark, you see. Not at that time – the time wasn't right then. If the Establishment – all they had to do was say: Well, I'm sorry we've got the wrong man and goodbye. They don't have to arrest anyone else. But if they had done just that it would have been all right. But they get someone else and charge him and – obviously they're waiting for someone to come forward. They get up to all sorts of tricks. As you say, they say 'black is white'. The onus is on the Establishment. Not on us. Me.
J. Well, the guilt of killing Gregsten is on you.
A. That's another matter isn't it? That's nothing to do with killing him. I mean if I – I killed Hanratty – well alright so in the olden days people killed one another and nothing was said about it. I killed Gregsten and the Establishment hanged Hanratty. Well it's the Establishment's fault. What have they done with me since? They almost acted like they knew that I done it ...

There were also some interesting exchanges about the murderer's clothes:

J. Where did you change your clothes?
A. That's beside the point.
J. It isn't beside the point.
A. What do you mean — change my clothes? There was no change of clothes at all. Well not for a day or two afterwards ... The only idea of doing a murder was when ... the motive was there. The essential thing was to get away with it. So we hardly undressed publicly did we? In any case, the clothes weren't changed for two or three days afterwards. There was no reason to change them ... There was no blood on them.

They also discussed the cartridge cases:

J. Where did you get empty cartridge cases, if you planted them first?
A. After shooting the bullets.
J. In the hotel?
A. Cumberland. Funnily enough I did shoot them. Well, anyway you can get cartridge cases easily enough.
J. Not that type.
A. Shoot the bullets out of them and the cases are there. You can't check and say that a bullet came out of a certain cartridge case, you know.

But by far the most important and interesting excerpts from the tape are those which deal with the five hours in the murder car and the motive for the murder itself. A few examples of these run as follows:

A. He had a chance to go ... chance to get out.
J. Who?
A. Gregsten. He had a chance to go. He could have gone and said goodbye, goodbye for good, there and then. He had a chance. He had five fucking hours chance to say goodbye and go back to his wife. He didn't take it. And he tried to get funny. He tried to turn the tables and he was shot. Dead. The other one wasn't anything to do with it at all. She just happened to be there: it could have been her, it could have been anyone else. This is Gregsten at fault, you've got to consider. She was the vital witness after all, so she was shot dead. I thought.

Later, he said:

A. If you come face to face with someone you've got the upper hand
on. It's nice to come face to face with someone who hasn't got
the upper hand. Someone like Gregsten for example. Somebody
who is so cocky in the end you feel that he's got the upper hand
on *you*. And then they die ...

J. Hanratty or whoever it was wouldn't let them go. They said
take the car — go away — we'll do anything you say ...

A. But there's one way of saying 'take the car and go away'. There's
a way of grovelling with tears streaming down your face and
saying 'I've got a wife and two children; for God's sake take the
car' and there's a way of saying 'Well, take the car I don't care
what you do — take anything — go ... ' You know ... 'it doesn't
matter to me.' It's the *way*, you know. There's a different way
of saying 'take the car.' You can say '*Take* the car, for God's
sake, take the car, I've got a wife and children, I mean it doesn't
matter to me, just take it and let me get back. I'm finished now.'
That's one thing. But the other way of saying 'all right take my
car, take my money it doesn't make any difference — me and
Valerie will still be there.' You see the difference now?

But, perhaps the most extraordinary statement of all was:

A. After all, we can't wait too long — the mission was to see ... *Let's
say the mission was to see that they were separated. Perhaps the
mission was to see that they weren't separated in the way that they
were, but the mission was to separate them and they were separated
weren't they? That's the point of it, and that's the only way they
could have been separated. I couldn't see any other way myself.*
Because after five hours, he had five hours and he couldn't do it
in five hours. So there's not much point in giving them any
longer is there? He was determined to be unfaithful. He was
going to go. If the man had just walked out with the gun and said
goodbye, they would have been in the cornfield the next night.
It wouldn't have done any good.
The mission was to see that the affair was finished. That was
the end of the affair.

These are only a few extracts from a conversation which lasted for
more than two hours, and whose transcript runs to more than
ten thousand words. The written words are a miserable substitute

for the voices. This tape records perhaps better than any other the swaying moods of Peter Alphon, switching from fear about a plot against him to the strange mixture of arrogance and remorse with which he describes the scenes in the car and the attitudes of his alleged victims. More than two years had passed since Alphon first met Justice, yet this was the first time, either person to person or on the telephone, that Alphon had spoken of Mr X or outlined any specific motive for the crime. It is the first time too that he had dealt in any detail with the events in the murder car, as he alleged he saw them. The tapes have to be read and heard in the light of the only two possible explanations for Alphon's confession — other than that he did the murder. The first is that he was inventing the entire story out of a perverse sense of mischief. The second, that he had convinced himself that he had done the murder. Neither explanation tells us why at so late a stage he involved someone else so blatantly in his fantasy or why he waited so long to develop his mischief in such a haphazard yet fundamental way.

At any rate, having named Mr X to Justice, he then proceeded to persecute him. Before long X was ringing Justice, complaining bitterly about the telephone calls which he was receiving from Alphon. He also assured Justice that he would be seeing Superintendent Acott about them. 'He's the only policeman I *can* talk to,' he explained. Mr X went on to affirm his belief that Alphon had nothing to do with the A6 murder, and that Hanratty was rightly convicted: 'If a man's got an *idée fixe* that he's done something and he's a lunatic to this degree, it's only as near as you'll ever get to doing it or something similar. This man is simply linking everything together here. It's something which everyone is wishing to forget.'

'I've never seen this man,' went on Mr X about Alphon. 'I've not got involved with this man. I know nothing about it. I've never met the man, and that's the great thing, I never have. And I've had no conversations with him.'

If all this was true, why was Alphon ringing Mr X? Was Mr X part of his *idée fixe*? Whatever the truth about this episode, Alphon soon stopped phoning both Mr Justice and Mr X, and turned his attention to a new victim.

The *Evening News* of September 9th, 1964 made two relevant announcements. First, Lord Russell of Liverpool had been commissioned by Victor Gollancz to write a book on the A6 murder.

Lord Russell, best known for his work on Nazi Germany, *The Scourge of the Swastika*, was, like Gollancz, an opponent of capital punishment. Unlike Gollancz, however, he opposed it not on moral grounds but because of the finality of the sentence. Russell's political views, unlike Gollancz's, were firmly of the Right. The other announcement, quite unconnected, was that Superintendent Acott had been promoted to the post of Deputy Commander of Scotland Yard's Criminal Investigations Department. 'He has', said the *Evening News* reporter, 'never failed to solve a murder.'

Almost at once, Lord and Lady Russell's flat in Putney was bombarded with silent telephone calls. At first, Lord Russell dismissed the calls as something to do with his previous work. 'It must be one of those Fascist people,' he told the *Daily Mirror* when that paper reported the first batch of 'nuisance calls' on October 13th, 1964.

Lord Russell was a new victim for Alphon, and an increasingly important one as the line to Justice was cut. Justice, who at the end of 1963 had stopped drinking (and who has kept off alcohol ever since), changed his telephone number at Half Moon Street and, a few months later, moved to a flat in Belgravia. Regular conversations between the two men stopped, and they have only spoken to each other twice since.

Alphon's calls to Lord and Lady Russell were substantially different to those received by Justice. There was very little discussion of the murder. When Alphon said, in a conversation in March 1965, 'I've never confessed to *you*, have I?' he was telling the truth. The calls were either silent, threatening or insulting, and their stated purpose was to stop Russell writing and publishing his book. Once, at his farm in Plaistow, Sussex, Lord Russell's phone rang thirty-three times in forty-five minutes. On another day, there were sixty calls in one and a half hours. The caller seldom spoke. When he did, it was to tell Russell: 'Your life hangs by a thread and I can cut it whenever I like,' or: 'If I thought you were alone on the farm, I'd come down and do you in,' or: 'It won't be long before I do you in and Justice too. Then you'll both be dead.'

Lord and Lady Russell were not a little irritated by these calls, and they complained to the police. They were advised to put in another line, and, when the man rang, to dial 999. This they did, and the calls were traced; but never, strangely, in time to catch the caller, though on one occasion the Russells kept him on the line for more than an hour. The police then advised Russell, as they had advised the Hanrattys, to change their telephone number, which Russell refused to do on the grounds that this would put him out of contact with friends and colleagues all over the world.

The police then suggested that there was evidence to sustain a private prosecution of Alphon by Lord Russell. Again Lord Russell insisted on police action. 'I am not all that wealthy,' he said 'and I believe it is the duty of the police to do it. I think I am entitled to the same protection as any other citizen in the country.'

Still the calls persisted. In the first year after the announcement of his book, Russell received some eight hundred calls. Still the police refused to prosecute. The identity of the caller was beyond question, as comparison between Russell's and Justice's tapes made clear. On May 2nd Russell received a letter from Scotland Yard. 'We regard this', said the letter, 'as not a suitable matter for police prosecution.'

Russell also received a letter from Sir Joseph Simpson, Commissioner of the Metropolitan Police, warning him that the defence in such a case might make much of the fact that Lord Russell was bringing the prosecution to advertise his book. 'This is something', wrote Sir Joseph, 'that may not even have crossed your mind, but it was a suggestion that would hardly be overlooked by a shrewd defence.'

Lord Russell finished his book in spite of these interruptions and threats. Victor Gollancz, however, decided that the book was too libellous. The decision was an odd one, for Russell's book does not argue or even suggest that Alphon did the murder. It does not describe events since the trial, nor even reproduce Alphon's confession notes as handed to Justice two years previously. Even the 1963 Commons debate is not touched on in Russell's book. It argues from the evidence given at the trial and nothing more.

This point was quickly grasped by Mr Frederick Warburg, managing director of the publishers Secker and Warburg, who agreed as soon as he read the manuscript to publish the book himself.

Peter Alphon, who had been delighted when Gollancz turned the book down, redoubled his activities on the telephone. Mr and Mrs Warburg were telephoned ceaselessly at their London home with threats and anti-Semitic abuse, in which Alphon has always excelled. Directors and even past directors were telephoned at home and at work and told to stop the book or take the consequences. The lines to Secker and Warburg's offices were jammed constantly with silent calls. The Warburgs contacted the police, and were greeted with a peremptory brush-off. 'One officer', said Mrs Warburg, 'suggested we were doing it for publicity.' (*Sunday Telegraph*, October 31st, 1965.)

Despite all this, the book, *Deadman's Hill: Was Hanratty Guilty?*, was published on October 21st, 1965. Alphon read the book, in some relief. It did not cast any aspersions on him, and it awakened public interest in the case. He phoned Russell and crowed about the book's lack of sting. Then, abruptly, the calls stopped, and no one, neither Russell, Justice, Justice's brother Frank nor Jeremy Fox heard from Alphon for six months.

In December 1965 Mr Roy Jenkins was appointed Home Secretary. Mr Jenkins was the first post-war Home Secretary with a reputation as a liberal reformer. He was a firm opponent of capital punishment which, by the time of his appointment, had been abolished for a five-year trial. With the decision came a Home Office concession to the families of hanged men to rebury their sons in civilian cemeteries. Permission to rebury the remains of James Hanratty was given on January 9th, 1966 and he was reburied on February 22nd. The reburial in a Wembley cemetery was made all the more macabre by the presence everywhere of Black Marias and plainclothes policemen who anticipated an 'incident' from sources unnamed.

Roy Jenkins had associated himself with Fenner Brockway's petition in 1963 for a public inquiry into the A6 murder verdict, and a precedent had been set by his predecessor, Sir Frank Soskice, who had commissioned a public inquiry under Mr Justice Brabin into the conviction and hanging in 1950 of Timothy Evans for the murder of his child. At an election meeting in Lewisham on March 23rd, 1966, Jenkins was asked by Mr Charles Irish, a friend of the Hanrattys, whether he would set up an inquiry into the verdict. He replied: 'My primary feeling was that there was some doubt about the Evans case, and some about the facts in the Hanratty case. I will look into the matter and certainly consider an inquiry.' (*Daily Express*, March 23rd, 1966.)

A lead was given to Jenkins to carry out this pledge by Lord Russell of Liverpool who, on May 20th, tabled a motion in the Lords calling for a public inquiry into the A6 murder. The motion was given some publicity, and it drew Peter Alphon to the telephone once more. Unable to ring Jean Justice or Russell or Warburg, all of whom had changed their telephone numbers in desperation, Alphon rang Frank Justice at his flat in Paddington. The first call was on June 6th, and the second a few days later. 'He said he was going to cut me up in the street and he would like to kill my brother,' said Frank Justice. 'And then he talked about black magic as he always used to ... He was more vicious than I ever remember.' (*Sunday Telegraph*, June 26th, 1966.) Justice told the Paddington police of the call and Lord Russell wrote once again to Mr Jenkins asking that the call be 'taken seriously by you and Scotland Yard'. Jenkins, in reply, set the police moving to find Alphon, and replied to Russell:

> There continues to be great difficulty in tracing the man who makes these calls ... What further action could be taken when he is traced would very much depend on what facts are established when the police find him.

When Lord Russell rose on August 4th, 1966, to move his motion in the House of Lords, he was not aware that the police had taken any action to find Alphon or interview him. The motion which he moved differed crucially from the one he had tabled three months earlier. It referred not just to the confessions of 'another man', but to the confessions of 'Peter Louis Alphon'. The Mr X fiction, so delicately maintained in the Commons in 1963, had been abandoned, and, as Russell explained to the Lords in the first part of his speech, there was now no longer any point in not naming the man who had made the confession and who had been ringing him up. Russell's speech dealt partly with the arguments of Lord Brooke three years previously, and partly with the Alphon telephone calls. He laid great stress on police reluctance to chase up the man who was pestering him. Lord Brooke, in a maiden speech, then repeated his Commons speech of 1963. Lords Brockway and Conesford made short, opposing contributions, and then Lord Stonham, Parliamentary Under Secretary at the Home Office, replied. He did not rule out an inquiry but he spoke against one. He too went over most of the ground which Brooke had traversed in 1963. He raised the question of the greyhound 'Mentals Only Hope', though for some reason (possibly the powerful arguments of Lord Russell) he did not talk about Alphon's driving ability. From Acott's thirteen points eliminating Alphon he selected the Cockney accent and the use of 'f' for 'th', stating bluntly and inaccurately that Alphon did not speak with such an accent and did not mispronounce 'th'. But the most curious part of Stonham's speech is that in which he enlarged on an alibi for Alphon on the night of the murder:

> I recognize that this, as has been said, depends partly on the evidence of the hotel manager, Mr Nudds, who has a criminal record, and who made one statement to the police, which was later withdrawn, in which he implicated Mr Alphon. The only point I want to make is that this, too, was before the jury, and it is difficult to see how they could have convicted Hanratty if they had not accepted the manager's withdrawal of the statement; and, as I have already mentioned, the prosecution produced the hotel register and the receipt book. (Houseof Lords, Hansard, August 4th, 1966.)

There can be no evidence that the jury accepted any of Nudds's statements. The jury most probably, and properly, decided to reject ALL Nudds's evidence. Such a rejection did not mean that Alphon was guilty. Equally, it did not mean that Alphon had an alibi for the murder.

Lord Stonham's speech went on:

> The whole crux of the matter which my Right Honourable friend the Home Secretary has to decide and which is really before the House is whether there is anything new in the noble Lord's arguments which have been adduced tonight which was not before the jury at the trial. These [Nudds's] statements were not the first evidence the police had in support of Mr Alphon's alibi. He was seen by them, first on August 27th, four days after the murder when he said he was with his mother on the evening of the 22nd, the fatal evening, and then went to the hotel. *This was verified with the hotel at the time and with his mother.* (Ibid., my italics.)

Let us recall what happened. On August 27th, 1961, Alphon was reported to the police for strange behaviour in a Finsbury Park hotel. He was asked where he was on August 22nd and he said he was with his mother and later went to the Vienna Hotel. A phone call to the Vienna Hotel verified his pseudonym in the hotel register. A brief interview with his mother on September 13th no doubt confirmed that he was with her on the crucial evening. That, for the moment, was that.

Then, suddenly, after Nudds had confirmed in his first statement that Alphon was in the hotel all night, Mr Acott and his colleagues descended on him once more. Nudds made a second statement, indicating that Alphon was out until after 2 a.m. Mrs Alphon, closely questioned again by Acott on September 21st, revealed that her son had not, in fact, visited her on August 22nd as he said he had. Then Acott unleashed a murder hunt for Alphon. The alibis of Nudds and Mrs Alphon had been discredited. Acott dared not repeat them in court. Two years after the murder, however, Brooke revived the Nudds alibi; and five years after the murder, Lord Stonham revived Mrs Alphon's alibi, pretending that both Nudds's and Mrs Alphon's alibis had been 'verified' by the police!

These were not the only areas where the unfortunate Lord Stonham strayed a long way from the facts. He went on to make a categorical statement about the abusive and threatening telephone calls to Lord Russell:

> I would assure the Noble Lord that I have seen all the correspondence which he has had with the Home Secretary, and the Commissioner has assured me that continuous, renewed and vigorous efforts are being made to trace the man who is making these calls. What action is then taken, if we trace him, must depend on what facts are established when we do find him ... I should have thought that before we could establish that this man has been making the calls we would have to find him and question him. (Ibid.)

Unfortunately for Lord Stonham, however, the 'continuous, renewed and vigorous efforts' had already borne fruit. Two days before the debate, on August 2nd, Peter Alphon had been 'tracked down' to his solicitor's office in Kensington, where he was interviewed by two senior police officers in connection with the calls to Lord Russell and Frank Justice. Although police authorities must have known about the House of Lords debate, and had been requested to keep in touch with the Home Office on developments relating to Alphon, the news that Alphon had been 'found' (by a phone call to his solicitor) and interviewed had not filtered through to Lord Stonham who proceeded to tell their Lordships that Alphon had not yet been traced. Three days later, Lord Stonham had to admit his error and tell their Lordships that a lot of what he had told them the previous Friday had been 'based on out-of-date information'. (House of Lords Hansard, August 7th, 1966.)

To the police, meanwhile, Alphon admitted making the calls to Russell, but claimed they were quite legitimate. Through his solicitor, he put out two further statements about the 'persecution' he was suffering from Parliament. The first, on the same day as the debate, read as follows:

> My client is most distressed that this matter has been raised again. He would certainly welcome a public inquiry so that he can once for all clear his name. My client has never at any time confessed or admitted to the murder. (*Daily Telegraph*, August 5th, 1966.)

The second, in the first person, read:

> I see no reason to repeat my previous denial of Lord Russell's allegations made in the House of Lords. I suggest he has been gravely misled. There has been a vicious campaign waged against me over a period of years by a group of people for reasons best known to themselves. (*Daily Express*, August 8th, 1966.)

Despite these denials, however, or perhaps because of them, the police eventually decided to move against Alphon in connection with the calls to Russell and Frank Justice. On August 20th, Chief Inspector Henry Mooney of Scotland Yard advised Lord Russell that Alphon would be charged under section 6 of the Post Office Act for making threatening and abusive calls and for wasting electricity in so doing.

The case eventually came up on August 25th – only three weeks after the Lords debate. Alphon was represented by Mr Sebag Montefiore. He admitted making the calls but pleaded not guilty on all counts, arguing that the calls were justifiable.

'I tried', he said, 'to give [Russell] an insight into the character of the people who were supplying him with evidence. Also, I felt that if I could hold him in conversation for a considerable time, being a man of a high standard of education, he would soon see I was not the murderer.'

Inspector Mooney gave evidence against Alphon, but assured the court that his department did not regard Alphon as in any way responsible for the A6 murder. The magistrate, Mr Nigel Robinson, found Alphon guilty on all counts. He fined him five pounds on the first two counts and conditionally discharged him on the other three. Alphon was bound over to keep the peace in the sum of fifty pounds, with his solicitor, Mr Michael Eden of Galbraith and Best, standing surety.

By the end of the trial, which I observed incredulously from the press gallery, I realized that I was well and truly hooked on the A6 murder. I had taken an interest since December 1965 when Richard Ingrams, the editor of *Private Eye*, told me that I ought to come and meet a man called Jean Justice who kept pestering him with documents about the A6 murder. I met Justice about three weeks later, and visited him one evening in his flat to hear some of his tapes. I was, at the outset, sceptical of his story, but found the voice of Alphon on the tape very convincing. I attended Hanratty's funeral and reburial in February, when I met Mr and Mrs Hanratty for the first time, and wrote two or three articles for 'Mandrake' of the *Sunday Telegraph* about the phone calls and Lord Russell's House of Lords motion. As I absorbed more and more information about the case, I determined to publish the full story of the Alphon confessions outside Parliament, with Alphon's name used openly. This proved a difficult operation. The *Sunday Telegraph*, for a start, were not interested. Nor were a number of other journals which I tentatively approached. The journal which eventually agreed to publish the lot was the magazine *Queen*, more usually associated with expensive restaurants, Ascot and noble families than with revelations about murders.

Partly due to the persistence of Gina Richardson, a journalist working on *Queen* features, who insisted from the moment she heard the story that *Queen* would publish it, partly to the patrician confidence of *Queen*'s editor and proprietor, Jocelyn Stevens (when I explained that calling a man a murderer was not merely civil libel but criminal libel which could result in a jail sentence, Stevens replied: 'I'd *love* to go to jail for this!'), partly to the deputy editor, Joe Scott-Clarke, *Queen* eventually published, on September 14th, 1966, a six-thousand-word, six-page article entitled: 'HANRATTY: The Case For An Enquiry'. In the article Alphon was named as the man who had confessed to the murder and long extracts from the March 18th, 1964 tape were reproduced. Protracted conferences with libel lawyers had only marginally changed the original draft and, as things turned out, there was nothing to worry about. There was no move from the Director of Public Prosecutions to proffer charges for criminal libel; and no reaction from Alphon's solicitors. The only reaction from Alphon himself was a familiar one.

'MAGAZINE RECEIVES SILENT CALLS' reported *The Times* of September 21st. 'The editorial office of the London magazine *Queen* has received dozens of "silent" telephone calls in the past week. It published an article last week suggesting there were grounds for an inquiry into the A6 murder.'

The Lords debate and the *Queen* article revived interest in the Hanratty case. On September 20th a Commons motion for an inquiry was put down by Joan Lestor and signed by about twenty M.P.s. Even the *Daily Express* reported, in a headline, HANRATTY A6 MURDER INQUIRY LIKELY—and this was before any revelations further substantiating Hanratty's Rhyl alibi. Although none of the newspapers had taken up the *Queen* article, B.B.C.'s Panorama team set to work on a fifty-minute programme on the case.

Peter Alphon, through his solicitors, agreed to appear on the Panorama programme and arrived at the B.B.C. for a taped interview on October 29th. At the start of the interview, John Morgan asked him why the police had regarded him as the first suspect. The question threw Alphon off guard and he mumbled something about having taken out a writ against Superintendent Acott for wrongful arrest and not being able to say anything which might prejudice that case. Much to Alphon's astonishment, Morgan then began to play him extracts from the tape-recordings which Justice had lent the B.B.C. Those of Alphon's replies which eventually appeared on the programme were as follows:

ALPHON. Well these notes were part of details for a book that Justice had suggested we collaborate on, it was to be a fictional reconstruction of the crime, and Justice put it to me that he ought to stress the psychological interest of the crime. But other than—the car for five hours ... nobody knows of course except Miss Storie, but obviously why should she go into details after what she's been through. And I used my imagination, and I used the first person as the most economical grammatical form ... a point which Justice, who is not a very well educated man, doesn't seem to understand. I'm writing to the Home Office in the next day or two and you've just had my explanation. I saw a senior police officer a couple of days ago and he said this is the first time we've had your explanation of it, and we don't like—it looks bad to us now. I put it to them that they should have come to me a long, long time ago for it. And I'm now writing to the Home Secretary, asking for compensation for the persecution which has gone on as a result of this man's activities, and I'm also asking them to charge him with criminal conspiracy.

MORGAN. The Hanratty family has stated that you went to them after the execution of their son and offered them money as compensation?

A. They stated quite a lot of untrue things and they—I'm afraid that I can't go along with that. I deny it—I'm afraid I haven't got money to spare to offer to anyone anyway.

M. Mr Alphon, you say that those notes towards a confession were intended as fiction—as something for a book. I'd like you to listen to this for a moment. [Background tape.]

A. This is an academic argument I'm having with Justice, that's what he's putting to me. I'm speaking to him in inverted commas.

M. You don't mean what you say on that tape?

A. I do mean what I say on the tape, I'm speaking to him in inverted commas, he's putting it to me and I'm putting it back at him. Look Justice—I'm the man ... I don't know what was said, something about being in the car, I'm putting it back to him, do you understand, I'm speaking back to him in inverted commas.

M. You say on the tapes 'I killed Gregsten the establishment killed Hanratty'—was that taking ...

A. Justice put it to me, he said that I killed Hanratty, I said what it— I killed Hanratty—I beg your pardon, I'll start again. I killed Gregsten, and so you say I killed Hanratty. But that can't be true even if I did kill Gregsten I didn't kill Hanratty did I. I mean the establishment did that. They hanged him. I don't go in for hanging people, that's what I'm saying to him in the context of his argument. You see?

M. Well what about remarks like—

A. The police understand it anyway. I don't know whether you do or not.

M. You also say that the man represented by yourself, your voice on this tape, that ...

A. That's me, that's me all right.

M. Right, that's established. But the people — 'they knew I wouldn't go to the police.' In your reading of the murder then, who are they? You're saying that someone sent the murderer to the field to meet Michael Gregsten and Valerie Storie.

A. Well that's what Justice is saying to me and I'm putting it back to him. This is the theory that we've concocted jointly together. I think he — obviously someone put the gun in his hand I mean, he didn't make the gun himself did he?

M. Why exactly did you suggest on the tapes that the purpose of the murder was to separate Michael Gregsten and Valerie Storie?

A. He did try to separate them, he sent Gregsten away ... to get some cigarettes didn't he, and Gregsten came back. I suggest that — I think he was a very brave man to have done so, but I think that perhaps if he hadn't come back things would have turned out very differently — he'd still be alive and I think probably Valerie Storie wouldn't have been in the predicament she is today. I mean she's rallied gamely from it, and I'm very pleased to have seen that, but I think that they conducted their business wrongly with the murderer, they didn't treat him the right way psychologically. In other words, let me put it to you point blank I think they should have pandered to him. I think they tried to be a little bit cocky and it got on his nerves.

M. These tapes Mr Alphon, the tone of voice on them, your voice, is excitable, almost hysterical. Now is that the tone in which people talk about a work of fiction?

A. I don't think we were discussing the writing of fiction explicitly by that time, I mean Justice made his motives well known to me, I was understandably wild, but I wouldn't say that — you say they're hysterical — I think it's a perfectly controlled hysteria, it's no good talking like a lamb to a man like that you've got to as I say, I told you before, intimidation. I don't mind admitting it. Why not?

M. On the tapes you say 'When I do a murder, it's not a murder it's an Act of God' — I mean do you yourself — were you imagining it or do you yourself have a sort of messianic ...

A. Oh my dear man, I'm not going to do any murders, I certainly — I think it's blasphemy absolutely. I mean, if I did a murder I think it would be an act of God, because I certainly wouldn't do one, under any circumstances — well I don't know, I think if I was paid by the State then of course I would do it, I would do it, I'm not a pacifist, or anything like that. But not private murder, certainly not.

This is, of course, a flat denial of any involvement in the murder, but the denial is an odd one. There is, first, the denial that he visited the Hanratty parents and offered them money for the death of their son—a visit for which there are three witnesses.

Then there is the suggestion that the confession was part of a fictional idea which Justice and Alphon were concocting. This is not corroborated by any of the tapes of the conversations between Alphon and Justice. The only mention of a book in the entire record of the conversations is when Alphon mentions Justice's plans for his book, *Murder versus Murder*, in contemptuous terms, saying: 'It isn't worth the writing.' With this exception there is no reference anywhere from either man to a fictional rendering of the murder. References to the A6 murder crop up at random in the conversations, almost as asides.

But perhaps the most interesting part of the interview is when Alphon answers Morgan's questions about the murderer wanting to separate Gregsten and Valerie Storie. It would have been easy for him at this stage to stick to his theme: to reply that he knew nothing about the crime. But he burst out:

> He *did* try to separate them! He sent Gregsten away, to get some cigarettes, didn't he, and Gregsten *came* back ... I think that perhaps if he hadn't *come* back things would have turned out very differently—he'd still be alive ... I think that they conducted their business wrongly with the murderer, they didn't treat him the right way psychologically ... I think they should have pandered to him. I think they tried to be a little bit cocky and it got on his nerves. (My italics.)

The use of the words 'come' and 'came' in this context is surprising. An objective narrator would more naturally have said 'went' and 'gone'. But Alphon's views about the development in the car that night are most extraordinary. They could not have been taken from the trial record or from any reasonable deduction from it. There is nothing in Miss Storie's evidence of the drive before the murder to indicate that she and Gregsten were 'cocky' to the murderer, or that they did not 'pander' to him. In fact, Miss Storie's account indicated the exact opposite: she had written (in *Today*, June 9th, 1962.):

When you have a definite feeling that one wrong inflection in your voice, one sudden gesture might get your brains blown out, you don't feel like being a toast-and-marmalade hero or heroine. Mike and I were scared stiff.

It is Alphon and Alphon alone who surmised that the couple in the car refused to co-operate with the murderer's plans to separate the couple, and were 'cocky' in their attitude to him.

Despite his assurances on Panorama that he was seeking compensation from the Home Office for the persecution he was suffering at the hands of Justice, he had already started to telephone Lord and Lady Russell once more — in breach of the assurance he had given to the court the previous August.

In September and October, Lord Russell received some fifty silent calls, interspersed with yells and heavy breathing. On February 5th, 1967, however, the caller finally spoke. He was, of course, Peter Alphon, and Lord Russell had his tape-recorder ready. The next day, he was writing again to the authorities and contacting the police with a view to summoning Alphon for a breach of recognizance.

Once more, the authorities refused to act, and on February 10th, Lord Russell took out a private summons for breach of recognizance against Alphon and Eden. On March 15th, the summons came to court, but Peter Alphon was not there. The magistrate, Mr Robinson, adjourned the case *sine die* until he could be found. The summons was finally served by the police on April 27th, eleven weeks after it was issued. The summons requested Alphon to appear at Marylebone magistrates' court on May 12th, 1967, to answer charges that he had broken his recognizance.

The game was up. Breaking a recognizance is, in normal circumstances a serious matter. The offence itself, making annoying or threatening telephone calls, is not usually regarded as a serious one (though, in February 1970, a young painter called Peter Wesley was sentenced to three months in prison at Folkestone Quarter Sessions for 'wasting electricity' by making a phone call to the police station asking for police protection — *Private Eye*, February 27th, 1970). But the deliberate baulking of a court order is regarded as monstrous.

Studying his summons, Alphon must have felt that if he answered it he would almost certainly be sent to prison. Such a prospect infuriated and terrified him. As before, when charged with stealing the handbag from Mrs Fedzuk in 1962, he began to think of ways in which he could avoid a prison sentence.

'If I'm convicted for this ... ', he had shouted at Justice four years earlier, 'I am going abroad and I'm going to tell the truth in a world press conference, and I'm going to shame British justice in the eyes of the world ... When I'm far away I'll tell the real truth. You tell your friends in the police that. Put the word around. It will involve someone else. Someone else.'

The idea had stayed with him. He had repeated it, for instance, to the Hanratty parents in one of his conversations with them. As soon as 'British justice' turned on him to the extent of imprisoning him he was determined to elude its clutches by going abroad and shaming it in the eyes of the world.

Early in May, Alphon walked into the London offices of the American magazine *Life*, and offered his life story, including a full confession to the A6 murder for payment. He offered to go abroad and make the confession in public. Miss Bacon, of *Life* magazine, interviewed him for about two hours. She was not impressed, but she wired her head office in New York with the details of Alphon's offer. The answer was No. If Alphon did go to Paris, he was told, he could contact *Life* offices there. He would, however, have to meet his own travelling expenses, and *Life* were not interested in paying large sums for his story.

In spite of this rebuff—and without any hope of any reward— Alphon decided to go ahead with his confession. On the evening of May 11th, Peter Stephens, the Paris correspondent of the *Daily Mirror*, was approached by Peter Alphon, who told him that the next day he planned to call a world press conference to confess to the A6 murder. The French press the following morning carried a substantial story to that effect, and Stephens included a few brief paragraphs in the *Mirror*:

> Alphon told me last night: 'I'm the real murderer. I was paid to do it. They got the wrong man.' The press conference, he said, would be held in the Louvre Hotel at 2.30. 'I'll make a full confession of the murder. I shall also produce proof,' Alphon added. (*Daily Mirror*, May 12th, 1967.)

Alphon arrived the next day at the bar of the Hôtel du Louvre, to meet journalists representing papers from all over the world, and two representatives from Scotland Yard, armed with a tape-recorder.

The press conference itself seems to have been rather a confused affair, partly because none of the press men knew anything about the A6 murder and the subsequent events. (My own heroic dash to Paris on reading the *Daily Mirror* that morning was cut short at London Airport when I discovered that I had left my passport behind.)

Alphon made three points at the conference: that he had committed the murder; that he had been paid to 'end the relationship between Gregsten and Miss Storie'; and that the gun had been given him by an intermediary.

While he was making his confession, Lord Russell and others attended at Marylebone court to deal with the case about Alphon's calls. 'Call Peter Alphon!' shouted the usher, dutifully. But to no one's surprise, since the *Daily Mirror* article that morning had been the talk of the court, Peter Alphon was not there. The magistrate promptly issued a warrant for Alphon's arrest.

The evening papers on the evening of May 12th were full of Alphon's confession. The *Evening News* in particular gave it great prominence. Across the front page was the banner headline: PETER ALPHON SENSATION.

The *News* report by Simone French from the paper's Paris office was the most extensive in the British press and is quoted here at some length:

'I have been persecuted,' he said. 'But now I want to drag British justice in the mud.'

Alphon ... announced that after his confession today he had no intention of returning to England. He expects to travel to Germany soon.

The only 'proof' he put forward after his statement was to state that a large sum of money — 'around £5,000' — was paid into his bank at the Law Courts branch of Lloyds Bank, in eight to ten instalments, directly after the A6 murder. The payments, said Alphon, began in October 1961.

'A man offered me a large sum of money — I am not prepared to say how much — and told me to end the relationship between Gregsten and Miss Storie. Another man, a mutual friend, then put a gun in my hand. I was not told in so many words to murder. It was just said. We will get you a gun ... take it from there.'

Said Alphon: 'I gave the couple in the car two chances. I spoke a lot of rubbish about morality and I gave Gregsten two chances to go away. He appeared to want to be got rid of. I sent him away twice. But each time the bloody man came back. Twice he came back.'

Then Alphon told his story of how James Hanratty was framed for the murder. He claimed that it was done by another man. 'But I', said Alphon, 'am a bit sophisticated. I did not know he was going to frame someone. I have no proof for this part of the story.'

Unfortunately, however, none of the British newspapers reported that Alphon had named the 'other man' who had framed Hanratty with the murder, even though the man was dead and therefore could issue no writs for libel. The framer, Alphon had said, was Charles France. France had put the gun under the back seat of a 36A bus. France had put the cartridge cases in the Vienna Hotel. And France had supplied Alphon with the gun.

I read the evening papers that day in a state of considerable frustration. So many crucial questions had clearly not been asked. There was, after all, no proof that Alphon had done the murder. The open confession was remarkable enough, but there was, according to the *Evening News*, 'no comment' from the Home Office or from Lloyds Bank. There was no way of telling, even, whether a large sum of money had been paid in instalments into Alphon's bank in the Strand.

Soon after reading the evening papers, I rang the Hôtel St Anne in Paris. I knew that Alphon was staying there because one of the journalists in Paris who had seen him the previous evening had rung Lord Russell and told him where Alphon was staying. I asked the hotel telephonist for Peter Alphon and almost at once I was listening to the familiar 'Hello' I had heard on so many tapes. I was worried that my *Queen* article would put him off, so I said my name was Birch and that I was a freelance journalist interested in the case.

After some initial hesitation, Alphon started to talk. He talked for about two and a half hours. The result, confirmed by Alphon during another telephone call two days later as an accurate record of what he said, appeared in the *Sunday Times* on May 14th, as follows:

I first met 'X' in The White Bear Inn in Piccadilly Circus about two years before the murder. He pretended to be an extreme right-wing Fascist and we agreed on a lot of things, specially about immorality among married people. 'X' talked a lot for months before the murder about Michael Gregsten and the affair Gregsten was having with a girl in the office.

I knew he had a plan to stop the affair once and for all. He approached one or two people in Soho to see if they would help, but no little Soho tiddler could do what he wanted. Anyway, I used to boast a lot about how easy it would be to frighten Gregsten. One day he said: 'If you're so clever why don't you do it,' and I said, 'I can do almost anything.' 'Like use a gun?' he said, and I replied, although I had never used a gun before, 'Of course you would have to use a gun.'

Then he talked about the money, and he offered me £5,000. You can check on this and as far as I am concerned the bank manager has my permission to disclose all the facts about my account. The money was paid into my account at the Law Courts branch of Lloyds Bank – £5,000 in five or six instalments, I think, starting in October, 1961.

Charles 'Dixie' France was a mutual friend of me and 'X' and Hanratty, especially of Hanratty. France was very broke at the time and he got money to get the gun and he gave me the gun a week before the murder. I wasn't very good with a gun and I had to have some practice so I shot two bullets into a cushion in a chair at the Cumberland Hotel, Marble Arch.

I took the two cartridge cases and gave them to France.

'X' had shown me the cornfield where Gregsten and Valerie used to go after work. I'd been there twice before the murder on a reconnaissance.

On the day I was at Slough dog-track and there was a book-maker there who knows me and who can confirm this, although I don't know his name. I left the track at about 8 o'clock and I walked all the way down through Taplow, cross-country to the cornfield. I know the area well because I was brought up there in the war. It's about seven miles and it took me about an hour and a half. When I got there the car [containing Gregsten and his friend Valerie Storie] was in the field.

I climbed into the back of the car and stayed there for five hours. Two hours in the field and three hours driving about.

My plan was to persuade Gregsten to get out of the car and run away. And then I would take the girl and rape her, and then she might feel: what sort of a man is he to leave me like that?

But that didn't work. Gregsten had two chances to go, when he got out for cigarettes and milk, but he kept coming back. When I complained to them about their immorality they laughed and told me to mind my bloody business. There was an awful lot of talking that five hours in the car. Gregsten was cocky the whole time, trying to take the micky. I knew that the only way to break up the affair was to kill them.

When I shot him, it was more in self defence. If I hadn't shot him I would have had it. He turned very quickly. But it wasn't accidental because I was going to kill them anyway.

I knew the way from Bedford to Slough but I didn't know the way back to London, and I got lost down a lot of side roads trying to find the A5. I left the car at Redbridge and walked to Ilford station. I got the train there, changed at Stratford on to the tube, changed again at Oxford Circus and went to Warwick Avenue, which was near the Vienna Hotel where I'd booked in the night before. I went into the hotel and went up to my room, had a wash, came down and had breakfast about 9.40.

I went to Paddington Station and left my case there. I was still wearing the same suit, but there was no blood on it and I had the gun in my pocket. I took the tube to Oxford Circus, changed and went east to Southend-on-Sea. I met France at Southend station and gave him the gun. We had drinks and a meal and then we left separately about five o'clock. I came back and booked in at the Alexandra National Hotel, Finsbury Park.

I was still staying there on the Sunday when the police came to interview me. They said it was a routine check-up because the hotel manager had reported my strange behaviour. But I don't believe it. I think I was shopped. They interviewed me for five hours, but I had a good alibi and there was nothing they could pin on me. The grey suit and the dark glasses I had worn for the murder I had put in a locker in Leicester Square Tube Station and destroyed the ticket.

They let me go then but they were obviously out to get me. I gave myself up on September 22nd after the police had started a nation-wide hunt for me. I was pretty sure I would be all right because Valerie wouldn't recognize me. She didn't recognize me. She never saw my face once in the car.

When I was in the clear I began to realize the plot against Hanratty. X had suggested to me that when I was in the car I could pretend I was Hanratty whom we all knew as a stupid little crook. That's why I said my name was Jim and I was on the run and I had done time.

What I didn't realize was that they meant to get Hanratty for what I had done. France put the gun on the bus where Hanratty had told him it was a good place to hide loot. And France put the cartridge cases in the Vienna Hotel.

I couldn't understand why they were so keen to fix Hanratty. I mean we had got away with it. But France took money from the press to give evidence against his friend and he went into the witness box against his friend. I can tell you that I put pressure on France. I used to ring him again and again after Hanratty was convicted telling him to retract his evidence and threatening him that if Hanratty died, I would see he died too. I think I had something to do with his suicide, but I don't want that on my conscience as well.

All the little bits and pieces of a confession at last became forged into a single, coherent story. Aspects of the A6 murder story, which had been unexplained in the court at Bedford, were explained by Alphon. There was a motive for the murder; an explanation for the long drive; and an account of what was said between the three people. There was the admission that no murder was intended either by the prime mover in the affair or by Charles France, and that the murder of Gregsten was 'more in self defence'. For the first time a meaning was given to those curious words in the original confession notes: 'Meeting my friend at Southend. Disposal of gun.' France had put the gun under the back seat of the bus, and indeed only France knew that Hanratty thought it a good hiding-place, and France had put the cartridge cases in the Vienna Hotel.

Alphon seemed resigned never to return to England. He clearly believed what he had said at the Louvre Hotel and was encouraged to talk to me at great length by my own assertion, quite justified by the facts, that journalists and commentators in England were not taking his confession seriously. Although I suggested to him that the results of our interview would appear in print, he did not at any time suggest that he might be paid for what he told me. Never once, in fact, through scores of telephone conversations and letters, and two meetings, although I have published a great deal about his statements, has Alphon been paid a penny or ever suggested that he should be.

The morning papers on the day after Alphon's Paris confession had lost a great deal of the interest shown by the evening papers the day before. *The Times* dismissed the confession in three short paragraphs; the *Express* in five inches; the *Mail* in two. The *Sun* reported that Scotland Yard were keeping an 'open mind' on Alphon's confession, and that any proceedings would have to be started at Bedford. The *Daily Sketch* crime reporter Peter Burden told his readers: 'Few people in authority are taking Alphon's claims seriously.'

To back this statement Burden produced five of Acott's original thirteen 'eliminating' points at the trial, including the fact that Alphon's christian name was Peter while the murderer had asked his victims to call him Jim. This difference, said Mr Burden, in whose world of crime no doubt murderers always identify themselves to their victims, was 'most important'.

The matter was taken more seriously by Independent Television News whose directors no doubt remembered the writ Alphon had taken out against them after Fenner Brockway's broadcast to the effect that 'Mr X' had done the murder. Alan Hart recorded a twenty-minute interview with Alphon which was shown in full on the I.T.N. feature programme, Dateline, the following Wednesday. Alphon summarized his confession in the Louvre Hotel, but there are two points worthy of notice.

In the first place, the transcript of the programme, twice, in the first two pages, has Alphon using the word 'fink' for 'think'. Transcribers record defections of accent or mispronunciations only when they are very obvious. Nor was the transcriber likely to have known or remembered that the A6 murderer pronounced 'th' as 'f'. Secondly, in his description of the murder, Alphon announced that he had fired only one bullet at Gregsten's head, and that he had not reloaded the gun when he fired at Valerie Storie.

Both these statements differed quite clearly from the facts of the murder. So much so, in fact, that Deputy Commander Acott was able to tell the *Daily Express* that if ever he had had any doubts about Alphon, those doubts were now laid to rest. Alphon's description of the shooting of Miss Storie, he said, clashed with the facts of the murder. Enough cartridge cases were picked up around the body to fill more than one revolver.

This fact, and the fact that Gregsten was shot *twice*, were well known to anyone with a marginal knowledge of the case, and certainly well known to Peter Alphon whose knowledge of the A6 case, whatever his involvement, was prodigious. Why then did he include in his confession such obvious inconsistencies?

The answer becomes clearer as the confessions of Peter Alphon proliferate over the next two and a half years. It is rooted in an essential contradiction which Alphon on more than one occasion admitted to me. On the one hand, he wanted to express his guilt, and to keep his guilt in the public eye so that 'British justice' would not escape the blame for the hanging of Hanratty. On the other, he was anxious to cover himself against possible prosecution.

This may be part of the explanation for the next development in the story. On Sunday, May 21st – only nine days after the Paris confession – the *People* led their front page with a story entitled: 'MY CONFESSION WAS A LIE – Alphon admits: "I wanted to sell my story for £5,000." '

In the story, Ken Gardner, the *People*'s chief reporter and one of the most experienced and able crime reporters in the country, quoted Alphon as follows:

That confession was nonsense.

I knew if I made a sensational enough statement it would be marvellous publicity for my life story. I am asking £5,000 for it.

Understand, I don't want money for myself, I want money so that I can sue all the people who have damaged my character by telling lies about me. But kill anyone? Not me, old man.

I hate England and everything it stands for. I have been hounded by the authorities, whose sole aim seems to be to get me into court on any pretext. I knew I would make the police sit up if I said I had done the murder. I hope they are enjoying a wild goose chase that will keep them occupied for a long time.

I said I had been paid £5,000 to do the killing and that it would be proved by a look at my bank account. If the authorities do that, they will find that the money was paid into my account. But the money had nothing to do with the murder. It was paid to me for something quite different, as I can prove if I want to.

The *People* article ended with a statement attributed to Mr Eden, Alphon's solicitor, suggesting that his client had 'sold his life story to pay for litigation'.

This conversation was reported to have taken place in 'a side-street bar in Dublin'. Alphon had moved from France to Dublin, and Gardner had discovered the name of the hotel where Alphon was staying.

The retraction of the confession had the effect of removing some of the credibility from Alphon's Paris statement. On the face of it, however, it seemed very odd indeed. If Alphon did in fact intend to lead the authorities on a 'wild goose chase which will keep them occupied for a long time', why should he tell a leading reporter of a mass-circulation Sunday paper that the confession was a lot of nonsense? If he was indeed asking five thousand pounds for a story which was false, why tell Gardner that it was false and wreck its selling price? If the money paid into his bank account had nothing to do with the murder why not tell Gardner there and then what the real purpose of the money was? Finally, if Mr Eden was right and the story was sold to get money for litigation, why has not Alphon since engaged in any litigation against any of his alleged persecutors? It also seemed odd that Gardner had not obtained a signed statement from Alphon retracting his confession, or a photograph of Alphon retracting.

At any rate, the following Thursday Alphon telephoned the *Sunday Telegraph* where I had said he could get hold of me under the pseudonym of Birch. Bobby Birch was the editor of 'Mandrake' where I was working a part-time stint every second week. By a stroke of luck, Alphon's call came to me and the moment I heard his voice I recognized it.

'Give me a ring this evening late,' he said, 'and we can have a few words about our friend, Gardner.' He then gave me the name and telephone number of a hotel in Dun Laoghaire.

That night I phoned the hotel and spoke to Alphon for another two hours. He started with a furious tirade against Ken Gardner, and vigorously denied ever having given Gardner the retraction as quoted. He also stated that the *People* had tried to get a picture of him, but he had dodged their photographers to avoid one.

Peter Alphon, incidentally, was not the only one to deny the words attributed to him in the *People*. Mr Michael Eden, his solicitor, when I spoke to him in July 1970, vigorously denied having said what was attributed to him. 'I've always been amused by that,' he told me. 'I wonder where they got it from. Certainly I never said it — or anything like it.'

I agreed to ring Alphon again the following evening, and the next two calls to Dublin I made from Justice's flat in Belgravia, because Justice's phone was fitted to a tape-recorder. As in the first conversation from Paris a fortnight previously, Alphon spoke at length about the A6 murder. He was in a depressed state, ringing from a strange country, with no friends and few acquaintances, uncertain about his future, and certain at that time that a return to England would mean imprisonment on the telephone calls charges. He spoke in a low key, often breaking off 'for a drink of water', and often interspersing his descriptions with the assurance: 'This will make you laugh.' Listening to those tapes again, and reading the transcripts of them it is very difficult to believe that they are based on fantasy.

This time his story was that he had travelled on the night of the murder to the cornfield from the Slough dog-track via the pub opposite the Old Station Inn. He had a quarter bottle of brandy in his pocket when he climbed into the car:

> The thing is that that was the sort of thing that kept me going. That was the kick about saying 'I'm thirsty, I'm hungry' and everything, and every time they turned round, I said, 'Don't turn round', because I had this flask of brandy and this is really what kept me going.

Alphon's plan, he repeated, was to get the man to leave the car of his own accord. He explains that once, driving around the Slough area, he told Gregsten to go for cigarettes and, on another occasion, for milk. Both times, Alphon says, 'he kept coming back'. Alphon stopped the driver at Deadman's Hill on the A6 at about 3 a.m. — five hours after he had first entered the car. He shot the man, raped the girl and then shot her:

> I'm sorry to say this, we had Miss Storie in the back of the car. She was very, very upset, but I think that at one stage there was a certain affinity. I like to think that, anyway. I don't know,

maybe that's a fantasy of mine. Some sort of affinity. I don't know. But afterwards, when that was over, I got out of the car and she got out as well and said, 'Leave me alone', and she was crying, you know, and terribly upset.

She said, 'Just go away and leave me alone because I'm not going to do anything.'

We were standing, it was dark, and we were standing face to face. She was pretty sharp in one way. Very, very sharp. I was turning it over in my mind, shall I leave her? And I almost persuaded myself that I would leave her, and, this is true, I said, 'One day you're going to pick me out on an identity parade.' It was pathetic. She said, 'No, no, I won't, I'll never do that.' Of course, she was still crying, I don't suppose she knew what she was saying.

I just stuffed these bullets in and pulled the trigger. Nothing happened. And then suddenly they all came out in a rush.

Then he climbed back into the car after shooting Miss Storie and drove by a roundabout route to the Ilford area. He abandoned the car and went back by train and Underground to the Vienna Hotel, Maida Vale, where he had booked in the previous night. He changed, had breakfast, and travelled to Paddington, where he left his suitcase. He set off for Southend from Paddington:

When I got to Liverpool Street, I was sick; not physically, I just felt I was going to be and had to get out, and got out, and sat down and had a bit of air. I got back in and I got as far as Stratford and got out again. Then I bought a paper and saw the midday lunch edition about 12 o'clock when it comes out [which contained the first news of the murder, including the fact that Miss Storie was still alive] and when I read that I just went into the pub just outside Stratford station and had a very large brandy and just couldn't take the whole thing in. You know, it so shocked me, really, as you can probably imagine just how shaken I was. I had the brandy and, this is going to make you laugh when I tell you this, I had it and got back on the train, you know, and got on the Southend line and got there about 1.30 p.m.

But it is in his description of the meeting with France at Southend that the narrative becomes most convincing:

When I got out of the station, I didn't feel good at all and I got another paper and it was the same; there was nothing new. I went and had a drink. I came back. I had to meet France at 2 p.m. — that was the original arrangement — to meet him there. When I came at two o'clock, he wasn't there. I went and had another drink and came back and at 2.10 and he was there.

Do you know what he said? He said, 'What the bloody hell are you doing here?' and he was white. He had a newspaper in his hand, folded up, but I knew that he had read it; white as a sheet. 'What the bloody hell are you doing here?' Well, that was the arrangement. This is not *trying* to play it big now, you know, the thing has been done and I'm *going* to be big with him. White as a sheet. I said, 'What are *you* doing here?' He said, 'I didn't really think that you would be here,' and he's got this crumpled up in his hand, and he said, 'You're mad.' He was sort of backing away from me at this stage and said, 'Why did you do it? Are you some sort of lunatic or something?'

This is going to make you laugh. I said, 'This is the arrangement — and you've got to take the gun from me.' He said, 'You haven't got *that*.' He didn't say it in so many words; he just looked what's in his mind; 'You haven't got this gun.' I said, 'I *have* got it.' He said, 'You must be mad. You don't mean to say you've got the gun,' and he started, he went to go away, but I grabbed hold of him.

There were a couple of women there and he — it was about 2.15 p.m. — I said, 'You're not going to run away, just calm down,' and we go into a pub. And this man was shaking. He was really going to pieces. I wasn't so fine myself. Anyway, I said, 'Let's go away and discuss the whole thing,' and we went into a pub near Southend station — go right and there's a big one on the left — I don't know if you know it. We went in there and he started carrying on, you know, all about his family and his kids, his girl and everything, and he started crying. I said it was nothing to do with me and got the gun out of my pocket.

And I gave it to him and he said, 'You must be mad.' He really looked at me and said, 'You're some sort of lunatic.' I said, 'This was the arrangement — to meet you at Southend.' I gave him the gun. 'There's the gun, do what you like with it,' and he went to go away again. I grabbed hold of him again and said, 'Just calm down, nobody knows anything about us. They're not looking for us at all. You've got the gun, I've done my part of the job and that's it, that's the finish of me.'

Now at this stage he's looking at me as though I were a lunatic and was looking at me like something out of another world, and I think I go along with him on that—deep down I think I was a little bit mad and still am—and he's really frightened and he's got the thing back and he's shaking, you know, and everything.

At 2.30, the pubs turn out and I said to him, 'Let's quieten down. We'll go along to Garons restaurant and have a steak and everything.' We go into Garons and we order a couple of steaks and he doesn't eat anything—he's just sitting there and he's just really white and ill. And, oh, I ate my steak anyway and we come out and we talk and it comes to about five o'clock and I said, 'Let's have a drink in Southend.' You see, this is a nice day. It's in August and was nice, a lovely day. He wants to get away; he can't bear to be with me a second longer. I can see that, and I say, 'What about going on Southend Pier, it's a mile-and-a-half long? Let's put the gun in the sea, in the bottom of Southend Pier.' He doesn't want to do that. Once he has got hold of it—this is the sinister thing—he doesn't want to do it.

When I said to Alphon: 'He had the plan about the bus, didn't he?', Alphon replied:

I knew in the back of my mind that there was a plan. I'm going to be sincere with you. Perhaps I knew a little bit, probably as much as he did. When it really came to me in black and white was when the trial started and I could see France there as a witness against Hanratty.

That's when the pressure really started and I just didn't go along with it, because when I was with France I was so sincere. I knew what was going on, I knew waht was going to happen, but I was so sincere that I said to France, 'Let's go to the end of the pier and put the gun and everything in the sea, and that's the end.'

These tapes confirm, in almost every detail, the story as told to me and published in the *Sunday Times* about his relationship with Mr X prior to the murder, and the motive for the crime.

Throughout these conversations Alphon knew he was talking to a journalist whom he had never met and whose responses and attitudes he did not know. There was no question at this stage of him taking me into his confidence. This was a continuation of his Paris confession – out in the open, and for the public at large. He knew perfectly well that I was taking notes, and may well have assumed that the conversations were recorded.

I felt, however, that it was wrong to continue with my pseudonym. So I wrote to Alphon, as he suggested I might do, care of the Post Office at Dublin, letting him know I was Paul Foot, and that I had written the article in *Queen* the previous September. Almost at once I received a cheerful note in reply:

> I have your *Queen* article in front of me as I write. I was very upset at the time of its appearance; mainly as regards some of the extraneous matter not directly relevant to the article's main implication, which as we both know is a just one.

Alphon went on to say that he did not know where he would be over the next few weeks but that he was happy to speak to me at any time. In another letter, a few days later, he wrote: 'I shall stand by my Paris confession whatever happens. Repeat, whatever happens. I cannot do more!'

Meanwhile, in London, Jean Justice had telephoned Mr X and asked what action X intended to take in view of the libels which Alphon had been perpetrating about him in Paris:

> The whole point is [Mr X replied] that the man's a lunatic. I can't get any damages out of it. He's a man of straw ...
>
> I can't think what he's got against an obscure person like myself ... and there's no damage in this. You see, I'm not the loser of anything. I mean I have lost, yes, I suppose over the years it's been a nuisance. It's cost me. But certainly the maximum I think of everything couldn't be more than about £2,500 – nuisance values one way and another of it, but I can't get a penny out of it in redress. It'll be very difficult to establish a damage of that description. I mean, *I* happen to know it but I'll find it very difficult to get anyone else to understand it.

'The pity is', I wrote in *Queen* the following September, 'that

Mr X is not available for comment as to how the murder cost him "in nuisance value' as much as £2,500."

At some stage during late July of that summer (1967) Alphon returned to London, and the silent calls to Lord Russell were resumed. A complete list of the next batch of calls was given in court later as follows:

1. 5.8.67 Approximately 12 up to 1.20 a.m. caller did not speak (silent calls).

2. 7.8.67 9.48 p.m. giving name Aguirre PRI 7958 when connected ended call.

   11.20 p.m. as Mr Johnson, from FRE 3729, when connected to Lady Russell made cackling noises.

3. 8.8.67 About 9.59 p.m. as Mr Rainbow, from FRE 7478, when connected ended call.

4. 9.8.67 10.45 p.m. as Mr Murgatroyd, from EMP 8946, when connected ended call.

   10.53 p.m. as Mr Prescott, ended call when connected.

5. 12.8.67 Three calls.

   8.30 p.m. as Mr Boram, from BAL 3177, made cackling noise.

   9.30 p.m. as Mr Crank, FIN 8113, falsetto voice, cackling noises, high pitched voice, mentioned Lord Bertram Russell.

   10.25 p.m. as Mr Looney, GLA 1862, mentioned 'Bertie' [Earl Russell], Waterloo and 1066.

6. 18/19.8.67 11.15 p.m. as Mr Nuttall, CHE 4288, cackling noise, talk of 'Bertie'.

   12.15 a.m. as Mr Singleton, PAR 4381, said mother dead, hysterical laughter, brain finished.

7. 15.8.67 10.20 p.m. mentioned Earl Russell, said he was at Finsbury Park.

8. 21.8.67 10.35 p.m. cackling, hysterical laughter.

   11.10 p.m. mentioned bullets at American Embassy.

9. 22.8.67 11.22 p.m. mentioned Bertie, Shoeman American Embassy.

10. 23.8.67 10.30 p.m. cackling, falsetto voice.

11. 24.8.67 3.14 p.m. cackling, falsetto voice.

12. 25.8.67 10.32 p.m. mentioned Holloway Road, etc.

13. 26.8.67 10.30 p.m. mentioned mother died, Shoeman.

14. 29.8.67 11.20 p.m. – 12.5 a.m. spoke in normal voice saying he had come back, rational.

Lord Russell informed the police that the calls had started again, and took recordings of the 'conversations'. Once again, Chief Inspector Mooney told Lord Russell that he and his men were hunting for Alphon.

The hunt came to an end in the early hours of the morning of Saturday, September 2nd, when Alphon telephoned Inspector Mooney at Scotland Yard and asked for the case against him to be tried. By arrangement, Alphon met police outside the call-box and was taken to Paddington Green police station, where Inspector Mooney arrived at 1.45 a.m. The two men were closeted together for the best part of the night. At first Alphon denied making some of the more absurd and abusive calls, but eventually agreed that he had made them all. Mr Mooney then took down a long statement from Alphon.

At about 8 a.m. that morning, the Russells were phoned by Mr Mooney with the news that Alphon had been found, and that he would be appearing before the Marylebone magistrate later that morning. There was, said Mr Mooney, no real need for Lord Russell to be represented by a solicitor. The case against Alphon was cut and dried.

I got to the court just in time for one of the most remarkable cases I am ever likely to witness. Lord Russell gave evidence about the calls he had received since Alphon's recognizance thirteen months previously. To his great embarrassment he was then expertly cross-examined by Alphon from the dock. Alphon asked for instance why Lord Russell had spoken to him at such length if he found the calls so intolerable, to which Lord Russell replied that he was bound to keep speaking for as long as possible to enable the police to trace the call, and to help identify the caller.

Chief Inspector Mooney then read out a long statement which, he said, he had taken from Alphon during the night. The statement started by saying that Alphon had had nothing to do with the murder, but that a group of people, headed by Justice, had set out deliberately to brand him with the murder. At one stage, the statement went on, Justice had offered Alphon five thousand pounds to confess to the murder – an offer which had been refused: 'For years they branded me as a murderer, and made my life a misery and they ate, lived and slept the A6 murder.'

The Paris confession, said the statement, was inspired by a desire to 'bring the whole thing into the open. These people were obsessed with the A6 murder and would not leave me alone. I thought I'd say I was the murderer, and perhaps that would clear the whole thing up.'

'He felt, Your Worship,' Mr Mooney explained, 'like this. If I can't beat them at their own game, I'll join them.' Mr Mooney said that Alphon was not represented in court (as he had been in the same court in August 1966), and that he, Mr Mooney, would have to read out Alphon's statement. Mr Mooney added a brief testimonial on Alphon's behalf indicating that he had gone to 'a good school' and 'kept very much to himself.' 'I am satisfied', concluded Mr Mooney, 'that Alphon did not and could not have done it [the murder]. I know where he was at the time of the murder.' Peter Alphon, at his most charming, then apologized to the court. 'I am sorry for the trouble,' he said. 'I won't phone again. It's outlived its usefulness.'

There was, of course, no one to cross-examine Alphon over his statement, and the magistrate, Mr David Wacher, was clearly impressed by it. He told Alphon: 'It is quite clear that what you have been doing has been done under a sense of grievance which appears to have some foundation in fact. I hope what has been said in court will finish for good and all these stories that are bound to be out and about with regard to your having a hand in the murder.'

He then fined Alphon five pounds on one count of making calls, two pounds each on three other counts, and ten pounds for breaking his recognizance. Alphon was given all the time he wanted to pay, and Alphon's surety, Mr Eden, was not called upon to forgo his fifty pounds. Never in legal history had the British magistrates' dubious reputation for leniency been so handsomely vindicated.

For some reason, however, the record of the trial is not complete. The transcript of the clerk's notes of the trial do not include the full statement by Alphon. The official record of the trial ends: 'Original statement returned to Chief Inspector Mooney'. No doubt the statement is now safely in the Home Office files of the case where it cannot be seen by the public until the year 2067.

The newspapers that evening and the following (Sunday) morning were full of the fact that Alphon could not have done the A6 murder. Mr Mooney's unequivocal statement about Alphon's alibi on August 22nd, 1961 (which had nothing to do with the telephone calls case in September 1967), had the effect of scotching any press suspicion that Alphon was the A6 murderer. Yet Mr Mooney did not produce evidence or witnesses to back up his statement, and did not say where Alphon had spent the murder evening.

The gap was filled to some extent by John Ponder, crime correspondent of the *Sunday Express*, who wrote the next day, under his story of the court case:

> *I understand* that Yard detectives have interviewed witnesses who say they saw Alphon in a Paddington hotel at a time on the night of August 22nd, 1961, that would have made it impossible for him to have got to Dorney Reach near Slough just after 9 p.m. when the killer first held up Michael Gregsten and Valerie Storie in their car. (My italics.)

Verification of Mr Ponder's 'understanding' came in an article in the *Sunday Times* the following Sunday (September 10th). Its author was Malcolm Southan, a reporter who travelled to Brighton to interview Alphon on Friday, September 8th. I was in Brighton that week myself (as a delegate to the T.U.C. Congress), and I joined Southan in the middle of his interview with Alphon, at the latter's parents' home in Marine Parade, Brighton. This was the first time I had met Alphon. He was cheerful and at his ease as Southan asked Alphon about his whereabouts on the murder night. The following, as reported in the *Sunday Times*, is what Alphon told him.

Shortly after 8.30 he went from the Volunteer pub in Baker Street to the Broadway House Hotel to book a room. He was booked for the night from there at the Vienna Hotel, and paid his 27/6. After another spell at the Volunteer, he travelled by tube and train to Streatham Common station, met his mother who handed him a case 'which he needed for a visit to Southend the next day'. He then gave his mother a drink at Streatham Common station, and travelled back to the Vienna Hotel where he was let in by the manager's wife, signed the register and stayed the night.

The *Sunday Times* report continued:

> Alphon believes the police have recently made a fresh inquiry into his alibi and found that it holds. But last week Detective Chief Inspector Mooney would not comment about Alphon's alibi.

Alphon's mother, her face clearly showing the strain of the last six years, talked about the alibi. *She said her memory had been upset after police questioning in 1961.* But she remembered meeting her son at 9.15 p.m. Alphon said: 'I spoke to two men at the Broadway House Hotel. They were Jews.'

And a Mr Frederick Pichler, proprietor of the Broadway House Hotel, said yesterday that he believed Alphon had visited the hotel that evening. He thought he had come about 9 p.m. 'One of the managers saw him and that manager later talked to the police. I think that the man who saw him is now dead.' (My italics.)

Then, towards the end of the article, Alphon said a most remarkable thing:

During the interview, Alphon refused to name the hotel. He gave the name in a telephone call yesterday. Even more mysteriously, he said that the police might shortly make known the alibi. '*If I tell you now, and the police tell a different story later*', said Alphon, '*well, I'm not going to look a gift horse in the mouth.*' (My italics.)

The only documentary evidence to support this story is Alphon's name in the Vienna Hotel register, which could have been written at any time on August 22nd, or even first thing on August 23rd, since it is the last entry for that night.

The story differs in several respects to the story told by Peter Alphon to Detective Sergeant Kilner at Highbury police station in Blackstock Road when he was questioned four days after the murder. In his signed statement then he said that he had been to the Broadway House Hotel at 'about 8 p.m.' – a crucial half an hour earlier than the time given in the story in 1967. Again, he had written for Sergeant Kilner that he had met his mother 'on the corner of Gleneagle Road' after ringing her up and arranging the rendezvous. He had met her there 'because I do not get on with my father'. There was no mention in Alphon's original statement at Blackstock Road of a drink with his mother near Streatham Common station. Both stories, of course, conveniently avoided introducing Alphon's father into the alibi, which relied entirely on his mother.

The murder hunt for Alphon was unleashed *after and because* the 'mother alibi' had been smashed. Without the 'mother alibi', the fabric of the Alphon story is torn to pieces. For even if Alphon did visit the Broadway House Hotel at 'about 8.30' on that evening (and there is no one alive, apparently, to prove it) he could still have been in a field near Slough at 'about 9.45' – 'about' an hour and a quarter later. Baker Street is two stations from Paddington on a direct Underground line (taking, at the most, five minutes) and a fast train from Paddington to Slough takes less than half an hour. The bus journey from Slough station to Taplow takes approximately twenty minutes. By car, the journey from Baker Street to Taplow takes less than an hour.

The Broadway House alibi itself is suspect. When was it 'verified'? The 'two Jews' were presumably a Mr Calman and Mr Christberg, assistant managers of the Broadway House Hotel at the time of the murder, both of whom have since died. If they had been interviewed by Superintendent Acott after the murder and had said that Alphon had visited the hotel at about 8.30 on the evening of the 22nd, Mr Acott would surely have mentioned it when explaining at Bedford why he had eliminated Alphon from his inquiries. In the Commons debate in August 1963, Home Secretary Brooke told the Commons that Alphon was in the Vienna Hotel. When asked whether this was entirely on the evidence of Nudds, Brooke agreed that it was. Brooke did not mention any confirmation of the alibi from the manager or managers of the Broadway House Hotel. Indeed he did not mention the Broadway House Hotel at all. The first time the hotel was mentioned in connection with Peter Alphon's alibi was in the *Sunday Times* (and, by implication, in the *Sunday Express*) more than six years after the murder. As for Mr Pichler's guess to the *Sunday Times* that Alphon had arrived at 'about 9 p.m.', Pichler admitted to me when I interviewed him on July 14th, 1970, that he had 'not the slightest idea about the time' as he was not in the manager's office when Alphon called. The truth almost certainly is that Calman and Christberg told the police that Alphon *had* called at the hotel – but at a time much nearer the 8 p.m. which Alphon himself first mentioned, and which clearly did not constitute an alibi. No wonder that Peter Alphon was reluctant to say too much about his alibi for fear of conflicting with any future police version and 'looking a gift horse in the mouth'.

In an article in *Queen* three days after the *Sunday Times* interview (September 13th), I commented on the apparent discrepancy between Mr Mooney's 1967 version of Alphon's alibi and Mr Acott's at the trial, and added:

> What a pity that Inspector Mooney's sensational revelations about an alibi for Alphon in August 1961 (which had nothing to do with charges against Alphon in September 1967) were not substantiated by a single witness or evidence of any kind.

To this and other comments in the *Queen* article there was a sharp reaction from Inspector Mooney. On November 28th, 1967, two months after the article appeared (and soon after interest in the case had been revived by the Frost Programme) Montague Gardner and Howard, solicitors, wrote to the proprietors of *Queen*, and to me, complaining of passages in the article which were 'highly defamatory' of Mr Mooney, for whom they acted. The letter demanded a printed apology, payment of costs and information about damages we were prepared to pay.

On December 5th my own solicitors wrote back asking for clarification. Which passages in the article were defamatory? A brief reply in January stated that, in the solicitors' view, the 'whole tone' of the article was defamatory. Still we pressed for details, which eventually came on May 27th, 1968, in another letter from Montague Gardner, which listed the defamatory suggestions as follows:

1. That Mr Mooney's statement that Alphon could not have done the murder was made without evidence to back it up.
2. That he had acted as 'devil's advocate' for Alphon.
3. That he had deliberately stood in the way of Lord Russell's prosecution of Alphon.

On the contrary, claimed the letter, Mr Mooney's statement about Alphon's alibi was not unsubstantiated. The alibi was 'thoroughly examined' at the trial. Secondly, Mr Mooney had only presented to the court what Alphon wanted him to present. Thirdly the article had wrongly stated that the police had refused to issue an arrest warrant, whereas arrest warrants are in fact issued by magistrates.

Nevertheless, the letter made it clear that Mr Mooney was prepared to settle for an apology, his costs and an undertaking not to repeat the libel.

Unfortunately, this letter, despite its length, did not shed any light as to what Mr Mooney meant when he told the Marylebone court: 'I know where he [Alphon] was at the time of the murder.' It is not the case that 'Alphon's alibi was thoroughly examined at Hanratty's trial in January 1962.' Nor was there 'ample evidence in support of it'. The *only* evidence in support of it was the third statement of Nudds, who, on his own admission, was a liar. Superintendent Acott did not mention an alibi for Alphon at Hanratty's trial; nor did any other witness. Neither Alphon's visit to the Broadway House, nor his drink at Streatham Common, nor his rendezvous at Gleneagle Road, nor his visit to a greyhound racetrack were mentioned.

I accept of course that Mr Mooney was doing his job when he spoke for Alphon as Alphon wished (though I am still not clear why Alphon's solicitors were not contacted to represent him). It is, of course, strictly true that magistrates, not policemen, issue warrants, but magistrates are known to take advice on such matters from the police. The *Queen* article did not say that Mr Mooney personally had obstructed the prosecution of Alphon. There is substantial evidence of delays in police action over his prosecution, especially in 1964 and 1965, before Inspector Mooney became involved.

On receipt of this letter, I told *Queen* magazine that, whatever their proprietors decided, I did not want to be associated with any apology. Mr Mooney's complaints, in my view, could all be answered satisfactorily.

In the event, no apology was printed in *Queen*, or anywhere else. No apology of any kind was made privately. Nor was a penny paid to Mr Mooney in damages or costs. No undertaking was given by anyone not to repeat the comments in the *Queen* article. The matter was dropped by Mr Mooney, but not by me. On April 8th, 1969, eighteen months after the *Queen* article was published, my solicitors wrote to Mr Mooney's:

> As it now seems clear that your client does not intend to proceed further with his unjustified allegations against our client, we think you will agree that it would be only reasonable for your client to reimburse our client for the costs which he has incurred as a result of those allegations which he now appears to have abandoned.
>
> We would be prepared to agree our costs at the nominal

figure of 15 guineas and we trust that in due course we may expect to receive your cheque for this amount.

Back came a reply a week later, making it clear 'with the greatest respect' that such a cheque would not be forthcoming.

My difficulty was then as follows: to continue to press Mr Mooney for my legal costs following his allegations would cost, merely in lawyers' letters, a good deal more than the costs to that date. Nor was my victory on so slender a matter assured. I abandoned the project, and paid my own costs which my solicitors agreed at ten pounds. I still think Mr Mooney owes me ten pounds.

The bulk of the *Queen* article had been written when I met Peter Alphon for the first time in Brighton on September 8th, 1967. After Malcolm Southan of the *Sunday Times* had left for London with his story, I spent a long afternoon with Alphon strolling around the Brighton beaches, talking about the A6 murder.

Ten days later, Alphon rang me to say that he was writing a letter to the Home Secretary demanding an inquiry into the A6 murder, without denying his guilt in it. He asked me if, in view of the interest which the *Sunday Times* had shown in the case, I could get anything in the *Sunday Times* about his letter. I agreed to try, and he sent me a copy of the letter he sent to Mr Jenkins on September 28th. Four weeks previously, Mr David Wacher, the magistrate at Marylebone, had told Peter Alphon in court: 'I hope what has been said in court today will finish for good and all these stories.' Little did Mr Wacher imagine that the next boost to the stories would come from Peter Alphon himself in a letter to the Home Secretary.

The letter, some of which was published in the *Sunday Times* of October 1st, 1967, started by 'petitioning you to order an enquiry into the A6 murder case *and its prolonged aftermath*.' (Alphon's emphasis.) There then followed a long attack on 'the campaign' which, Alphon alleged, had been waged against him, with particular reference to Justice's book, *Murder versus Murder*.

'Having written the foregoing', the letter continued, 'I must now state – without I hope being faulted for any imagined paradoxicality – that while I deplore the campaign, the people connected with it, and the techniques and machinery they have sometimes used, I concur completely with the saner commentators, *not* actuated by any personal animosity towards me, who express dissatisfaction with the murder investigation, prosecution evidence and arguments, trial verdict and subsequent execution.'

Alphon had many other complaints about the conduct of the trial – notably about identification and Charles France's role. His letter went on: 'there were many other aspects of the case which left one with a very nasty taste in the mouth indeed. I hope that I never again witness a major trial where the prosecution is so unsoundly based.'

Finally the letter restated the role of Mr X in the murder. Throughout Alphon used the words 'Mr X' and did not name the man.

However, perhaps the most unnerving consideration in the whole case was the complete failure by the police to *thoroughly* investigate the man who has been referred to, in press articles of the last few months, as 'Mr X'.

'Mr X' later, perversely enough, became 'friendly' with the instigator of the previously-mentioned campaign, encouraging him in his efforts, and attempting to channel his energies *exclusively* against my own person.

As a result of this inherently illogical strategem 'Mr X' enjoyed complete anonymity as far as the public was concerned. I note that, until last May, none of the propagandists for the campaign (with the invariable singleness of mind that has characterized them throughout) mentioned even the existence of such a figure in any guilt-implying connotation; *nevertheless, the belief was commonly held, privately among them, that 'Mr X' was, in fact, the 'prime mover' in the affair.* Such was the measure of their integrity.

I remedied their omission at the Paris Press conference. That was the *real point* of my conference; that it was held in the 'spirit of truth' (and it is important that full semantic consideration be given to that phrase, to avoid any misunderstanding). I would hardly have blasted a man's whole reputation unless I knew it to be deserved.

I would ask you to disregard any misrepresentation of my motives for holding the conference by unscrupulous reporters, intent on implementing the policies of their papers; or by employees of your own departments, whose supererogatory endeavours to preserve the police image from further deterioration should be placed in their proper perspective.

Needless to say, I should attempt to gain the widest publicity for any *further* coercion or malpractice directed against me.

Finally, I might draw your attention to the fact that, since my conference, 'Mr X' has sadly compromised himself in a tape-recorded (presumably without his knowledge) telephone conversation, extracts of which appeared in a magazine recently.

It would appear that the only parties vociferous in rebutting demands for a public enquiry are 'Mr X' and the police. They, of course, are the ones who stand to lose most. (Alphon's emphasis.)

Mr Jenkins did not take Peter Alphon's assurance that the Paris confession was made 'in the spirit of truth' very seriously. A month later, on November 1st, when he turned down the demand for an inquiry into the A6 murder he referred only briefly to Peter Alphon:

Mr Peter Louis Alphon has withdrawn his earlier confession that he committed the murder of which Hanratty was convicted. His involvement in the case was an issue at Hanratty's trial, and neither his confession nor other allegations about his part in the case are supported by new material of substance. (House of Commons Hansard, November 1st, 1967.)

The rejection of an inquiry stirred some influential interest in the case. David Frost, the television personality, had started a series of programmes on commercial television entitled The Frost Programme. On November 16th he devoted his entire programme to the A6 murder.

Frost's researcher for the programme was Peter Baker, a former assistant editor of the *Daily Express* whose journalistic flair was one of the main reasons for the success of Frost's programmes. Baker, who became convinced of Hanratty's innocence during work on this programme, approached Peter Alphon and asked him to appear on the programme. After some discussion, Alphon agreed and made clear his intention not to repudiate his Paris confession.

All the arrangements for Alphon's dramatic appearance on the programme, including a fee for Alphon, were negotiated and finalized. Two days before the programme date, Baker again got in touch with Alphon and pressed him with a number of further questions. Alphon was flustered by this approach, and, in the event, did not appear at the Wembley studios. The programme went on without him.

The incident is an important one, for the conventional explanation for Alphon's behaviour is that he confesses for money and publicity, and then withdraws his confession for more publicity and more money. Here, however, was probably the best chance he would get for publicity, and the offer of a substantial fee. Both were turned down in a last-minute panic.

Alphon was, however, irritated by Jenkins's Commons statement about his confession. On December 15th, he posted another letter to the new Home Secretary, appointed in the wake of the Government's sterling devaluation, Mr James Callaghan:

> I must deny the validity of the statement obtained from me by police upon my return from Paris, and produced in evidence at Marylebone Court. The statement constitutes the only ground that Mr Jenkins could have for referring to a 'withdrawn confession' ...
>
> Secondly, in respect of the three belated 'alibis', I must state categorically that they are unsound. They are all based on a statement made soon after the murder and were *flatly rejected* by the officer in charge of the investigation, Supt. Acott.
>
> Further, it is noteworthy that the superintendent did not mention any alibi when, at Hanratty's trial, he was called upon to give his reasons for dropping me from his inquiry. And, definitively, Mr Jenkins, in his Parliamentary statement, although it was made close on Inspector Mooney's widely-reported dogmatic assertion of an alibi — scrupulously refrained from accrediting me with one ...
>
> In conclusion I again ask you to order a public inquiry into this case; the procrastinatory attitudes of your predecessors will *inevitably* be confounded. (Some of this was reported in the *Sunday Times*, December 17th, 1967. Alphon's emphasis.)

If anything, Mr Callaghan was even less impressed by Alphon's demands for a public inquiry than Mr Jenkins had been. The above letter was answered with the same starchy negative as were all the others.

The following May (1968) press interest in the case was revived by the Hanrattys' discovery of more relevant evidence in Rhyl. In his telephone conversations during the period, Alphon was invariably irritated by mention of Hanratty's Rhyl alibi. There seemed to be two reasons for this irritation. Firstly, he was angry that the case was no longer focused exclusively on himself. Secondly, he was worried that the Rhyl alibi might be proved beyond all doubt. The desire to prolong the mystery of the A6 murder is one of the most common characteristics of Alphon's approach to the case.

He did not write again to the Home Secretary until the following autumn. This time, once again, he 'upped the ante', and for the first time wrote an unequivocal confession to the murder:

> I killed Gregsten, the Establishment murdered Hanratty: and have since acted against me as though they knew I was guilty.
>
> These words spoken by me nearly five years ago sum up the whole case in a nutshell. I see no reason to qualify them except that undoubtedly my well-known political views have been a factor in my persecution ... With respect, you can have no valid excuse for any further delay in ordering a public inquiry into the case.

Once again, the letter started with a long account of developments in the case, complained bitterly of the 'campaign' being waged against him and called at the beginning and end for a public inquiry. Once again, it was treated with indifference by the Home Secretary. Six weeks later, on November 5th, 1968, I had my second and last meeting with Peter Alphon.

Despite endless and countless telephone calls, I had noticed that Alphon was reluctant to meet me face to face. At least three arranged meetings in London were cancelled by him at the last minute. He was, however, happier about meeting in his home town of Brighton and so I spent a bizarre day striding up and down a deserted and freezing Brighton promenade with Peter Alphon filling in the details of how he committed the A6 murder.

The story Peter Alphon told me then was essentially the same as that told to me on the phone from Paris. He repeated in detail the plot with Mr X; describing a meeting with Mr X in the Manor House pub, Finsbury Park, where the sum of money for 'the job' was discussed. The money, he said, was not handed over until after the murder, and not by hand. Charles France had supplied (and planted) the gun and planted the cartridge cases. The shooting of Gregsten was an accident, he repeated. The rape of Miss Storie, which he described with much hesitation and embarrassment, was a cover for his real motive; and the shooting of Miss Storie was inevitable, as she was a witness to the original crime.

At the start of 1969, Alphon started to talk once more of writing to the Home Secretary, this time naming 'Mr X'. A further demand for an inquiry by Lord Brockway had been turned down on November 28th, 1968, by Lord Stonham, and Alphon was determined not to let the matter drop.

The letter which he eventually wrote, dated March 7th, 1969, was uncharacteristically short. It argued that the Home Secretary's delays and obstinacy in not holding an inquiry had forced the issue. He wrote:

> I name 'Mr X' [this time using a real Christian name and surname] as the prime mover in the three-man conspiracy I have alleged was behind the A6 murder.
>
> The identity of the middle-man in the plot has already been made known: he was of course the Hanratty trial Crown witness who committed suicide, Charles Dixie France, a former strip-club employee ... The relationship between the prime mover and France is an open secret among police officers, journalists and others.

This was a very important development. By writing to the Home Secretary in a private letter, and, more important, by showing me the letter before it was posted with the deliberate intention of getting it published in the *Sunday Times*, Alphon was openly courting an action for criminal libel.

Criminal libel is a public accusation of criminal behaviour. There is no defence, as there is in civil libel, of justification. In criminal libel, 'the greater the truth the greater the libel'. It is not a common charge. But neither is it obsolete. In 1965, for instance, a Mr Peter Forbes was convicted of criminal libel after writing a letter to the Prime Minister complaining that a police officer was harassing him. Mr Forbes was convicted for criminal libel and sentenced by Mr Justice Melford Stevenson to three years' imprisonment. (*Private Eye*, October 1st, 1966.)

Alphon's letter to the Home Secretary was much more libellous than Forbes's. It cast grave aspersions on a respectable citizen, and branded him as a plotter who had set out to frame Hanratty for the A6 murder and had watched in silence while the latter hanged. It is difficult to imagine a more monstrous libel. Yet the authorities took no action. They took no action when Mr X's name was mentioned again in public on a number of other occasions.

In April 1969, the A6 Committee acquired a new and unexpected member: Mr Michael Fogarty-Waul. Mr Fogarty-Waul, it will be remembered, had been living at the time of the murder in a caravan in Pecks Farm field, off Marsh Lane, only a few hundred yards away from the field where the murderer surprised his victims. He had told the police soon after the murder of a strange man he had given a lift down Marsh Lane about a week before the murder, and had seen someone he thought was this man meddling with his car in Marsh Lane in the middle of the night about ten days after Hanratty's conviction. Once again, he had told the police, and the police had taken no action.

That was in February, 1962. Jean Justice and Jeremy Fox had taken a statement from Mr Fogarty-Waul the following month, which described the man in the lane as looking like Sidney Tafler. Since then, Mr Fogarty-Waul had played no part in the case. He attended the April 1969 meeting of the A6 Committee which was attended by Justice, Fox, the Hanratty family and myself, and asked us how he could settle in his mind whether the man whom he had seen in 1961 and 1962 was Peter Alphon. We hit on a solution which would not satisfy a court of law, but which, in the circumstances, seemed the best possible. We told Mr Fogarty-Waul that Alphon's parents lived in Brighton, in the Marine Parade. We did not give him the number of the house. We said that the house where Alphon lived was between numbers 150 and 170. We also told him that Alphon was likely to be in Brighton over the Whit holiday.

Mr Fogarty-Waul drove to Brighton on Whit Saturday, and, according to his story, after walking about Marine Parade for several hours, noticed a man looking out of a top window, and recognized him as the man he had seen in Slough and Marsh Lane. He also spoke to the man, who was Peter Alphon, in the street. According to Fogarty-Waul's story, Alphon recognized him, and agreed that the two men had met at Slough dog-track.

After this first encounter, the story goes on, Fogarty-Waul continued to walk up and down outside Alphon's house, and, the next day, Alphon called the Brighton police and tried to persuade two officers to arrest Fogarty-Waul. The officers, somewhat nonplussed, could find no reason for such an arrest, and, with Alphon screaming abuse at them to the effect that 'this man is a friend of Justice's!' the policemen left.

Mr Fogarty-Waul's story is no doubt a little exaggerated, and in any case would be useless in a court of law. Alphon was recognizable by several photographs in the press previous to the Brighton confrontation, and there are a number of ways in which Fogarty-Waul could have discovered his exact address. Yet the fact remains that, to satisfy himself, Mr Fogarty-Waul undertook to make the journey to Brighton, and, at any rate to his own satisfaction, identified Peter Alphon as the man whom he met in Slough and Marsh Lane in 1961 and 1962.

Peter Alphon, needless to say, contradicts Mr Fogarty-Waul's story. He says that Fogarty-Waul sat outside his window until he was forced to respond, and denies totally that he had ever seen Fogarty-Waul before that day. Alphon has since phoned Fogarty-Waul several times to discuss the case.

The A6 Committee redoubled its activities through the summer of 1969. Meetings were held every Sunday in Hyde Park to popularize the case for Hanratty's innocence. On July 14th, 1969, several members of the Committee paraded in front of St Stephen's Gate of the House of Commons bearing placards naming Alphon as the murderer and making serious allegations as to the way the case against Hanratty had been run. Despite the strictly enforced rules banning all demonstrations within a mile of the House of Commons, the demonstration was allowed to continue for several hours without hindrance. At the end of August, two members of the Committee took the placards to Brighton and paraded them outside Alphon's parents' house. Again, Alphon called the police, but no action was taken against the demonstrators.

All this upset Peter Alphon considerably. On September 6th he wrote an angry letter to the Home Secretary once more demanding action against his persecutors and a public inquiry into the A6 verdict:

Failing this and in the absence of any other fitting action by the authorities, I shall call a press conference of British and foreign journalists for 22nd October in London to reiterate and uphold the substance of what I said at the controversial 1967 Paris one and in letters since to you or your predecessors, and present more new evidence in the case, mostly of police misconduct; afterwards I shall sign affidavits confirming my murder allegations and make a written statement embodying them to the police.

This promised press conference, like Alphon's appearance on the Frost Programme, never came off. At first, there were the usual excuses: 'I'm preparing another letter for the Home Secretary,' he explained to me in one call. Then he started to insist that he would hold the conference only if it was attended by all the witnesses from Rhyl. When I refused to organize this on the grounds that the Rhyl witnesses had been heard before, he flew into a rage and blamed the cancellation of the press conference on myself and on Fogarty-Waul. The truth, however, was obvious. Peter Alphon was not prepared to go through with a public confession to the murder in Britain.

On November 26th, Mr Justice, Mr Fogarty-Waul and Mrs Edith Whicher, a new member of the Committee who had joined after listening to speeches in Hyde Park, were finally arrested for demonstrating outside the House of Commons. That weekend, Mr and Mrs Hanratty went to stay at the Ascot home of their nephew, a young, successful antique dealer called John Cunningham.

Cunningham offered to help his aunt and uncle by approaching his neighbour, John Lennon, the popular singer. The Hanrattys immediately did so, and a meeting was arranged between Mr and Mrs Lennon and the Committee on Tuesday, December 9th.

The meeting was followed by a press conference the following day in which the Lennons promised to make a film about the A6 murder. Details about the proposed film were vague. The promise, however, got a great deal of publicity, and revived public interest in the case.

All this unnerved Peter Alphon. The promised press conference was forgotten about. His telephone calls became much less confident, and more frequent. My telephone conversations with Alphon up to November 1969 had been irregular and unrecorded. During the two years since he first started to ring me we must have spoken at least fifty times. Almost all the conversations were late at night, and few lasted less than half an hour. With one exception, all his calls are marked by an elaborate courtesy.

Relations between Alphon and myself in all the time I have known him have remained essentially formal. The dialogue has been between the investigator/journalist on the one hand and the interviewee on the other. In fact, what was going on was not an interview but a game of cat and mouse in which we swapped the title roles. Alphon's aim was to maintain my interest without my finally establishing the case against him. He was keen to talk for hours about irrelevant and unprovable details, but nervous always of any evidence or possible evidence which might prove the case against him. For my part, meanwhile, I tried to prise out of him some nugget of new information. The winner of this game, on every occasion, was Peter Alphon.

In the entire two years I was able to acquire from Alphon only one piece of documentary evidence. In the spring of 1969 he wrote to his former bank manager at the Law Courts branch of Lloyds Bank in the Strand giving me permission to see his accounts for 1961 and 1962. The accounts were then sent to me in August.

The accounts were described by the assistant manager in his accompanying letter (August 21st, 1969) as 'duplicate statements of his accounts for the years 1961 and 1962'. They do not unfortunately include information about names on cheques paid to or paid in by Alphon. All the bank's photographs of cheques are destroyed six years after they are drawn. Paid-in cheques are lumped together as 'sundry credit' and paid out cheques as 'payments' under the cheque numbers. Nevertheless the following facts can be deduced from the accounts.

Peter Alphon was released from Mortlake magistrates' court on Tuesday October 3rd, 1961, after having been cleared of the charge of assaulting Mrs Dalal. Most of the previous week he had spent on remand in Brixton prison. Until September 25th, and probably later, the police still regarded him as a suspect for the A6 murder. After October 3rd, he was no longer a suspect.

The following Monday, the fourth weekday after his release, Peter Alphon opened a deposit account in Lloyds Bank with a payment of £750. In the next six weeks £3,300 was paid into this deposit account in cash payments as follows:

October 9th: £750

October 24th: £150
October 30th: £250
November 1st: £400
November 14th: £150
November 17th: £300
November 21st: £800
November 22nd: £100
November 24th: £400

In this period, only £150 was transferred to his current account. After November 24th (which was, incidentally, the third day of the hearing at Ampthill) no further payments are made into the account. The balance of £3,150 on November 24th gradually dwindles as payments are made into the current account, until the deposit account is finally closed on April 2nd – two days before the execution of James Hanratty.

Ten days after opening his deposit account Alphon also opened a current account with a £150 payment from his deposit account. In October and November £2,050 was paid into this account in cheques and cash from outside (that is, *not* from his deposit account). All the money was paid in units of £150, £250, and £300. There seems to be a weekly payment of £250, plus a few extra payments of £300. On December 1st, he paid in £1,000 and on December 4th another £800. After that, until the account was finally closed on June 22nd 1962, there were only three major payments in 'sundry credit' from outside: £445 on February 8th, £150 on February 23rd, and £120 on March 2nd. The assistant manager has confirmed to me that Alphon has not reopened his account since.

In all, £7,569 was paid into Alphon's two accounts in large blocks of money in between October 1961 and June 1962 – the bulk of it in the first ten weeks. This was a staggering sum for a man of Alphon's means. I have been unable to find whether Alphon has ever had any other account at any other bank, but I am inclined to believe his own statement to me that he normally copes with his financial matters without bothering with banks. He lives on a small fixed income from an annuity, a shrewd gambling sense built on detailed knowledge about greyhounds, and, occasionally, on odd jobs. For long periods during 1967 and 1968, for instance, he lived in a small room in an unpretentious hotel not far from King's Cross station, for which he paid one pound a night during summer and twenty-five shillings a night during winter. Even when his gambling was at its most successful, however, Alphon could hardly hope for a sustained income the size of which he suddenly got in the late autumn of 1961.

Where did the income come from? Unfortunately there is no clue in the bank books. No record is kept of paid-in cheques, and, at any rate, according to Alphon, most of the money was paid in cash. Alphon had, of course, had a very good run with the newspapers following his release. The *Daily Express* had paid him £1,000 for their feature 'My Ordeal, by Peter Alphon' on the day after his release (which would account for the £1,000 received in one lump on December 1st). The *Daily Mail* had, according to Alphon, paid £800 for rather less exclusive rights to his story. The *News of the World* had paid £150 for his impressions of the Hanratty trial, which were never published. Altogether at least £2,500 of the money paid in almost certainly came from the newspaper proprietors. What about the rest? There is no doubt that Alphon was a successful gambler, and some of the sums can be attributed, no doubt, to spectacular wins at the races. But the roundness of most of the figures of payment and their regularity suggest that there was some other, more reliable source.

Almost as surprising as the sudden flow of funds into Peter Alphon's account, following his release as a suspect for the A6 murder, is the fact that, as far as it is possible to judge, all of the £7,500-odd which he paid into these accounts was spent in the same period. The expenditure is colossal—and again it is at its peak in the early months. On November 3rd, for instance, he paid out £470 in two cheques; on November 29th and 30th, £1,389 in four cheques; on 6th, 7th, 8th and 11th of December £2,332 in seven cheques. On 16th December he paid out £1,000 in one cheque.

At some stage in this period, Peter Alphon had bought a grey-hound—which could account for the £1,000 cheque. We know, too, that during those months, Peter Alphon was living in fine style, staying at the four-star Ariel Hotel for four months and hiring cars to London almost every day. He also had to pay substantial fees to Galbraith and Best for their prolonged legal activity on his behalf. Living grandly, he could easily spend up to and even more than five hundred pounds a month—but even that luxury living would account for only half the money which he paid out from his small fortune.

The accounts constitute my one real clue after two years of incompetent sleuthing on the telephone. Otherwise, the telephone conversations were consistently frustrating. The more I tried to construct a coherent story from Alphon's conversations with me, the more his story crumbled. Key facts were swapped and replaced with malevolent abandon. The Slough dog-track, the Vienna Hotel, the role of Nudds, the shooting and rape at Deadman's Hill, the role of Mr X, the details of the car ride and the conversation in the car have been displaced, replaced, chopped and changed.

Towards the end of 1969, I began to weary of the hunt, and for the first time and without Alphon's knowledge, started to record a few of the conversations. A typical extract in which Alphon talks about the murder runs as follows (November 21st, 1969):

Q. Well what do you think their [Michael Gregsten and Valerie Storie] attitude to you was all this time? I mean do you think their attitude was serious—I mean do you think they were worried?

A. They didn't seem it to me, Paul. They never seemed it to me—they never seemed worried to me. I must say that. It never struck me after five hours—they didn't seem terribly worried. I think Gregsten seemed—he seemed a bit tense. Well, I suppose they were both tense—and I was tense too. We were all tense. But they never seemed terribly worried, no. In fact, I sum their attitude up as being cocky.

Q. So when you are getting on to the A6 now and you're sort of driving up there—what are you thinking? Your mind is racing around is it, trying to work out some kind of solution to this thing?

A. Well, yes. I don't know. Yes I suppose—there is no solution really to it. The only solution I felt at that time was to have left them—to have driven them as far away as possible. I did think of taking their clothes you know. One hears of tarring and feathering people, you know, that sort of thing. Well of course I didn't have any tar and, as I say, I wouldn't do anything like that, but just to humiliate them and really expose them and do as much as I could possibly do so that I could justify myself to Mr X [Alphon, of course, used the real name here]. But, I did think of doing that. And we got to Deadman's Hill and, as I say, I was still mulling it over in my own mind, when he turned round and tried to get the – get the gun. And as I say, I have never fired a gun, it's quite true, never fired a gun before, and I tried to hit him in the shoulder. But I misfired completely. The whole thing, the bloody thing was hopeless. It hit him – I could see that it hit him in the head and I realized that the whole thing had, well, misfired in more ways than one. So I shot him again quickly. I am pretty quick thinking and I realized the damage that had been done and I fired straight away. Killed him. Killed him the first time probably. I don't know which – whether the first one was the fatal shot or not. Don't know whether you know that?

Q. Well, I don't think anyone knows that.

A. No. Well perhaps the medical experts do. I shouldn't imagine it did him much good anyway, the first one. But I am afraid that's how it was. It was almost instinctive you know, the second shot upon the first shot. But they're both instinctive but I think certainly the second one was, anyway. I mean the first one – it wasn't that instinctive it was just accidental. I just shot him in the head. And, you know, when someone lunges at you over the seat of a car like that, I mean that's the biggest part of them really, the head and the upper half of the body. You aim at the shoulder. Completely missed it, and that's what happened there. And of course, the girl – she was the only witness to the murder. Well, I've told you that before haven't I? [Yes.] And I felt I had to disguise the motive – it was true that I put this bit about pleading love in the notes and all this business. There might be a certain amount of truth in it. It's very subjective, though. The motive really for her was much more objective – but I did try to disguise the motive to make it look like that of a murderer chance-rapist, you know. I realized that there would be signs that she had been molested if I did that ... And then of course I had to get rid of her. Shoot her. Of course we know now that it was unnecessary. But I couldn't know that at the time.

Perhaps even more remarkable than these vivid descriptions of the murder is Alphon's account of 'the plan' behind the murder – the motive for what at Hanratty's Bedford trial had been described as a random sex murder. The motive had been stated countless times by Alphon since the conversation with Justice in March 1964, and was repeated again in this recorded conversation in December 1969:

A. One of the ideas we had — one of the fundamental ideas was to get rid of him — to separate the two physically at that time.

Q. And then do what?

A. Well that's quite — I see what you mean yes. That's rather — that's something that obviously I don't like to bring up. But of course that was the idea. To get the girl and well, that's quite true, after all she had been carrying on an adulterous affair with a married man. I mean what happened to her after was something which she deserved probably. But —

Q. Get the girl and do what though?

A. Well. I suppose that — the type — done the same thing as he was doing.

Q. Yes. I see, yes. What you mean drive off and do it?

A. Oh yes. I would have left there. Well, he had a chance to get away. I mean let him get away and then said to the girl — well you've been — you see what's happened. You see it would have depended on what attitude she took. If when he had gone and when I had done with her and she'd seen that he had sort of left her in the lurch, I would have had to have given her time. I should have had to be very careful on the timing of it. I mean, I couldn't stay too long because he would obviously have gone and alerted the police straight away. And if it had sunk into her what had happened and she had been left and I felt she was repentant that would probably have been good enough for that night, anyway. It could always have taken place on another night, couldn't it, after that you see. Do you understand what I mean? [Yes.] I mean if she had been tremendously repentant and said 'There, you see what sort of man he is. He's just left there. What are you going to do?' — that would probably have been good enough. If she had started being bitchy and the way they had been all along, the pair of them, then I would have tried to make my point more plainer — or more plain. You know, it was so tricky, such a tricky business really. You have to take into account so many different factors. It was really a crazy scheme from start to finish, really. When you look back on it it was — well it was doomed to failure right from the start. But I never knew it would end like that.

Later on in the same tape, I returned to 'the plan':

Q. The plan was to get him to get out — was that the position? And to leave altogether.

A. Yes. That was the idea of it, yes. So that he'd leave voluntarily —
not be forced to go because otherwise he wouldn't have any sort
of recriminations then. If anyone's forced at gun point to go
obviously the pressure is upon a fellow. But if he could be moved
to forsake her altogether — just go — and then — yes, that was the
plan.

Q. And then what? Then you were going to drive off? Or was she
going to drive off?

A. No. I was going to drive off.

Q. Where were you going to go to?

A. Well just about quarter of a mile — half a mile away — that was
all. The nearest point where I would think that it was safe to do
— to do — fulfil the plan.

Q. Yes. And then how were you going to get away?

A. Well, I would leave her there and drive the car on again. Of course
everyone would be at sixes and sevens by that time.

Q. It was a very dangerous operation, wasn't it?

A. Of course it was, yes. It was a dangerous operation but you've
got to remember that they were also carrying out a dangerous
operation too. I mean, he — the faithless husband. They are not
all that keen on publicity, you know. I mean there was no
murder or anything like that in the offing at that time, was
there? Wasn't that dangerous you know. Well, it was dangerous,
but, I mean, it wasn't as dangerous as it was at the end. I mean,
we all know it's dangerous now, don't we? So that there's no
question about it not being dangerous. I mean it's very dangerous. It was dangerous for Hanratty too in the end, wasn't it?
I mean, it's rather — if you're mulling over in your mind the
question of my not doing it because it was dangerous, I mean,
it's demonstratively dangerous now. We all know that — there's
no point in arguing about the fact that it was dangerous. But it
was less dangerous than it was at the point when they were
murdered. It wouldn't have been quite as dangerous as that —
say that Gregsten had been made to leave the car and say that
Miss Storie had been molested and then the car driven away —
and then say I was caught — what would it have been? Who's
going to give evidence, first of all? Gregsten and Miss Storie.
Well, what sort of evidence would they have given? Would they
have been too willing to give evidence? We don't know what
sort of evidence it would have been. First conviction — what

would it have been? Two or three years—very most. Well, you've got to take chances, some sort of chances.

Q. Yes, but I mean, it just seems to me that the plan was a little vague, you know. I would have thought that being a resourceful fellow you would have thought it out a bit more carefully than that.

A. Well, I mean, the point is that if I was going to think out a plan I probably would think it a bit more carefully than that. But the thing is that it wasn't the sort of plan that I would normally make. You have got to realize that—I am carrying out someone else's plan for them. I mean, I don't know really. When you look at it—what else can you do? I mean, the idea was to separate these people. I can't see even now, much other way of doing it. It was just a daring plan, really, that misfired. I think it was a pretty good plan really, if it had worked.

I recorded these last four conversations in November and December 1969 in order to have in my hands a credible and representative record of Peter Alphon's conversation. Another reason, however, was that I sensed his nervousness increasing. There was no obvious reason for this change of mood, and Alphon exaggerated out of all proportion the impact of the A6 Murder Committee's public meetings or even of Mr and Mrs Lennon's brief involvement in the case. During January 1970, Alphon started to talk more and more about the Committee's campaign, and to ask about the possibility of his being hunted by thugs hired by the Hanratty family. Ever since I have known Alphon, he has been haunted by physical fear that he might be searched out, beaten up or even murdered in revenge for Hanratty. The confrontation with the demonstrators at his home in Brighton during the summer of 1969 exaggerated these fears. When Mrs Whicher, who, like Mr Fogarty-Waul, also engaged in a long telephone relationship with Alphon, told him one evening that I was taping his calls, he rang me in a violent temper which I only just managed to calm. He seemed convinced that the Committee had hired a man 'with 127 stitches in his head' (Alphon's description) to beat him up. The following evening, Alphon telephoned me and, when I told him that the story of the man with the 127 stitches was a lot of fantasy, launched into twenty-five minutes of magnificent abuse. This was the only time during the three and a half years I have known Peter Alphon that he has given me the sort of treatment to which Justice, Russell and others had become accustomed.

'If I hear the slightest thing', he shouted, 'if I get a letter or any little word out of place, I'm going to come for you! I'll tell you straight! And it's not going to be very nice!'

After working himself up into a terrible, and, as far as I could see, quite unjustifiable rage ('I'd have you in the gas ovens!' he shouted), he told me that he did not want to speak to me any more, and slammed the telephone down.

Some weeks later, in March 1970, he rang again and apologized for the more personal abuse of the previous call. He was, in this call, his former friendly self again. When I suggested that I would like to meet him again before completing work on the book, he agreed instantly and we tentatively fixed up a meeting for May.

Since then, I have not heard from Peter Alphon. In the three and a half years I have known him, he has never let so many months go by without contacting me. On April 4th, 1970, the eighth anniversary of Hanratty's execution, Jean Justice and another member of the Committee travelled to Brighton once more to demonstrate outside Alphon's parents' house, but on this occasion there was no trouble, and Alphon did not appear. His silence during all these months is surprising. Publicity about and public interest in the case were lower in the first nine months of 1970 than at any other time since the murder. As in Brighton in 1967, I got the very strong impression that his two enraged calls in January 1970 were inspired more by instructions from someone else than from any genuine fear or shift of mood.

I expect that Peter Alphon will ring again. Perhaps, particularly after the publication of this book, he will not ring *me*. If not he will find someone else with whom to discuss the A6 murder. For all the tantrums, contradictions, inconsistencies, confessions, retractions of confessions, threats, abuse and humour which have plagued Peter Alphon's conversation about his part in the A6 murder over eight and a half years, one characteristic has remained unchallenged and beyond argument: his obsession with the murder and his determination publicly to return to it.

SUMMARY:

The most common public reaction I have encountered to Peter Alphon's part in the A6 murder case goes like this: 'I agree that there was doubt about Hanratty's guilt. But as for Alphon: he's just a crank. He's a loony. I'm sure he had nothing to do with it.'

There is one flaw in this approach. The A6 murderer, whatever else he was, was not 'normal'. If the prosecution was right, he was provoked to his crime by lust. On another view, he was putting into practice a hideous plan to separate the couple from one another, which, whether or not it originally involved murder, can only have been the product of a sadistic and deranged mind. If Peter Alphon is a crank, so was the A6 murderer.

The word 'crank', however, does not explain very much of the complex character of Peter Alphon. A proper analysis requires some knowledge of psychiatry, a science in which I am both untrained and ignorant. All I can say, after three years of conversations with him, is that the workings of Peter Alphon's mind are far out of the ordinary.

Various spokesmen from the Home Office and the police over the years have taken the argument that Alphon is a crank a step further. Cranks, they point out, often confess to murders, especially sexual and highly publicized murders. Alphon, it is suggested by these spokesmen, is one such.

This view is supported by the inconsistency of Alphon's confessions over the years. The greyhound 'Mentals Only Hope' ran too late in the evening for a man to walk to Dorney Reach after its race at Slough, as Alphon suggested he did in his confession notes. Two shots were fired at Gregsten's head, not one as Alphon said on Dateline. The gun was reloaded during the shooting of Miss Storie. Alphon, on the Dateline programme, said that he did not reload. The safety catch was not on the handle, as he suggested. Then there are the changes in his story: the inclusion of the visit to the Slough dog-track in the confession notes, in the Paris confession and to me on the telephone from Paris and Dublin, followed by its removal from the story later in the same year. There are contradictions in his story about leaving the case in the Vienna Hotel; different times given for the visit to the Broadway House Hotel; clear denials — on Panorama, to the *People*, to the Marylebone magistrates' court — that he had anything to do with the murder. Mr X and France are withdrawn on two occasions from Alphon's confession. These and several other examples demonstrate that the confession is in no way consistent, and that on occasions Alphon is prepared to withdraw his confession altogether.

All this proves that the confessions, if taken together, are, in detail at any rate, contradictory. But does that necessarily mean that Alphon can be written off as the A6 murderer?

Most genuine confessions to murder are made after the murderer himself has been convicted of another murder or of some other crime. John Christie, for instance, having given evidence against Timothy Evans in the latter's trial for the murder of his baby daughter, confessed himself to the murder of Evans's wife only after he had been convicted of other murders, and was certain to hang.

Free men who make genuine confessions of murder are not necessarily bound by the laws of logic. Their confessions may be inaccurate or inconsistent, and yet still be genuine. In such instances, the murderer's motive for confessing is not necessarily only to convince others that he committed the crime. He may feel neurotically impelled to raise the matter in public (or in private), but still want to save his skin. In such circumstances, the details of his confession will be fudged by deliberate mistakes; essentials of it altered as the confession's credibility increases.

The inconsistencies and obvious flaws in Peter Alphon's confession prove nothing more than that the confession is inconsistent and has flaws. It does not prove that Alphon did not do the murder. Indeed, the very fact that Alphon throughout the last eight years has blown hot and cold with his confessions fits the murderer more closely than if the confession had been accurate and consistent.

Final elimination of Peter Alphon as the A6 murderer requires more than the assertion that his confessions are sometimes inaccurate or inconsistent. Some credible motive has to be found for Peter Alphon's returning again and again to his guilt in the A6 murder, though warned by policemen, magistrates and politicians not to do so.

The first possible motive is publicity. Yet the first confessions were made, not in public, but in the course of a close, and (Alphon hoped) private relationship with Jean Justice. All the original manifestations of confession – the McDougal drawing, the notes and the tape-recorded conversations with Justice in October and November 1962 – were made in private and were intended to be confidential. At the outset, Alphon did not know he was being taped on the telephone and would not continue the conversations until he had assured himself that Justice was alone. In those early months he was terrified of any public association of himself with the murder, and avoided journalists and television men like the plague. The persecution of Lord Russell and Mr and Mrs Warburg in 1964 and 1965 was clearly designed to stop publication of Russell's book. Until his Paris confession in 1967, Alphon's attitude to any public reference to himself as the murderer was to issue denials and writs. It is only after the Paris incident, with his letters to the Home Secretary, that Alphon attempted to get publicity for his confessions and then only for letters carefully worked out in private.

A second possibility is that Alphon confessed for money. Yet, apart from the single, half-hearted and unsuccessful attempt to blackmail Justice in early 1963, Alphon has never tried to make money out of his confessions. His attempts to interest *Life* magazine in 1967 in his 'life story' based on his confession were pathetically inadequate. Never once in the last three years has he suggested that he should be paid a penny for his confessions, as retailed by me in *Queen* magazine or the *Sunday Times*. The chance to make a large sum out of his confession on the Frost programme was summarily turned down (as was the publicity on that occasion). Alphon has made a fair amount of money from the media out of *denying* his association with the murder (£1,000 – at least – from the *Daily Express*; several hundred pounds from the *Daily Mail*; £150 – at least – from the *News of the World*; £50 from Panorama), but nothing out of confessing to it.

The third possible motive is that the confession was made originally to maintain his close relationship with Jean Justice. This does not explain why, after Justice left him and betrayed his confidences to the authorities, Alphon continued to return to the subject of the murder, and to confess to it. Nor does it explain why the motive for the murder, by far the most convincing part of Alphon's confession, was held back from Justice until Alphon believed that Justice and Mr X were in league against him. The terror expressed by Alphon on that tape in March 1964 is un-characteristic of a man who made up Mr X's part in the murder in the first place. A fourth explanation arises out of the third, as follows. In the first instance he wrote his confession notes and confessed to Justice in order to maintain Justice's interest and retain the company and affection of Justice and Fox. After Justice left him, however, he decided to continue with a macabre game by persecuting people who had anything to do with the murder or with writing about it. When this persecution caught up with him, in the form of the magistrates' summons, he went to Paris and made a phoney confession. When I rang him, he was forced to continue with the confession, and, as he got to know who I was and what I represented, he delighted in baiting and humiliating a journalist with extreme left-wing views who stood for everything he detested.

If Peter Alphon did not commit the A6 murder, this is a very credible explanation of his confessions over the last eight years. Yet even this does not fit all the facts. First, as early as 1962, Alphon assured Justice that he would one day go abroad, tell 'the truth' and 'involve someone else' in the murder. Secondly, his attitude towards Justice and Russell since the latter entered the case has always been one of contempt. 'There's people like Justice and Lord Russell and these people,' he told me once. 'These people are anathema to me. They are a load of rubbish. If I were in power, they would be in the bloody gas ovens.' If he was trying to convince me that Justice had the truth about the murder, why speak so consistently of Justice with loathing and contempt?

There is, however, a fifth explanation of Alphon's behaviour which is more convincing than any of the others. It runs as follows.

Alphon was interviewed by the police in connection with the A6 murder because he was staying in the Vienna Hotel on the murder night. The interview made a profound impression on his over-wrought and highly strung mentality. Gradually, over the months he began to *see himself* as the A6 murderer. As Hanratty's guilt appeared questionable at the trial, so Alphon's belief in his own guilt took firmer root, and when Justice started to cross-examine him, he developed his belief in himself as the murderer to a point from which he could not return.

The theory is supported by the fact that Alphon stayed in the Vienna Hotel on the murder night. If his confession story was right, if the plan was to frame Hanratty – why did Alphon stay in the same hotel as the man he wanted to frame? If he knew Hanratty was staying there, the hotel would surely be the last place to approach – and if he did *not* know it, the coincidence seems impossible. Alphon himself, incidentally, has never given an adequate explanation for this coincidence.

The explanation, in short, is that Alphon was unhinged by his interrogation in connection with the murder into believing that he was the murderer and has acted ever since as though he was. Such an explanation, because its central figure is a madman, does not allow for rational rebuttal. Certainly there is nothing rational about the chronology of Peter Alphon's confessions: the six months' silence following the murder, broken only by the appearance of Jean Justice; the slow extraction of a confession by Justice; the holding back for two years of any mention of accomplices or motive; the public confessions delayed until nearly six years after the murder, followed by their withdrawal for his own protection. This chronology could fit someone who sincerely but mistakenly believed himself to be the murderer. (Although it could also fit the A6 murderer, who was clearly unbalanced.)

All these explanations assume that Alphon had nothing to do with the murder, and that any connection between Peter Alphon and the murderer is entirely coincidental. If this is so, the list of coincidences between the appearance and characteristics of Peter Alphon, his behaviour after the murder and of other relevant circumstances and of those of the A6 murderer, is long enough to stretch the credibility of the most redoubtable sceptic.

1. Alphon looks startlingly like the Identikit picture drawn up by Valerie Storie. The main features of the face — the hair and the eyes — are strikingly similar. Alphon closely fits the description of the murderer put out from Bedford Hospital after the murder, of a man in his thirties, with dark hair and deep-set brown eyes (though his eyes are hazel).

2. When excited Alphon mispronounces 'th', as the murderer did.

3. Alphon spent much of his childhood in the Slough and Taplow area, and knows it very well.

4. Superintendent Acott, who was in charge of the inquiry, had evidence suggesting that Alphon was the murderer. The alibis which Alphon had provided clearly did not satisfy Mr Acott.

5. The probability is that Mr Acott proved that Alphon lied about where he was on the night of the murder.

6. For four or five days after the murder, Alphon behaved so oddly that guests at the Alexandra Court Hotel reported him to the manager, who in turn told the police.

7. The motive Alphon presents in his confession is far more credible than the 'lust' motive attributed to Hanratty at the Bedford trial. The character of Charles France exactly fitted the role attributed him in Alphon's version of the crime.

8. Alphon's bank account, opened soon after his release, shows large

sums of money paid in the six weeks following his release. The sums are out of keeping with Alphon's financial standing and way of life.

9. Alphon's driving ability fits that of the murderer almost exactly.

10. Alphon was identified by Mrs Dalal as the man who had assaulted her shouting: 'I am the A6 killer.'

11. Alphon's 'completely lunatic and unstable disorder' in the Regent Palace Hotel as Hanratty awaited execution was, even for him, unprecedented.

12. Alphon had been advised to press ahead with legal action against Superintendent Acott for wrongful arrest, and against the *Daily Mirror*, the *Daily Mail* and other newspapers for libel in connection with the murder. He also sued Lord Brockway and Independent Television News. His lawyers advised him that he stood a very good chance of winning substantial sums in damages in all or some of these actions. All these actions were abandoned, and Alphon's cause of action in them was effectively removed by his Paris confession.

13. Mrs Lanz and Mr Fogarty-Waul have said that Alphon was seen in the Old Station Inn and in Marsh Lane shortly before the murder.

14. The attitude of the authorities towards Alphon has always been equivocal. If he was indeed a crank who without any justification resurrected ghosts of a case which was settled, the authorities, surely, would have been more than keen to hound him until he stopped. Throughout, however, Alphon has been treated with kid gloves by the authorities. Summonses against him have been refused, and searches for him delayed. When finally tried, he has been let off with surprisingly light sentences. On two occasions – the Regent Palace drunk and disorderly case and the Hanratty assault case – he was found not guilty after powerful evidence had been presented against him.

If Alphon's was indeed a chance arrest, if he was indeed a man whose name was plucked from a hotel registry without any justification, it is more than remarkable that he should in so many ways resemble a man who, in his own words, had killed Gregsten and been treated by the Establishment as though they knew that he had done so.

To sum up, I am as sure as it is possible to be that James Hanratty did not commit the A6 murder. I am quite certain that any jury presented with all the evidence now available would not convict Hanratty.

As for Peter Alphon, either he committed the A6 murder, or he has been leading all of us, and me in particular, a fantastic dance. I tend, perhaps naturally, to the former view, but I have not the power to find the facts finally to prove or disprove it. That can only be done by a public inquiry with power to subpoena all the relevant witnesses and documents. In the meantime, I can do no more, and the case, temporarily and uneasily, must rest.

Postscript, July 1972

During the last week in April and the first in May 1971, this book was serialized in ten parts in the *Sun* newspaper, which campaigned the while for a public inquiry into the A6 verdict. The serialization brought with it considerable public interest in the case, and the *Sun* was flooded with letters, the vast majority of them supporting the paper's call for an inquiry. The book itself was widely reviewed. Writers in *The Times*, the *Guardian*, the *Evening News*, the *Daily Mail*, the *New Statesman* and the *Spectator* wholeheartedly supported the call for an inquiry, as did some forty-five local newspapers throughout the country. The review which probably gave the greatest pleasure to the A6 murder committee was written in the *Observer* by Louis Blom-Cooper, whose Penguin book eight years previously had done so much to allay public disquiet about Hanratty's guilt. Mr Blom-Cooper wrote (the *Observer*, May 9th 1971):

> [In my book] I expressed the conclusion that Hanratty was the killer. Mr Foot takes me to task for the reasons I advanced for so thinking. He has convinced me at least that in some respects I was either rash in my judgment or overlooked countervailing arguments. My conclusion was based on all too slender a review of the accumulated material . . .

And he concluded: 'Should the Home Secretary, even now, unbend and concede that there is something to inquire into? I think he should.'

There was, however, one influential reviewer whose mind was not changed. Mr Dick Taverne Q.C., Labour M.P. for Lincoln, had been Parliamentary Under-Secretary at the Home Office when Mr Roy Jenkins turned down the demand for a public inquiry into the case in 1967. In a long review in the *Sunday Times* on May 9th, Mr Taverne restated his view that Hanratty was guilty beyond all reasonable doubt and that an inquiry into the case was unnecessary and undesirable.

In support of this view Mr Taverne attached most importance to the evidence of Roy Langdale, taken together with that of the prison officer, Eatwell, who had overheard Langdale's account of Hanratty's alleged confession in a prison coach on November 22nd, 1961 – the first day of the committal proceedings against Hanratty. Langdale, it will be remembered, had been all day in the court cells at the Guildhall, London, waiting to be tried on a forgery case. In the coach on the way back to the prison, Eatwell overhead Langdale blurting out to a fellow prisoner that Hanratty had confessed to him in the prison yard at Brixton.

Mr Taverne writes:

> The prison officer's original report shows that Langdale referred to Hanratty saying he had made Valerie Storie drag Gregsten's body out of the car. This had not, as far as I know, been reported at the time when the remarks were overheard and could only have come from the murderer.

On the contrary, however, the early editions of the London evening papers *that same afternoon* had carried detailed reports of the prosecutor's opening statement at Hanratty's trial at Ampthill, Bedfordshire. The *Evening Standard* had: 'Hanratty then forced Valerie to get into the back seat and raped her. He ordered her to drag Gregsten's body outside.' And the *Evening News* recorded: 'Later . . . Valerie Storie was forced to drag Gregsten's body from the car.'

It is true that Mr Eatwell stated in evidence that, as far as he knew, Langdale had not had access to the evening papers while in the court cells. Yet we are left with the remarkable coincidence that Langdale chose the very evening when the details about the A6 murder were splashed across papers and news bulletins all over London suddenly to recall that Hanratty had confessed to him some three weeks previously.

Mr Taverne scoffs at the suggestion that Langdale's light sentence (three years' probation, which he received the day after revealing Hanratty's confession) could have been related to his conversation in the prison coach. Such things cannot happen in the innocent world which Mr Taverne imagines is that of the British courts. Meanwhile, the uncharacteristic leniency with which the courts dealt with the recidivist Langdale on that occasion seems to have continued. On January 22nd, 1971, Langdale was sentenced to eighteen months' imprisonment for yet another robbery. On May 3rd, when the Hanratty case was very much in the news, his sentence was unexpectedly halved by the Court of Appeal after a moving appeal from Mrs Langdale.

In his review, Mr Taverne introduced an entirely new element into the case in order to attempt to explain the coincidence between the story told by Mrs Dinwoodie, the sweetshop-minder in Liverpool, and that of Hanratty.

'After the trial,' wrote Mr Taverne, 'it was found that Hanratty had been seen outside the sweetshop on another Monday, in October.'

The strength of Mrs Dinwoodie's evidence from the defence point of view had been that the man she identified as Hanratty must have entered her sweetshop on Monday, August 21st, or Tuesday, August 22nd (the day of the murder). Since Hanratty was definitely in London on the Monday, her evidence seemed to suggest that Hanratty's story (that he had been in the sweetshop on the day of the murder) was true. Now Mr Taverne was suggesting for the first time in public, that the incident might have taken place on a Monday in October.

This was never suggested by the prosecution. It must have come from unseen evidence, available only to the privileged in the Home Office. Mr Taverne, who re-examined all the secret Home Office evidence before writing his review, introduced this new piece of information without attempting to corroborate it. Was Mrs Dinwoodie in the shop on that Monday in October when Hanratty was seen outside it? Was there a little girl with her that day, as Hanratty testified? If not, of course, the statement is entirely irrelevant.

Mrs Dinwoodie was interviewed by the police less than a fortnight after Monday, October 9th – the only October Monday when Hanratty can have been seen in Liverpool. Had the sweetshop encounter taken place only a fortnight previously, surely Mrs Dinwoodie would have remembered so. On the contrary, however, Mrs Dinwoodie always insisted that the event took place in August, when the sweetshop proprietor's family were on holiday.

The introduction of secret, uncorroborated evidence without any attempt to relate it to other facts which would have made it relevant demonstrated how deep into the barrel Mr Taverne had to scrape in order to justify his and his Minister's decision to keep the Hanratty file closed. His review clearly did not persuade the people in charge of the paper in which it was printed. The *Sunday Times* on the same day (May 9th) published a long, powerful leader, which ended:

> The case will not lie down, and the only antidote to the haunting suspicions is the truth, the whole truth and nothing but the truth. For all these reasons, Mr Maudling should set aside the legitimate scruples about reopening the case. He should take the courageous step of instituting a public inquiry.

The *Sunday Times* that day carried yet another article about the A6 murder. Mrs Charles France, the wife of the prosecution witness in the case, allowed *Sunday Times* reporters to see some of the letters which her husband had written to her and her family on the night he committed suicide. 'The family,' wrote the *Sunday Times* reporter Philip Jacobson, 'is adamant that Mr France killed himself because of his horror and remorse at having introduced a sex murderer into his home where he became a friend of the family and its three daughters.'

The France letter, reproduced in full by the *Sunday Times*, ran as follows:

> My Darling Wife,
>
> One day you will understand that what I have done this night I have done for you and my darling children. They are going to crucifie us all. You in your innocence of anything wrong. As for Carole my heart bleeds to think what I am leaving you to face. But I sincerely promise you it will be much better than having the stigma of bearing the the [*sic*] fact that I have done what was honestly write but will be so twisted as to make it look as though I was an associate of this filthy act.

My petty acts of wrong will be magnifide to make it look as though I knew all along that this *man* who I took to be a freind, as turned into a monster and should pay a just penalty. Oh my darling Family *forgive me*, if you think that I have taken the easy way out you are so wrong. I wont you to find peace with your dear family who I know will stick by you all the way. While I am here nobody wants to come near but now you will find some happiness.

God Bless you all

Bobbie xxx
Brenda xxx
Carole xxx
Mummy xxx

Daddy

At first sight, the letter appears to bear out the sincere feelings of the France family that France killed himself in innocent remorse. A closer look, however, leaves many questions unanswered. What does France mean when he writes: 'They are going to crucifie us all'? If France was indeed an innocent bystander in the case, why should he believe that things 'will be so twisted as to make it look as though I was an associate to this filthy act'? I have, as I wrote in the introduction, seen most of the letters which France wrote, and the letter reproduced in the *Sunday Times* serves only to strengthen my view that France wrote these letters to shelter his family from an association with the crime which he could not live with.

These matters were the subject of furious discussion on the evening of the *Sunday Times* publication (May 9th) when the Hanratty family and a large body of supporters arrived in Rhyl for a public meeting about the case. The hall was packed with some three hundred people. After the speeches, a woman rose in the audience to say that she had material evidence which had always been on her conscience.

Mrs Pearl Hughes, of 161 Ceffynd Road, Rhyl, then told her story. In the summer of 1961 she had been walking to work one evening (she did a night cleaning job) with her mother, when a young man approached her and asked her to help him find his friend. He did not know the friend's name, but remembered that he was swarthy and had a mark on his forehead. After some discussion, Mrs Hughes identified the 'friend' as Terry Evans, who lived close to where the conversation was taking place. The man then asked her to knock on the 'friend's' door, while he waited in the road to see if he could identify him. Mrs Hughes, who was late for work explained that she had no time for this rigmarole, and went on her way. The man Mrs Hughes told us, had very clearly identified Evans, Evans's features, Evans's house and Evans's wife.

After so long a time, of course, Mrs Hughes could not possibly remember the date of this event, which her mother, who was also at the meeting, confirmed. But she did say, to the amazement of the meeting, that the man who approached her bore a strong resemblance to Richard Hanratty, who was on the platform. Of the three Hanratty brothers, Richard most closely resembles James.

Here was further evidence of a man, looking like Hanratty, wandering around the streets of Rhyl in late summer, 1961, searching for Terry Evans. The behaviour which Mrs Hughes described to us precisely fits that of a criminal on the run, who has forgotten the name and address of a possible fence.

After a few hectic days in Rhyl, during which they interviewed a barber, Mr Gerald Murray, who said he may have been the barber who shaved Hanratty in 1961, the Hanrattys returned to London to hear the Court of Appeal dismiss their action against Mr R. A. Butler for negligence in not studying all the available evidence before deciding that Hanratty must hang in 1962. The Court ruled that no action in negligence can lie against a Home Secretary in respect of the manner in which he carries out his task of advising the Crown how to exercise the prerogative of mercy.

By now the case was beginning to cause a stir even in Parliament. On May 3rd, 1971, three Labour M.P.s, including Mr Patrick Gordon Walker, a former Foreign Secretary, put down a motion stating grave doubt about Hanratty's guilt and calling for a public inquiry. By May 20th, the motion had been signed by some thirty-six M.P.s, including one Conservative, Mr Ernle Money (Ipswich). On that day, Mr Philip Whitehead and Mr Charles Loughlin, two back-bench Labour M.P.s, had questions down to Mr Reginald Maudling, the Home Secretary, asking whether he would set up a public inquiry into the case. Mr Maudling replied:

I am having a full analysis made of the latest publication on this subject, and I shall then have to determine whether it brings out any new facts not previously known. I cannot make a decision on that until I have been fully advised. (An Hon. Member: By whom?) By my advisers of course. There are voluminous documents which I have to study.

Mr Whitehead replied by emphasizing the importance of a public inquiry which would have the powers to subpoena witnesses and Home Office documents. Mr James Callaghan from Labour's front bench, who as Home Secretary had turned down an inquiry only a year previously, weighed in with the news that if Maudling decided on a public inquiry, he, Callaghan, 'should not want to dissent from that merely because a different conclusion was reached earlier'.

On May 27th, just before the Whitsun recess, Mr Frederick Willey, another former Labour Minister, spoke in an adjournment debate calling for a public inquiry into the case. The Home Office Parliamentary Under-Secretary at the Home Office, Mr Mark Carlisle, replied that Mr Maudling was still considering the case, and reminded Mr Willey that only new evidence could be taken into account.

There is some evidence that at this time Mr Maudling was favourably disposed to those campaigning on behalf of Hanratty. He told a prominent political correspondent that he was determined to get to the bottom of the case and imagined himself 'like Maigret' in his detective work. A letter from the Hanratty parents to every Member of Parliament brought a sharp increase in the number of M.P.s signing Mr Gordon Walker's motion. On June 9th and 11th respectively, two amendments were put down to Mr Gordon Walker's motion, one by Liberal M.P.s, the other by Conservatives. The amendments removed the reference to the possibility that the verdict might have been different and called for a public inquiry into the case 'in view of the evidence which has since become available' (Liberals) and 'in view of the widespread and serious public doubts about the verdict' (Conservatives). Two Liberals and eight Conservatives signed the amendments, bringing the total number of M.P.s eventually calling for an inquiry to eighty-two.

On June 24th Miss Joan Lestor, Mr Loughlin and Mr Willey

again questioned Mr Maudling about the case. Maudling's answer on this occasion showed an interesting shift of emphasis. After saying that he had read the book and studied the Home Office analysis of all the information available, he went on:

> It is not my function to retry a case on the basis of evidence and arguments previously considered by the courts, but only to consider whether there is any information that was not before the courts *which might justify me in recommending the exercise of the Royal Prerogative of Mercy.* (My italics.)

No one has asked Mr Maudling to recommend the Royal Prerogative of Mercy for Hanratty. The motions and questions had all demanded a public inquiry. In this answer, Maudling hinted that he was considering by-passing an inquiry and granting a free pardon to Hanratty. This would have been an honourable course which would have avoided a tedious public inquiry. It would also have removed the necessity of accusing another man. At the same time, it would clearly have satisfied the Hanratty family. Mr Maudling went on to say that he was asking me for a note of all new evidence on the case. In response to this request I sent him a long letter of about 4,000 words on July 1st. He replied at once, thanking me profusely for it.

On the day I posted the letter, a further important piece of evidence came to light. Mr and Mrs Hanratty received an urgent telephone call from Mrs Lanz, the proprietress of the Old Station Inn at Taplow, where Valerie Storie and Michael Gregsten had had their last drink together. Mrs Lanz said she had been disturbed by all the publicity about the case and felt she must make a statement about something which had been on her mind for a long time. Accordingly, Lewis Chester of the *Sunday Times* and I went down to Taplow and took the following statement from Mrs Lanz, which appeared in full in the front page of the *Sunday Times* on July 4th:

1. On the night of Tuesday, the 22nd of August, 1961, I was serving as usual in the bar at the Old Station Inn, Taplow, Bucks.
2. On that night, Michael Gregsten and Valerie Storie came into the saloon bar, and sat in their usual seat under the

arch. They used to come in three or four times a week. They were well known to me and my family.

3. Also in the pub that night was a man who I now know to be Peter Louis Alphon.

4. This man had been in the pub on several previous occasions. Usually he was alone, but on this occasion he was accompanied by a blonde woman who was, I would say, in her early thirties.

5. I recall Michael Gregsten and Valerie leaving after nine o'clock. The man who I now know to be Alphon left with the blonde lady about half an hour later by the back exit.

6. At the time I did not attach any significance to the presence of this man. The public house was packed that night with people coming and going all the time.

7. When police officers from Slough came the next day to make inquiries about the murder of Michael Gregsten, I did not mention this matter because it did not seem in any way important.

8. However, the man who I now know to be Alphon did come into the pub subsequently. I distinctly recall one evening shortly after the murder he came in and asked whether he could book in for the night. The man gave the name Louis Henecky.

9. Some time after this, during the trial of James Hanratty, a Mr Jean Justice brought this man who I then knew as Louis Henecky into the pub. Mr Justice asked me if I recognized him. I said yes. Mr Justice then told me that the man was in fact Peter Alphon, who had been a suspect for the A6 murder.

10. I was naturally very worried about this and after Hanratty's appeal failed became concerned that an innocent man might hang for murder. Although I had seen a number of local police officers, neither I nor any member of my family was interviewed by Det. Supt. Acott, the man in charge of the murder inquiry. And although we were the last people, apart from the murderer and Miss Storie, to see Michael alive, none of us ever gave formal statements to the police or were called at the trial.

11. I became so worried about the possibility of a miscarriage of justice that I decided to tell the authorities what I knew

about Mr Alphon. I therefore visited Slough police station with a member of my family a few days before Hanratty's execution. I was there until the early hours of the morning, making a statement along the lines of the one that I have made today.

12. I feel I did all I could to stop the execution.

13. I have refused to talk publicly about the Alphon incident because I did not want to involve my family in unnecessary publicity. It has, however, always preyed on my mind. I am only giving this statement now because there seems to be some possibility of the Hanratty case being reopened at an official level. I have received no money for it, nor want any. I know that I shall sleep easier now that I have made this statement.

The significance of the statement needs no emphasizing, and was dealt with at length by the B.B.C. television programme, 'Twenty-four Hours'.

Mrs Lanz's statement gave an impetus to the Parliamentary campaign, and M.P.s pressed for a decision on the case by the summer recess, which was to start on July 23rd. On July 22nd, Mr Whitehead and Mr Willey had questions down to the Home Secretary about the A6 murder. The day before, July 21st, two and half months after the book was published, Mr William Ewer, Michael Gregsten's brother-in-law, issued a writ against me and the publishers of this book, alleging libel. When Mr Maudling rose to answer the M.P.s' questions, therefore, he astonished them by saying: 'I cannot make any further comment as I understand that a writ has been issued in the High Court in respect of certain published material relevant to this matter.'

Pressed about a possible meeting with me, Mr Maudling added: 'If it is useful to have a meeting, I will arrange one. I do not think it would be useful to comment further because I have not seen the terms of the writ which has been referred to.'

When he had studied the terms of the writ, Mr Maudling clearly made up his mind that the whole matter was *sub judice*. On August 13th he wrote to me as follows:

Dear Mr Foot,

   As you may have noticed from my recent replies in the House of Commons, while I was looking forward to a meeting with you about the Hanratty case, the position has been complicated by the issue of a writ against you by Mr Ewer.

The issue of the writ will not preclude me from continuing my researches into the Hanratty case and my consideration of the points made in your book. Your letter of 1st July sets out quite clearly and sufficiently the detailed points on which you are mainly relying, and I am advised that in these circumstances it would be inappropriate to ask you to discuss with me matters which you have already drawn specifically to my attention and which have now become the subject of the pending libel action.

The above was typed. In his own hand at the bottom of the letter, Mr Maudling wrote: 'I'm sorry about it, but all this seems pretty definite.'

There was not time in Parliament to challenge this novel interpretation of the *sub judice* rule, whereby, apparently, discussions between Ministers and private citizens on matters of public importance can be ruled out by the issuing of a writ for libel. Parliament was by now in recess for the summer.

By one of those remarkable coincidences which has dogged official reaction to the campaign for a public inquiry into the A6 murder verdict, the matter next came up in Parliament on a day when the press, television and public opinion were obsessed with the vote in the House of Commons on British entry into the European Common Market. Questions to the Home Secretary were something of a formality that day, and Mr Maudling chose to answer further demands for a public inquiry into the A6 murder from Philip Whitehead, Fred Willey and Joan Lestor. Maudling's reply took the form of statement which must be repeated in full:

James Hanratty was convicted in February 1962, after a long trial in the course of which the jury heard extensive evidence and argument. It was for the jury to reach a verdict upon that evidence. The Court of Criminal Appeal subsequently dismissed Hanratty's appeal. It is not for the Home Secretary to set aside the verdict of the Courts. But I have considered whether there are any grounds for my intervention on the basis of material which was not before them.

The case has already been closely reviewed on that basis by successive Home Secretaries, and over the years a great deal of information has been accumulated. After full examination of all the information available to me I cannot find that Mr Foot, despite his very extensive research, has brought out any significant aspect of the case which has not already been thoroughly considered.

Mr Foot has not had full access to all the available material, and in some respects his arguments are based on premises that are not supported by the facts. I cannot, for example, find any basis for the suggestion that Miss Storie materially altered her description of the murderer, and accordingly I cannot accept any inference sought to be drawn from this suggestion. Nor is it the case that the police were put on the trail of Hanratty as a result of information received from Mr William Ewer.

Other material which has been described as new evidence has proved upon examination to relate to matters which have already been the subject of investigation. I find, for instance, that inquiries were made of Mrs Lanz at the time of the crime and shortly after the trial about persons she had seen at the Old Station Inn, Taplow, and her present recollection of events is not consistent with the statements she made nearer the time.

My predecessors gave special attention to the possibility that Hanratty might have been at Rhyl at the time of the murder, and I have for my part examined with care all the additional evidence tending to support this alibi. At a trial, alibi evidence is subject to searching cross-examination to verify its relevance and reliability; and after close scrutiny I remain unpersuaded that any of the evidence produced since the trial could stand up to such a critical examination, bearing in mind that the recollection of witnesses must necessarily become impaired by the passage of time.

I recognize and entirely respect the doubts which still remain in many minds, and I have considered carefully whether the appointment of a public inquiry would help to resolve the issues. I have concluded for two reasons that it would not. I do not believe that any judicial tribunal can be expected to arrive at a convincing opinion as to the facts on the basis of the recollection of witnesses as to specific details ten years after the event. Mr Justice Brabin, in his report on the Evans case, has graphically described the fallibility of any such process. Secondly there are fundamental objections to the use of such a procedure as a means to the informal trial of some other person outside the normal processes of the law which would be inevitable in this case.

After an exhaustive review, I have therefore come to the conclusion that there is no further action which I should take in a case which, I fully recognize, has given rise to much genuine anxiety.

Early in his statement, Mr Maudling comes close to criticizing me for not considering material to which he and successive Home Secretaries before him have consistently denied me access. The call for a public inquiry is based precisely on the complaint that crucial information about the A6 murder is not available to the inquirer. It is, however, difficult to believe that there is, as Mr Maudling suggests, 'no basis' for the suggestion that Valerie Storie materially altered her description of the murderer. How else is one to explain the police description of the murderer printed in hundreds of different newspaper reports all over the country for six days after the murder, that the murderer had 'deep-set brown eyes'? Where did this description come from, unless from Miss Storie, who later decided that the murderer's eyes were 'icy-blue' and 'saucer-like'? No one who knows about these two descriptions is going to be satisfied with a bland assurance from the Home Secretary that he 'cannot find any basis' for the suggestion that Miss Storie changed her description. What is needed to satisfy these doubts is a copy of the statement made by Miss Storie at Bedford a few hours after the murder, and a full explanation of the police description about 'deep-set brown eyes'. The same goes for Mr Maudling's 'assurance' about how the police were put on the trail of Hanratty. If it was not through Mr William Ewer, then who was the man whom Ewer suspected and trailed in Swiss Cottage? Again, there is an assurance without evidence to support it. The same goes, too, for Mr Maudling's criticism of Mrs Lanz. In order to add substance to the point that Mrs Lanz contradicted herself, why could

Maudling not produce the statements she made previously and demonstrate the alleged contradictions?

As the *Sunday Times* put it in another powerful leader criticizing the decision (October 31st, 1971):

> Mr Maudling could have stilled the doubts if he had made a full and detailed statement to the House, quoting at least some of the documents which his Department has so far sedulously withheld. He chose not to do so; and he has thereby made certain that public unease will persist.

In dealing with the Rhyl alibi, Mr Maudling told the Commons that he remains 'unpersuaded' that any of the evidence about the alibi produced since the trial could 'stand up' to the 'critical examination' of an inquiry. On the face of it that is most surprising. Both Mrs Walker and Mr Larman, the strongest witnesses, have both indicated that they are prepared to testify in front of an inquiry. The same goes for most of the other witnesses. Mr Maudling's worries about the 'recollection' of witnesses after so many years is one which applies to many court cases heard years after the relevant incident. It is indeed less relevant in this case than in many others since most of the statements on which the new evidence is based were made at or around the time of the trial. For the Home Secretary to decide in advance whether such evidence would stand up to cross-examination at an inquiry is to prejudge the inquiry, and to remove the chance of the evidence to be *publicly* tested.

The most remarkable part of Mr Maudling's statement is the final paragraph. All other Home Secretaries had turned down demands for an inquiry on the grounds that there was not a scintilla of doubt about James Hanratty's guilt.

Henry Brooke, for instance, had been quite clear:

> If I thought that there was anything in the memorandum I have received, I would not hesitate to appoint a public inquiry. Indeed, I go further than that. If I thought that on any reasonable view there could possibly be anything in it, I would welcome an independent investigation. (Hansard, August 2nd, 1963.)

This, in rather less forthright language, has been the position of Sir Frank Soskice, Mr Roy Jenkins and Mr James Callaghan —the three Home Secretaries to succeed Henry Brooke.

Mr Maudling's attitude, however, was quite different. 'I recognize and entirely respect the doubts which still remain in many minds,' he told the Commons. For 'Maigret' Maudling, there *is* doubt, but unfortunately no way of resolving it. A public inquiry, he complained, is no good because of the dangers of witnesses' recollection after so long a time. The judges, apparently, are not intelligent enough to make allowances for that. Then there is the problem of Peter Alphon. He might be tried by an independent inquiry – 'outside the normal processes of law'.

The implications of these statements must be spelled out. They mean that *no* injustice committed in the courts can *ever* be put right by independent, public examination unless the matter is fresh in people's minds and any likely criminal in the case is dead. No injustice a long time ago, if the real criminal, or a likely real criminal, is still alive, is, according to the Maudling doctrine, capable of public rectification.

Thus Mr Maudling can 'fully recognize' the 'genuine anxiety' which exists about the Hanratty case. It is, because of the wealth of evidence now available, no longer open to him to claim that the court's verdict was right beyond all reasonable doubt. 'Genuine anxiety' has at last been established to the satisfaction of the Home Office, but there is apparently no way in which that anxiety can be laid to rest.

This arresting doctrine was repeated even more blatantly in a debate in the House of Lords on June 14th, 1972, initiated by Lord Goodman, who asked for an 'impartial review' of the Hanratty and Bentley cases. Several peers spoke in the debate, which was replied to for the Government by Viscount Colville of Culross. Lord Colville restated that a public inquiry was an unsatisfactory way of finding things out when they happened a long time ago, and went on to speak on behalf of Mr Peter Alphon:

> I should have thought that there was the gravest danger that public inquiry into this case would be likely to turn into a para-judicial trial. And I am afraid that the person who would be very liable to be tried would be Mr Alphon. I feel that this is an exceedingly dangerous thing to encourage, and I am very much afraid that this is what would happen.

In other words, if a man makes a confession to a crime, it is impossible to have a public investigation to test that confession for fear that the confession may turn out to be correct.

Mr Peter Alphon, after all, has confessed to this crime at a public press conference in 1967, and on many occasions since in letters to newspapers and in private conversation. If a public inquiry were to test his confession, he could hardly complain that he was being tried 'outside the due processes of law'.

Alphon, incidentally, has been almost silent since the book was written. For a brief period during its publication, he telephoned me a number of times, spitting with rage at the reviewers who had written him off as a crank and an exhibitionist. He told me that he was writing a long letter to the *Sunday Times* and the *Sun* restating his confession in detail. He read out passages from the letter. Then, suddenly, on the day he was to ring me with the full text, he broke off contact, ringing me only intermittently from then on. I have not heard from him since Christmas 1971.

The libel action with Mr William Ewer has been settled. Nothing in the book has been changed as a result of the settlement. I was invited to lunch at Mr Ewer's house in Golders Green, where Mr Ewer explained to me how the curious article in the *Daily Sketch* about his and his sister-in-law's 'sighting' of Hanratty in Swiss Cottage came to be written. He had, he said, been chatting to the *Sketch* and *Mail* journalists after the conviction of Hanratty at Bedford. He had mentioned casually that Hanratty had gone into the cleaners' shop opposite his umbrella shop in Swiss Cottage, and had remarked on the coincidence. He had, he agreed, taken the journalists to his shop the next morning (a Sunday) and allowed them to take photographs. The story which eventually appeared, he said, was a farrago of nonsense. There had, he said, been no 'sighting' of Hanratty by his sister-in-law. He did not know whether a man he had reported to the police was, in fact, Hanratty. And he had never known Mrs Louise Anderson. All these facts, he told me, were invented by the journalists on the *Daily Sketch* and *Daily Mail*.

Mr Maudling's shabby statement in the House of Commons on October 28th, 1971, caused a great deal of gloom in the Hanratty family and in the A6 Murder Committee. They have, however, continued their campaign at Hyde Park and at various public meetings. On April 18th, 1972, there was another glimmer of hope.

Mrs Shirley Williams, Labour's Shadow Home Secretary, was on the Radio 4 programme 'Its Your Line'. Mr Hanratty phoned her to ask whether she would set up a public inquiry into the case if she became Home Secretary. Mrs Williams replied: 'I myself believe that the evidence which has been brought forward both in the book and in the television programmes and elsewhere is so disturbing that a case for a public inquiry is now made out.'

There are two old people in North London who are hoping that Mrs Shirley Williams will be Home Secretary after the next General Election and that she will not change her mind.

Postscript, April 1988

In the spring of 1974, partly as a spin-off from libel action taken against the *Sunday Times* by Mr X, the A6 Murder Committee got hold of *another* statement by Valerie Storie – a statement, which, incredibly, had not been available to James Hanratty's defence at any stage before he was hanged.

The statement is in the form of an interview which Valerie Storie gave to two police officers, Det. Sgt Douglas Rees and Woman Police Constable Rutland, on the morning she was shot – within an hour of being taken to Bedford hospital. What she said was recorded by Mr Rees and Miss Rutland in a nine-page statement.

The fact that she made a statement to police officers so early in the morning, when the horrific events of the previous night were so fresh in her mind, was clearly evidence of the highest importance. A number of matters were mentioned in the statement which would have had a considerable impact on the prosecution case. For instance, she said that 'Mike' (Gregsten) had split up with his wife the week before the murder, that he had taken lodgings in Maidenhead to be nearer Valerie and that as soon as the divorce was out of the way, 'We were going to get married.'

This news might have given added thrust to the gunman's talking of Valerie and Michael as 'man and wife' and of offering them a threepenny bit 'for a wedding present'. The proximity of the break-up of the marriage, the impending divorce proceedings and the fact that Gregsten had already got himself lodgings in Maidenhead – all this, which the jury never heard, must surely have given strength to the argument that the gunman was not in Dorney Reach that night by chance but had been sent there as part of a madcap plan to frighten the lovers apart and weld together the Gregsten marriage. No one expanded on this argument in court, but might they not have done if Valerie Storie's frank and immediate admission had been made available?

The recollections of Valerie Storie that morning would also have damaged severely Mr Acott's already fragile 'twelve points' for eliminating Peter Alphon from the murder inquiry. Two of these points were that the gunman had called himself Jim, while Alphon's first name was Peter; and that Acott's suspect was 'in his mid-twenties', while Alphon was 31 (in fact, Alphon was 30).

Valerie Storie told the two police officers in that first interview: 'After he shot Mike, he told me to call him Jim, but I don't think that was his real name.'

Secondly, when asked to give the man's age to Sergeant Rees and W.P.C. Rutland, Valerie Storie replied, 'Thirty' – exactly Alphon's age! Two of Mr Acott's points were entirely destroyed by his own chief witness, in a statement which he had seen but which, for reasons which have never been explained, was deliberately withheld from Hanratty's defence lawyers.

The publication of the statement in 1974 caused an outcry, which the newly elected minority Labour Government moved quickly to soothe. Eight years earlier, in 1966, a Labour Home Secretary had set up a public inquiry into the case of Timothy Evans, who was hanged in 1950 for the murder of his wife and child. The dreadful miscarriage of justice in that case was dragged out of the legal establishment in the glare of publicity, and Timothy Evans was (posthumously) pardoned. The Home Secretary who finally signed the pardon was Roy Jenkins. Now Roy Jenkins was Home Secretary again, yet, on the Hanratty case, he decided to move cautiously. After an 'inspired' all-party House of Commons motion, he set up a secret investigation under a criminal barrister, Mr Lewis Hawser, Q.C. Mr Hawser operated on his own. No one could see the documents he could see. He interviewed witnesses behind closed doors. Though the A6 Murder Committee and the Hanratty family could make submissions to him, they had no right to cross-examine witnesses or to study evidence. The whole secretive process was a replica of the Scott Henderson inquiry into the Evans case in 1955, which predictably found that Evans had been guilty.

Hawser's report was published in April 1975. It found the case against James Hanratty 'overwhelming'. The Home Secretary, in great relief, announced 'no further action'. It was another victory for the legal establishment but no victory at all for truth or justice. The Hawser Report was flawed from start to finish not merely by the secrecy of the inquiry from which it flowed, nor even by its reliance on 'notes' and 'documents' released to Hawser but not to anyone else, but also by a series of quite blatant errors and innuendos, all of which overstated the case against Hanratty or understated the case for him.

Three examples of Mr Hawser's method are worth noting.

1. In paragraph 50, dealing with the re-tinting of Hanratty's hair when he was on the run from the police, Hawser writes: 'On the 3rd October, 1961 (at a time when the police were looking for a dark-haired man), he had the tint removed from his hair, restoring it to its original auburn.' This is wrong. On October 3rd, as can be checked from the narrative in this book, Hanratty knew the police were looking for *him*. For the many reasons outlined here, he did not want to give himself up. So he changed the colour of his hair. In August and September, when the police were looking for a man with dark hair as the A6 murderer, Hanratty *kept it dark*.

2. In paragraphs 154–6, Hawser deals with the curious coincidence that there were two or three more bullets found at Deadman's Hill than there were cartridge cases, and two cartridge cases from bullets fired by the murder weapon were found at the Vienna Hotel. This suggested that two of the cartridge cases *not* found at Deadman's Hill stayed in the gun (or were picked up by the murderer) and were eventually dropped or placed in the Vienna Hotel.

If they were left there after the murder, however, Hanratty could not have put them there, since he stayed at the Vienna on the night *before* the murder night. Mr Hawser wrestled with this dilemma. He satisfied himself, fairly convincingly, that there were, in fact, *three* cartridge cases not accounted for by bullets at the murder scene. He stated (paragraph 154): 'If, indeed, as is suggested, the gun was "broken" at the Vienna Hotel after the murder and re-loaded [it was carefully loaded with six live bullets when found on the bus], three cartridge cases would have fallen out. It is almost inconceivable that the murderer would have taken one away and left the other two.'

Why was that inconceivable? If the cases had been *placed* in that room at the Vienna Hotel in order to put the scent on Hanratty, then, of course, it is perfectly possible that the murderer kept one cartridge case up his sleeve. Perhaps he has it still.

To state, as a serious point, that it is 'almost inconceivable' that two cartridges cases should be dropped or placed because these cases were left in the gun is an extravagant non sequitur which would not stand up for a moment to public scrutiny (such as at a public inquiry).

However, Mr Hawser goes on to make another brick from this rather mangy bit of straw. In paragraph 156, he concludes: 'In my view, it is not possible to reconcile the two cartridge cases found at the Vienna Hotel with the three left in the gun after the murder. If anything, these facts tend to suggest that the two cartridge cases in the Vienna Hotel were placed or dropped there before the murder.'

The reasoning appears to be as follows. The murderer had three cases in his gun after the murder. If he had dropped or left any of them in the hotel, it is 'almost inconceivable' that he should only drop or leave two out of the three. *Therefore*, by logical progression, we can deduce that the cases were left in the hotel before the murder, by poor James Hanratty!

3. In paragraph 373, as part of his case for ruling Peter Alphon out of his reckoning, Mr Hawser wrote: 'Alphon mentions the safety catch of the gun on two occasions . . . the murder gun has no safety catch.'

Q.E.D. What a devastating refutation of the Alphon confession! In her evidence in the trial Valerie Storie herself had said: 'On two or three occasions there was a click. When I asked him what he was doing, he said he had put the safety catch on the gun so that it would not go off. Then a little while later there would be another click and when I asked what he was doing, he would say: "I have taken the safety catch off."' (Vol. II, p. 49.)

The murder gun, in fact, had a hammer device to prevent it from going off accidentally, and the man in the car, for one, described it as a safety catch.

Such matters are only examples of the way in which Mr Hawser proceeded. The report is at its weakest, however, where it deals with Hanratty's claimed alibis in Liverpool and in Rhyl. I dealt with these sections in an article in *Private Eye* in 1975, and I can barely improve on this today.

1. The Sweetshop

Hanratty said he had called at a sweetshop in Scotland Road, Liverpool, on the late evening of the murder and had asked the way to Carleton or Tarleton Road. Mrs Olive Dinwoodie told the court that a man, whom she identified as Hanratty, had come to a Scotland Road sweetshop where she was serving on August 21 and 22, and asked for Carleton or Tarleton Road.

The murder took place on August 22. The prosecution tried to persuade the court that the incident took place on the Monday – the 21st. Mr Hawser agrees: 'My assessment is,' he writes (para. 209) 'that the incident took place on the Monday.'

Yet there were no less than *seven* prosecution witnesses who told the court that Hanratty was in London on the Monday. A London cleaner's shop had records that showed that Hanratty left his suit in the shop at 11 a.m. on that Monday. Mr and Mrs Dixie France and their daughter Carol say that Hanratty spent the afternoon in their house in St John's Wood. The daughter remembers the date because she had just come back from the dentist – and her appointment with the dentist that Monday is on record.

There is documentary evidence that Hanratty stayed the Monday night in the Vienna Hotel, Maida Vale, arriving about 11.30 in the evening. A bar girl in a London night club also supported Hanratty's story that he had gone there during the Monday evening.

If Hanratty was in London all that day, he couldn't have been in the sweetshop. So he must have been in the sweetshop the following day, and could not have done the murder. Mr Hawser gets himself out of this difficulty by assuming that the three members of the France family and the bargirl were 'wrong or unreliable' (in spite of the dentist appointment).

His considered view, therefore, is that Hanratty handed in

his suit at a London cleaners, dashed to Liverpool, called in at a sweetshop in the Scotland Road, and dashed back again to London in time to be at the Vienna Hotel at 11.30 p.m.

The entire case against the sweetshop alibi rests on the casual disregard of three prosecution witnesses' evidence (all of whose evidence on other matters helped to hang Hanratty) and the above unlikely itinerary. The suggestion, floated some three years ago by a former Home Office Under Secretary Mr R. Taverne, that the sweetshop incident took place at some other time – in October 1961 – is curtly dismissed by Mr Hawser.

To this I add one more point.

The Hawser report on the sweetshop alibi suggests that Hanratty went to Liverpool on the Monday in order to fix himself up with an alibi for the Tuesday. Indeed, if Mr Hawser is right about the hurried return journey to Liverpool that Monday (and there are plenty of witnesses to prove him wrong), there was no time for Hanratty to do anything else in Liverpool except visit the sweetshop, make his inquiry about Tarleton or Carleton Road and dash back to the station in order to be at the Vienna Hotel by eleven o'clock. Trains to Liverpool took much longer than they do now, and a return journey to Liverpool leaving after 11 a.m. (when Hanratty certainly went to the cleaners in Swiss Cottage) and returning by 11 p.m. (when he was certainly at the Vienna Hotel) left very little time for the traveller to spend in Liverpool. Hawser makes no bones about this. It is plain that he believes that Hanratty went to Liverpool on the Monday to cover himself for his dirty deed on the Tuesday.

Yet the central plank of the prosecution case in the A6 murder trial was that it was not premeditated, that Hanratty was wandering by chance through an area he had never been in before when he happened across a car which put thoughts into his mind of sex and petty robbery and, perhaps, even of murder. How can an alibi in Liverpool be fixed up on the day before an entirely unpremeditated crime on the Tuesday? Such a question might have baffled a public inquiry, but, of course, Mr Hawser never had to face up to one.

2. The Rhyl Alibi

Hanratty told the court that, after the inquiry in the sweetshop and a fruitless search for Tarleton Road, he travelled to Rhyl to look for a fence to sell stolen goods. He arrived late in the evening, and searched around for digs. He stayed in a lodging house for two nights – and he described the house in some detail. A landlady gave evidence that a young man looking like Hanratty had stayed two nights in her house, which fitted in every detail, including a green bath in the attic, Hanratty's description. The prosecution managed to discredit her evidence because she wasn't sure of the date.

During the trial another Rhyl housewife, who lives in the street behind this boarding house – Mrs Margaret Walker – came forward and told the police that a young man had come to her house looking for digs. In her first statement she was not absolutely sure of the date, but when she was interviewed by the defence only eleven days later – while the trial was still on – she confirmed that it was Tuesday, August 22. She remembered the date with total certainty – her son had visited her that day to tell her that an unhappy family incident would take place the following Friday, August 25. He always visited her on Tuesdays, and the Tuesday before the 25th was August 22nd.

Ever since that day more than thirteen years ago – in numerous statements to the press, to the police and to the Hanratty family – Mrs Walker has stood by this statement. When she was first shown pictures of Hanratty while his trial was on, she replied: 'They are very like the man who called here, but the hair was dark.' The photographs were of Hanratty with his hair its natural colour. At the time of the A6 murder, Hanratty's hair was dark.

Mrs Walker's statements from February 19, 1962, until now have been constant on all the main points: the date of the encounter, the suit, the colour of the man's hair, his likeness to Hanratty.

Hawser's attempt to discredit Mrs Walker's evidence is confined to a single paragraph (319). It refers to the 'plain conflict' between what she said when she first went to the police (February 8, 1962) and her written statement eleven days later (February 19, 1962). In the first statement she said the incident took place during the third week in August. By the second she had remembered the exact date – the Tuesday of the third week of August. That is the only 'conflict' which Mr Hawser can find!

The paragraph ends with a simple mistake. Hawser writes: 'A crucial point is the question of the luggage. If Mr Hanratty went to Rhyl he must have taken his suitcases with him. He made it clear in his evidence that he did so and stated twice that on returning to Liverpool from Rhyl on August 24 1961 he put his case in the left luggage office at about midday. In her statement of 8th February, 1962, Mrs Walker says: "The man had no luggage at all."'

This is the lynch-pin of Hawser's case against Mrs Walker. But there is a clear explanation for the lack of luggage, given by Hanratty himself, voluntarily, before any witnesses had come forward, when he first described his visit to Rhyl to his lawyers in February 1962. In the lawyer's notes, scribbled on a rough piece of paper, there appears a passage: 'Left little leather hide case. Landlady about 50 like my mother. I wearing the double-breasted striped suit. *Said could I leave my case, I will pick it up later*' (my emphasis).

So, *he left his case in the boarding house while he searched in the streets around it for better accommodation.* That is Hanratty's own explanation – in the record. Hawser ignores it, and (twice, with some vehemence) argues that the 'lack of luggage' destroys Mrs Walker's alibi for Hanratty! Hawser does nothing to shake Mrs Walker's firm story. And that story is the key to most of the other evidence of Hanratty's Rhyl alibi.

Four women in separate houses in the same street – none of whom appeared at Hanratty's trial – have stated that a young man in a dark suit with dark hair came one night in late August 1961 asking for lodgings. Mrs Walker remembers the date – and has been quite firm about it for thirteen years. Mrs Ivy Vincent, Mrs Betty Davies and her mother-in-law Mrs Margaret Davies say that the incident took place on the same night as the visit to Mrs Walker.

Add to this the evidence of Mr Christopher Larman who recognized Hanratty's picture in the papers as the man he had directed to lodgings in Rhyl on a night late in August 1961, and the coincidence with Hanratty's story is inescapable.

Hawser has not sought to explain this coincidence. He has tried to discredit each individual witness by showing differences in minute detail between statements made to different people over thirteen years. That method may satisfy lawyers – always the last group to accept that their legal system can make lethal mistakes. But it does not answer the simple question: how was it possible for Hanratty to invent a story about travels through the streets of Rhyl, a green bath in an attic, etc., etc., etc., when all the details of his story are subsequently backed up by fourteen independent people with no axe to grind?

The title of my article was 'Hung, Drawn and Hawsered'. There was no reply to it.

Mr Hawser became very famous the following year when he defended Peter Hain, the anti-apartheid campaigner, who was charged with robbing a Putney bank. Mr Hain's defence was one of mistaken identity, and Mr Hawser waxed eloquent on the dangers of false identification. Peter Hain was triumphantly acquitted, and Mr Hawser became a judge in 1978.

In that year, James Hanratty senior died after weeks of pain and discomfort from lung cancer. To the end, he continued to ask for news of 'the case'. It was shocking enough to see such an indomitable spirit broken, but doubly shocking that he should have died when his son's name had still not been cleared.

In 1980 Mary Hanratty was clearing out an old cupboard when she came across some of her eldest son's belongings. Among them was a 'blood card' from Maidstone prison, where Jimmy had given blood. She noticed, to her surprise, that Jimmy's blood group was O group, rhesus negative. The fact that it was O group was common knowledge. It had told against him, since the murderer too had had O-group blood. The forensic scientists had found that out from the semen he had left behind in Valerie Storie. Yet the fact that James Hanratty's O-group blood was in the rare category rhesus negative had never been disclosed. For a brief, delirious moment we all felt we might be able to prove his innocence once and for all. If it was possible to establish from semen whether blood is rhesus positive or negative, then perhaps the murderer's blood group could be proved to have been positive.

Hanratty's lawyers took advice. They were told that nothing in semen can possibly disclose whether a blood group is rhesus negative or rhesus positive. Once more, hope of a new breakthrough faded. There remains, however the mystery of why the forensic evidence and the prosecution lawyers were so silent on the rare quality of Hanratty's blood group.

The Hawser Report, the dashing of this revived hope and the death of the old man put an end to the A6 Murder Committee. I still get half a dozen letters or so every year from people who have read this book in a library and who ask anxiously what has happened since. Can it really be, they inquire, that the whole subject is still dormant and that the hanging of James Hanratty is still upheld by the Home Office and by government as right and proper? I have to answer yes. I have to say that very little has come to light in the last thirteen years to force the case once more into the limelight. One anonymous man once rang my Ansaphone machine at the *Daily Mirror* to say that he knew the bus conductress, Pat, on the 36A bus and could put me in touch with her. He never rang again nor left any means of my contacting him. There has been, in all these years, nothing from the France family, nothing from the Gregsten family, nothing from Langdale, nothing from Nudds (who must now be dead). There has been almost nothing from Peter Alphon. Once, when I wrote about the case for a partwork magazine entitled *Unsolved*, I got a strange, silent phone call in the middle of the night and thought I recognized the heavy breathing. At the same time, Jean Justice, who keeps all the case papers with an ever-burning passion, got a silent, midnight phone call too. I have a feeling that Peter Alphon is still alive and kicking. I am always happy to talk to him, as he knows.

If he wants to send me that third cartridge case, I would like to see it. Even the Establishment, which, in his words, has acted as if it knows he did the murder, would find it difficult to explain that away.

Index

A CHOICE OF PENGUINS

The Big Red Train Ride   Eric Newby

From Moscow to the Pacific on the Trans-Siberian Railway is an eight-day journey of nearly six thousand miles through seven time zones. In 1977 Eric Newby set out with his wife, an official guide and a photographer on this journey. 'The best kind of travel book' – Paul Theroux

Star Wars   Edited by E. P. Thompson

With contributions for Rip Bulkeley, John Pike, Ben Thompson and E. P. Thompson, and with a Foreword by Dorothy Hodgkin, OM, this is a major book which assesses all the arguments for Star Wars and proceeds to make a powerful – indeed unanswerable – case against it.

Somerville and Ross   Gifford Lewis

Edith Somerville has a talented artist and illustrator, her cousin Violet Martin had a profound political insight. Together they created the masterpiece *The Real Charlotte* and the witty tales of *The Irish R.M.* This is Gifford Lewis's colourful account of their lives.

PENGUIN CLASSICS OF WORLD ART

Each volume presents the complete paintings of the artist and includes: an introduction by a distinguished art historian, critical comments on the painter from his own time to the present day, 64 pages of full-colour plates, a chronological survey of his life and work, a basic bibliography, a fully illustrated and annotated *catalogue raisonné*.

Titles already published or in preparation

Botticelli, Caravaggio, Cézanne, Leonardo da Vinci, Manet, Picasso, Piero della Francesca, Raphael, van Eycks, Vermeer.

FOR THE BEST IN PAPERBACKS, LOOK FOR THE

A CHOICE OF PENGUINS

The Diary of Virginia Woolf
Five volumes edited by Quentin Bell and Anne Olivier Bell

'As an account of intellectual and cultural life of our century, Virginia Woolf's diaries are invaluable; as the record of one bruised and unquiet mind, they are unique' – Peter Ackroyd in the *Sunday Times*

Voices of the Old Sea   Norman Lewis

'I will wager that *Voices of the Old Sea* will be a classic in the literature about Spain' – *Mail on Sunday* 'Limpidly and lovingly Norman Lewis has caught the helpless, unwitting, often foolish, but always hopeful village in its dying summers, and saved the tragedy with sublime comedy' – *Observer*

The First World War   A J P Taylor

In this superb illustrated history, A J P Taylor 'manages to say almost everything that is important for an understanding and, indeed, intellectual digestion of that vast event . . . A special text . . . a remarkable collection of photographs' – *Observer*

Ninety-Two Days   Evelyn Waugh

With characteristic honesty Evelyn Waugh here debunks the romantic notions attached to rough travelling; his journey in Guiana and Brazil is difficult, dangerous and extremely uncomfortable, and his account of it is witty and unquestionably compelling.

When the Mind Hears   Harlan Lane
A History of the Deaf

'Reads like a suspense novel . . . what emerges is evidence of a great wrong done to a minority group, the deaf' – *The New York Times Book Review* 'Impassioned, polemical, at times even virulent . . . (he shows) immense scholarship, powers of historical reconstruction, and deep empathy for the world of the deaf' – Oliver Sacks in *The New York Review of Books*

A CHOICE OF PENGUINS

Trail of Havoc   Patrick Marnham

In this brilliant piece of detective work, Patrick Marnham has traced the steps of Lord Lucan from the fateful night of 7th November 1974 when he murdered his children's nanny and attempted to kill his ex-wife. As well as being a fascinating investigation, the book is also a brilliant portrayal of a privileged section of society living under great stress.

Light Years   Gary Kinder

Eduard Meier, an uneducated Swiss farmer, claims since 1975 to have had over 100 UFO sightings and encounters with 'beamships' from the Pleiades. His evidence is such that even the most die-hard sceptics have been unable to explain away the phenomenon.

And the Band Played On   Randy Shilts
Politics, people and the AIDS epidemic

Written after years of extensive research by the only American journalist to cover the epidemic full-time, the book is a masterpiece of reportage and a tragic record of mismanaged institutions and scientific vendettas, of sexual politics and personal suffering.

The Return of a Native Reporter   Robert Chesshyre

Robert Chesshyre returned to Britain from the United States in 1985 where he had spent four years as the *Observer*'s correspondent. This is his devastating account of the country he came home to: intolerant, brutal, grasping and politically and economically divided. It is a nation, he asserts, struggling to find a role.

Women and Love   Shere Hite

In this culmination of *The Hite Report* trilogy, 4,500 women provide an eloquent testimony of the disturbingly unsatisfying nature of their emotional relationships and point to what they see as the causes. *Women and Love* reveals a new cultural perspective in formation: as women change the emotional structure of their lives, they are defining a fundamental debate over the future of our society.